Clepsydra

STANFORD STUDIES IN JEWISH HISTORY AND CULTURE

EDITED BY *Aron Rodrigue and Steven J. Zipperstein*

Clepsydra
Essay on the Plurality of Time in Judaism

Sylvie Anne Goldberg

TRANSLATED BY BENJAMIN IVRY

STANFORD UNIVERSITY PRESS

STANFORD, CALIFORNIA

Stanford University Press
Stanford, California

Clepsydra: Essay on the Plurality of Time in Judaism was originally published in French in 2000 under the title *La Clepsydre: Essai sur la pluralité des temps dans le judaïsme* ©2000, Albin Michel, Paris.

This book has been published and translated with the assistance of the Jewish Federation of Greater Hartford, the French Ministry of Culture—National Center for the Book, the Fondation pour la Mémoire de la Shoah, and the Centre de recherches historiques (CRH—CNRS) de l'École des hautes études en sciences sociales.

Printed in the United States of America on acid-free, archival-quality paper

Library of Congress Cataloging-in-Publication Data

Names: Goldberg, Sylvie Anne, author.
Title: Clepsydra : essay on the plurality of time in Judaism / Sylvie Anne Goldberg ; translated by Benjamin Ivry.
Other titles: Clepsydre. English | Stanford studies in Jewish history and culture.
Description: Stanford, California : Stanford University Press, 2016. | Series: Stanford studies in Jewish history and culture | "Originally published in French in 2000 under the title *La Clepsydre: Essai sur la pluralité des temps dans le judaïsme*." | Includes bibliographical references and index.
Identifiers: LCCN 2015048592 (print) | LCCN 2015049042 (ebook) |
ISBN 9780804789059 (cloth : alk. paper) | ISBN 9780804797160 (electronic)
Subjects: LCSH: Time--Religious aspects--Judaism--History. |
   History--Religious aspects--Judaism.
Classification: LCC BM729.T55 G6513 2016 (print) | LCC BM729.T55 (ebook) |
   DDC 296.3--dc23
LC record available at http://lccn.loc.gov/2015048592

Typeset by Bruce Lundquist in 10.5/14 Galliard

For my children and grandchildren,
who give meaning to time.

To the historian Bernard Lepetit,
whose life did not leave him the time . . .

Contents

viii   Contents

Acknowledgments from the French Edition

This book would never have seen the light of day without the generous help lavished upon me in countless ways by loyal friends and charitable souls, who contributed to the life of this work by encouraging me, making documents available, reading and rereading draft after draft, making relevant suggestions, and providing information. My thanks especially go to Hélène Monsacré, who welcomed the book enthusiastically. I also owe thanks for assistance with my research to Alain Boureau, Albert Ogien, Alessandro Guetta, Alex Derczanski, Alex Szalat, Arnaud Sérandour, Bernard Goldstein, Chayim Milikowsky, Eli Yassif, Éric Vigne, Étienne François, Floriane Azoulay, François Hartog, Gad Freudenthal, Israël Goldberg, Marc Bregman, Maurice Kriegel, Michael Riegler, Morgane Labbé, Moshé Idel, Nancy Green, Nissan Rubin, Nurit Shahar, Olivier Munnich, Perrine Simon-Nahum, Pierre Vidal-Naquet, Reuven Bonfil, Sacha Stern, Tony Lévy, Véronique Gillet-Didier, Yosef Hayim Yerushalmi, and Zeev Harvey. Each one knows how much I remain beholden to them. Those who attended my seminar at the École des hautes études en sciences sociales deserve special mention for their patience and attentiveness, and my family likewise put up with my inaccessibility, absences, and constant "running out" of time. This research also benefited from support from the Lady Davis Fellowship Trust, which made my stay as visiting professor at the Hebrew University of Jerusalem all the more valuable by allowing me time to immerse myself in the National Library of Israel.

The clepsydra is a water clock. Devised to measure changing, relative time, its flow is adjusted depending on the season to take into account the length of the day. The amount of water in the clock must be calculated to achieve an unequal flow, but one that nonetheless conveys the passing of the hours and duration. This varying, mobile time can serve to represent our lived experience of it, in which, inasmuch as they impinge on us more or less intensely, hours are not to be judged by the same measure. Our relationship with time involves multiple perceptions, which do not weigh equally in the balance. Beliefs, hopes, and fears burden the passage of time all the more if they arise from systems of thought in which it is a key concept. The past, present, and future form temporal flows that, although differently sensed, constitute a whole in which memory, history, hope, and faith blend into a vast, unchanging present. Our awareness of time past emerges from that of the present. The present asks after the future, and with this in mind turns back toward the past.

The history of the West delineates a unique relationship with time, which is both "told as a tale" and "tallied." This book endeavors to highlight the importance of the theme, somewhat overlooked by history, of the multiplicity of temporal registers. It shows how this multiplicity may be used and "adapted" to suit historical requirements and their evolution over the course of centuries. What better device than the clepsydra to embody the amazing ability of human beings to make use of their temporality?

This book is an essay. It has no philosophical ambitions, although it sometimes aspires to reflect on the use of categories of thought. It denotes a moment in the research of the historian, who has spent years gathering archival documents, materials of all kinds, based on sources in religion, culture, law, and folklore. Some of these texts belong to the sacred, others to the profane. They all convey ways of doing or thinking, and assertions by pedagogy, theology, or philosophy. After this process, we may wonder how the data harmonize to form a cultural *ensemble* specific to a given time or group. In choosing to work on Jewish temporality, I aimed to dig beneath the ambient clichés, the more or less vague and implicit approaches to the history of the Jews, as well as their past depictions of the universe. Tired of the repeated invocation of teleological, essentialist, political, anti-Judaic, and other singular agendas that still permeate Jewish studies, whether unconsciously or in all frankness, I came to feel that a sufficient toll has been paid to our history for us finally to pursue ordinary research about it. To be sure, anything dealing with religion is tricky to handle in terms of historical work. And also to be sure, Jews are denominationally defined. In earlier societies, however, a person was Jewish in the same way that every human being was "something": it was a matter of being enrolled in a social order, a group, a community, a form of civilization. The Ashkenazi universe, like the Sephardic one in its locations, belongs, just like the Christian one, to a conceptual order much vaster than that controlled by a synagogue or Church. Although organized according to its own laws, the system of thought specific to the Jewish world is interrelated with the development and evolution of the cultural milieu from which it descended, as well as the environment in which it evolved. Equipped with the Halakhah, a corpus of distinct laws held to be a normative structure governing Jewish life in its public and private aspects, Jews subjected every realm of life to ethical reasoning. Halakhah governs both ritual and religious subjects and social, civic, and penal issues. It might have been the law of the land had the Jewish people not been dispersed to a multitude of nations. It possesses the powers and contours of such a law, with the difference that from the talmudic era on, rabbis have decided that "the law of the kingdom is the law" (dina de-malkhutah dina), meaning that they fully and entirely accept the external laws of the countries they have inhabited since the loss of the ancient Jewish state and the resulting Diaspora.[1] Accepting a double standard of jurisdiction, to which they only referred with respect to generic penal matters or in a limited way to avoid transgression, Jews likewise employed it in regard to temporality. Possessing their own method of computation, they also acknowledged the conventions common to their surroundings, sometimes participating in calculations by scholars of their day of calendar tables (such as those of Tycho Brahe or Kepler). Playing with time as with laws, they thus continually employed a double register of references. The process of secularization and the separation of Church and state led to a crystallization of the religious realm. Members of Jewish society thus became citizens whose religion was Judaism. Their ways of thinking shifted: from what had been models of representing the universe, they drew notions that would be taken as belonging to a strictly confessional order.

The historical breach during the twentieth century that also caused the demolition of the dynamics of continuity and discontinuity of the bygone Jewish world contributed in a major way to the loss of its codes. These "codes," which allow organic transmission of a social and cultural patrimony, were usually filed away in family and local lore, storehouses of memory of secular tradition that were irremediably lost. Since the end of the nineteenth century, the Jewish world has been, for the most part, wholly uprooted from its historical and geographical milieu; furthermore, it has experienced the modification, followed by the disappearance, of its points of reference and forms of internal communication. Notably, the Jewish languages that provided *ex tempore* access to its varied traditions have ceased to be used. As a result, the endlessly repeated connections between past and present Jewish worlds are now only inscribed in a system of consistent readings for Jews who are aligned with the Orthodox religious tradition, even though the latter scarcely escaped the widespread upheavals that affected other Jews. If the transformations in contemporary Judaism can be gauged in light of the relationship of Jews with temporality, how are we to grasp the structuring of time in past Jewish societies? How did Jews devise a relationship with time and space so singular that it has spanned oceans and epochs? Was this also the case for Jews before rabbinic Judaism appeared? Doubtless that transition led to changes as profound as those to which Jews have been exposed over the past two centuries. And doubtless, too, in order to understand this phenomenon, we must make a detour by way of antiquity, when the seeds of the structural elements of Jewish thought were sown, prefiguring future structurings and informing the genealogy of Judaism for future centuries in a relationship with Christian time as half-hearted as it was unchanging. It is to find answers to these questionings that I have chosen to analyze the origin of structures of time in the Jewish world of antiquity and the High Middle Ages.

Temporality is approached here in a dual aspect. On the one hand, it is a matter of understanding the questions of time asked during a given era in response to a specific historical, cultural, or social situation; on the other, it is a matter of trying to understand how in every era and situation, a dynamic principle is put in place to convey or recreate a truly Jewish temporality, whatever the context. This Jewish temporality, which operates according to liturgical and calendrical rhythms or other ways of appropriating space, is a social fact. As such, it can be studied by the historian with appropriate means. Sometimes changes that occur in approaches to temporality are subject to other questionings. The latter belong to a different cultural apparatus, more diffuse because it extends beyond a specific group. The present study aims to draw attention to the way in which times intersect for various groups, forming a set of "questions of time," rather than to teach anyone anything about time per se. What is more, it aspires to bridge the concepts of time and temporality, which, according to current thinking, the compartmentalization of academic fields has made seemingly irreconcilable.

This study has two parts. Part I, "Narrated Time," suggests an approach to the conceptual universe that makes up what is called "time." The structure of a Jewish time is analyzed by weighing the arguments expounded in contemporary texts and speech. This first part seeks, by describing the means by which it was constructed, to demonstrate the kind of bricolage upon which the standard view of Jewish time is based and its lexicon, which combines a diversity of ideas rooted in historical, philosophical, and theological traditions. Starting from standard perceptions of time in the Bible and the history of Israel, it examines some of the central notions governing the approach to these two sources of interpretation, which lead to the conclusion that Judaism invented a form of temporality that is forever being reenacted by the reseeding of the past in the present, and that denies Jews any relation to history.

The purpose of Part II, "Time Counted Down, or the World Order," is to prove the historical relevance of this finding. It seeks to understand the affiliation between the idea of time and the collective experience of it within a group. Specifically, it seeks to test the validity of the theory that a break occurred between Jews and history after the destruction of the Second Temple. This section takes the form of an archaeological survey of the relics of Jewish antiquity. It aspires to identify traces of the development of a connection between time and history before rabbinic Judaism appeared. Studying the way in which the meaning of time changed the direction of historical consciousness means rediscovering the pathways that led to the double construction of a unique understanding of time and a unique temporality. Study of the many "scansions," or orderly repetitive temporal patterns, shown in the sources makes it possible to examine how the permeation of religious and social spaces structured itself during the invention of a principle of temporality. From biblical chronologies to rabbinic judgments of time past, including texts that structure thought, we can try to assemble a mosaic. A temporal jigsaw puzzle can perhaps be (re)constituted by means of bricolage and mosaic assembly.

Historians will not be surprised to find the analysis of philosophical and theological ideas in Part I subject to contradiction by the reading of sources in Part II, which aims to highlight the difference between theoretical and practical constructs. Nonetheless, it is true that our contemplation of the past, especially when it is so distant that analysis of the traces of it that remain is inevitably hypothetical, is encumbered with traditions and proprieties that the centuries have laid down as confirmed principles. It may be hoped that reading these pages will call into question some common certainties about both Judaism and its "prehistory." The bond that connects ancient Judaism with that of today may then seem less stable than it did a priori: rabbinic Judaism did not suddenly appear only after the destruction of the Second Temple but emerged from a national question that history bluntly settled in its own way. By establishing a new temporality, Judaism managed to perpetuate itself among the nations. Through this unique temporality Jews were enabled to continue living in the midst of other peoples, as much by the rhythms of Judaism as by a time that was not theirs. This structuring of time rooted in the most ancient Jewish texts reappears nowadays among all the minority groups in our so-called multicultural societies. The genealogy of the pyramid of time dealt with here may thus, perhaps, help us better understand the role Jewish time plays today.

*

"Every generation writes its own history of past generations," Salo Baron writes.[2] In conceding that the vision of the past reinvents itself from age to age in light of current issues, the search for time undertaken here must necessarily be a "matter of time." It perhaps supplies the basis for an account of the construction of Jewish time, but I confess that I am not entirely sure yet how to formulate the question . . .

Scriptural Abbreviations Cited

Books of the Bible

Dan.	Daniel
Deut.	Deuteronomy
Eccles.	Ecclesiastes
Est.	Esther
Exod.	Exodus
Ezek.	Ezekiel
Gen.	Genesis
Hab.	Habakkuk
Hag.	Haggai
Hos.	Hosea
Isa.	Isaiah
Jer.	Jeremiah
Judg.	Judges
Josh.	Joshua
Lev.	Leviticus
Mic.	Micah
Neh.	Nehemiah
Num.	Numbers
Ps. (pl. Pss.)	Psalms
2 Sam.	2 Samuel
Zech.	Zechariah

Apocrypha and Pseudepigrapha

Bar.	Baruch
Jub.	Jubilees
1 Macc.	1 Maccabees
2 Macc.	2 Maccabees
Sir.	Sirach (= Ecclesiasticus)

Rabbinical Treatises*

Arakh.	Arakhin
AZ	Avodah zarah (Foreign worship; a talmudic tractate in Nezikin)
BB	Baba Batra
Ber.	Berakhot
Git.	Gittin
Gen. R.	Genesis Rabbah
Hor.	Horayot
Hul.	Hulin
Ket.	Ketubot
Koh. R.	Kohelet Rabbah
Lev. R.	Leviticus Rabbah
Meg.	Megilla
Ned.	Nedarim
Nid.	Niddah
Pes.	Pesahim
RH	Rosh Ha-shanah
Sanh.	Sanhedrin
Shab.	Shabbat
Sota	
Ta'an.	Ta'anit
Yad.	Yadayim
Yal.	Yalk
Yev.	Yevamot
Yoma	

* Unless marked "(JT)" the treatises cited are from the Babylonian Talmud.

Clepsydra

Introduction

> I was born in the week of the life of Sara, in the year 390 of the small chronological table.
>
> This happened during the Holiday of Weeks, forty years ago.
>
> Dead the seventh day of the comforting month, in the year 550 . . .

Inquisitive readers lacking the proper indices who wish to translate into "universal time" the above calendrical references, shown according to forms typical of (imaginary) speakers in traditional Jewish society, must proceed to some basic calculations. To begin with, add 5,000 to 390 and subtract 3,760 from the result, which takes us to the year 1630. Or add 240 to 390 to get 630 and then add 1,000 to arrive at the same place. Since the day is not specified, the week must be dated. It appears in the weekly parashah (section of the Torah) "Hayei Sarah," a passage about the life of Sarah. It is placed in the fifth position after the start of Bereshit, the first weekly portion of the Torah in the annual Jewish cycle of reading the complete Pentateuch, following the celebration of the High Holy Days, enshrining the yearly numeric change. In that year, 1 Tishri, the first day of the civil year and the seventh month of the religious year, was on September 18. The reading of the life of Sarah was on Saturday of the week starting November 4. So our speaker was born between November 4 and 10, 1629, since the Gregorian calendar only changes years on the first of January.[1] For the speaker who indicates an event occurring during the holiday of Shavuot forty years before, our research need only find that in 1959 Shavuot fell on June 12 and 13.[2] As for the person who died on the seventh of Av (traditionally referred to as Menachem Av, or Av of Comfort)[3] in the year 5500, by similar calculations we arrive at July 18, 1789.

These data take us to the heart of a system of temporal references underutilized by conventional standards, which make of time an idea equally distributed in society. Time quantified by the Jewish era, *annus mundi*, is calculated from the estimated date of the creation.[4] It inserts between the latter and the present day an additional span of 3,760 years not supplied in the Western Christian convention. In the world of Jewish observance, which in today's society represents one choice among many,[5] the year follows the rhythm of the liturgical cycle transmitted by old-age tradition, whose temporal customs recall the conventions of ancient society. In our day, these accepted distinctions between religion and civil law delineate places reserved for the public and private, confession and citizenship, while introducing an unchanging principle of twofold temporal reference.

Questions of Time

Whether liturgical or quotidian, Jewish time speeds along in a weekly cycle, annually repeated in readings of parashiot from the Torah, yet anchored in the ever-renewed deliberateness of the eternity of the first day of creation, which marks the arrival of moving time. Tradition locates the creation of the world in the autumn of a year between 3760 and 3758 BCE. Over the centuries, *annus mundi*, a unique calendar and double insertion in time and history, promoted the feeling of the uniqueness of Jews amid the sociability of the world in which their lives unfolded. Could the passage of days resembling those of others, yet different in their temporal course, be seen merely as convention, without further effect?

Inherited from ancient civilizations, especially that of Chaldea, the Jewish calendar is lunisolar in principle and function. It differs from the solar Julian calendar, based on the ancient Egyptian one, and the later Gregorian calendar in use today. Like its Christian counterparts, however, the Jewish calendar is based on the convergence of religious and civic principles in yearly proceedings.

The cyclic Jewish disposition of the year comprises various divisions in the succession of months. The new spiritual year begins in autumn, whereas the calendar year starts in the spring. Calendrical divisions juxtapose eschatology, based on biblical tales, with laws emerging from both scriptural orders and rabbinic readings. Biblical tales arrange time in regular cycles, from weekly timekeeping regulating the week into seven days to extraordinary units of nineteen years, including jubilee years governed by seven-year cycles.[6] These temporal conventions that cadenced the life of a farming population to the rhythm of the Palestinian seasons in an era before the Diaspora were inherited with hardly a change by the "remnant of the people of Israel,"[7] geographically dispersed to highly diverse climates. They result from crafting a life cycle that allows the survival of the group amid other peoples, a phenomenon seen since the first Babylonian Exile.[8] At the same time, Hebrews, and later Jews, readily accepted Persian or Seleucid conventions for general external dating, used to denote the reigns of the monarchies of the time.

Dating conventions seem separate from procedures that account for forms of ritual that regulate daily life. The *annus mundi* was only fully adopted in the Jewish world around the eleventh or twelfth century, whereas the cycle of ritual life had rolled on mostly unaltered since the dawn of the Hebrew religion.[9] The life cycle and dating finally met in a specific ordering of time imposed in the Middle Ages. While forms of "traditional society" based on normative rabbinism grew and stabilized, a new symbol of Judaism was implemented, guided by historical convergences that pushed it toward differentiation and self-containment.[10] Turning away from surrounding societies that were gradually growing more hostile, the Jews drew on privileges[11] granted them by princes and nobles to reinforce their uniqueness. Caught up in this historical process, the Jews became so singular that in a few centuries they formed an autonomous microsociety within some countries, at the same time creating an intellectual world of which understanding and time-related customs were but one reflection. By ignoring the calculation of time in common use and opting for a chronology more reliant on guesswork than on objective computation, medieval Jews located themselves in a temporality that kept them outside the social norms of the countries in which they dwelled. This attitude was affirmed over the centuries, until in modern society it became one of the key markers of the distinctiveness of Jewish identity. Whether one ascribes this temporal enrollment to a resolve not to yield to the usual historical conventions that govern the system of dating or, from an altogether different point of view, regards it as the expression of a kind of national and political autonomy, it reveals a special relationship to temporality. For as we know, the notion of time is a social construct that calls for putting to work the sum of experience accumulated by members of the same group over centuries.[12] In light of the fact that "all culture is primarily a certain experience of time," as the anthropologist Alban Bensa observes, the uniqueness of an era results from the tension caused by the entanglement of "the contemporaneity of attitudes inherited from the past and conduct induced by new concerns."[13] A group's communication and commerce with its environment might well depend on the time scale it adopts.

Yet measuring time is only one aspect of understanding and using it. The relationship with time is an essential social indicator. It allows us to be part of a plan, to allocate social tasks, and to alter social rhythms to those of nature. It provides a way of distinguishing what is human from what is superhuman, the earth from the heavens, and to contemplate the divine. Whether taken as an idea, stored in a system of categories, or studied as a variable conception, ever since St. Augustine's meditations on eternity were brought up to date,[14] time has most often been relegated to the class of perceptions. It haunts the realm of the undefinable. In traditional society, a person is born, lives, and dies in a temporal order seen as divine. This conception implies splitting human activity into divine and human times. Sacred and profane time both shape the use of what I call a characteristically Jewish "space-time." Based on a topographic structuring of space, the physical place where Jews are located, this space is governed by the time-related plan conveyed by tradition that traces a space-time framework for daily life. To be sure, this temporality takes shape through use of the calendar, but even more by an arrangement of rhythmic temporal scansions that differ from those adopted by Western Christianity. These distinct rhythms share a border. They meet, and they sometimes even make use of one another, but without ever blending; they are separate yet belong to the same cultural plan. In contrast to the West, which, deeming heathen times obsolete, takes as its benchmark the birth year of the Christian Savior, the *annus Domini*, Jews take as theirs the origin of time itself: the creation of the world, based on biblical chronologies.[15] Between these two temporal scales a whole realm of sociability opens up, fluctuating in the encounter of two modes of belief, two religions. Ways of coexisting and interacting are also decided here.

Insofar as one's perception of the world shapes one's idea of time, one's way of belonging in the world and conceiving of it depends on one's relationship with time. There is no doubt that time impinges on us differently if it is seen as cyclical, always beginning again, or as propelled into the future or toward some objective. The certainty of inevitable progress toward a final goal involves a process of human action or expectation. Such is the conclusion of many scientific studies of the question. For the historian of religious orders Alphonse Dupront, "Eschatological time is innate certainty of salvation, therefore a conspicuously human time of deliverance and achievement; perhaps it is the only one, made to man's measure if the human condition is accepted, sought, and experienced in the fullest scope of its force." Dupront backs up these statements by noting that, essentially, "eschatological time is . . . the time of the communication between the worlds of history and being."[16]

Another idea is advanced by Marc Bloch, who defines "historical time" this way: "This real time is in essence a continuum; it is also perpetual change."[17] When historians confront time, to construct a "historical" time to be studied for their own use, they must recapitulate the evolutionary course of its transformation into a convention, which inevitably returns them to antiquity, toward what are taken to be humankind's first encounters with the notion of eternity. In his introduction to *L'ordre du temps*,[18] Krzysztof Pomian inventories options such as "chronometry, chronography, chronology, and chronosophy" for translating time into signs.[19] To delineate his objective, Pomian conceptualizes structures in time, with each defining either its own kind or a specific social construction: psychological time or the time of lived experience; solar or seasonal time pertaining to dwellers in the same land; a liturgical calendar for believers in the same religion; a political calendar for citizens of the same country. This list contains some exact usages of time, all of which fit into the implicit assumption of a shared engagement with the convention establishing a flow and method of dating based on quantitative standards. If we are to believe the historian of traditions Philippe Ariès, the title of his book *Le temps de l'histoire* (The time of history) suggests that in some sense, historicism creates temporality: "Classical antiquity . . . had no need of the continuity that has since Creation linked contemporary man to the chain of time. Christianity added the idea of a close interdependence of man and history."[20]

In a way, the present book seeks to test the validity of this statement by trying to answer the following question: Can the idea of temporality inferred from Jewish thought be understood in terms of a similar relationship of interdependency between humankind and history?

Evaluating Time

From the eighteenth century on, the upheavals in Jewish life profoundly transformed Jews' perceptions regarding their worldview, on the one hand, and Judaism, on the other. Their relationship with, as well as conventional usages of, time changed radically as a result. By taking an interest specifically in this relationship and these usages, my research seeks to analyze the conflict within Judaism between opposing desires for the perpetuation and the transformation of traditional society. Thus, studying Jewish approaches to time also means examining the reinterpretation of Judaism by Jews during confrontations with their environment. To pinpoint the modalities of participation in society by the Jews that serve as an indicator of their relationship with time, the historian can refer to calendrical conventions. Yet insofar as the calendar is exclusively dedicated to its function of scheduling the liturgical cycle, there is a risk of obtaining only factual, erroneous, or incomplete data. Are there concrete indicators of the relationship with time that are more appropriate? Epigraphy tells us that in the Jewish world it is usually tombstones that convey the most reliable information about conventions in dating an era or community; it is often easier to identify dates of death on grave markers than to find exact the birth dates of people in Jewish society of long ago. Studying dating practices, we find that two historical periods display significant variations from the *annus mundi* model. The first, appearing fleetingly though frequently during a certain period, consists in using the date of the destruction of the Temple (70 CE) for inscriptions on gravestones or in catacombs;[21] the second occurs in revolutionary France, with the advent of the republican era.[22]

The use in dating of a combination of the *annus mundi* and the common era, or else of the common era alone, can be traced from that time up to the present, fluctuating according to the rhythm of Emancipation. What takes shape through funerary dating practices, then, is a space for the representation of temporality. The analysis in this essay focuses on genealogy during this long phase.

This vast space-time unfolds on a stage set between the destruction of the Temple and the Emancipation. It contains a series of theological, philosophical, and historical events between the Middle Ages and the end of the modern era that shed light on the relationships among dating practices, conceptions, and customs of the day. Yet the shaping of these practices occurred during the development of rabbinic Judaism in the years that preceded, accompanied, and followed the fall of the Temple. These conceptions and customs are capable of outlining a possible relationship of Jews to historical time that is continuous but also ever-changing, as in Marc Bloch's definition of it cited above.[23] Another path is opened up by examining the dialogue between the Bible and its users, revived in large part by the Jewish Enlightenment movement, the Haskalah, which, because it grants a major role to the struggle between rationalism and faith, belief and knowledge, and to both Jewish and Christian readings, offers a special vantage point for studying these disputes. Built on scriptural readings during the biblical era, this exegesis continued down the centuries, but because it is established as a source of interpretations in antiquity, it is on antiquity that the first part of this study will focus.

This history of time aims to be an inquiry into temporality, sidestepping historical duration. But this project presents some difficulties that cannot be avoided. How not, for example, to uncover a unique time in any specific history? Likewise, how to avoid questioning anew the division of Jewish history into periods by the historians of the Wissenschaft des Judentums movement, launched in nineteenth-century Germany,[24] who extended the Middle Ages up to the Emancipation?[25] How to understand, without denying history, those historians' proposition that the Jews be seen as existing in a space-time out of sync with their environment? These questions form the background to this study, which aims to understand how traditional Jewish society perceives and structures time—the way in which, in the long term, it perceives the world. By treating the predominant essential texts, whether religious or secular, that this society has produced, used, and transmitted through the ages as historical sources, we risk compiling a sort of digressive reading of the Jewish social and religious phenomenon through time and history.

Aside from temporal conventions, understood as agents of Jewish singularity, two other elements permeate this study: time and history. They meet, avoid each other, and are set within ideas that are contiguous or associated with them, remaining inherent in the relationships between the imagination and attitudes of the Jews. Time may mark the sudden entrance of an external element or phenomenon, not to speak of a portion of the divine, whereas history, with its cohort of acceptances and refusals—as much a purely terrestrial progression as a profane narrative—remains the prerogative of human purpose. The point of this reflection is neither to devise nor propose a specific meaning hidden behind rites, practices, or even attitudes. More prosaically, it is about realizing how ideas of time and historicity determine, through their objectification in daily life, a way of belonging in the world. Far from explaining or even discussing the beliefs of Jews in traditional society, this analysis rather consists of locating their grounding (*ancrage*) in a system of references that in turn refers to an imaginary world and a social reality, conveyed by their attitudes and developments. Without seeking to endorse any sort of deep-rooted religious tradition, my goal is to identify effective action in the religious domain of the Jewish world, a world understood as being the fruit of a civilization and a culture preserved—intentionally or not—by objective historical conditions, but also crisscrossed by dealings with foreign mind-sets. In other words, the second objective of this study is to grasp the changes occurring in Jewish attitudes about temporality during their transition from so-called traditional to so-called liberated societies. These working hypotheses allow for tracking the boundaries of the categories of thought; they may also permit us to avoid standard ways of understanding the history of the Jews.

In each era, unremitting strain may be discerned within Jewish societies on many grids, be it religious conflicts, theological movements, or cultural or social changes. All might find expression through a typology that would operate by means of different approaches toward and conventions of time. To talk about the decisive stages in Jewish history, we might choose a periodization based on the appearance of cultural and religious elements that mark clear-cut changes; we could also choose a periodization with a factual basis, comprising neatly cut slices of history. One study of the relation to temporality opens other horizons that some may find fruitful, but others risky. Understanding the relationship between Jews and temporality through their temporal conventions requires the implementation of a grid that cannot be summed up in mere chronology. Certainly, one may construct a history of time limited to a critical scholarly study focusing on temporal indicators found in liturgy, rites, and responsa[26] from biblical times to a given era, reducing them to a saga about time. Such is not my purpose here. The present undertaking seeks to delineate the layers deposited by the centuries in Jewish "cultural baggage," or, in other words, in its cultural and religious patrimony. This jumble of customs, beliefs, integrations, and rejections portrays a society sealed in its singularity by surroundings at times foreign, hostile, or even more dangerous to its survival because tolerant, if not friendly.

It may almost be commonplace to say that Jewish society does not remain fixed, although it perpetuates the pronouncements of its founding documents by continually reintegrating them into its developments. This vitality also keeps it from avoiding broad changes in the societies that surround it. This form of action, the continual infusion of the past into the present, introduces a paradoxical dynamic of the perpetual and the permanent to change whose relationship with temporality is intriguing. It would be easy to interpret this, without further clarification, as a characteristic feature of "traditional" societies according to the now-classic accounts of these severally provided by Mircea Eliade and Aron Gurevich.[27] Yet the cyclical model of the ancients and the linear one of the moderns seemingly coexist without friction in a temporality that rejects the usual conceptual conventions. The cultural approach argued by Efraim Shmueli allows us to reread Jewish history while keeping a distance from the monolithic forms created by linear history.[28] All the developments in the history of the Jews—even if obviously in the past, such as the biblical or talmudic eras—are thus always at work in the current models constituted by modern rabbinic, philosophical, mystical, or rational systems. They meet or separate briefly before merging into the modalities of a present that calls together a multiplicity of specific conceptual models of the idea of time. In order to document them according to the stereotypical conventions of the linear/circular distinction assumed to shape the traditional or theological models of Western Christian societies, we might easily index odd or incomplete systems, each of them being at any given moment in conflict with the others and thus providing evidence of a barely perceptible rivalry among conceptions that are nonetheless inevitably entangled by their unchanging interdependence. For its heuristic utility, I prefer to adopt a typology organized around the importance given to the idea of present time in the most essential concepts of the Jewish world—a somewhat abstract universe, located outside any clearly delimited temporal space—but constantly engaged with the transformations that reach it in restructuring a Judaism fitting its aspirations and ontological requirements. Our dialectical model suggests analysis of the status of the paired concepts of *'olam ha-zeh* (this world) / *'olam ha-ba'a* (the coming world). The starting point is provided by a parameter: the concept of waiting for redemption that characterizes Judaism through the ages. The correlations and cross-fertilizations of the Jewish concepts of *le-'atid lavo* (in the future that is coming) and *b'olam ha-zeh* (in this world) in the different models of conceptualization and interpretation circulating in Jewish societies, which confer on them their distinguishing features in various environments and eras, are key to these objectives. These two elements, drawn from basic principles of Jewish eschatology, allow us to clarify its relationship to the notion of time as well as its conventions: real time, whether absent or present, but always assumed to be hurled between past and future, that is, understood as a momentary rescission from projections into the past or future. Far from being limited to philology, the analytic view held here tends toward an anthropological approach: I shall not track down the frequency of these terms in the relevant texts, but instead try to gauge their impact on attitudes.

One of the general ideas of this study is signaled in the reading by Jewish tradition of the concepts "this world" and "the coming world." We can distinguish between these two concepts the rift in the idea of redemption that separates the concept of resurrection from that of "the coming world" because one pertains to historicity and the other to mystical expectation. In the first case, the "world to come" must arrive at a given point in time in order to inscribe itself in the course of humankind's progress and extract it from history. It is destined for everyone, it is universal, and it unifies the common heritage of the West. In the second case, however, it is not certain that resurrection is promised to all or guaranteed,[29] since God alone holds the key.[30]

This idea, keenly debated throughout the ages of Judaism, remains open to interpretation, whether from the perspective of a national event or as a worldwide phenomenon. It was challenged directly as to its factuality, notably by Maimonides, the most eminent thinker of medieval Judaism, who in the twelfth century refused to see anything in it but a metaphor for the immortality of the soul.[31]

To grasp their subject, historians of time must develop categories of analysis that fall outside of theological ideas and create a taxonomy of their own as regards the temporal order. The endeavor here is to develop a model of interpretation that combines aspects of quantification (employing the historical approach based on chronologies and the archaeological finds that validate them); of speculation (acquired from theological discourse, using textual criticism to place texts according to the era in which they are presumed to have been written);[32] of religious phenomenology (reflecting the mystical approach, dismissing temporal elements to keep only the account of the meeting with God); and of intratemporality (deriving from Jewish tradition, which gives access to the Bible through the accumulation of exegeses and interpretations).[33] Applying this model is a matter of analyzing texts and judging them as documents illustrating a general phenomenon, the function of categories of thought. This will take us far from exegesis or biblical commentary, although the objects analyzed are the same.

Part I   *Narrated Time*

In the late twentieth century, assisted by digital watches and clocks, Westerners enjoyed a purely functional use of time, seen as a means of optimally quantifying and scheduling activities on a daily basis. This view of time, doubtless the most familiar because the most nonchalantly practiced, still prevails. For millennia, measuring time seemed to depend, not on mankind, but on the stars, before becoming for many centuries the privilege of the Church. If the fragmentation caused by temporality today seems a given, its source and determining have been relegated to unfathomed depths that science has yet to clarify. It is thus paradoxical that the more humans believe that time has been mastered, tamed, and integrated into our lives as a given, the more its direction seems vague. In traditional societies, the sacred dimension of time was taken for granted: its measure was neither precise nor a commonly known fact, or even seen as essential. Its origin, destiny, and recurrence were perhaps more consistently known. Ever since Einstein radically overturned the approach to time by breaking with the ancient idea of an absolute time, understanding has, however, depended on a range of methods and fields. Some temporal functionalists take refuge in books such as David Landes's *Revolution in Time* (1983) and Ilya Prigogine and Isabelle Stengers's *Entre le temps et l'éternité* (Between time and eternity; 1988), in writings by astrophysicists and biologists, or in appealing to earth scientists, archaeologists, palaeontologists, philosophers, theologians, and specialists in the philosophy of history. My approach is somewhere in the middle; it is neither strictly speaking history, since the terms of the historical contract are not always respected, nor philosophy. I would not dare try to develop a general review of time, and even less one of the philosophy of history!

Yet would it be sensible to seek to capture the relationship of the Jews with temporality without using philosophy; that is, by ignoring any progress in thinking about time? Is it possible to avoid taking into account the positioning that religions assign to the human sense of being in time? Are theological movements not markers that from the start express considerable changes? In a similar way, how to avoid analyzing the role played by the philosophy of history? Was it not the key driver of the first progress in the science of Judaism? Somewhere between the two, domains entrenched in the social sciences sail onward, hoping not to founder in a backwash of disorder, boredom, or drought.

The first section is intended to grasp the way in which the question of time is considered. No matter what questions researchers may have today, their ideas derive from knowledge stockpiled since the nineteenth century. In a certain way, understanding is insidiously guided by all the work done in the field. So an inquiry into perceptions and the use of time in a specific group related to a cognitive system preceding our own requires the deconstruction of the analysis grid that makes it intelligible to us today. The categories of thought in traditional Jewish societies appear obscure to us, as much due to the process of secularization that altered them as to changes in models of understanding the world.

The present work is primarily an essay; in this sense, it offers an occasion for thinking about what currently makes up the complexity of approaches to time and Judaism. Whether accepted or rejected, these approaches are shaped by a group of ideas belonging to the observant or secular Christian conceptual world, as well as to the Jewish conceptual world, adapted to its entry into the City [i.e., into the Western civilizational context in the wake of the Emancipation]. Let there be no mistake about my approach. No nostalgia for Atlantis should be sought in it; it is simply the report of a researcher working on a social world vanished barely a century or two ago, whose sources, to be intelligible to current generations, require a learning process akin to palaeography in the study of the Sumerian world.

This first section is oriented by two major debates. The first philosophizes in pursuit of the preliminary Aristotelian question: "What is time?" Long seen as masters of thinking about time, philosophers devised varied approaches to this, with the help of which I shall try to explain the positions of Jewish thinkers. The other debate, in tandem with theology and the philosophy of history, asks: "What is Jewish time?" Both draw a distinction between Greek (Indo-European) and Hebrew temporalities based on ideas of cycle and linearity. The Quarrel of the Ancients and the Moderns is surely just a step away from debates about the Greeks, which we shall try to span by using our own instruments. Starting with the Western convention that there is such a thing as "universal" time, we'll investigate its meaning. Readers who don't jump ship during the crossing are invited on an excursion around several questions, commonplace to all comers: Is time really the same for everyone? How should temporality be approached? What are the historian's tools in this realm? In thinking about time in the Jewish world, what do we seek to deal with exactly? Representations, to be sure, but of what? Might it involve calendrical rhythms? Social otherness? Religious differentiation? History or events? Or, for that matter, ideas that the Jews have developed over the centuries about their past, present, and future?

Whether we intend the idea of "universal time" as a commonly accepted principle for perceiving time or an arbitrary convention, different conclusions will be drawn about its meaning. In the first case, it would be difficult to sidestep the pitfall of making the history of time into a historical tale as a rough outline of the progress of Western history. By relegating ancient epochs to before the year 1, which divides time into a series of eras, cycles, and scansions determined by reigns and genealogies, we implicitly follow a kind of theological evolutionism, conceived as the feeling of being able to control temporality in some form. After dating became a social marker, the measurement of time had the upper hand. By contrast, the second case opens perceptions to the whims of arbitrariness. From this one may, as the historian Daniel Shabetaï Milo expects us to, merrily blow away the centuries, shake up chronologies, and reflect analyses and historical tales pertaining to unconstrained contradiction.[1] Both perspectives seem critically to lack efficacy for building time in traditional Jewish society.

How do we advance to an outline of building universal time in contemporary efforts? Citing Plato and Aristotle, the Polish historian and philosopher Krzysztof Pomian sketches his thoughts about what he calls "time visible and invisible."[2] He starts from the idea formulated by Plato that "time is born with the Heavens, so that born together, they also dissolve together . . . the Sun, Moon, and Five other stars . . . are born to define the numbers of Time," representing night, day, the lunar month, and the year.[3] Time imitates eternity even though the immutability of the invisible world makes the creation of the visible into an act located outside time: "days and nights, months and seasons existed not at all before the birth of heaven . . . for . . .

these are divisions of Time."[4] To back his formulation of the research question, Pomian quotes three main objections by Aristotle, which distinguish between circular movement and time, as well as between change and movement. The objections conclude that time is in the instant, in the thing that changes. Change is linked to the visible object, whereas time is universal. Without any ties to the visible, "it is simultaneously the same everywhere."[5] Controlled in this manner, the inverse of the Platonic model of creation, the Aristotelian world, is in fact intemporal: "Its total duration had no beginning and will have no end; on the contrary, it contains and embraces in itself the infinity of time."[6] For Pomian, this says it all. What Aristotle advances as problematic about time will remain so until the arrival of relativity in the twentieth century: "An invisible twin of movement that affects them, it was deemed a metaphysical intrusion into the heart . . . of the physical world."[7] According to Aristotle, movement is what defines the passage of the instant between the before and the after, what happened in the instant preceding what would happen, which only the soul can detect. Aristotelian time is only perceptible due to the invention of the idea of physical movement, which in turn demands to be associated with intelligence and soul: "Because instants are in time, likewise the before and the after are in time, for where the instant is, the dislocation from the instant is also found,"[8] which takes into account the simultaneity of the confrontation of the moving body and the soul. Aristotelian time, captured between movement and instant, multiplicity and universality, qualitative and number, illustrates unity, identity, universality, and uniformity; by extending the notion of the eternal movement of the First Cause, it might be referred to the idea, however separate from the eternal life of God.

Yet for people, time is destructive and irreversible, just as "it also applies to other things that possess [within them] natural flow, creation, and destruction."[9] Pomian conceptualizes Aristotelian time by blending it with chronosophy, psychological or lived time which is short, linear, regressive, and irreversible; cosmic, solar time whose last trace is found in daily life, is indefinitely long and cyclic, for which a return is reserved only for certain species; and religious time, that of eternity, unchanging and stationary. The underlying question of the *imitatio dei* (imitation of God) slips between changing time and eternity, which

Pomian classes respectively as psychological and religious time. For the Stoics, cosmic time is divine; humanity should contemplate and strive to conform to it. Time is endowed with a religious dimension, which inevitably subsumes the time of a sage who knows how to live in harmony with nature. If Plotinus breaks with this approach by refusing primacy or independent reality to cosmic time, it is the better to formulate his vision of links existing between eternity and time. Since as a totality never to be completed, eternity is perceived as consubstantial with the reality of God, for which there can be neither past nor future, it is identical to itself in its unchanging perfection. In Plotinus, meditation is the means by which the soul relates to eternity.[10] Plotinus thus accords preeminence to religious time, leaving no room for cosmic time, it being recognized that the visible, apparent measure of time established by the celestial revolution is nevertheless only the soul's time, preceding the time that engenders and activates it. In this depiction of eternity, Pomian notes an integration in magic and religion that makes time "congenitally incomplete, always in need, refusing to be grasped in its entirety, which has no point of life; the present falls into the past, into nonbeing, where the future still abides."[11] Pomian thus relies on Aristotle here, who asks how best to classify time, whether among beings or nonbeings.

Based on the schism introduced by Plotinus, perhaps influenced by gnosticism, cosmic time is relieved of the sense of mediation between eternity and psychological time. This is particularly the case for Christians, who see time as the expression of God's will. Every event is presently responsible for the totality of a destiny (*devenir*) that in essence contains past, present, and future. History may thus be conceived of as a divine design, of which the Incarnation is the central point, around which everything is organized and explained. In other words, only the mediation of the Christian approach makes possible the concordance of archaic and modern ideas that superimposes the conventional concept of a time underpinned by a history irreversibly progressing toward universality upon the ancient, pagan, and Greek.

In *Categories of Medieval Culture*, Aron Gurevich devotes a whole chapter to showing that time and space are the crucial parameters of life and human experience.[12] However, time is not meant here as duration, an irreversible sequence of the flow of events, and time and space are objective data whose qualities are separate from content. Gurevich also reminds the reader that time and space are categories that cannot apply identically to nature and society: "Few factors in a culture express the essential nature of its world picture so clearly as its way of reckoning time: for this has a determining influence on the way people behave, the way they think, the rhythm of their lives and the relationships between them and things. . . . The comparison [of ancient Eastern and classical societies with the apocalyptic conception of the world's evolution from creation to destruction] underlines the importance of making a thorough study of the problem of time in the historico-cultural place; but it does nothing to help us to understand the category of time as apprehended by medieval man."[13]

Gurevich rightly notes that Judeo-Christian civilization was not the only influence on the categories of medieval consciousness, and his history of approaches to time includes the agrarian society of the ancient barbarians. Its pattern formed by nature, the farming calendar in an agrarian society reflected the changing of the seasons and the succession of agricultural tasks. In Scandinavia, summer was designated as the time "between ploughing and stacking," May was dubbed the "time for gathering eggs" and the "time when sheep and calves are rounded up." For Germanic tribes, July was the "month of mowing." June was for setting aside a "month of fallow," and September the "month of sowing."[14] The years and time in general constitute a circular movement, signaling periodic repetition, rather than being directionless slots devoid of content. Governed by the cycles of nature, time in agrarian society both shapes the mutual interdependence of humanity and structures the subjugation of human consciousness to it. Far from being change, in this case, movement is repetition, and only acts repeated at intervals, as sanctioned by tradition, are deemed real. Denying any worth to individuality or innovation, archaic society considered it natural to behave as it had from time immemorial. Following tradition alone conferred moral strength on human endeavors. Drawing on the work of Eliade, Gurevich deduced that people in traditional societies had tirelessly to imitate the first people, deities, and heroes, who lifted them up toward the heavenly model. People forcibly gained authenticity from being bound to deities: "All human activity, productive, social, family, intimate, becomes significant and is endorsed in so far as it participates in the sacral order, and follows the ritual established 'at the beginning of time.'"[15] Traditional man moved in a mythological time in which festivals and ceremonies stood in direct relation to the tales that dictated proper conduct. The archaic conscience and history contradicted each other, because collective memory changed into myths events that had actually occurred, reducing them to ideas and people to archetypes. The emphasis was on repeating facts relating to the "beginning of time," which had preceded life; by relating yesterday to the actual content of today, and rooting both deeply in eternity, this made any distinction between past and present even more opaque.

Archaic society marks the scansion of time by numbering generations belonging to lineages, which build and reproduce human groups, which the individual naturally joins. Genealogies and family legends organize a tribal or clan time, always local, further strengthened by seasonal rhythms of nature, which act equally on the same land. Yet Gurevich thinks that barbarian time falls within a spatial concept, expressed by the weak appearance of cyclical time, in which the only meaning of the future is as renewal of the past in the present. The magical action, if it permits a return to the past, also permits influencing the future by changing the course of events. This is why time may be considered concrete, indeed tangible. It is a phenomenon that may be felt, like other objects in a world. So time and space involve places and times divided between sacred and profane, the former being festivals and ceremonies, the latter temples, tombs, burial mounds, or homes consecrated to the gods. Time thus has no life of its own, being wholly subject to consciousness; but it embodies the "chain of human generations."[16] With the passage from paganism to Christianity, medieval Europe discovers a self-contained meaning for the idea of eternity. This discovery involves a thorough overhaul of depictions of temporality without cancelling the archaic relationship with time that would henceforth nourish what Gurevich calls the "lowest layer of popular awareness." As an example, he notes that Christian liturgy returns to the pagan calendar, based on cycles of nature, adapting it to inherent needs. Pagan festivals were reinterpreted, recharged with new meaning, and adapted to the Church. Calendrical time becomes liturgical time, with the year adjusted to the pace of the events that marked the life of Christ and the feast days of the saints. Whereas the calculation of time works according to the number of weeks before and after Nativity, depending on the country, the year does not begin at the same moment. It opens with Nativity and follows with Holy Week and Annunciation. Day and night are not divided into equal numbers of hours, but respond to sunshine by splitting into hours of day and night, varying by season and region.

Without any precise measuring instrument,[17] the flow of time depends on the clergy who, calling the faithful to daily prayer, chant the hours of light as the bells toll,[18] marking canonical hours that control people's daily lives to the rhythm of Christian liturgy. Outside any context of dominion, medieval man accedes to nature, which in turn subordinates time to light and dark. Henceforth, everything is organized perfectly for the arrival of the "metachronic time" that Hervé Barreau considers the "final avatar . . . of that mythical time that was originally the only time in representations of the world, then the time of this world, inasmuch as it outflanks and informs ordinary time, and that finally becomes the eschatological time that nourishes the hope, or the despair, of those who think about the world and know that death is unavoidable."[19]

Whether philosophical, historical, or psychological, the few paradigms cited above to trace the emergence of a time taken as universal in the West are all based on a perception of Christian origin. Is it imaginable that in an identical conceptual space, the idea of time might have been drawn from other sources?

A Time for the Jews

Assimilating the works of Émile Durkheim and Marcel Mauss, and later Marc Bloch, Fernand Braudel, and Jacques Le Goff, French historians were confirmed in the belief that temporality, the perception of time, and the representation of its passing are the raw materials of their discipline and the means of articulating their métier. Henceforth, they were equally convinced that their own system of cultural and scientific references tends toward ways of interpretation probably not shared by past societies. How could one grasp the course of time when the concept of the earth's rotation was merely a heretical fantasy? How could one depict infinity when the idea of a light-year was only an

expedient due to ecstatic experiences? How could one imagine duration when that of seasons, days, and years was imprecise? Acting as one
of the elements of nature, the individual moves in the seasons, forming
part of the cycles.[20] Raising itself above the natural order extolled by
the theological model, the being is located at a given moment of its
unfolding, between genesis and *parousia*,[21] creation and redemption,
the beginning and end of time. From the circle to the line, the link to
time proves to be one of the basic criteria for deciphering beliefs and
value systems. Yet may we think in terms more nuanced than circular
and linear? As we shall see, starting with Mircea Eliade's, most studies
of time focus on the opposition between ahistorical pagan, barbarian,
and primitive times, on the one hand, and modern time, conceived of
as a historical continuum, whether vertical or horizontal, on the other.
Studies of specific groups have shown that these general distinctions
may be far too simplistic. The timeworn paradigm of Greek cyclic time
was overturned by Pierre Vidal-Naquet, who clearly demonstrated
that we cannot understand time among the Greeks without taking
into account the overlapping of linear and circular ideas and gaps
possibly existing between philosophical speculation and the average
Greek person.[22]

The same is true for Jewish society, which combines circular aspects
of traditional societies with linear aspects of theological societies. What
algebraic symbols would be adequate to express this case? Is it conceivable given current thinking about time, and when whole libraries have
been written on the subject, that one might be able to escape from the
beaten path and imagine time moving in curves, rather than circles,
and triangles instead of lines?

Awareness of Time and the Sense of History

Jewish historiography has not avoided dispute over time. A debate was
born around highly attractive theses by Lionel Kochan[23] and Yosef
Yerushalmi[24] with regard to Jewish society. Both assert that in their
approach to the past, Jews have preferred inscription in memory to
history for a period stretching from the closing of the biblical canon
in the first century CE to the appearance of the so-called science of

Judaism in Germany in the nineteenth century, with the brief exception of the Italian Renaissance in the sixteenth century. This seems to run contrary to the usually accepted Western historical model and features reiteration in the present of certain events that occurred in the distant past, raised to the rank of historical archetypes, whereas other, more recent happenings are doomed to oblivion or vanish into the archetypical. A tale recounted by Manès Sperber of Jews hunted down in a Polish town during the dark hours of Nazi oppression who greet a messenger by remarking that he comes from the "martyred community of Vienna," alluding to the tragedy that had struck that city's Jews fully 520 years earlier, exemplifies this proposition.[25] Other Jewish historians and thinkers have argued against this idea for various reasons, including Amos Funkenstein[26] and Abraham Joshua Heschel.[27] Funkenstein contends that since Judaism is, above all, a historical religion, Jews certainly possess historical consciousness.[28] For Heschel, because the God of Israel expresses himself by events and more often with actions than in places or objects, his historical unfolding must have been constantly in the process of becoming.[29] Furthermore, Heschel goes so far as to define Judaism as a real "architecture of time."[30] In some sense, this viewpoint identifies the Jews as a key component of history. In this way, the debate between advocates of the torch of memory and those of history create obvious lines of division.[31] It is symptomatic of divisions in Jewish historiography that Jewish historians should be engaged in an impossible dialogue about a misunderstanding. Although all may study the position of Jews with respect to writing history, when one resolves to point out characteristic traits in the attitudes of Jews in traditional or contemporary society, another relies on the religious forms of ideas inherent in Judaism since the remotest eras, while a third reintegrates the approach of Jews into a Western medieval context. We might resolve this dispute by suggesting that in presenting itself as *the* historical religion par excellence, and history's veritable incarnation, Judaism exempts Jews from any interest in it. Between the burden (which might be better described as a "weight," "duty," or "value") of memory and the task (which might likewise better be called a "function," "value," or "role") of history, an abyss of misunderstandings gapes, which are simultaneously methodological, conceptual, and disciplinary, if not philosophical. The outline of a pertinent approach to temporality eludes the content of fashion-able polemics about memory in Jewish studies.[32] A time-related influ-ence anchored in memory is inescapably linked to the circular model produced by the return of the past into the present, which it finally sanctifies, while since Spinoza and Vico, the idea of an historical tem-porality has rested on a clear separation between sacred and profane realms.[33] To grasp the elements of misunderstanding that oppose these introductions of attitudes in Judaism, it would be interesting to verify whether the content imputed by both sides to the idea of temporal-ity might help to clarify this debate. These approaches seem frozen in an inability to think of ideas of time and temporality together, owing to the division between labor on the idea either of purely abstract, philosophical, or eschatological time or of temporality that is con-crete, measureable, and approachable by history or anthropology. The omission of thought tends to make living people into either acrobats lacking a vision of time or visionaries of time without temporality. Still, temporality is organized through constant interactions involving experienced time and the consciousness of time.

"Since the Greeks did not conceive of time as a straight line, the field of actions of Providence could not be history as a whole but only the destiny of individuals," Oscar Cullmann writes. "To satisfy his needs for revelation and deliverance, man had no alternative but to have recourse to a mystical conception for which time did not exist, expressed with the help of spatial concepts."[34]

Stated thus unambiguously, the division between curved and straight visions helps us observe that the debate over the place that is or is not given to history is filled with a basic dispute about what is reserved for religious phenomena, as allowed by history. Jacques Le Goff is supremely clear: "The dialectic of history seems to be summed up in the opposition or dialogue between past and present (and/or between present and past). In general this opposition is not neutral but subtends or expresses an evaluative system, as for example, in the oppositional pairs antique/modern, and progress/reaction."[35] To emerge and escape from this false debate, we might try to reshuffle the playing cards by reconsidering the relevance of conventional allega-tions about the approach to temporality among the ancient Hebrews and that of the Jews. Even more, changes issuing from the transition from biblical to rabbinical religion, from the Diaspora to medieval Europe, from modern times to the Emancipation, were strained through a series of filters until usable data necessarily seem biased. But then, does granting memory a leading role in religious functions and Jewish identity really make an intimate enemy of history? Or is it a question of something else entirely?

Two   Where Does Time Come From?

To try to untangle this web of ambiguities, we must look to the Bible, the source upon which all approaches to Judaism are based. It is presented by Jewish tradition as a paradigm of the history of humanity, although the distinction is clear-cut between the Israelite biblical religion and rabbinic Judaism, which followed it. Yet how is it possible to approach the Bible in terms of our goal? It requires an especially formidable approach, since the Bible is considered as the original patrimony shared by religious worlds that diverge about its use, history, and meaning. For the Protestant theologian Gerhard von Rad, an Old Testament expert, European time is marked by an "infinite line" along which all events are arranged, while he terms Israelite time a "filled" concrete time, leaving scant room for the arrangement of periods.[1] The development from ancient ideas of time to monotheistic visions is crucial for grasping the concept of events, which amount to the growth of historical time. We can easily see the difference between a repetitious ceremony about the myth of origins in which the Creator intercedes as the main actor and a quantitative measure of time that recalls this. Yet the relationship to eternity that results from it is doubtless more difficult to perceive. So that time be imaginable based on the idea of eternity, the human element that gives it full scope must, by contrast, be fleetingness because of mortality. While time may be measured in its passing, it also forms part of the destruction of beings and species, without being changed by the process, for it follows its own course. We have seen that in ancient times Aristotle grasped it as change in a visible object, but independently of it, since time is the same everywhere. For Plato, time stems from the creation of the visible, "days and nights, months, seasons did not exist before the heavens were born . . . these are the divisions of time."[2] Caught between movement and moment, Aristotle's time resembles monotheism's eternal life of God, but is destructive and irreversible—whence its autonomy in terms of mankind and things. If changing time is experienced or psychological time, the time of eternity is eschatological time. Yet how to take account of a time that for Aristotle inclines toward nonbeing? Saint Augustine may have ushered in modern Western thinking about the measurement of time, and his doubts became archetypes.[3] We cannot measure what does not exist, so if we measure time, it must exist, notwithstanding its Aristotelian existential flaw and Plotinian immutability.[4] Augustine, and Christianity after him, found time to be inherent to the soul, which alone can perceive it in three dimensions: past, present, and future. However, this concept excludes dependence upon physical motion. In a monotheistic vision, God himself may change the course of temporal motion, just as Joshua did by halting the sun's progress. Time is independent, but still had been the object of creation. All speculation on time is thus meditation on eternity, Paul Ricoeur affirmed, insisting on the Augustinian vision according to which eternity resembles time in that while the fact of its existence is unproblematic, the way in which it exists remains perplexing.[5]

Judaism proposes no solution to these questions. The Bible pronounces a tale, tells a story in which time, as we shall see, plays a secondary role. Yet between the books of the Torah and the Prophetic Books, we can clearly discern time's variation, and Daniel and the Apocalypses recognize even more flagrant discrepancies. The Jewish reading of the Bible, which begins each week with a parashah and a prophetic reading (*Haftarah*) thus continually redirects Jews toward ideas enriched by multiple sources of added commentary, bearing the marks of the era in which they were written. So for example, we read Genesis with commentaries written by Rashi (Shlomo Yitzhaki) in the eleventh and twelfth centuries,[6] retaining the biblical story and its medieval exegesis, amplifying earlier commentaries from the Talmud and Midrash. What is more, if the Haftarah refers to the prophetic text, we can see a relaying of tradition that, even when based on the archaic concept evoked by Eliade, is revisited each week by the *derashah* to the congregation from the rabbi, who in turn chooses, mixes, and interprets texts to make them comprehensible to listeners in the light of actual events in their daily lives.[7] In this way, Bible reading became part of the contemporaneity of Jewish temporality. Narration is based on a search for or approximation of eternity through time. Far from erasing the difference, the latter continues to increase, for the achronic tale does not draw nearer to eternity, whose most illuminating contrast is, as Paul Ricoeur notes, temporality itself.[8] The historical element is not only what happens, but what can be told or what has already been told in chronicles or legends.[9] Biblical accounts can thus be read in several ways with respect to temporality. One can reorder chronologies and organize passages according to the presumed date of their composition to clarify historical narratives, as do biblical criticism (and researchers). Or one can set aside temporal elements and retain only stories of en-counters with God from which lessons can be derived, as does the exe-gete. Or, finally, exegeses and interpretations of Bible stories can simply be welcomed and accepted, as for the ordinary observant believer.

With regard to eternity and time, the concepts of Jewish thinkers of the Middle Ages are divided into two major choices, as described by Aristotle and Plotinus. Yet ideas about time are also closely linked to basic notions of Judaism. To think about eternity, we must address the notion of immortality and retribution, which relates to the other world, '*Olam ha-ba'a*. However, those who accept Plato's point of view on the existence of time "before time" must resort to interpre-tations of the creation of the world, while immortality of the soul, a key Greek and Maimonidean concept, cannot be perceived without recourse to the notion of resurrection, itself tied to ideas about the end of time and the advent of the Messiah. I shall focus on these inter-twined notions and concepts in an attempt to untangle and grasp what may be called the function of time in the world of Jewish observance.

The Times of the Bible

Marcel Proust's *À la Recherche du temps perdu* (*In Search of Lost Time*) may well be the most frequently cited fictional reflection on time, but for present purposes I prefer Thomas Mann's *Der Zauberberg* (*The Magic Mountain*), where Mann observes that

> stories, as histories, must be past, and the further past, one might say, the better for them as stories and for the storyteller, that conjurer who

murmurs in past tenses. But the problem with our story . . . is this:
it is much older than its years, its datedness is not to be measured in
days, nor the burden of age weighing upon it to be counted by orbits
around the sun ; in a word, it does not actually owe its pastness to
time . . . [10]

In Mann's novel, the reader is faced with the question of literary time,
always caught between two forms of temporality. One covers the time
of the story, while the other belongs to the reader, the time spent
reading the book.[11] It is somewhat the same with analyzing biblical
time. Two approaches to biblical temporality are possible. The first (a)
is rooted in the quantifiable, or measure, and may relate to the periodization of the biblical text. The second (b) less obviously elucidates
the Bible's concept of time, but explains how the Hebrew Bible has
been reconstructed by (Christians) critical scholarship. Both play a role
here in understanding the Bible's role in attitudes developed over the
centuries by Jews to identify with, and find their bearings in, temporal
continuity.

(a) The Period of the Bible

The Jewish Bible, or Tanakh (an acronym for Torah, Nevi'im, and
Ketuvim),[12] consists of three parts. The first, the Pentateuch, or Torah,
comprises five books: Genesis, Exodus, Leviticus, Numbers, and Deuteronomy. The second, Prophets (Nevi'im), divided into Former and
Latter Prophets, contains the books of Joshua, Judges, Samuel, and
Kings, along with other prophets, great and small. Finally, Hagiographa,
or Ketuvim, gathers together diverse writings, such as Psalms, Proverbs,
Job, the Song of Songs, and the books of Ruth and Esther, Lamentations, Ecclesiastes, Daniel, Ezra, Nehemiah, and Chronicles.

Did the "biblical period" ever exist? Divided over the pertinence of
the scriptures as a historical document, some archaeologists classify the
Bible among national literary myths.[13] Only rarely does scientific consensus occur in biblical matters. Nevertheless, the chronological table
of the history of Israel may be cut into historical slices, even if these become the subject of bitter debates over dating in view of archaeological
digs or philological analysis. The first of these periods is the pre-Mosaic
era. It locates Abraham during the time of Hammurabi, king of Baby-

lon, around 1700 BCE. Then came the Mosaic period, identified, as its name suggests, with the person of Moses, dated to around 1300 BCE. After which is the period called the Conquest, described in the Book of Joshua, and that of the Philistine invasions, which places Samuel in approximately the eleventh century BCE. After that, the Period of the Kings began, with the reigns of Saul near 1029 BCE, David toward 1004, and Solomon between 965 and 926, defined by the building of the Temple. The next period was that of the Two Kingdoms, which starts with the division of Jeroboam in the eighth or ninth century BCE and ends with the taking of Samaria ca. 721–722. The period of Judah consists of the reign of Hezekiah; the prophecies of Isaiah and Micah, 701–699 (or 742–697) BCE; the reign of Manasseh, ca. 699–645 (or 696–642); the prophecies of Jeremiah and Second Isaiah, between the sixth and fifth centuries BCE; the reign of Josiah, ca. 629 BCE, marked by efforts against paganizing, interrupted by such events as the discovery in the Temple of the Book of the Law, ca. 621–622, the first deportation (598–587), the arrival of the prophet Ezekiel between 598 and 586, and, finally, the Fall of Jerusalem ca. 586 BCE.

The so-called Babylonian Exile, even though the deportation extended over three sequential steps, began around 587, only ending in 538 with Cyrus's edict permitting the Hebrew captives to return to Palestine to rebuild the Temple. The prophecies of Haggai, Zechariah, and Malachi, ca. 520, fall into the subsequent Persian era, as does the completion of the Second Temple in 515. The key figures of Nehemiah and the scribe Ezra take precedence ca. 445 BCE,[14] and the first public reading of the Torah occurred around 444. The schism between Samaritans and Jews may have happened approximately in the fourth or third century BCE.[15]

In one way, biblical history ends, chronologically speaking, with the last words of the Book of Nehemiah: "And for the wood offering, at times appointed, and for the firstfruits. Remember me, O my God, for good."[16] The next era is already postbiblical. After 332 BCE, the fall of the Persian Empire is followed by the Hellenistic era, marked by the Syrian persecution of Hellenized Jews in Judea and the Maccabean revolt in 168.[17] Maccabean rule continued from 165 BCE until 63 BCE, when the Roman general Pompey subdued Judaea in 63 BCE, announcing the end of its independence and the start of Roman rule, which began in 37 with the reign of Herod the Great, during which the two scholars Hillel and Shammai stand out, representing two rival schools of thought. A primary turning point was the destruction of Jerusalem and burning of the Temple in 70 CE. Between 132 and 135 CE, the Bar Kokhba revolt against the Roman Empire preceded the completion of the Mishnah around 190, which opens another stage in Jewish history by ushering in rabbinic Judaism.

Although extensive, the period covered by the Hebrew Bible is finite. Starting with creation, it concludes with the Book of Chronicles.[18] The story begins, as it were, in Mesopotamia and develops until the end of the Persian period and the dawn of the Hellenistic era, since the books of the Maccabees are not included in the Jewish biblical canon.

One of the first observations made by every reader of the Bible is that the temporal principle governing its books is not a matter of chronology. Made up of descriptions of sequential, repetitive, or remembered events, it would be unthinkable to integrate them into a coherent period by a simple graduated reading. For although the story follows a historic continuity, it does not deal with narrative scheduling. Drawing up a biblical division into periods calls for implementing salient points outside the Bible itself. The Jewish canon provides a conundrum about whether narrative forms of temporal balance are valid in the religious realm. How, for example, are we to understand the absorption of texts such as the Book of Daniel, written under the reign of Antiochus IV Epiphanes[19] or the Book of Esther,[20] describing events occurring during the time of Xerxes I of Persia, which both seem substantially later than the historical body of the Hebrew Bible?

The inherent problem in dividing the biblical text into periods is primarily the question of its composition. When were the books written that later made up the canon, and by whom? Traditionally, a key indicator was given by a *baraita*[21] reported in the Talmud:[22]

> Our Rabbis taught: The order of the Prophets is Joshua, Judges, Samuel, Kings, Jeremiah, Ezekiel, Isaiah, and the Twelve Minor Prophets. Let us examine this. Hosea came first, as it is written, God spake first to Hosea. But did God speak first to Hosea? Were there not many prophets between Moses and Hosea? R. Johanan, however, has explained that [what it means is that] he was the first of the four prophets who prophesied at that period, namely, Hosea, Isaiah, Amos,

and Micah. Should not then Hosea come first?—Since his prophecy is written along with those of Haggai, Zechariah, and Malachi, and Haggai, Zechariah, and Malachi came at the end of the prophets, he is reckoned with them. But why should he not be written separately and placed first?—Since his book is so small, it might be lost [if copied separately]. Let us see again. Isaiah was prior to Jeremiah and Ezekiel. Then why should not Isaiah be placed first?—Because the Book of Kings ends with a record of destruction and Jeremiah speaks throughout of destruction and Ezekiel commences with destruction and ends with consolation and Isaiah is full of consolation; therefore we put destruction next to destruction and consolation next to consolation.

The order of the Hagiographa is Ruth, the Book of Psalms, Job, Prophets, Ecclesiastes, Song of Songs, Lamentations, Daniel and the Scroll of Esther, Ezra, and Chronicles. Now on the view that Job lived in the days of Moses, should not the book of Job come first?—We do not begin with a record of suffering. But Ruth also is a record of suffering?—It is a suffering with a sequel [of happiness], as R. Johanan said: Why was her name called Ruth?—Because there issued from her David who replenished the Holy One, blessed be He, with hymns and praises.

Who wrote the Scriptures?—Moses wrote his own book and the portion of Balaam and Job. Joshua wrote the book which bears his name and [the last] eight verses of the Pentateuch. Samuel wrote the book which bears his name and the Book of Judges and Ruth. David wrote the Book of Psalms, including in it the work of the elders, namely, Adam, Melchizedek, Abraham, Moses, Heman, Yeduthun, Asaph, and the three sons of Korah. Jeremiah wrote the book that bears his name, the Book of Kings, and Lamentations. Hezekiah and his colleagues wrote [mnemonic YMSHK] Isaiah, Proverbs, the Song of Songs, and Ecclesiastes. The Men of the Great Assembly wrote [mnemonic KNDG] Ezekiel, the Twelve Minor Prophets, Daniel, and the Scroll of Esther. Ezra wrote the book that bears his name and the genealogies of the Book of Chronicles up to his own time.[23]

To this image of composition handed down by tradition, the French rabbi Lazare Wogue (1817–1897) added: "Every hypothesis in the Talmud about the order of the Nevi'im [Prophets] and even more of the Ketuvim [Writings], leaves much to be desired."[24] Without venturing onto the highly specialized minefield of dating biblical texts, we may nevertheless observe with Wogue that the order provided by scholars of the talmudic era hardly corresponds to a desire to attribute authorship to the works mentioned, but rather to supply indications about the collection and a "final draft" of surviving texts, in their final transcription. The traditional point of view, in this case the talmudic corpus[25] and Rashi's commentary, is built on this *baraita* to find that the writing and transcription of the texts were divided in this way. The Pentateuch has God as its author and Moses as transcriber (apart from the eight last verses written by Joshua). Some books were written by eponymous authors, which means that Joshua, Samuel—aided by Gad and Nathan—Jeremiah, Ezra, and Nehemiah themselves personally wrote down their books. By contrast, Isaiah and Proverbs, the Song of Songs, and Ecclesiastes were put together by members of Hezekiah's academy; the texts of Ezekiel, Daniel, and the Minor Prophets were retranscribed by *soferim* of the Great Assembly;[26] the Psalms may have different authors but were collected by David. Then there remain books whose authorship is not associated with their titles, such as Judges, attributed to Samuel; Kings, to Jeremiah; Job, to Moses; Ruth, to Samuel; Lamentations, to Jeremiah; and Esther, authored by the scribes of the Great Assembly. This established view did not prevent each attribution to an author or transcriber being discussed by the codifiers, even into the Gemara, rabbis, and finally by scholars, philosophers, and philologists. Likewise discussed were the books themselves as well as their divisions, with the exception of the divine author of the Torah of Moses.

It was long believed that the Jewish canon was fixed along the lines established by Ezra at Yavneh under Roman rule. At this time, whatever might be the destiny of the sum of extant works, it was decided that the Torah would remain tripartite, and that nothing more would be added.[27] On the contrary, the right would be reserved to cut from the corpus everything that seemed dubious or dangerous in this era, when issues about Judaism and many dissident sects (including Samaritans, Sadducees, and Essenes) proliferated, as well as the Jewish Christian sect.

The supposed official fixing of the Jewish biblical canon at Yavneh in the first century determines in a fairly precise way what can be assumed in a broad sense about the length of the biblical period, decontextualized from its narrative alone. Two or three millennia are counted from the working out of creation to the era of Nehemiah. From this measure of temporality partly arises the discrepancy of 3,760 years between Jewish and Christian computations.

(b) Time in the Bible

Of what time does the Bible speak? During the biblical period, historical temporality could not be accountable for the measurement of time seen in biblical narrative. Figures appear one after another all through the books without the order of their declarations or appearances being clocked by timekeeping. This lack of temporality is emphasized even more by the interpolation of texts apparently set down during more or less distant times by scribes whose writings were merged with the *seder* (order) of the gatherers. How then can time be situated in the Bible? The very term "canon" suggests a way to solve the problem. Currently bearing a Christian connotation, the Greek word apparently still bears a Semitic root; the Hebrew *kane*, a reed or measuring stick, a benchmark,[28] then includes a Jewish connotation. Jewish sources establish that it is permissible to remove a work from the canon by hiding it in the *genizah*. Hidden this way, it becomes apocryphal and while still circulating in private for the personal edification of readers, may no longer be read aloud in public. This canonical practice started the gradual disappearance of works transmitted in Greek translation or that were rediscovered in the Cairo Genizah and at the Qumran site.[29]

If everything is language, every language is also discourse. Yet reading books in the order in which they were collected removes all relevance from the chronological approach. The Book of Chronicles ending the Ketuvim section of the Hebrew Bible concludes by mentioning Cyrus II of Persia, who, Prophets and the Book of Ezra inform us, authorized the captives at Babylon to return to Palestine to rebuild the Temple. The story does not end there, for its next episode is placed earlier. To follow the continuity of the history of Cyrus, the reader should return to the first chapter of the Book of Ezra. This characteristic form of unpredictable narration is also found in the order that directed the placing of the Book of Ruth,[30] an ancestor of King David, into the last book of Ketuvim, while the Book of Kings is integrated into the prophetic portion that precedes it. Consequently, how to interpret the message about time conveyed in these books that present Jewish tradition as a model for humanity?

'Olam means time in the aggregate, in the largest sense possible. In the manifold nuances related to it—it appears 460 times in the Hebrew Bible[31]—it evokes many things. In ordinary language, it means the universe as eternity. In dictionaries of the Bible, it is translated as "hidden time" or "unknown time," with multiple meanings:[32] eternity, as indicated in Genesis;[33] "days of old," or yemot 'olam;[34] "time to come," even an entire lifespan; and, finally, the totality constituted by the world. Jastrow's talmudic dictionary unhesitatingly translates it as variously as "nature," "existence," "world," "life-time," and "eternity."[35] So a single term covers all the potential meanings of time: eternity as the limited duration of human life; the earthly world as the world to come; limited time as infinity; measurement as the immeasurable, hidden, or unknown. Did the ancient Hebraic language make light of temporality?[36]

The origin of time, in the order of biblical discourse, takes shape with the creation of the universe, the story of which opens the first two chapters of Genesis. The idea of creation, however, proposes a notion of time that is both cyclic and linear. Creation is repetitive and forever in motion; this is reproduced by the intermediary of revelation, introduced in the cycle of the weekly and annual liturgy. For its part, the occasion of primordial creation indicates the origin of horizontal time, which unfolds from it, while historical time takes hold with the expulsion of Adam and Eve from the Garden of Eden: "Creation is regarded as a work of Jahweh in history, a work within time. This means that there is a real and true opening up of historical prospect," Gerhard von Rad writes. Therefore "Creation is itself a sequence in time, exactly marked out into days."[37] We have seen that for Aristotle, the Prime Mover established the temporal idea, transposed into a monotheistic vision, and this first element, this unique mover, is the essence of essences. It may correspond to the God of gods who possesses and organizes all powers, including that of acting on time and the elements. The first postulate states that God, the construction manager of temporality, is located outside the latter. Hence, an eschatological view of time is necessarily dual, implying, on the one hand, a fixed period for creatures, and, on the other, the transcendence of their Creator.

Understanding the biblical story depends in Jewish tradition on its commentaries and later interpretations. Deprived of its exegeses, the Jewish message of the Bible remains incomplete. Devoid of the elements that enable it to be grasped in the totality of what it must disclose, it remains hermetic. Commentary is thus an inexhaustible source of riches, and revelation is not a single, fixed event, but a historical continuum: "They [the rabbis' statements] make absolute the concept of tradition in which the meaning of revelation unfolds in the course of historical time—but only because everything that can come to be known has already been deposited in a timeless substratum."[38] Knowing that Judaism is based on and spread around the idea of revelation (God appears and expresses himself in historical time)—which adds linearity to the circularity of his replication in his ritual function—the biblical story offers two variants in formulating the act of revelation. Two stories convey a sort of direct personal revelation, and two others present it indirectly, working through the intermediary of an event. All four end by promulgating a covenant contracted with mankind at God's instigation. Following a development in biblical continuity that depends on a significant change in the idea of revelation itself permits a division into periods that differs from the common temporal measures. This other dividing reveals a first period that, starting with the creation of the world, continues until the personal revelation made to Abraham in Gen. 12:1: "Now the Lord had said unto Abram, Get thee out of thy country, and from thy kindred, and from thy father's house, unto a land that I will shew thee"; then to the agreed-upon covenants in Gen. 15:7–21, and finally chapter 17: "And God said unto Abraham, Thou shalt keep my covenant therefore, thou, and thy seed after thee in their generations. This is my covenant, which ye shall keep, between me and you and thy seed after thee; every man child among you shall be circumcised."[39] The second period runs from the Patriarchs through the personal revelation of God to Moses in Exod. 3:3: "And Moses said, I will now turn aside, and see this great sight, why the bush is not burnt." The phenomenon culminates in the collective revelation of the giving of the Torah by the utterance of the Ten Commandments that mark the forming of the people of Israel in Exod. 19–20: "And the Lord said unto Moses, Thus thou shalt say unto the children of Israel, Ye have seen that I have talked with you from heaven."[40]

The third period determined covers the entry into the Promised Land, the formation of the Kingdom, the period of Judges and Prophets, and that of the monarchy, continuing until the reign of Josiah around 621–622 BCE, when the first element of indirect revelation occurred. In 2 Kings 22–23, with respect to a copy of a book of the Law that had been misplaced, we are told: "And the king went up into the house of the Lord, and all the men of Judea and all the inhabitants of Jerusalem with him, and the priests, and the prophets, and all the people, both small and great: and he read in their ears all the words of the book of the covenant which was found in the house of the Lord."[41]

Finally the last period, starting with the Book of Kings, extends until after the return from the Babylonian Exile when, around 441 BCE a hitherto unknown ancient book is discovered in turn, in Neh. 8–10: "And all the people gathered themselves together as one man into the street that was before the water gate; and they spake unto Ezra the scribe to bring the book of the law of Moses, which the Lord had commanded to Israel."[42]

The structure of direct revelation may be grasped in a perspective approaching a "mythic time" during which events occur that penetrate the symbolic order by changing into rites and cultural forms. In this case, they resemble the myth of origins that they symbolize. To generations who never witnessed it, they convey the story of the founding event in the unity of the people. To capture the effects of the Jewish idea of creation drawn up from the story of Genesis, we must seek out forms of its celebration during the United Monarchy.[43] Rituals such as lighting the great menorah of the Temple or the ceremony of Simhat Beit Ha-sho'evah, the water-drawing festival during Sukkot that appears in the Book of Psalms and in Sirach, also called the Book of Ecclesiasticus or Ben Sira, and in Prophets, are alone likely to indicate the way that reiterating creation may work in the social planning of religious life at that time.

As for the two events described in indirect revelations, they introduce an outside element that, by highlighting another possible form of revelation of the divine to mankind, adds a mediator between the sacred word and its reception by mankind. From then on, without intercession at that moment from the strength of the word, these "discoveries" insist upon the primacy of the written word, induced by the sanctification of the book. Like the first revelations, these indirect ones have power to bring people together in a new covenant. They again pick up the original promise by reiterating the revelation of the past. In turn, they lead to massive changes in rites as well as attitudes. With the first, pagan rites reinstated over time (e.g., altars dedicated to the moon and sun, statues, pillars, columns, children sacrificed to Moloch) will be abolished, leading to centralization of worship, which can no longer be done other than in the Temple of Jerusalem. With the second, priestly laws will be decreed. Revelations "by intermediary" renew the first divine word spoken to Abraham and then to Moses. Operating, as was the case, by the intervention of the rediscovery of the Book of Deuteronomy, they intervened like brutal separations in spaces of profane time where the people move. Once again God intervenes, albeit indirectly, in mankind's linear space during a solemn shared reading in public, to remind them of His sacred orders which over time had been "lost" or "forgotten."

The Bible and History

The arrangement of books of the Bible relates to a space-time defined by the eras in which they were written and collected. The history of biblical times can be built upon the chronology handed down in tradition, as well as by one suggested by biblical criticism, although the two offer contradictory readings of the temporal approach. Max Margolis notes that tradition invites us to follow the Bible and relevant talmudic treatises.[44] To help understand the makeup of the biblical tale and its scheduling, this traditional vision implements a temporal measure heralded by the Prophets. As presented in biblical stories, the prophet is neither a seer nor a medium, as suggested today. He is able neither to read the past nor to predict the future. The Prophet is a man of God, who possesses him and speaks through his mouth, making him prophesy in his name. He allows God to intervene and communicate with his contemporaries. Whether he eagerly accepts his burden or seeks to refuse it, like Jonah,[45] he cannot escape the role assigned him, and however reluctant, he must submit to his destiny. Accompanying the prophet, sometimes sharing a body with him, is the priest, the other man of God who teaches the divine doctrine and judges in His name. The priest handles ordinary matters of everyday life, while the prophet intervenes only in critical situations and exceptional times. The priest is sober and measured, while the prophet is tumultuous, impulsive, and ecstatic. Sometimes priest and prophet clash, and if the former embodies authority and institutional power, the latter remains isolated, armed only with his ranting; like Hosea, he easily passes for a lunatic; like Jeremiah, he curses and is loathed by his contemporaries.[46] Their domain of competence differs and also differentiates their relation to divine law. The prophet considers that the law of God concerns social justice more than Temple sacrifices or distributing tithes. Yet prophets also clash with one another. Jeremiah and Ezekiel constantly bluster against false prophets. Yehezkel Kaufmann suggests that the common evaluation of messenger-prophecy's agency in the history of Israel tends to obscure the effect of prophetic teachings. It gives the impression that each new prophecy instantly begins a different period of religious life, and, what is more, that no version of the monotheistic idea developed without a prophetic element. However, a number of accounts show that the messenger-prophets' influence was minimal in their day and only became obvious long after their deaths.[47] The Book of Kings shows that their prophecies do not differ from other religious phenomena, and they in no way appear as harbingers of a new interpretation. It is thus the moral force of their prophecies, extending beyond the piety of the priests of later eras, that justifies the chronological priority accorded Hebrew messenger-prophets.

Somehow, in the traditional approach, the books gathered in the biblical canon seem to stem from declarations by prophets who follow one another in the history of Israel. So the organizers of the canon would have used as criterion the fact that when prophecy ended in Israel, the content of the Bible had to be fixed, because "biblical times" were over. After that, the only books to achieve holiness were exegetical studies of a lesser rank in the scale of the sacred. From this perspective, the tripartite Jewish division of the Bible is based more on a thematic, rather than chronological, idea. In the process of sacralization and fixing of the holy books, chronology hardly matters. What counts is what is said, and the way it is said. For scribes, the importance of the tale lies mainly in the transcription of the divine word, not in its temporal unfolding, but in its perpetual reproducibility, no matter what time it may be for the recipient hearer or reader.

Understanding, Locating, Transmitting

This didactic way of recording temporality beyond the binding framework of chronology has its own pedagogical virtues. By distinguishing different approaches to time (eschatological, historical, cyclical, or linear), we can untangle complexities of Jewish temporality that blithely confuse its cyclical and historical dimensions. The transcendence of divine time that frees God from temporal constraints may be echoed in the fact that birth and death, which mark the beginning and end of these created beings, cannot be treated as self-perceptions. It is always someone else who is seen to be born or die. Based on our own experience, we might well consider ourselves eternal. Yet it seems that awareness of death and birth is shared knowledge basic to humanity, each person knowing that his or her own time on earth is limited, even though this knowledge cannot be experimentally confirmed. For Aristotle and Augustine, the existence of time may be demonstrated by measuring it, but this approach to the idea cannot be satisfying, because it implies an end. By formulating it in contemporary terms, Martin Heidegger's *Being and Time* may be more useful in helping us answer the question being asked here:[48] How, given that it eludes temporal measurement, notwithstanding that it involves duration and motion, are we to understand biblical time?[49] Heidegger proposes to divide what for him is the basic structure of human experience. He assumes that the individual is not *in* time, but *is* himself time, which hearkens back to some extent to concepts of the ancients, for whom time remains a perception of the soul. Yet our sense of time is not exclusively determined by its calculation. According to Heidegger, existentialism refers to the three modalities of human experience, namely: (1) *Verstehen*, understanding, which is not reason but may relate to the future; (2) *Befindlichkeit*, the situation that links the individual to the past and his origins; and (3) *Rede*, speech or parlance, originally a link to the present, also representing the inner dialogue that we conduct with ourselves or the structure of thought. I shall use these three mediations of existential perception to try to grasp the structure of the biblical tale, as much for its distinctive division into periods as for its message about time. The three dimensions of understanding time proposed by Heidegger are highly useful here. That of *Verstehen* indicates that to comprehend, it is first necessary to know what one is discussing. The Bible offers a narrative of events reflecting the aspects of "how" and "why." That of *Befindlichkeit* helps locate the issue, but to do so, we must know what happened and where we find ourselves in this story. The Bible incorporates the tale in a repetitive way. Finally, as a last resort, the extent of *Rede*, or speech, is doubtless what matters most. In order to be heard, perceived, and transmitted, the Bible perpetually reorganizes its iterative message by upending time and chronology. However, conceived in the tripartite way as suggested here, it still manages to convey three different types of message. The first bears the divine word, suggesting the voice heard during revelation or its reiteration; the second is the historical account of the events that led there, guiding and proclaiming it. As for the third, it is made up of conclusions that must be drawn, or laws that must be obeyed. Seen from this angle, biblical times take a cyclical form as much as a historical one in Jewish life, organizing complex rituals, notably New Year and Passover "get-togethers." Not participating in the transcendence of time, Jews must position themselves for continuity if they are to observe the revealed laws and find their places. In this sense, for tradition, the two or three millennia that comprise the biblical era were a time in which fusion was deliberately maintained through eschatological tales—revelations and prophecies—and historical ones, which support and vouch for the truth of described events by rooting them in common human experience during the relevant age.

Biblical criticism offers a wholly different way to approach biblical time.[50] Although often appealing, efforts to locate biblical works in historical time by dating them remain unconvincing, let alone drawing any consensus from specialists of different schools. Already in its time, the Mishnah indicated the difficulties that Jews faced when they were forced to include or ban different works from the canon owing to the presumed authenticity of the sources. During the time of the Second Temple, there seems to have existed an ancient canon of scripture, and hard-fought discussions took place over the rejection or admission of texts such as Ecclesiastes, Proverbs, the Song of Songs, and the Book of Esther.[51] Sirach is also supposed to have been included, before being rejected.[52]

Biblical times saw both chronological advances and throwbacks, acceptances and rejections. These are commonly seen as definitively decided at the hypothetical Council of Jamnia (Yavneh) in the late first century, marking the supposed closing of the Jewish biblical canon. Yet the calling into question of temporality raised by the advance of biblical criticism was not easily resolved. If we accept that the corpus consists of tales arranged in the Bible over the ages by including oral tradition and adding laws, we note two dates mentioned above, which allow chronological benchmarks to be obtained. The first is just before the fall of the Kingdom of Judea, around 621 BCE, marked by the finding of the Book of Deuteronomy by Josiah. The second is around 444 BCE, imposed by the public reading of the Priestly Code, or the Book of Deuteronomy, by Ezra. Advocates of the critical method who support the documentary hypothesis offered by Julius Wellhausen state that Ezra published the Torah in its definitive form.[53] According to this hypothesis, the production process occurred in three separate stages over two- or three-century intervals. Begun around 621–622 BCE and completed around 444 BCE, they were finalized by scribes in about 100 CE. From this perspective, the most singular premise is not the chronology as suggested. Not being considered the oldest part of scripture, the Torah acquired primary status because of its mythic content. Certain parts of the prophetic books might have been written earlier and circulated as personal writings. In this hypothesis, subsequently ruled out, Margolis writes: "*The prophets* antedated the *Torah* and both the *Psalter*," with the Law (Leviticus) being placed in the middle.[54]

Wellhausen's documentary hypothesis rests on the delimitation of distinct biblical corpuses, based on philological analysis and especially on spotting the use of the theonyms Jahveh and Elohim, as Ibn Ezra had done previously. The different documents of the Hebrew Bible are distinguished by stages of their production. The oldest identified source is J, in which the narrator or Yahwist is so named because he uses the tetragram (Yahweh) to indicate God. This first source of the

Torah was written around the ninth century BCE. Written about a century later and next in the determined order comes the E source, so called because the elohist narrator uses the theonym Elohim. Then comes the D source, highlighting the Book of Deuteronomy, written at the time of Josiah in the last quarter of the seventh century. The subsequent P source comprises the Priestly Code, written during or after the Exile at the time of reinstatement, from the sixth to the fifth centuries, offering a Jewish constitution for the Persian Empire. The entire Torah was finally published after the Babylonian Exile, in the time of Ezra (around 444 BCE), by a priest connected with the P source.

Amid an abundance of critical theories about the Bible, another school dates it according to the text and pushes back the writing of the Priestly Code to before the Book of Deuteronomy. Given such reevaluations of the coherence and, to an extent, authenticity of the biblical text, Jewish—as well as Christian—tradition sought scientific reasons. Since the Wissenschaft des Judentums school, Jewish scholars also remain divided over these problems. Leopold Zunz, for example, placed Ezekiel after Ezra and saw the Book of Leviticus as the latest of the corpus. He maintained that the whole Torah had been compiled three centuries after Josiah. The religious reformer Abraham Geiger accepted the precedence of Leviticus over Deuteronomy, but willingly accepted post-exilic additions. Heinrich Graetz dated the writing of the Book of Ecclesiastes to the reign of Herod the Great and some Psalms to the time of the Maccabees.[55]

While readily admitting that this hypothesis is currently "on its last legs,"[56] biblical scholars accord preponderant importance to the intervention in written form of priestly texts (tales or laws) in the arrangement of the Torah. For between the narrative and legal sections, there is a major difference in treatment. The tales are discursive, scattered throughout the books, whereas laws form virtually separate entities. Yehezkel Kaufmann notes the corpus of the Exodus Code from the J and E sources, and the Priestly Code (P) as found in Exodus, Leviticus, and Numbers, as well as the Deuteronomic Code.[57] Differences of opinion remain about the steps of composing elements in the total corpus. Ziony Zevit concludes with the hypothesis that document P precedes the Exile, in line with recent trends in critical method that now postulate that the writing of biblical texts must have extended over a much longer time than previously suggested, and that their division into periods is consequently more enigmatic than the first scientific investigators suspected.[58]

This approach to biblical times becomes essential during the modern confrontation of Jews with historical time, determining their attitudes and scientific viewpoints. Yet for our purposes, we need only assume that, like the divine Word that it incarnates, biblical discourse arose in an indeterminate time and age and cannot be submitted to a temporal harnessing of eschatology. From this type of functionalist perspective, "biblical times" do not require the authenticity of strict calculation. That the Kings era is duly certified by archaeology and that the Psalms of David were written during the Maccabean Revolt in no way changes the force or meaning of their scriptural message. In this case, the notion of real time, if such is conceivable in the structure of the Bible, has no intrinsic value. What matters for biblical design is to demonstrate that a God exists who is part of the history of mankind, proving by the transcendence of His Word that He can reformulate His message and His covenant across all the epochs of humanity.

Creation and the Origin of Time

God possesses three keys: to rain, birth, and the resurrection of the dead.

Ta'anit 2a

The above epigraph, drawn from the Mishnah, signals that two stories from Genesis teach that the creation of the world occurred in three steps: first, the separation of the waters from original chaos; second, childbearing and birth, which also mark an integration in time; and a third, not found in Genesis itself, that of resurrection, which is the ultimate way out of time.[59] In shaping time, the creation of the world is based on the matrix principle as applied to water. In return, people grant it different statuses and attribute to it different descriptive terms according to its functions and degrees of holiness. Among these are natal, divine, primordial, diluvian, lustral, or even purifying streams. Water figures in many rituals of reactivation of creation or birth, identifiable in most civilizations. Even today, before proceeding to a Jewish ritual, the flow of water is required, whether a ritual bath or hand-washing.

Water has a large place in the first biblical tales; there are waters of separation, of creating regions, and the Flood. It is also significant in Deuteronomy and Leviticus where lustral water, oblations, and other methods of purification are mentioned. Waters also appear in the rites of the Temple, when during the festival of Sukkot, the creation of the world is reiterated by celebrating Simhat Beit Ha-sho'evah, "rejoicing at the place of the water-drawing."[60] At the turn of the year, it reenacts the water miracle that shaped the world and fed it by fertilizing it with rain: "Therefore with joy shall ye draw water out of the wells of salvation" (Isa. 12:3).[61] Without water, no birth is possible and everyone knows that the fetus floats in the womb until the mother's water breaks, after which it enters the human life cycle. Thereafter, the individual can no longer escape linear time except by divine decision, which alone holds the power to suspend time and make it eternal. The creation described in the Bible is also a paradigm. We find it again with few changes in the Epic of Gilgamesh,[62] as well as in many myths of origins that recount in a similar way the original separation of the elements, the Flood—destruction/regeneration—followed by the new creation of the universe, more refined than before.

Every casual reader will be struck by the fact that the Bible gives successive and inconsistent versions of the tale of the creation in the first two chapters of Genesis. The second chapter seems bound to continue the description started in the first, yet it returns to the order of creation and in doing so, offers another version. Unsurprisingly, the documentary hypothesis as adopted by Sir James George Frazer, for example, attributes them to two different sources joined by a clumsy scribe who failed to take the trouble to reconcile them: "The flagrant contradiction between the two accounts is explained very simply by the circumstance that they are derived from two different and originally independent documents, which were afterwards combined into a single book by an editor, who pieced the two narratives together without always taking pains to soften or harmonize their discrepancies," Frazer says.[63] Wellhausen states: "What are generally cited as points of superiority in Gen. 1 over Gen. 2:3 are beyond doubt signs of progress in outward culture. The mental individuality of the two writers, the systematiser and the genius, cannot be compared, and the difference in this respect tells nothing of their respective dates; but in its general views of God, nature, and man, Gen. 1 stands on a higher, certainly on a later, level."[64] For Jewish philosophers and exegetes, two accounts were provided because two discourses of creation exist with two messages to decipher. Rashi is positive:[65] there can be no question of a chronological story; the first verse of Gen. 1 states, "In the beginning, God created . . ." giving us no concrete indication about the order of creation, but making us reconsider.[66] For purposes other than those discussed here, Raphael Patai is one of those who have drawn up a typology of the order of creation that shows variations between the two chapters.[67] Light, heavens, earth, firmament, land, plants and trees, lights, sea creatures, birds, cattle, and reptiles, wild animals, man and woman appear in turn in Gen. 1, whereas in Gen. 2 the order of creation is as follows: the earth, the heavens, mist, man, trees, flowers, wild animals, cattle, birds, and woman.

In what concerns us in these stories, we see that the forms of temporality instantly fall into place; lights are destined to take hold of time and its measurement, with the Sabbath as the day of rest. In the first story, God saw that it "was good," and "he rested." These two versions offer suspended time. In the first, time emerges in the beginning from the first day, by appearing out of darkness and light: "And the evening and the morning were the first day." On the fourth day, time is defined by the future incarnated in celestial bodies: "and let them be for signs, and for seasons, and for days, and years. And let them be for lights in the firmament of the heaven to give light upon the earth." The function of time is clearly indicated here. Its scansions are already present with the mention of festivals, days, and years. It is destined for mankind first and then for Jews.

While giving the impression of following the first story (by opening with these words: "Thus the heavens and the earth were finished, and all the host of them . . . and he rested on the seventh day from all his work which he had made"),[68] the next verses of the second return to the origin of the creation of the universe, to present them in another order. The relationship between man and woman differs between them, as does the order of the appearance of nature. The "Holy Spirit" of the Shabbat and the Garden of Eden dominates this chapter overall, while these two elements refer to a concept of eternity, according to the interpretation of Jewish tradition based on the fact that any explicit mention of death is missing from these creation tales. The creation so described may be verified, but as yet has no duration. It is "perfect," "eminently good," and death there is only in a latent condition. As Rashi affirms, the creation of the world eludes chronology, just like the three attributes of the divine cited in Ta'anit 2a:[69] rain, childbirth, and resurrection of the dead, because they preceded it. Whence the classic interpretation of the observance of Shabbat as "zekher le-ma'asseh be-reshit," or a reminder of creation. "The observance of the Sabbath is itself an acknowledgment of His omnipotence, and at the same time an acknowledgment of the creation by the divine word," Yehudah Halevi writes. "He who observes the Sabbath because the work of creation was finished on it acknowledges the creation itself. He who believes in the creation believes in the Creator."[70] In this way, from the start of Genesis everything is said about the orders of divine and human, including the seminal human limit, mortality, which is still in the realm of potential danger: "But of the tree of the knowledge of good and evil, thou shalt not eat of it: for in the day that thou eatest thereof thou shalt surely die."[71] Coming after preexistent immortality and eternity, the capacity for dying will create the sense of temporality.

In the first account of Genesis, each day of the process of creation is marked by its explicit mention: "And the evening, and the morning were the first day" (Gen. 1:5), and so on with remaining days. The fourth verse sketches a time already cadenced by the days, seasons, years, and festivals that Jewish tradition observes in its ritual phenomenology. This is how the typical metaphor of creation operates in interpretation—implying that everything is already present from the first moment on—whose revelation is a redundancy or extension, as seen from the fact that God revealed to Moses the entire Torah, already containing all the commentaries and exegeses added by sages and scholars who were not yet born according to strictly human temporal rules.[72] Only in Genesis 3, with the cursing of Adam followed by his Fall and expulsion from the Garden of Eden, do death and the span of lifetimes of mankind and animals dramatically change by shattering temporal transcendence. It is reasonable that the birth of the first child (emergence of the human race) and death follow, begotten from the cursing of both the male (he must work the earth from which he came) and the female (the pain of childbirth).

The creation of the world is reflected in the ritual celebrating the New Year. At Rosh Ha-shanah, the liturgical year begins and with it, rereading the original text reiterates the creation by an intermediary in everyone's life. Simhat Beit Ha-sho'evah fell into disuse after the destruction of the Temple. Yet Passover, commemorating the escape from Egypt as described in Exodus 12:11, "And thus shall ye eat it; with your loins girded, your shoes on your feet, and your staff in your hand; and ye shall eat it in haste: it is the Lord's Passover," has persisted in every era. Today it is celebrated as a historical event that penetrates individual time each year. This escape from Egypt is explained in countless ways in Jewish society, since the desert may be a useful metaphor for spiritual wandering, just as slavery, which will endure until the Redemption of Israel, represents an approach to the Covenant as described in Deuteronomy: "The Lord made not this covenant with our fathers, but with us, even us, who are all of us here alive this day."[73] And later: "Neither with you only do I make this covenant and this oath; but with him that standeth here with us this day before the Lord our God, and also with him that is not here with us this day."[74] If advocates of the critical method are to be believed, Deuteronomy is indeed the book "found" during the reign of Josiah, during the reconstruction of the Temple. The Covenant, which it describes as perpetually current for "all of us here alive" and not just "with our fathers," marks the cyclic reintroduction or repetition of an event seen as historic, but that happened some centuries or millennia before. Von Rad, upon whose work Steensgaard would base his studies,[75] clearly accepted the documentary hypothesis. For the former, this injunction betrayed the upsurge of a linear consciousness of time. According to him, cyclical time in primitive societies was definitely over by the era of the Judges (1200 to 1025 BCE) during the writing of the first biblical books seen as "historical." This breach in creating the perception of time would suggest that events can no longer be repeatable through the intermediary of celebrating a festival, but instead must be reenacted. From the symbolic point of view, this approach to biblical time certifies that the dominant idea is that of a God who constantly intervenes in mankind's cycle of times of life. Following

Rashi's interpretation, we might also add that a distinction was introduced as early as the first two chapters of Genesis between "universal" time and "Jewish" time, in which nuances owing to traditions of translation play their role; the seasons belong to all humanity, but festivals only to the Israelites.[76] This leads us to the idea that God and Jewish time have historical functions. Paul Ricoeur writes of how the levels of temporality foreseen by Augustine were organized into a hierarchy: "by interpreting the extension of time in terms of distension and by describing human time as raised beyond its inside by the attraction of its polar opposite, eternity, Augustine gave credit in advance to the idea of a plurality of temporal levels." Among these, the "Intervals of time do not simply fit into one another according to their numerical quantities, days into years, and years into centuries." Even more than the quantitative aspect, the question of human time looks to be addressed by a qualitative aspect that Ricoeur expresses in terms of "graduated tension" that leads to these questions: "For how long a time? During how much time? In how much time?"[77] To which one might reply that people try to find answers in the Bible.

Three   Where Is Time Going?

Alluding to the qualification "very good" (*tov me'od*) applied to death in Genesis's first account of creation in Midrash Rabbah—"and behold death was very good [*tov me'od*]—and behold death [*maweth*] was good"[1]—tradition explains the use of this superlative in terms of death's preexistence; it is inherent to the order of the universe. Interpreted this way, this qualifier follows the direction of human temporality, which, heading toward death, will be followed by redemption; it is therefore "good." Created for the exclusive use of people and animals—who are born, live, and die, and whose nature is "generation"—time implemented by the Creator remains apart from Himself. Morning liturgy begins with a series of blessings and praises evoking this extratemporality. "He was, He is, He will be," proclaims the hymn *Adon 'Olam*,[2] one of the very first prayers uttered in the morning just after waking, which affirms: "He is Lord of the universe, who reigned ere any creature yet was formed. . . . And after all things shall have had an end, he alone, the dreaded one, shall reign."[3] The hymn adds: "Who was, who is, and who will be in glory. / And he is One, and there is no second to compare to him, to consort with him: / Without beginning, without end: to him belong strength and dominion."[4] This declaration of God's presence in the past, present, and future underlines the notion that His existence may not be understood in terms of motion. Eschatological time cuts a path between the time of God and the time of mankind, allowing people to free themselves from human time and judge in terms of eternity *ad 'olam*. The strictly human temporal rhythm is defined by the triad of past, present, and future. Franz Rosenzweig offers further thoughts along these lines.[5] Considering the theologies of the three monotheistic faiths, Rosenzweig offers a genuine principle that makes it possible to grasp the basis of Jewish temporality: ideas about creation, revelation, and redemption represent the past, embody the present, and foresee the future. They appear in a series that enables us to draw a chronological line between elements that defy all linear representation of time a priori. For Rosenzweig, the idea of creation is only present in finished form. When humans appear, it is already there and can only be calculated as part of the past. Yet creation is fulfilled by the dialogue begun in everyone's present time, as substance of the revelation disclosed to mankind. It is likewise revelation that, while returning the past to the present, foresees the promise of future redemption: "In this manner, Revelation gathers everything into its contemporaneousness, it knows not merely itself; rather: there is 'all in it.'"[6] For Rosenzweig, these are the three times which create the chronology relevant to consciousness which must be in the present, always located between past and future, set on the path which leads from one to the other. Once this dialogue is established, the temporal series can be inverted. The world may only experience an awakening of consciousness as a thing created during redemption, which would allow it to gain lasting durability and permanent life. In this way, for worldly things, wakening precedes being, and this very inversion of the temporal sequence "establishes the life of the eternal people," anticipating the end in order to make it blossom. In this game structured around a space in between, time is in this way denied. By reclassifying "after" as "before," taking its end for a beginning and its beginning as an end, time is tested on the eternal path.[7]

Between Eternity and Mortality

Among human beings, the passage of time is viewed by its flowing, which like a river constantly pours forth. The movement of the past toward the present, as of the present toward the future, creates a perception of temporality that points to an incessant reminder of the past in what is permanent. Conversely, sacred time is defined by the absence of movement, inasmuch as its immobility and perpetual fixedness need not be concerned with the present or future, not being subject to change. The time of God, supposing that it may be defined by human beings, is eternity. It seems paradoxical that Hebrew should be a language that curiously ignores this term. To speak of eternity, Hebrew must seek metaphors. For "eternal," it uses "constant" (*tamid*), "for always" (*le'olam va'ed*), or *netsah*, which is also close to "victory" or "conquest"; in the Middle Ages, "without end" (*'ein sof*) was used. The fact that Hebrew words are clearly unaware of eternal fixity shows that eternity did not appear in the Hebrew lexicon, because it lacked its own specific connotation beyond permanence, conquest, and "without end." Eternity, which represents the true alterity of what is human, is not conceptualized in this vocabulary, which only includes forms of passing, becoming, and change. The human language contains no linguistic attribute capable of representing or even characterizing God. Perhaps this is what induced Maimonides, in his battle against any attempts at anthropomorphism, to declare Him unknowable and unimaginable for mankind, whose skills in understanding do not rise to the divine. These statements, even though rather convenient, because they avoid any confrontation between the divine and human orders, are far from showing the range of representations devised by Jewish thinkers. Hasdai Crescas, the head of the Jewish community of Aragon (ca. 1340–1410/11 CE), constructed a philosophical argument in his *'Or Adonai* wholly directed against Aristotelian thought as represented by Maimonides, which he repudiated in the name of Jewish tradition.[8] For Crescas, human intelligence is surely capable of grasping and conceiving metaphysical facets. The talmudic exegete Gersonides, who lived in southern France (1288–1344),[9] had held that it is impossible for time to be without "beginning,"[10] because the notion of an infinite past is unthinkable. Crescas responded to this that a genuine infinity exists, that time is conceivable and possible even without any beginning. For according to him, the past remains at a finite distance from the present day. Infinite time only means that before each section of time there was a previous section, which makes it permissible to think of infinity being expressed in terms of "completion." Crescas also asserts the causality of the universe, for matter has not been created from any substance separated from the divine. God is the sole, absolute cause of it, although that has no bearing on the question of whether the world had an inception or not in terms of temporality. As a result, Crescas reaffirms the Aristotelian principle of creation ex nihilo, advocated by the Persian polymath Avicenna, or Ibn Sina (930–1037),[11] and also in the Christian scholastic philosophy of Saint Thomas Aquinas (1225–1274), well before the Spanish-Jewish rabbi.[12] Crescas insisted that the universe, in the plenitude of its being, stems from God and cannot be founded in a separate existence. He held that the idea that space is an infinite receptacle of things, and as such the "archetype of divine omnipresence,"[13] permits the concept of conceivable infinity. Crescas again acknowledges his differences here with Maimonides, who only refers to the God of the *'olam*, or time,[14] of the universe and not of space.[15] For Crescas, the meaning of the idea of creation lies in deriving being from things, starting with God. In effect, this rejects the issue of the temporal creation of the universe as an idle question. From this perspective, and still contra Maimonides, a world conceived as eternal insofar as it is a product of divine will is not just possible in the absolute sense, but equally conceivable by mankind. According to Crescas, human intelligence is likely to conceive that we may combine the idea of the eternity of the universe with the biblical doctrine of miracles that illustrate God's direct intervention in the earthly macrocosm. Nevertheless, the question of immortality remains unresolved for Crescas, although for Maimonides it is linked to that of eternity by the concept of the immortality of the acquired intellect. Another choice about time was made by the Spanish rabbi Joseph Albo (ca. 1380–1444),[16] a disciple of Crescas. Starting with the latter's Aristotelian postulate of God's eternity and autonomy with respect to time, Albo nevertheless arrives at a dogmatic relativization. Apart from the three fundamental principles of the existence of God, revelation, and divine rewards and punishments, the remainder of his doctrine, notably that which concerns us about creation ex nihilo, is not fundamental and does not lead to heresy if denied.[17] Albo's essential originality lies in the fact that he sees time as a perception of the imagination: "even if time is the unmeasurable duration imagined in thought."[18] Departing from Crescas's key notion that "the existence of time is in the soul," although it remains a quantifiable continuum, measurable by movement, Albo distinguishes two concepts. The first is the "order of time"—*seder ha-zmanim*—measurable by diurnal movement. The second is that of "time" in itself, neither generated nor created, but found in eternity. This comes down to asking whether there is a time of the intellect like that of the imagination, which requires that a "before" and "after" exist in the order of time, notwithstanding that there is neither a "before" nor an "after" in eternal "time."

The abiding conflict between the idea of a purely human temporality, which God surely surmounts, because He created it all, and a divine extratemporality to which man always aspires, whether he can grasp it or not, is strongly conveyed by this dialectic. Situated apart from human time, God is also outside the process of creation. He generates but is not generated, counts but cannot be tallied. Existing in an unmoving time, God thus truly constitutes the meaning of eternity. He abides in the Jewish tradition of the unspeakable, of the Name humanity does not know or no longer knows, the tetragram. Maimonides and Crescas propose two, related approaches to the question. The former believes that people cannot rationally have an idea or knowledge of the divine, the latter affirms that it is precisely human rationality that makes it possible to understand God from a philosophical as well as religious point of view.

What Is Temporality?

"Relationship with the future, the presence of the future in the present, seems all the same accomplished in the face-to-face with the Other," Emmanuel Lévinas writes. "The situation of the face-to-face would be the very accomplishment of time; the encroachment of the present on the future is not the feat of the subject alone, but the intersubjective relationship. The condition of time lies in the relationship between humans or in history."[19]

In responding to Heidegger's *Being and Time*, Lévinas's stance, which is closer to contemporary approaches, allows for progress in the quest for time being pursued here. Postulated in a relationship between people or history, temporality is decided by the relationship of Jews to the divine. Based on monotheistic understanding of a willful God viewed as "the Lord of history,"[20] it establishes the ties of Judaism to time and history; temporality is thus entirely located in experience. Yet at the same time that it redirects the specificity of the relationship between God and man, the notion of a willful God leads to that of an individualistic God and moral philosophy of the will. The personalist nature of biblical religion stands in opposition to the other, more spiritual and more impersonal form of religiosity represented by mysticism and pantheism. In the relationship that exists between mankind and God, a sort of fracture will occur. An escape opens up by the intervention of mysticism, which considers God as a hidden source from which beings emanate, or the vital power of the cosmos. Instead of individual moral communion, mystics install the *unio mystica*.[21] The interpersonal relationship is replaced by the abolition of personal individuality, the barrier that separates mankind from God. We could formulate this difference in theoretical terms, following Julius Guttmann.[22] For mysticism, the divine "foundation" and "source" do not create the universe, but rather expel or emanate it from their own substance. In religious terms, this means that God is not a will who directs and determines the world, but a transcendent being secluded within Himself. To raise oneself to God's level, one must leave what is worldly, achieve detachment of the soul, and cross barriers that stand between the macrocosm and God, as well as the soul and God. For the mystic, the universe can only be perceived as a divine manifestation. While the creator is above the cosmos and against it, the God of mysticism is the underlying principle of the world imperceptible by the senses; the soul's ascent toward God is only the final step on its path. However, the idea of creation marks the breaking, or separating, point between myth and religion. In excluding all evolution or emanation by which the universe is derived from God and accepting that the will of God is the sole, unique cause of the world's existence, nature loses its divine quality. From the abode of the divine, it becomes the work of divine hands. Humanity is thus superior to nature, which is stripped of all "natural" or divine essence.

The Israelite religion always considered its God as the unquestionable and absolute master of the macrocosm and its history.[23] History, for the ancient Israelites, originates with the covenant signed between God and his people. This covenant is maintained by the intermediary of human observance of the Commandments, for which, in turn,

God grants them Providence. Understood this way, the history of the people itself is raised to the level of "a locus wherein God might be known."[24] For the Hebrew prophets, this historical conception rises to the universal level. Great nations become instruments to accomplish divine purposes. Having designated God as master of history and then of the universe, the divine perspective embraces both past and future. Thereafter, the dimension of prophetic consciousness is mainly oriented toward the future, while the personal and historical dimension is anchored in the past. On the other hand, the extant relationship between God and Israel which longs for renewal and rebirth, or, in other words, redemption, cannot only concern Israel. It must be universal and shared with other nations. The appearance of this eschatology also demonstrates a singleness of purpose that includes all peoples and leads them together toward the point of historical convergence. This process of building a unicity of historical advance must arrange past and future in a single vast vision. We can see a metaphor of the stretched thread of temporality lying ahead.[25] Yet a difference is brought to light between the biblical God and mystical God. For the biblical religion, the temporal world does not dissolve in the void. The Bible sees the universe as the site for accomplishing the divine order, a moral order that will bring about a moral life. On the contrary, mysticism conceives of a God who dwells in himself, very much beyond time.

The Eschatological Word in Time

Next, how to understand the Jewish eschatological model? The transcendence of God stems from the fact that nothing created is contemporaneous with God. All of creation takes place in historical time, and no created element exists in the "nontime" of the divine kingdom.[26] The exteriority of the relation of God to his creation is absolute, but that absolute is destined to reproduce itself at the end of time. When history is over, creation as an unfolding must disappear. Only God and his attributes will remain in this nontime. In eschatological terms, the idea of ending echoes the cosmology of origins. Although creation is not contemporaneous with the creator, He Himself is a contemporary of his creation. In this way, the universe is only a parenthesis, which

God penetrates, impregnates, and identifies with Himself. Such is the meaning of the idea of biblical panentheism, which is opposed, like a Hebraic reply, to philosophical transcendentalism and pantheism. This panentheism—which generally expresses space but which must be taken here in the strict sense of time—appears in Genesis, where the terms "spirit" and "word" are found. Spirit hangs over the waters, the surface of which covers the chaos and obscurity of the void. The confrontation between God and nature is symbolized in this way, according to André Néher.[27] The waters confront the spirit; created matter is amorphous, opaque, immobile, and massive. Flying over it, spirit is in motion, keeping watch around and calling for life to awaken. The image suggests that the divine Spirit embraces the world without penetrating it. Only the word manages this kind of entry. When God speaks, the Word as speech immersing the cosmos appears in the created chaos.[28] Each new word from God evokes a new stage, which adds rhythm to creation. With the sudden entrance of speech, confrontation stops being mute and turns into dialogue. The universe replies to the Word by creating itself from it, and "becoming." Creation no longer features only God but follows his gradually progressing movement, adding part to part of creation, day after day. The creation takes shape by the Word, making and absorbing its contradictory facets and powers: light/darkness; heaven/earth; earth/water; cosmic/stellar myth; and finally a living category, nature/human.

In this system, God's relationship to the world is not mythical but historical. The Bible refers to historical time through the intermediary of "days," *yamim*, and "times," *divrei yamim*, which highlight history in the sense of the telling of the *yemot 'olam*, "the "days of the world," which in turn define history in the broad sense as becoming: "Remember the days of old, consider the years of many generations."[29] Here, *'olam* means precisely *zman*, or "time." This terminological gathering accompanies the *toledot*, the "generations," which, from a literal point of view summons up the image of history conceived as begetting, an evocation of the past that links fathers to children and inversely, children to their elders. The expression *shenot dor va-dor*, the "years from generation to generation" also refers to history, as expressed in the remainder of the verse cited above: "ask thy father, and he will shew thee; thy elders, and they will tell thee."[30]

This terminological pairing may also be sought in the account of the creation. In Genesis, this is divided into seven days. The three different meanings mentioned above are related to it in this way: "God saw that the light was good, and he separated the light from the darkness."[31] The first "day," *yom*, has a cosmic meaning here as an element of the pair of opposites light/darkness. Yet elsewhere it includes an astronomical meaning, which reflects the complete daily cycle: "divide the day from the night,"[32] meaning from one sunrise to the next. Everywhere, the word *yom* underpins a period, a space-time that heralds and precedes the next one. The days of creation are chronometric days, suggesting mobility and movement. Thereafter they belong to a different category, historical time.

Days are the first elements of the series that accompanies creation. Yet they are also the subject of biblical stories; these follow a logical sequence starting with the dawn of history and not from an idea about prehistory. The dual terminology of "day" and "generation" used by biblical narration to describe the creation of history and its development is also used for its historical culmination, *be-reshit*, the "beginning of days" which finds its counterpart in the pronouncement about the end of days, *aharit-ha-yamim*: "Gather yourselves together, that I may tell you that which shall befall you in the last days."[33] Here again the problem of translation and interpretation exists. This "series" of biblical days announcing a historical future is interpreted by tradition as the "consummation"[34] of days unveiled by Balaam.[35] Days of history are an announced beginning and end, which lead back to the starting point of creation. In the same way, generations of history head toward a paradoxical goal, since they yearn for their own end.

Where Is Time?

Starting with the relationship that Jews established with God, how are we to grasp their link to a time conceived essentially for them, outside of which He is located? Is God distant, impenetrable, and inaccessible, as Maimonidean thinkers suggest? Or on the contrary, is he an interventionist historical God who acts deliberately during human lifetimes? The Jewish scansions of time may be invoked in turn to outline a reply to these questions. Placed in the perspective of Mircea Eliade, the Jewish eschatological calendar keeps repeating creation, making humankind "contemporary with the cosmogony and with the anthropogony because ritual projects [it] into the mythical epoch of the beginning."[36] The first of these scansions is provided by Shabbat, inherent in *imitatio dei*[37] since the Shabbat day of rest copies the primordial gesture of God, who rests after His works are accomplished.[38] Yet for humans, *imitatio dei* is a mutable obligation, for copying the divine is not only a matter of following an example but also, and above all, a command. The principle of this form of "repetition" is based on a simple observation. Insofar as an action acquires a certain reality by the reproduction of actions that become paradigmatic owing to ritual repetition, it leads to the implicit suppression of profane time, or the suspension of historical duration. "He who reproduces the exemplary gesture thus finds himself transported into the mythical epoch in which its revelation took place," Eliade asserts.[39] The suppression of profane time and the projection of mankind into mythic time only occur in essential intervals, which are ritual moments and important life actions, such as ceremonies and feeding. Other daily actions must take place in profane time, which, devoid of all meaning, forms a kind of temporality that can move in the "becoming." So that the application of the rite taken as a way of suspending time may also express an attempt to abolish the "passage" from time that makes it possible to rediscover the original prototype of temporality, *illud tempus*.[40]

Jewish temporality, however, aspires to something entirely different, included in the perspective introduced by Gershom Scholem. The foretaste of the next world given by the Sabbath suspension of profane time can be integrated into the quest for *ma'aseh be-reshit*, an inquiry into the nature of the works of creation.[41] Instead of rushing toward the end and consummation of historical time as mentioned above, this is fleeing toward the beginning, such as Rosenzweig also alludes to— toward the original Genesis, in some way embodying an "inner homeland."[42] The messianic hope, generally based on the idea of the collapse of history that marks the end of exile and freedom from the yoke of the empire of nations, is also expectation of divine intervention. The notion of a new world constructed in this way finds its completion by restoring its original perfection from the time of creation.[43]

It may well be that scrupulous observation of traditions materializes and reproduces the past in the present. Yet the future also participates in this present. People look to and become involved in it because of the supernatural nature of prophecy. Temporal duration is no longer a useless abstraction, but is filled, as von Rad affirmed when he evoked the image of "filled" Israelite time,[44] by all the rites that fulfil it. This is all the more true because this duration marks the tie between human generations who follow one another and return in the mystical tradition. These include the cycle of seasons, through "reincarnations," or *gilgulim*.[45] Perceived this way, time becomes as concrete and tangible as the rest of the world.[46] This concept reflects the feeling of fullness of being that is not a function of the analysis of categories. Time and space are regarded as an integral part of human experience. Yet the chronological series formed by the past of daily life clearly differ from mythical time. For ancestors and descendants coexist in two different forms of the perception of time, with two ways of approaching reality, in which festivals and rites form the link joining these two different visions of the temporal race. Yet this experience of linear time does not predominate in the individual consciousness. It is just as much conditional on a cyclic perception of the phenomenon of life as on the mythical image of the universe. Perceptions and representations of temporality reflect the essence of cultural life. When cyclic time dominates linear time in the social consciousness, this means a specific relationship between static and dynamic elements of the historical process, Aron Gurevich explains.[47] In daily life, time passes, but it is only one of the guises of the cosmos. "Real" time is that of superior reality, which is not subject to change and constitutes eternity. In the universe, sprung whole from the hand of the Creator, past and future unite in the life of the present. However, the idea of time conveyed by the Hebrew Bible connotes yet another eschatological task as well: waiting for the arrival of the messiah-savior that will fulfil and complete history as a prelude to messianic times.

Four God's Time, Humanity's Time

By attributing the merit of having been the first historical religion to the religion of Israel, Christian theologians confer the paternity of the idea of temporal creation upon it. Yet they, with Gerhard von Rad first and foremost among them, refuse to concede Judaism the ability to develop an "absolute" notion of temporality: "Today, however we are beginning to realise that her [Israel's] experience of which we call time and ours are different," von Rad writes.[1] To be sure. Yet for von Rad and his adepts, this means that the ancient Hebrews were unable to project themselves into the future and lacked the skills to think about an idea as abstract as chronology. Countless studies based on that premise contrast the supposed incapability of the Israelites to depict time other than through perception of an event to the skill of the Greeks in distinguishing between "absolute time" and "space-time." This charge reasonably irked Arnaldo Momigliano, who responded with a stimulating, incensed article.[2] James Barr demonstrated the limits, flaws, contradictions, and bias of such theological approaches based on linguistic methods and biblical philology as long ago as 1968.[3] Yet this idea continues to circulate in a diffuse way and inspires all sorts of studies about representations and perceptions of time and space by the Hebrews, sometimes even spreading into an approach to the history of the Jews.[4] While seeking to avoid theological squabbles not worth revisiting, one is obliged to admit that an ambiguity does exist, linked to the formulation of time in the Bible. The sages of the Mishnah had already pointed this out: "There is no real difference between what is here and what is beyond in the Bible." This observation was commented upon by Rashi as a matter of lacking chronological order.[5] From absence to incapability, there is nevertheless a determinant element for our discussion that seems to have eluded this debate: the ability of the biblical tale to find its place in the reader's temporality rather than in that of the tale itself. To grasp this kind of determination of time, I shall proceed cautiously and gradually. Now it is a matter of examining the key ideas that allowed the Israelites, and then the Jews, to find their bearings and situate themselves in history, as well as chronology, by trying to recount visions referring to the functions of past and future allowed to surface in certain texts. As we have seen, the idea of creation remains linked to that of revelation, which tirelessly recalls God's original intercession in the progress of human time. The God of Israel shapes a history within which He takes action. He intervenes directly by coming forward in the course of events, reveals himself by acting on individuals and their future. This is why A. J. Heschel asserted that Jewish ritual can be described as an "architecture of time,"[6] since its rites, Shabbat, Rosh Hodesh,[7] and festivals depend on being observed at a clearly determined time. Evenings, mornings, and afternoons are for prayer meetings, while seasons and the number of years determine celebrations. The idea of holiness is only evoked in Genesis to be applied to the rhythm of temporality. The very first sanctification settles on the tale of the creation of time: "And God blessed the seventh day, and sanctified it."[8]

Architecture of time or religion of history? For von Rad, the "theological radius of what Israel said about God is conspicuously restricted compared with the theologies of other nations—instead, the Old Testament writings confine themselves to representing Jahweh's relationship to Israel and to the world in one aspect only, namely as a continuing divine activity in history."[9] For him, the Law of Israel relies in its totality on a historical theology. Based on points of history, it is "fashioned and formed" by events in which the intercession of God's hand may be deciphered. It is in this context that the prophets intervene recounting historical facts—with the nuance that instead of being prior, already done with and belonging to the space of the past, these facts allude to matters after the time of the witness who announces and describes them. This uniquely complex aspect of the historical tradition of the Hebraic Bible emerges from the continual reflection to which the people of Israel have devoted to themselves throughout their history. Each generation finds itself facing the task, simultaneously similar and always new, of understanding itself and defining itself as being Israel.

Each generation must again "become" Israel. Every link in the chain of generations is assigned the duty of recapturing the status of essential choosing, being "singled out" again, and "chosen" afresh. This process of permanent updating is at the heart of the principle of revelation and choosing. This is how von Rad explains the gap between the biblical tale and its analysis by critical method—which, as we have seen, overlap with great difficulty. The biblical tale, continuously reinterpreting the ancient story, reconstructs and reformulates it, while using it for new purposes, and sheds light on duplications, where reiterations are found, while making it possible to explain the variations in the stories. By taking ownership of a historical construction that is handed down, each generation can divert it to present-day purposes. The Elohist takes action after the Yahwist, and the Deuteronomist reorganizes what was created and heralded by the Chronist. By this form of narrative construction, historical data of the biblical system is presented in mixed guise, as an object of faith, interpretation, and preservation.[10]

The Movement of History

In this typology of narrative order, the first exile marks a clean break from the dynamic of continuity of God's actions vis-à-vis Israel, such as occurred in ancient history. It remains to be resolved what happened during this period of the history of Israel. No description or prophet confirms it. The silence would only be broken when the God of Israel brought his people back to its land, and history regained its narrative flow. It resumes, to be recorded in the Book of Nehemiah (chapter 9) and the deuterocanonical Judith (chapter 5).[11] In this linear flow, which for von Rad is entirely a "history of salvation,"[12] the intercession of prophets is meant to prepare the people for imminent great changes: "The prophets seek to convince their contemporaries that for them the hitherto existing saving ordinances have lost their worth, and that, if Israel is to be saved, she must move in faith into a new saving activity of Jahweh, one which is only to come in the future," von Rad says.[13] In his view, then, the Israelites' alleged belief that everything that had happened prior to their appearance on the scene was obsolete thus finally puts them outside this history of "salvation," such as it had been understood by Israel, he avers, until then. The sermons of the prophets were persuasive in shattering the previous life of Israel before Yahweh and opening other horizons to a new historical drive in the history of God's salvation with regard to Israel.

The description of time in the Bible assumes a pattern that may be considered characteristic.[14] Two examples will suffice: first, in Judges, the standard formula is used to describe what followed the death of Abimelech:

> Thus God rendered the wickedness of Abimelech, which he did unto his father. . . . And all the evil of the men of Shechem did God render upon their heads: and upon them came the curse of Jotham the son of Jerubbaal. . . . And after Abimelech there arose to defend Israel Tola the son of Puah, the son of Dodo, a man of Issachar; and he dwelt in Shamir . . . . And he judged Israel twenty and three years, and died, and was buried in Shamir. And after him arose Jair, a Gileadite, and judged Israel twenty and two years. . . . And Jair died, and was buried in Camon. And the children of Israel did evil again in the sight of the Lord . . . [15]

Kings presents the circumstances of protagonists in time:

> In the fiftieth year of Azariah king of Judea, Pekahiah son of Menahem became king of Israel in Samaria, and he reigned two years. Pekahiah did evil in the eyes of the Lord. . . . One of his chief officers, Pekah son of Remaliah, conspired against him. . . . So Pekah killed Pekahiah and succeeded him as king. The other events of Pekahiah's reign, and all he did, are written in the book of the annals of the kings of Israel.[16]

> In the second year of Pekah son of Remaliah king of Israel, Jotham son of Uzziah king of Judea began to reign. He was twenty-five years old when he became king, and he reigned in Jerusalem sixteen years. His mother's name was Jerusha daughter of Zadok. He did what was right in the eyes of the Lord. . . . As for the other events of Jotham's reign, and what he did, are they not written in the book of the annals of the kings of Judea? . . . Jotham rested with his ancestors and was buried with them in the City of David, the city of his father. And Ahaz his son succeeded him as king.[17]

Kings offers more widely documented historical relationships than Judges, with external stories more often mentioned and annals brought to bear, as well as stories of the prophets and excerpts from the Temple chronicles. Still, the narrative process remains identical. The rulers of Israel take action in a qualitative area of heavenly judgment; in consequence, they "[sleep] with [their] fathers" or are slain with the sword. It is unsurprising that some biblical scholars date the writing of Kings to the Babylonian Exile, as the following mention indicates: "And it came to pass in the seven and thirtieth year of the captivity of Jehoiachin king of Judea, . . . that Evilmerodach king of Babylon in the year that he began to reign did lift up the head of Jehoiachin king of Judea out of prison."[18] This dates back to the year 561 BCE.

The fall of the two kingdoms shows that God's word was carried out in history. By punctuating it, many prophecies incorporated into the narrative provide its rhythm, setting standards and marking the boundaries of its flow. Prophecies, followed by their fulfilment, form the historical process in which the history of Israel becomes the flow of time. The dominant factor is a result of the tension produced by the fulfilment of continually renewed prophecy. Instead of directly intervening in the course of events, as in the Torah, God now directs history through the mediation of the word. The tension provoked may be short-lived, such as when Adoniah declares himself king, despite Nathan's prophecy promising the kingdom to Solomon.[19] It may also unfold in a tale that affects several generations and different books: "I see a prince that is to come, born of David's race, Josiah by name"; Josiah asks: "'What title is that that I see?' And the men of the city told him, It is the sepulchre of the man of God, which came from Judea, and proclaimed these things that thou hast done."[20] Succeeding to the throne becomes an integral part of the tale of fulfilling the explicit word of God, which announced the order of events through Nathan's prophecy, securing the kingship for David and his offspring.[21]

Placing the writing of Deuteronomy in exile as von Rad and his followers do, at a moment when the history of salvation was merely marking time, requires implementing a theology of history. Israel ponders events that affected it and principally why God denied his people. Whence the observation that Israel is at fault and had ruined its own well-being, having conducted the experiment, both constructive and destructive, of the Law, which nonetheless contains the promise of re-habilitation, with the promise of Nathan. God acts through language, which works in two ways: as Law, it destroys if it is not obeyed, while as promise it saves—if it is heeded. The divine Word is rationalized this way and demonstrates its power of effectiveness. What fulfils general history is not decisive for matters regarding Israel. The determining factor for the life or death of the people of God is essentially the Word spoken in history. The content of the "history of salvation" becomes clear. It is about the series of events fashioned by the ongoing inter-vention of God's Word, which judges, saves, and leads to fulfilment.

Characterized by the gift of free will, however, humans see the free-dom granted them as limited precisely by the divine Word. This reveals an odd paradox. Since the creation, God has constantly put humans, and later Israel, to the test. Starting with Genesis, He exposes them to many temptations: speculation, by putting Adam near the forbidden fruit of the Tree of Knowledge; power, as in the tale of the Tower of Babel; dis-obedience, all through Exodus; and, finally, before the downfall of the kingdom, even rejecting His possessive religion. Is it to impose His Law all the more effectively? After all, as with individuals in their personal capacity, Israel as a people may choose to "return" to God and His land. The prophetic Word works in a coherent framework. By allowing divine speech to be disseminated to humankind, it confronts them with the "free" choice between its fulfilment and their own destruction.

The divine Word channels the current of history and structures its torrent. It gives biblical time a specific meaning. The time described by the prophets of the biblical period is brief in relation to that sepa-rating Genesis/Creation from redemption (for Christians, from the Second Coming and the end of time). It follows the progress of the divine Word and human doings. Between laws and rebellions, human history unfolds in a time fashioned solely by divine will and justice. Passing time is a tale that imperatively leads to the redemption that the prophets believe must take place during human history, in the time of human experience. For as the prophetic texts proclaim, the liberation of Israel as a nation will occur in historical time;[22] the monarchy will be reestablished,[23] Israel's enemies will be vanquished,[24] the exiles will re-turn,[25] and the glory of Jerusalem will be restored.[26] Justice and God's kingdom will extend over the earth,[27] which will be fertile,[28] and all the people will return to Zion to honor God,[29] while violence will disappear, even among animals.[30]

Concern about the measure and flow of past time is ignored by models of biblical temporality. Inscription in years indicates the begetting of primordial generations. It dates primarily from the appearance of the divine Word through the intermediary of a human being, the prophet, who is introduced as being a certain number of years old, living in a specific year during the reign of a given king, without these details seeming of particular importance. A change occurs with Chronicles, placed at the very end of the Jewish Bible, as the last book of the Writings whose author, probably writing the P document around the fourth century BCE, is according to biblical scholars the same person who wrote the books of Ezra and Nehemiah. A reading of Chronicles thus shows that the history of Israel has been entirely rethought as part of a continuum from Adam to Saul. The book lists genealogies, pointing for the first time to the direct lineages of Israel, describes the founding of the kingdom and the reign of David, and stops with the post-exilic period under the rule of Nehemiah and the scribe Ezra during the fourth century.

"By the rivers of Babylon, there we sat down, yea, we wept . . ."

Reading the biblical text offers an infinite domain for inquiry, since "for the philologist, the text is a profound, invisible entity, to be reconstructed independently of material data," Carlo Ginzburg observes.[31] This applies to prophecy just as much as it does to the rest of the biblical corpus. Helmer Ringgren can thus affirm that Jeremiah is the first prophet consistently to use the idea of the Covenant, which previous prophets seemed to take as a trifling idea or one of scant interest.[32] Typifying the difference between classical prophecies and those of Jeremiah and Ezekiel, the latter bring the tragic message of the ineluctability—indeed necessity—of the Fall. Until then, pre-exilic prophets presented themselves mainly as messengers of judgment. They announced that God, the Lord of history, would send powerful people to fight Israel, who would crush it, that He would make the great powers of the day His instruments to magnify the judgment that He would deliver against His people. History may tell us that the fall of the kingdom of Judea was owing to the defection of its allies on the field and the sheer size of the Babylonian army, but biblical tradition says otherwise. Since the destiny of Israel is directed by the divine hand, an event as extraordinary as its fall can only have been providential. It can only be understood in terms of retribution for failure to adhere to the Covenant between God and Israel.[33] In short, until the Exile, prophets are primarily preachers who proclaim the word of God in a given situation without becoming either historians of the phenomena that occur or seers who map a future according to a pre-established historical pattern. Yet their preaching is undeniably based on a concept of history as God's field of action. This is certainly true of the prophecies of Jeremiah and Ezekiel. It is visible first and foremost in the announcement of judgment spoken by the oracle about the people, and next in the announcement of final redemption. Prophets who announce the return of Israel to its homeland indirectly refer to exile and the fall of the kingdom of Samaria, whereas other messianic prophets announcing the arrival of an ideal king do not necessarily imply that the Davidian dynasty no longer exists. The idea of repentance, which sometimes—but not always—abuts that of return, may also be related to the underlying idea of a "remnant of the people of Israel" or a "New Covenant" announced by Jeremiah.[34]

Historians, biblical scholars, and New Testament theologians agree in thinking that the fall of Jerusalem in 587 BCE greatly influenced the later evolution of the religion of Israel. The destruction of the Temple forced the Jews to seek new forms of worship, while the loss of the royal dynasty dealt a fatal blow to those who relied on its permanence because of the Covenant between David and Israel. The ruin of Israel may be seen as a failure of its God or theology. The religious and political power elite, deported to Babylon, left those who remained in place without guidance, since religious traditions followed the elite into exile. The ambient state of mind in the province of Judea is described in Lamentations. There are plaints over the destiny that has befallen them, the destruction of the Temple, the lack of places of worship, and, finally, bewailing the fall of the monarchy. Having directed the annihilation of the kingdom of Israel, God has turned into an enemy. Yet heavenly rage swept over Israel only because it compromised itself looking for trouble and provoking God's wrath.

Abandoned, the Israelites fall back in despair on sundry other forms of worship and gods.[35] Yet in Babylon the situation is different. Well-read people try to preserve the uniqueness of the religion of Israel by focusing on everything that preserves their coherence as a people without the Temple. Naturally, sacrifices and festivals must be renounced, but to compensate the burden of domestic and individual religious duties, the *miqdash me'at*, will be increased. These conditions lead to the imposition of practices of religious differentiation. Circumcision evolves into a sign of fidelity and recognition; observing Shabbat is henceforth de rigueur; ritual purity is scrutinized.[36] Probably most of Israel's laws were compiled in exile, if not drafted there. The fall of the Neo-Babylonian Empire during the era of Cyrus allowed the Jews to return to Jerusalem and Judea in 539 BCE. According to Ezra 3, the first things the Jews did were rebuild the Temple and require the celebration of Sukkot, the Feast of Tabernacles. Begun in 520, exhorted by the preaching of Zacharias and Haggai, reconstruction of the Temple took five years, and it was consecrated in 515. Despite the inexact chronological indicators of the work and although the roles of the protagonists are not clear, it transpires from the text that Ezra was likely a charismatic religious leader, highly influential in the Persian world.[37] Knowing how to bring the people together, he gave public readings of the law brought from Babylon in which exogamy was banned.

History Silently Pursues Its Course

Israel now possessed sacred laws that it had to obey. They formed the cornerstone of its religion, notably those dealing with ritual purity and the forbidding of mixed marriages. Until the Samaritan schism (in the second or third century BCE), the biblical source dries up again and a silence falls on events.[38] From the chronology of the kingdom of Israel, we can sketch a linear approach to time as translation of the divine Word in human space. God had chosen his people and forced them to submit to his Law since the exodus from Egypt. In spite of repeated warnings from prophets, translators, and mediators of the divine Word who threatened it with obliteration, Israel had made bad use of its free will. Having preferred disobedience to docility, its ruin occurred as forecast. At this point, a New Covenant as promised by Jeremiah was established under the auspices of clerics: "And I will make an everlasting covenant with them, . . . I will put my fear in their hearts, that they shall not depart from me."[39] Still, the Israelites are not satisfied and refuse to obey the laws strictly. They sin consistently and inevitably find themselves under the yoke of nations that will impose the just punishment of divine wrath. Persian and Roman tyrants are God's instruments of justice and vengeance. Chastised, the Jews will encounter Hellenism and the Diaspora. An entirely different history begins.

Historical narration resumes—without inclusion in the Bible—by the writing of the two books of the Maccabees, which recount events occurring during the reign of the Greek ruler Antiochus IV Epiphanes.[40] Their composition is dated to the Hasmonean dynasty, with the first book having been written during the reign of John Hyrcanus (134–104 BCE) and the second before the end of the second century BCE, a time that also produced the Book of Daniel. The period that now begins is marked by fleeting national independence, followed by Roman domination, during which the Apochrypha and Pseudepigrapha were composed. Sources that finally become the rabbinic legal system, the Oral Law, were simultaneously codified under Roman and later Christian rule by the writing of the Mishnah in Palestine and the compiling of the Gemara, which would form the Babylonian and Jerusalem Talmuds.[41]

The little that is known about this era derives from the testimony of Flavius Josephus.[42] Born into a priestly family related to the Hasmoneans, Josephus seems to first be noted for his knowledge of Halakhah, religious law. In 66 CE, at the start of the revolt against the Romans, he headed the government in Galilee, in conflict with Zealots. Recalled by the Sanhedrin, he refused to comply. Yet when he was under siege, after forty-seven days of battle, he took refuge in a cave with the plan of committing mass suicide. Left alive with a single companion, he traveled to see the emperor Vespasian and became his protégé. He was present in the Roman camp during the sack of Jerusalem and the destruction of the Temple. Next he moved to Rome, where in exchange for his surrender,[43] he received an imperial pension to become historian of the conquest. His literary work is unique. The only surviving account, his narrative of events is the basis for what we know about the occurrences and background in Palestine at this time.

Moreover, his *Jewish Antiquities* collects a literature based on biblical and oral sources. The corpus had not yet been drawn up in his time, and he recounts traditions that have since vanished or changed. His contribution to our limited knowledge of the history of this period is all the more precious because it remains exclusive.[44]

In all probability, the perception of time was profoundly transformed by the impact on Jews of the Diaspora and the destruction of the Temple. These two historical events must have changed the relation to temporality that takes shape in later transmission in Jewish writings. No matter how we interpret the attitude of the Israelites after the fall of the Temple in terms of the interventionist God of the Bible, reading *The Jewish War* highlights the role that Josephus grants to the interposition in historical time of God, who intervenes directly in order to punish or save His people. The main theme of the tale is the history that leads to the destruction of Jerusalem and the ruin of Israel. Josephus asks how his God could have permitted this, which naturally sends him back to the idea of punishment.[45] From this perspective, Rome is the instrument of divine judgment, and the revolt by the Israelites against it amounts to a rebellion against God Himself. This is why Josephus encourages his fellow Jews to surrender.[46] By submitting to divine will and judgment, presently embodied by the Romans, the Israelites would bow to the will of the divine lawgiver and testify to their infinite trust in His word. As Isaiah had proclaimed, this word would surely be more powerful help than any military alliance.[47] Accepting that Roman rule was a just punishment, Josephus has no doubt that the Jews should resign themselves and accept the situation. The duration of punishment remained unresolved; when would it end? Josephus consulted the ancient prophecy of Balaam in the Book of Numbers, which states: "Surely there is no enchantment against Jacob, neither is there any divination against Israel: according to this time it shall be said of Jacob and of Israel, What hath God wrought!"[48] Josephus sums up: "From which completion of all these predictions that he made, one may easily guess that the rest will have their completion in time to come."[49]

Five   The Time to Come

> What is above and what is below, what is before and what is behind?
> You may speculate from the day that days were created, but you may
> not speculate on what was before that.
>
> Babylonian Talmud: Tractate Hagigah 11b;
> Midrash Rabbah: Genesis, 1:10[1]

Representations of time employ all types of cultural, scientific, and religious metaphors. The ancient world evoked time by winged beings
who show its brisk flight, a set of carefully balanced weighing scales,
or symbols of power and fertility. From the end of the Middle Ages,
metaphors of destruction and decline introduce an element of decay or
senescence in the image of representing time.[2] In terms of conceivable
representations in the Jewish world, the image of time to be deduced
from the Midrash cited above would tend to exclude any vision, rather
than kindle one. Symbolizing time is forbidden here before it even
starts to show. The universe glides between before and later, forbidden
to human questioning. It is only permitted to observe what has been
created for man simultaneously in time. We might almost conclude
that with these three dimensions prohibited, spatial representation itself cannot be conceived. If we could have used a linear image above—
the thread of history stretched between past and future—the scales
would currently be relevant. Implemented time would allude to the
allegory of weighing scales upon which are balanced the past, on one
side, and the future, on the other. The latter is maintained by the present, which itself is articulated by the past and sustained by expectation
of the future. The whole thing is structured between two interdictions,
the before and after of creation, which Jewish mysticism constantly
examines nonetheless. How is the balance between these two levels
controlled by the historical present, so that one or the other of these
directions is not overemphasized?

On a daily basis, how to be part of a time which has not yet come,
although wholly determined by its future? Projection into the future is
a commonplace matter, often seen as the driving force behind human

actions. It helps us to tolerate the present and invest in tomorrow. Yet, when transcending individual desires to be made collective, this projection is put in the perspective of a redemption, it becomes eschatological. Within Judaism, two eschatological visions coexist on parallel paths from distant periods to the contemporary era. One, articulated around two ideas of redemption and the world to come, projects *geulah*, or the future of redemption, into an "other world," which cannot be clearly defined, since the *'olam ha-ba'a* is difficult for mortals to imagine. The other takes on the vision of redemption in "this world," whose expectations are expressed in different phenomena such as the Shabbetean sect, the Polish Hassidim of the eighteenth century, and the Jewish revolutionaries of the nineteenth and twentieth centuries. All of these may be seen as consecutive avatars.[3]

In Judaism, messianic hope is to some extent a manifest duty. It was through the Covenant that God established with Abraham and later sealed with his people that the Jews gained the certainty that this promise would be carried out in the future. The biblical books embody this promise and are in some way the collateral guaranteeing the divine word, an expression of His power to intervene in and on history. The pact made of Abraham's descendants a people established on their land and recognized among the nations as being the people of God. In Judaism, this goes with the idea of judgment, which also reflects what is found in references to the "day of the Eternal" and the "day of Judgment" in the Bible, and to the "day of the Messiah" in later tradition.

As we have seen, biblical narrative expresses temporal tension by stressing three moments, those of creation, revelation, and redemption. They form the structures of temporality, such as phenomenology describes as well, with the categorical terms of origin and end.[4] In this way, the starting point reflects on the narrative method of creation—which might seem to refer to the cycle of biblical readings. The present is revealed through a word that denotes the event as a reference. The future is determined by the imperative form of guideline and appears or is heralded in prophetic conduct. This grasp of time runs throughout the history of the Jews, just as it defines messianic expectations. Rabbinic temporality experiences a shift in the use of the biblical term *'olam*, which, starting with the idea of the eternal in biblical writings, comes to be used in the sense of "world," "universe," and "everything." Subsequently, this temporality is indicated, not as a given, but as something constantly "becoming": this world insofar as it is coming—literally, in the Hebrew *'olam ha-ba'a*,[5] the messianic universe qualified as such by the arrival of an envoy-Messiah—and refers us to the cemetery, with the phrase *beit 'olam*.[6] Presented as the son of man, the Messiah outlines the future of humanity. He represents the interplay of specific history with world history, the succession from individual history to collective history, from inwardness to exteriority, from waiting to what is postulated, that shapes the thought aimed at resolving the aporia[7] and enigma of time. In this way, the Messiah embodies the future of humanity, but letting rest its actuality, which is suited to a temporality "in the making," according to Hans-Georg Gadamer's concept of the "internal historicity of experience."[8]

Telling Time

The keys to understanding this interspersion may still be provided by four terms that date back to biblical times.[9] Apart from *'olam*, already discussed,[10] the Hebrew language uses three other terms to define and indicate temporality: *zman*, *mo'ed*, and *'et*. In today's speech, the word *zman* is most often used. It conveys an image of time that is passing, measuring, counted by showing an indefinite time, like that perpetuated by Ecclesiastes,[11] available in the form of *zamin*, temporary, or fleeting, with *zmani*. It specifies the instant of summoning with *hazmanah*, or *zimun*, the invitation to say grace after meals.[12] This is a time that completely eludes the idea of eternity, since it is so inclined toward passing and motion. Still, its infrequent appearances in the Bible show that it is also marked by the time of happenstance. It appears twice in the Book of Esther,[13] as well as in the Books of Nehemiah[14] and Daniel,[15] just when the history of Israel intersects with that of other nations.

The term *mo'ed* derives from the root indicating testimony. It implies and proceeds from the meeting or appointment. *Heh 'id* means "testify" but also "warn"; in Exodus we read: "ve-yassem ha-Shem mo'ed lehemor mahar ya'asseh" ("And the Lord appointed a set time, saying, To morrow [*sic*] . . .").[16] Meanwhile, *hit h'oded* means "to dare" or "become bolder." The tent of meeting—an encounter with the divine—called *ohel mo'ed*, is the place or tabernacle of simultaneous confrontation and testimony.[17] The temporality reflected by *mo'ed* bears duration, providing continuity. It is defined with reference to the era and time that structure and signify, suited to indicate liturgical time. It is a fixed temporality. In its plural form *mo'adim*, it refers to festivals which extend cosmic time, as in Genesis 1:14, "let them be for signs, and for seasons."[18] They are torn away by memories of experience attached to the latter and settle in a future that opens and extends beyond: "And Moses declared unto the children of Israel the feasts of the Lord."[19] *Mo'ed* also reflects a passing time or moment of change: "And he shall . . . think to change times and laws."[20] There is even sudden change: "the new moons and sabbaths, the calling of assemblies, I cannot away with; it is iniquity, even the solemn meeting."[21] It is the time of an epoch that has passed, an era still present which is passing even while it remains, the incessant time of *immer schon*,[22] a moment of irreversible duration.[23]

The subtlest of these three names for time is that covered by the word *'et*. The Torah says *ba'et ha-hi'*, "at that time," which the Vulgate translates as *in illo tempore*: "And it came to pass at that time, that Abimelech . . ."[24] It is also found in "la-kol zman ve-'et . . . 'et laledet ve-'et lamut," famously paraphrased as "To every thing there is a season, and a time to every purpose under the heaven: A time to be born, and a time to die."[25] This fleeting time that must be seized when it is here, time with the urgency of now, is also indicated by its absence: "lo 'et bo 'et bet-Adonai lehi-banot" ("The time is not come, the time that the Lord's house should be built").[26] In this sense, it also indicates the time that eludes the decision or will of people because it corresponds to the hour chosen by God, as affirmed by the expression *b'et ratson*. This ensures that time is not a matter of chronology and only finds its full meaning in a prophetic reading of time, comprehensive biblical interpretations based on sources leading to a conclusion that remains sealed, but is on the way.

Wait, but How?

After the destruction of the Second Temple, the Judaism of presence that had characterized the religion of the ancient Israelites was replaced by the Judaism of expectation. Infused with constant stress between these two categories, Judaism would constantly waver in messianic hope, between a tragic outlook, marked by apocalyptic and destructive visions, and a peaceful viewpoint. The intensity of these movements may be gauged from the periodic flare-ups of messianic agitation throughout Jewish history. It may also be discerned in exegeses and Jewish texts.[27] These periods marked by clashes between divergent trends are often treated with reluctance by rabbis opposing the excesses to which the certainty of the imminent arrival of an apocalyptic Messiah may lead.

Trying to locate apocalyptic messianism in the dialectic framework of Jewish temporality as discussed leads to grasping it as a rationalized and time-varying historical vision "in this world." This messianic approach—some scholars called it "political messianism" because it aims to form a society—remains linked to the position of Maimonides, who projects messianism into everyday life. From this point of view it is wholly contained in obeying the Torah and the commandments. Yet beyond his articles of faith, Maimonides retains an explicit reference both to a personified Messiah and to his "day."[28] Inverting the apocalyptic proposition by neutralizing its tragic aspect, Maimonides also changes the direction of the course of time. Human actions with potential to "summon" the Messiah are those belonging to faith in Judaism in everyday life. It becomes unnecessary to watch and wait for disaster, seeking signs, reckonings, and calculations about the end of time as apocalyptic mystics do. Yet Maimonides' stance is far from abandoning the constant resonance based on the talmudic statement that the Messiah will come only when Israel is either wholly virtuous or entirely sinning.[29] This leaves the debate between different expectations unresolved and prone to be revived. For Maimonides, messianic times must be those of Israel's independence. They will be composed by the reversal of current time; it will mean a return to the time of nations according to the time of Israel, when the latter will once again become the theme of its own history and rediscover its lost identity. From the Maimonidean point of view, messianic identity is to be grasped as an expression of the true identity of Israel, finally free to devote itself fully to the study of the Torah.[30]

With this in mind, the arrival of the Messiah is tantamount, as a historical and political outcome, to a political solution, as well as to a way out of politics and history. The Passover Haggadah recalls that formerly, during a *seder* celebrated at Bnei Brak, rabbis discussed the extent of the revelation made by God to Abraham about the Messiah. Doing so, it includes the tale of the Exodus in an ahistorical context. Sages discuss the future of Judaism against a background of the recent destruction of the Temple, followed by the Diaspora. These discussions about the persisting possibility of the "day of the Messiah," indicate that no matter what the time, Jews always think about messianism, whether reinterpreted in apocalyptic terms, negated, or just relegated to the stage of a delayed history. The traditional alternatives—the Messiah son of David[31] or son of Joseph[32]—are placed on the scales and weighed yet again. These two emblematic figures also represent the historical or metahistorical paths offered by the warlike public Messiah and peaceful hidden Messiah. The Messiah son of Joseph is the Messiah of the present day; he fights for freedom, paving the way for the Messiah son of David, who is peaceful, more spiritual, and embodies the future.[33] In linking messianic time with the end of the oppression of Israel and obliterating the coming of the Messiah, the miracle that includes it, Maimonides relativizes these two figures. For him, the Messiah will accomplish nothing visible or spectacular. He will not revive the dead, but mark the end of the "time of nations."[34]

Writing the History of God . . . the History of Humanity

This new perception of the "time of nations," experienced in terms of the trials and tribulations of Israel, brings us back to the conceptual moment where we had left Josephus. Expecting the Messiah and believing in the resurrection of the dead combine to merge into a single hope for redemption. Provided by Pharisaic doctrine, it enters into texts of Judaism during the first two centuries of the common era.[35] The emergence of an eschatological concept within a religious system is not easily explained in historical terms, although its development may be traced. Messianic turmoil and its counteraction participate in a constant process in Judaism that for convenience is traced back to the rift caused by the destruction of the Second Temple and the defeat of the Bar Kokhba revolt in the second century.[36] The fall of the

Second Temple brought about such profound changes that Judaism as we know it came into being as a result. The most striking aspect of this is the cessation of historical transcription by Jews. Given that the fall of the First Temple not only inspired new scriptural books but prompted the formalization of the biblical canon, why was the destruction of the Second greeted with such deafening historical silence? Those who address this question explain the silence as a sign of the exit of Jews from history. The Christian theological schema accommodates such an escape very well: better than any discourse, this aphasia shows that henceforth history switched protagonists for the time being. However, Jewish reasoning follows a different logic: shocked to the core and feeling rejected, Jews henceforth strove to accept the only choice they saw offered them, repentance and insularity, while awaiting the arrival of the redeeming Messiah.

How to come up with a comparison of the two destructions that simultaneously permits us to understand the emergence of rabbinic Judaism and the suspension of narrative forms used until then by Israel? Von Rad and Jacob Neusner—from opposite theological positions—agree in minimizing the harshness of the conditions imposed on the Jews during the fifty years of their forced stay in Babylon. Let us follow their respective arguments, starting with the idea that they come to the same conclusion, notwithstanding that the former defends a Christian viewpoint and the latter a Jewish one. Von Rad highlights the negligence of the neo-Babylonians in not dispersing the exiles or planting settlers in Judea. He sees the Exile of 586 BCE simply as a "sort of internment" in Babylonia, while those who remained behind in Judea were left to their own devices.[37] To be sure, this was an era of dejection. The Temple was in ruins, and sacrifices and festivals suspended. As the prophet Zechariah makes clear, it was a period of fasting and mourning.[38] The Book of Lamentations also describes hardships faced by the survivors, focusing on self-criticism and the justness of their punishment. Yet for von Rad, all of the P source—written during the Exile, according to Julius Wellhausen—shows that "page after page of history was here scrutinized and the result was quite unambiguous: the disaster was not due to Jahweh, or to the failure of his patience or of his readiness to forgive. On the contrary, Israel had rejected Jahweh and his commandments. For that reason judgment had overtaken Israel and Judah, the judgment which Jahweh had threatened if the commandments were disregarded—here the chief thing in mind was certainly the curses in the concluding section of Deuteronomy (Deut. 28)."[39] The prophets Ezekiel and Jeremiah both insist on the need for a new covenant and a new Jerusalem, and we know that the exiles effectively accepted the prophecies.[40] The conquering swathe cut through the ancient Orient by the Persians, and their imposition of a new regime that was appreciably more tolerant of subjected peoples in religious matters, aroused a messianic fever led by Haggai and Zechariah, who urged rebuilding the Temple and restoring the Davidic dynasty by anointing Zerubbabel.[41] Yet it would take almost a century between the return of the exiles in 538 and the first public reading of the Torah in 444 BCE under the leadership of the scribe Ezra for new, hard-line forms of Judaism that were definitely more purist to develop, directly promoted by exiles who remained in Babylon. For von Rad, this is when Judaism appears in its full diversity, the outward sign of this being the fact that Israel "threw off the vestment of her statehood together with her kingdom with surprising ease and without apparent internal crisis."[42] According to von Rad, belonging to the people of God had been a clear-cut matter until the Exile. After that everything changes, because "Israel now no longer appeared as a people determined by nature and history; it was the Law that more and more began to define who belonged to her [Israel] and who did not."[43] This is why outsiders were excluded, mixed marriages nullified, and laws of ritual purity stressed, since the Law became the only way by which to recognize and identify who belonged. This was an absolute reality, destined to be permanent, and no longer relying on contingencies of any kind, whether in time or history.[44] For von Rad, the introduction of the Law caused Israel to "emerge from history," and more specifically, from the "history that it had experienced until then with Yahweh." By serving its God in an "enigmatic place beyond history," it definitively cut itself off from any solidarity with other peoples, who became wary and hostile.

Jacob Neusner published prolifically, especially on Jews in the Babylonian era and the Mishnah.[45] For Neusner, the process of emerging Judaism is somewhat different. Although he also believes that the destruction of the Temple in 586 BCE led to reevaluating Israelite history, which finally led to collecting the biblical texts, Neusner is mainly surprised that nothing similar happened in first-century Palestine or third-century Babylon.[46] Apart from the account by Josephus, no writing from the contemporary rabbinic corpus bears witness to events in Palestine before the year 70, any more than talmudic sources contribute to the knowledge of the Babylonian period in the third century. Information about the destruction of the Temple derives only from apocryphal and pseudepigraphic texts in which historical connotations are offered in the form of apocalyptic visions in the style of the Book of Daniel or the Sibylline Oracles. Neusner wondered about the strange paradox of silence from Jewish sources.

Yohanan ben Zakkai (30 BCE–90 CE), a master of Pharisaic Judaism, flees the burning city of Jerusalem to make a pact with the Romans that allows him to reopen his school at Yavneh. There he can convene the lawgiving power and religious authority of the ruined sanctuary. Little is known about his attitude in the years before the siege of Jerusalem, apart from assuming that he could have confronted rebel zealots with Roman authority. Ephraim Urbach argues that the school of Jewish law known as the Academy of Hillel took a negative view overall against those who fought Roman rule.[47] Yohanan ben Zakkai's personality only emerges with his rebuilding work. While most texts from this era lead us to think in eschatological terms against a background of the ruin of Jerusalem and the Temple, Yohanan ben Zakkai resolves to take action in the present, maybe hoping to take care of immediate needs of the "remnant of the people of Israel." He tries to create a program for survival and reconstruction for the Jewish people and their faith. Little heeding past sufferings, which tended to lead to an obsessive search for the secret of the coming redemption, he stubbornly persists in the present with the sole aim of preserving what can be saved from the tragedy of disappearance. Others try to console Israel, with the comforting assurance that He who punished them would offer salvation, and it was just a matter of waiting for the undoubted redemption. By contrast, Yohanan ben Zakkai offers a concrete program for this waiting period.[48] Like ben Zakkai himself, Romans, apocalyptic sects, loyalist Jews, and Judeo-Christians give answers pointing to the trespasses of Israel when asked by the people about the reason for their sufferings. Yet the replies differ in assessing these trespasses. Josephus believes that Jews sinned in taking up arms against the Romans, who currently embody divine will. It was precisely this Jewish transgression that ensured the success of Roman rule. From the Roman point of view, it was an appropriate price paid by the Jews for their revolt against Rome. Israel sinned with war, and it was punished by conquest. Over the decades, many Jews also came to see things that way, especially some sixty-five years later, after the rout that followed the suppression of the Bar Kokhba uprising.[49] During this time, the Judeo-Christians keep their distance from Judaism, considering that the punishment meted out to the Jews was justified by their refusal to accept the Savior and signaled the victory of Christian belief over Jewish belief. Along the same lines, the apocalyptic sects criticize Israel's transgressions, meditating on their nature, while promising future redemption.[50] They focus on the prospect of the Last Judgment, when the Messiah will finally come to destroy Roman power and God will reign. The Jewish Apocalypse of Ezra affirms that the ways of the Lord are unfathomable.[51] On all the evidence, then, the disaster was caused by sin and, more specifically, mankind's innate inability to fulfil the will of God. Ezra prays for forgiveness and bases his hope in the future, when human hearts will change and finally be able to heed God.

In the same way, the pseudepigraphal scribe Baruch reaffirms the promise of future redemption, but offers little advice for holding on until then. The text contains five chapters in which an explanation in three points can easily be discerned. First, God acted justly in punishing Israel. Second, the disaster was provoked by Israel's transgression. Third, just as surely as God punished Israel, he will deliver it.[52] Far from these stances, Yohanan ben Zakkai takes on the duty of teaching Jews to repent and return to God, explaining that this is the key condition for the redemption to occur. Whereas Baruch saw this as a true hope, certain and nearly accomplished, Yohanan ben Zakkai apparently only mentioned it in his final days. Surviving texts show him as quite skeptical about the power of messianic movements, as this representative maxim shows: "If there were a plant in your hand and they should say to you: 'Look, the messiah is here!' Go and plant your plant, and after that go forth to receive him."[53] Yohanan ben Zakkai offers no immediate hope, only a conditional promise. Just as punishment follows sin, so redemption will follow repentance. Yohanan ben Zakkai's program of rebuilding involves the social and political life of Palestinian Judaism. It is meant to comfort, to be sure, yet also to show people what must be done to avoid transgression by enhancing the meaning of the divine service without a sanctuary, and above all, construct a religious life capable of facing and overcoming historical mutations.

By promoting focus on the present time and imminent problems, Yohanan ben Zakkai paves the way to transcending history, without the least eschatological mediation being involved, solely by the intervention of concrete actions in the world of daily life. The comforting message that talmudic tradition conveys in the name of the leading Pharisee is clear:

> Once, as Rabban Yochanan ben Zakkai was coming forth from Jerusalem, Rabbi Joshua followed after him and beheld the Temple in ruins.
>
> "Woe unto us!" Rabbi Joshua cried, "that this, the place where the iniquities of Israel were atoned for, is laid waste!"
>
> "My son," Rabban Johanan said to him, "be not grieved; we have another atonement as effective as this. And what is it? It is acts of loving-kindness [gemilut hasadim]."[54]

For Yohanan ben Zakkai, since sin led to disaster, virtue must lead to redemption. He rejects all consolation in the form of an eschatological vision and suggests that Jews work upon themselves. This creation of an ethical model of expecting redemption will equip Jews to survive as a people in transition.

The Time of Nations

In previous eras, standards were set forth in the books of the Bible. Temple rites and acts of devotion naturally emerged, but for the moment, it became necessary to lay the foundations for study of the Torah and observing the commandments, while pious and charitable actions counteracted the violence of the war years. The most typical example of Yohanan ben Zakkai's position in this respect is the episode in the form of an anecdotal proverb in which he meets ascetics who shun meat and wine, telling them: "He said to them, 'My children, come and I shall teach you. Not to mourn at all is impossible, for the evil decree has already come upon us. But to mourn too much is also impossible, for one may not promulgate a decree for the community unless most of the community can endure it."[55] He admitted that despite everything, efforts were being made to hasten the arrival of the Messiah, but not by political or military action, which had proven futile and wasteful. He believed solely in the virtue of reform based on study, good deeds, and acts of devotion. To follow this path, people must be helped to transcend despair and dependence, and he took on this task. He apparently adopted an approach created some centuries before by Jeremiah and Ezekiel, who had shown, during the previous disaster, that people must be changed from within to accept individual responsibility. Neusner believes that Rabbi Yohanan ben Zakkai conveyed a scriptural message suitable for his epoch. In this regard, teaching meant not just preserving the social order and public well-being, but also a way to achieve redemption. If he actually believed that the Messiah would come soon, hoping for God's intervention in history, he surely did not suspect that he was offering a long-term program of political passivity. Trying to sustain social stability against all odds, he did not target religious irresponsibility, but rather aimed at radical change and healing for a people decimated and vanquished by years of civil war and continued fighting. In this guise, the Jews could continue to participate in the drama of redemption, albeit reduced to a secondary role.

We find this attitude again one hundred and fifty years later, when the Jews of Babylon faced a similar situation. The Sassanid takeover in Babylonia in the third century CE threatened the political, religious, and theological security of Jews in Babylon. Wars between the Roman and Persian empires reach their apex with the conquest of Syria and Asia Minor by the Persians and the capture of the Roman emperor Valerian in 260 CE. The rulers of Palmyra, allied with Rome, occupied the eastern provinces from 260 to 272. To undermine pro-Persian Jewish opposition, they sacked the Jewish city of Nehardea on the Euphrates (in modern central Iraq), a vital cultural and economic center, which had one of the largest rabbinic academies. During the fifth and sixth centuries, subsequent religious persecution would result in banning the observation of Shabbat,[56] ending Jewish autonomy, and closing rabbinical schools.[57]

In the Jewish world, messianic turmoil generally accompanies times of persecution. This agitation can foment two reactions with specific features. The first resorts to conjecture about signs and calculations for the expected arrival, while the second seeks historical paradigms or models in scripture that can be adapted to the present day. Some Jews fully believe that the end of days—which must come—will be hastened by the advent of a new world order, as the Book of Daniel states. They naturally focus on identifying signs as evidence of the messianic age and seek to identify the circumstances preceding the coming of the Messiah and the time of his arrival. In second- and third-century Palestine, messianic hope underwent far-reaching changes. Yohanan ben Zakkai's new concept, having eliminated any attempts at military or political subversion, was henceforth spiritual, entirely composed of passive expectation. In view of this, Roman rule might continue indefinitely, and those trying to fight it by prematurely hastening the arrival of the Messiah and redemption were inexorably doomed to failure.

To extricate the evolution of these ideas from talmudic literature, it suffices to consider the positions held by protagonists such as Abba Arikha (known as "Rav" [master]) and Samuel of Nehardea.[58] Both adhere to the attitude determined by Yohanan ben Zakkai in his day and recommend calm. Objectively, there seemed to be no military solution to the situation in Babylon, where the Jews were a tiny minority without land or allies. Moreover, Neusner comments, nothing in their past or present history in the Diaspora had prepared them to rebel against a dominant power. Samuel and Rav tried to channel the messianic fervor among Jews in Babylonia with prayer and spirituality, reaffirming that only individual merit could hasten the arrival of the Messiah. This attitude, characteristic of Pharisaic and tannaitic Judaism, led them to affirm that whatever happened, Israel must bow to divine will so that no nation could dominate it. Until the arrival of the new divine order, Jews must submit and reconcile themselves to history's vicissitudes. To pave the way, in practice, good deeds, intensified study, and prayers must replace sacrifices and sanctuary. Neusner asserts that at this time, no other position could compete with this one within Judaism.[59] This process of ethicization and spiritualization of messianism may be seen in this type of statement by Samuel: "When Israel throws the words of the Torah to the ground, the pagan kingdom expands its decrees."[60] Rav explains that Israel had lost its statehood and possessions by sinning, rather than for metaphysical reasons. Only by improving moral life could historical conditions be changed.[61]

This teaching, intended to replace messianic expectations, promoted an ethics devoid of subversive potential, but did not prevent discussion of how to speed the arrival of the Messiah: "Rab said: All the predestined dates [for redemption] have passed, and the matter [now] depends only on repentance and good deeds. But Samuel maintained: it is sufficient for a mourner to keep his [period of] mourning."[62] For Samuel, exile would be a better guarantor of redemption than repentance. This dialogue nonetheless shows that both Rav and Samuel believed that repentance and the coming of the Messiah were not necessarily linked, and that only patience and obedience would actually work. This discussion echoes another one a century and a quarter earlier, between Rabbi Joshua ben Hananiah and Rabbi Eliezer ben Hyrcanus, two disciples of Yohanan ben Zakkai: "Rabbi Eliezer said: if Israel repent, they will be redeemed; if not, they will not be redeemed. R. Joshua said to him, if they do not repent, will they not be redeemed! But the Holy One, blessed be He, will set up a king over them, whose decrees shall be as cruel as Haman's, whereby Israel shall engage in repentance, and he will thus bring them back to the right path."[63]

The teachings transmitted in the name of Samuel are intended as dissuasive and warn not to desire the coming of the Messiah too ardently, for it will inevitably be preceded by a host of disasters and persecutions. This focus on sufferings to come is another attempt to neutralize messianic expectations. At the same time, Samuel affirms that the only difference between the present world and the messianic era is Israel's servitude to the rule of a government,[64] for the golden age will have neither miraculous healing nor affluence. Affirming his faith in the radical inversion of the present and future, as well as the resurrection of the dead,[65] Rav has a favourite saying: "[The future world is not like this world.] In the future world there is no eating nor drinking nor propagation nor business nor jealousy nor hatred nor competition but the righteous sit with their crowns on their heads feasting on the brightness of the divine presence."[66] By its wide-ranging social importance, the messianic hope as expressed by Samuel brings a full revision of postapocalyptic messianic conjecture, wholly redirected toward ethics.

Biblical exegesis of the day must also take part in comforting people perturbed by events. The importance given to the story of Esther finds its place in this framework of reappraisal. Commentaries grow heavier with pacifying teachings, such as telling how Providence had already saved Jews from the Persians' oppression and attempts to destroy them, while carefully avoiding any discussion that might relate to eschatological promises by prophets or interpreting them mainly in an ethical or worldly way. They become guides to conduct devoid of any messianic activism. The Book of Daniel, which becomes paradigmatic of salvation worked by God, grasped and offered as the proof and assurance of the coming redemption, remains exceptional in being the object and subject of all kinds of pro- and anti-messianic conjectures. Neusner notes that this type of exegetical approach differs from the apocalyptic writings of prior centuries and from the third-century Sibylline Oracles; according to him, it is an evasive tactic to avoid confronting the ordeals of the time.[67] To further clarify, he cites the example of the fall of Caesarea (modern Kayseri), or Mazaca, the largest city in Asia Minor, concerning which the rabbis of Babylonia debate only whether there should be mourning for the twelve thousand Jews who had died during the siege of the city. Similarly, an army sacking Nehardea is only recorded in Babylonian rabbinic literature because of question about where prayers took place the following day, since troops occupied the houses of study. In this anarchic era, during which the Persian Sassanid Empire succeeded that of the Parthians, Rome itself was undermined, and Jews were subjected to great tribulations, such omissions must have been deliberate rather than negligent. During these dark years, sages diligently wrote and clarified laws. They reviewed all the legal opinions and dissents of the masters, finding compromises for their differences of opinion. "May the fear of dominant power always be before you," the first-generation Amora sage Rabbi Yannai says.[68] Knowledge of the past, or of current events, becomes of secondary importance. The primary role is reserved for scrutinizing events to draw moral teachings and useful references for the idea of redemption.[69]

Time (or History) Suspended

Detached from the vagaries of history, rabbis likewise absolved themselves of other concerns. Preferring memories of the past to fitting in with the present, they lived in a time of stasis, suspended by choice in a "non-epoch," so to speak.[70] Henceforth, a mythical treatment is applied to biblical readings by twisting heroes of scripture into emblematic figures for the study of Torah. After the fall of the First Temple, the Israelites were interested in history because it seemed to hold the keys to divine will and explained the course of events. In contrast, the fall of the Second Temple illustrates the deep-seated self-deception of the rabbis regarding the history of their era. By projecting themselves into rethinking the past, they obscured the present. In midrashic literature, King David may be a sage, and Rabbi Akiva studied with Moses.[71] Not only do the lines between generations become clouded but temporality itself takes on a mythic quality in which everything shares in eternity. Rav and Samuel report episodes that occurred during the period of the Tannaim—which was over by their time—but are careful not to mention anything related to their own day. Their interest in the past may be contrasted with that of the Greeks,[72] for although perhaps illuminating the scriptures, their propositions are not historical. Instead, they develop an abstraction that finally allows them to avoid any constraints, extracting them from their own historical framework. Having set themselves up as the companions of biblical characters, they are immersed in a static time, in a universe without concrete temporality. For Neusner, this attitude of negation or refusal may be seen as deriving directly from skepticism about the messianism of Yohanan ben Zakkai and his disciples.[73]

Does this type of analysis, typical of the most common approaches, ascribe too much weight to the role played by messianism in the history of the Jews? Doubtless a study of the Jewish relationship to temporality may offer data likely to shed light on many edifying implications. Since Gershom Scholem, all analyses of the position of Jews in history have taken messianic hopes as an indicator, conceived of as an essential and undeniable driving force of Jewish action in the world.[74] To be sure, it is possible that this is the right approach. Yet although it has the capacity to explain events clearly, it nonetheless deserves reevaluation. If the Jews are a historical people—inasmuch as the Hebrew Bible is the work of the demiurge of History—they shed that status through the determined abrogation of their messianism, seen as the cause of their earthly trials, or even worse, as a barren practice. In this context, messianic politics are avoided when history and events are defused by merging ethics and eschatology, freed from any historical contingency. In addition, if it is forbidden to calculate the moment of the Messiah's arrival, the advent of his time, what use is history? Stripped of this ultimate interest, it will be seen much later by Maimonides as a "waste of time."[75] Consequently, why not follow Neusner when he claims that rabbis will barter history for eternity?[76]

The books of the Talmud may in fact suggest that the Babylonian sages became more and more involved in questions of codification. If prophetic teaching conveyed the notion that the state of society is key to its national history, the conclusion to be drawn is that even the lowliest of matters must be handled with the strictest equity and piety. Yet the importance simultaneously given to the eschatological role of observing laws makes things take a different turn. If redemption were based on social change and fulfillment of the Torah, doing justice and charity would establish God's mandate on earth, according to His demands transmitted in scripture. Israel was thus nevertheless fulfilling its part of the messianic contract with God, but doing so by means of prayer, study, and good deeds, somehow become authentic responses to the historical disasters of the time, the instruments of a reinterpreted messianism.

Yosef Hayim Yerushalmi suggests another approach to this process. Although also of the opinion that the jumbling of biblical heroes among different times and ages typical of tales in the Aggadah clearly relativizes the findings and knowledge of history, he concludes, differently, that the rabbis of the day were so to speak historically surfeited— "too full." Their attitude, based on the need to create a consecrated nation and form a Jewish society that hinged on ideals, precepts, and hopes, expressed discord linked to the present: "Contemporary history must have seemed a realm of shifting sands. The biblical past was known, the messianic future assured; the in-between-time was obscure."[77] Only messianic activism was capable of arousing the rabbis' interest in historical events. From this also follows the repression of activism that became the rabbinic norm in the following centuries, after three collapsed revolts, strongly influenced by eschatology, against Rome: "Blasted be the bones of those who calculate the end, for they say that since the predetermined time has arrived and yet he has not come, he will never come. But [even so]—wait for him, as it is written: Though he tarry, wait for him . . ."[78]

History has a beginning, middle, and end. The history told by the Bible is dominated by the Sinaitic Covenant, the repudiation of which led the Jews to disaster. If one of the results of the Covenant might have been the emergence of a historical religion for the Israelites, its abandonment may have resulted in the opposite. Having drawn from history all the teachings that it could offer, Jews who followed them would be turned toward clarifying other questions more crucial for their time.

Having followed the transformation of biblical characters—the recital of their heroic deeds, the intercession of prophets who evoke God's active role in history—such as Josephus conceived it as well, conjuring up the static time of the tales told in the Midrash and Aggadah in the early centuries, we must now turn to what is commonly called "Hellenistic Judaism."[79] In fact, this somewhat problematic term indicates both a broad concept and a narrow slice of historical time, running from Alexander the Great (died 323 BCE) to the death of Cleopatra and the annexation of Egypt to the Roman Empire (30 CE). During this era, Palestine and the Mediterranean Basin were under the political and cultural rule of the Hellenistic empires. Dominated variously by the rule of Rome or Persia, the peoples of Judea, of Egypt (all the way to Macedonia), and of Iran were split between those who spoke Hebrew or Aramaic and those who spoke, and doubtless thought, only in Greek. In a broad sense, the notion of Hellenistic Judaism also refers to communities that for some seven or eight hundred years practiced the Jewish religion while using the Greek language, even in synagogue services. This long period sometimes referred to as assimilation was marked by wars, intense nationalistic and religious clashes. It was marked by the emergence of dissident Jewish sects, of Gnostics and Pharisees, but also by the appearance of the sages. It served as a fertile source of a literature that became basic to the Jewish patrimony, with the books of Daniel and Esther and the Mishnah, as to the world's patrimony with the Septuagint—a translation of the Hebrew Bible and related texts into Greek *koinē*—including books outside the Jewish canon, the Apocrypha, Pseudepigrapha and Deuterocanonical books, Tobit and Judith, 2 Ezra, the two books of Maccabees, Sirach, and the Wisdom of Solomon. The saga of Hellenistic Judaism provides a backdrop and context for the composition of the books of Maccabees and the writings of Josephus and Philo of Alexandria.[80]

Like the works of Josephus and the books of Maccabees, those of Philo the Greek were neither transmitted nor preserved within the Jewish patrimony. Their surviving the centuries was wholly due to diffusion by the Christian world.[81] Philo's thinking has a bigger influence on Christian theology than on the Jewish world. We know nothing about any possible impact on his contemporaries, and he was ignored by later rabbis. An outstanding example of the civilization of which he is one of the jewels, Philo of Alexandria lived at the turning point of an era, from around 20 BCE to 54 CE.[82] Imbued with Platonic pronouncements on time and space, Philo paves the way for grasping the thought process followed by Judaism during centuries that saw the Diaspora taking place as a typical phenomenon of the Jewish condition. A great reader of the Bible, doubtless the Septuagint rather than the Hebrew one, Philo always discusses the messianic era in terms used by Isaiah to stress the overturning of the violent, brutish natural order: the wolf will lie down with the lamb, peace will reign between mankind and animals, and the earth will be filled with gratitude to God.[83] These concepts tap into highly conventional Jewish tradition, combined with the equally canonical aspect of divine retribution against the enemies of Israel: "Everything shall be reversed, God will turn [His] curses against the enemies of these penitents, the enemies who rejoiced in the misfortunes of the nation and mocked and railed at them";[84] those "who have mocked at their lamentations, proclaimed public holidays on the days of their misfortunes, feasted on their mourning, in general made the unhappiness of others their own happiness."[85] Philo conceives of the messianic era through Ezekiel. It will be preceded by the ingathering of the exiles, but also by the war between Gog and Magog.[86] Stating that, based on the Bible, the promised ingathering of the exiles will only occur "[i]f they shall confess their iniquity,"[87] "[a]nd shalt return unto the Lord thy God,"[88] Philo describes and understands this admission and this return in terms of what for later Judaism would amount to the crux of repentance: a feeling of shame and self-reproach, admission and acknowledgment of sins. He uses the Hebrew meaning of the term *shavim* to indicate them in Greek using the root word meaning "to return," which will later be associated with "to repent." For him, pardon and redemption are promised to Israel by the merits of the Patriarchs. God will doubtless recall the promise made to them, but as advocates of reconciliation, three instruments of intercession are nonetheless present, wholly devoted to the volition of the Jews: the clemency and goodness of God; the sanctity of those who founded the nation; and, last and seemingly most useful in guiding the other two, repentance. These conditions will also be found in the Talmud,[89] where stressing the importance of repentance, they complete and fulfil the conditions needed to prepare for the coming of the Messiah and final redemption. For Philo, as later for Maimonides, the messianic era is conceived of as a time during which Judaism, finally recognized internationally, will become a world religion. Mosaic law, taken as "eternal law," should then last forever. Yet even more, with the restoration of Israel, each nation will abandon its specific life and ancestral customs to honor only that Law. He expresses this based on verses from Isaiah and Micah,[90] yet this inspiration is the same one that motivates the Sibylline Oracles.[91] Naturally, there are parallels with the Stoic ideal of the messianic age, popular in the era of Philo, who expects "an age . . . during which Judaism will become a universal religion."[92] As Harry Austryn Wolfson emphasizes, "in this Stoic Messianic ideal all differences of nationality or historical states" will vanish, merging with and being replaced by a world law that leads to a reign of tranquility; there will no longer be any difference between races and religions, and all people will form a single community and nation.[93] Superficially, the Stoic influence seems obvious and unequivocal, but the promise to which Philo constantly refers is conveyed by Jewish prophetic writings. The Universal Law mentioned by Philo is that of Moses, which he sees as eternal and perfect. By keeping his distance from Plato on laws and Aristotle on politics, both of whom assert that no human society can be perfect, Philo affirms that a state based on the divine law revealed by Moses would be perfect and ideal. In it, obeying the law is akin to submitting to the authority of God. For Philo, the Mosaic state would arise from combining the best aspects of all the necessary elements: royalty, democracy, and aristocracy. In this way, the underlying idea is sanctity. Nonetheless, only the divine will to establish the messianic age would allow such a state to exist, which amounts to affirming the eternal truth of the divine, which permits transcending, at a time willed and chosen by It, the history of nations. Philo's main contribution remains having reconciled the two aspects of culture—Jewish and Greek—that nurtured him. With an allegorical reading, he attests to the passing of Greek philosophical conceptualization into Jewish culture. Yet he maintains that the teachings of Mosaic law preceded Greek thought. The meeting of these two elements works a kind of universalization of Judaism, thereby transcending the framework of the national history of the Jews.[94] This allows some to state that the "epoch of Philo was the last in which the ideal of a brotherhood between Greeks and Jews could still be seriously envisaged."[95]

✳

Time thus pertains to the consciousness of the elusive, and Jewish time once again instantly slips away. . . . Part I has attempted to make intelligible one of the modalities of the structure of Jewish temporality. Probably the most common one, if not the most widespread, since it consists of defining a group of descriptions, mixing more or less scientific notions, conventions, standardized responses, and commonplaces. Gleaned from historians, anthropologists, philosophers, sociologists, exegetes, and theologians, whether Jewish or Christian and advocates or not of a school of thought, a religious or ideological choice, each has a viewpoint on time in general or Jewish time specifically. The proposition that I have sought to sustain here is that this group forms a kind of conceptual world, on which modern thinkers draw when considering how to think about time. The structure of Jewish temporality arises from a change in the perception of a celestially modelled history. Due to its tribulations, this history would lead to the ultimate concealment of the integration of events in contemporary time. The leading position about the attitudes of the Jews on writing history may be summed up in one sentence: the destruction of the First Temple led to the idea of the closing of biblical time (and to the creation of the canon), while the destruction of the Second Temple led to the end of history itself.[96] The first historical religion, once dispersed, will be cut off from all taste for history, preferring instead to savor the Law, playing the present tense of events against eternity. It basically mattered little whether this structure was genuine or not, because the belief that it was so is the source of attitudes—very real ones—about the transmission of the distant past of the Jews. This structure is the basis for much research about the Jews. Much later,

Heinrich Graetz may have still been using this argument when he noted: "Judaism is not a religion of the present, but of the future."[97] Rightly so? Perhaps. Before verifying this opinion, which the scholarly community also seems to hold, from source material, let me conclude this attempt to analyze the evolution of Jewish temporality with the words of Friedrich von Schelling from the Introduction to his *The Ages of the World*: "What is past is known, what is present is discerned, what is future is divined. The known is retold, the discerned is represented, the divined is foretold."[98]

Part II *Time Counted Down, or the World Order*

The Course of Eras and Calculations of Time

> For a thousand years in thy sight are but as yesterday when it is past, and as a watch in the night.
>
> Psalms 90:4

By building a way of life articulated by an experience of time expressed in liturgy and literature, Jewish groups endured while overcoming geographic dispersion and the end of rituals linked to the existence of the Temple. This experience of time was rooted in principles derived from age-old Judaism that broke through in the three or four centuries before the fall of the Temple. What is known about ancient Judaism stems from the transmission of the Bible and the production of rabbinic texts. The singular expression of rabbinic literature filtered the information that it reports. Stated in the form of teachings and not as tales, these texts construct a history that, while not linear, asserts itself as a series of "lessons." As such, history is repeatable and tractable, its actors being the eternal protagonists of a course for which they are partly responsible. Rabbinic Judaism is born of this possibility of endless reformulation of these "lessons."

Resulting from meetings and changes tied to cultural and historical impacts which it experienced, Rabbinic Judaism is the fruit of centuries during which it confronted other civilizations and abandoned politics. In these showdowns, often injurious and sometimes tragic, systems of thought were developed which set traditions. Made of a dynamic of integration and rejection, innovation and invention that enrich a central core of biblical material, this allows rabbis to produce a history that springs from a break with the past. Rabbinic thought strives to rebuild a kind of continuity between a time gone by, an unsure present, and an inviolable future. In other words, to establish an ordonnance of time. If this thought is contemporary to the events that affected the Jewish world after the destruction of the Second Temple, the process it pursues is already in use in the Judeo-Hellenistic world in the period sometimes called "intertestamentary."[1] As the sources unfold, we follow these developments in thinking about tradition that structures an approach to the world.

Over the past century, however, the rereading of history begun for this period has been substantially enriched by finds in the Cairo Genizah[2] and archaeological digs in Palestine. The vision of the past, until then transmitted by rabbis, became more complex for historians. Henceforth, there was room for different currents and leanings that threw Judaism in Palestine and the Diaspora into a turmoil. Opening onto long-overlooked horizons, this new knowledge illuminates many aspects of activities conducted by rabbis in the time after the fall of the Temple. The image of cultural and religious diversity that emerges from this recent textual input to some extent helps us understand attempts in that era to unify co-existing contemporary currents in Judaism. Formulating the oral law gave Judaism the dimension it maintained everywhere until the eighteenth and nineteenth centuries, and subsequently as well in the Orthodox world. This is why it may seem useful to return to that source. It explains how the ideas that still serve as a base for Judaism, and by which we continue to grasp it, are constituted.

By refining these divergent readings, exegesis played a key role in forming an idea of the unity of the Jewish people. By mitigating dissent liable to lead to schisms, counteracting messianism also served rabbinic activity. I hope that I have established that a temporal model can be found in the Bible from the earliest times, without really referring it to any specific era. Conversely, consider the temporal leads that led rabbis, at the conclusion of a long process that only ended in the Middle Ages, to imagine the age of the world based on biblical sources. It may be observed that the crystallization of links between Jewish groups occurred around historical benchmarks. Changing the status granted to history plays a key role in the perception of time. Events likely to be included in the framework of prophetic history recounted in the Bible possess symbolic impact as stages of time, serving in this way as a base for the future. And this is owing to the idea that since promises of punishment were kept, those of redemption will be as well. I shall try to show that the phenomenon of transforming an event into a sign of temporality is one of those that allowed Jews to endure through centuries. This phenomenon, far from being peculiar, is commonplace in the manner that Jews and Christians, in their own ways, built themselves a patrimony of differentiation within world history.

If on the scale of the terrestrial journey Judaism is only a minor part of history, the biblical story, setting down memories of the emergence of monotheism, extends the evolution of humanity from its origins by the unfolding of a national history. Far from being written in a day, the Bible was shaped over centuries after a slow maturing process, ultimately reflecting its finality in the mirror image of the creation of the world. The authors of the biblical account, by settling on a canon, also defined axes in the onward march of time, measuring the stages leading to the future in increments. Solidly attached to the time scale, these axes direct forward motion in the flux of human temporality. Fixing a point of origin, they guide the outcome. One of the goals of Part II will be to study the deployment of these time axes, which locate and integrate historical events in a "Jewish" course of things, thereby seizing ongoing time in which various temporal scansions form a chain that is simultaneously historical, mathematical, and eschatological. The mosaic of time is devised in the interlacing of history and eschatology, but also for functional purposes. Some of the objects studied here are linked to the genealogy of history, others to its apocalyptic change, and still others to an arithmetical survey.

Like the elements studied here, this section is offered in mosaic form. It aims to retrace the complexity of the conceptual framework underpinning the conceptualization of a "Jewish time." The texts and sources presented and discussed in the following pages were chosen because they could attribute features to time and build approaches to history passed down over the centuries, ignoring all other aspects of their approach. They were determined for their narrative and interpretative value for characteristics allotted to time. Grasping the rabbinic formulation "Jewish time" is only possible by proceeding in a genealogical way. To answer the questions developed since the nineteenth century about rabbinic thought requires focusing on analyzing phenomena that emerged in antiquity. The rhythm of original temporal scansions is followed, from day to month, week to the "sabbaths of years,"[3] in tallying time past. Yet this tally varies according to different axes and scales used differently by Jews in Palestine, Babylon,

Alexandria, and other places of the Diaspora. That is because at the dawn of the rabbinic period, neither the calendar nor the biblical text was fixed. The calendar still had not struck a balance between revelation and astronomical observation; chronological systems depended on circulating many versions of the Bible. Chroniclers, prophets, historians, sages, and messiahs divided the approaches to history and time. Versions of the Bible betrayed numerical differences that would be the basis for Christians and Jews in early centuries to behave like bickering heirs. One outcome would be the emergence of the principle of the era. The other goal of Part II is to study the circulation of texts, disputes about time past, and the emergence of the era, which meant a sort of "conquest" of historical time for both Jews and Christians. The body of work done here consists of scrutinizing the way in which Jews assembled different temporal principles that determined their past history from within the rabbinic tradition. The interlaced designs of events and concepts of time within the same framework betray the multiplicity of experiences in lived time. There are references here to developing practices that, while seeking to unify representations of time, support the principle of a double temporality that guided Jews across the centuries.

Six Temporal Scansions

What Day Is Today?

There is a scansion of time whose recurrence requires neither advanced calculation nor uncertain estimates of its duration. It is said that in six days the Lord made the heavens and the earth, and on the seventh he rested. The weekly break forming the pattern of the life of Jews is fixed by the model of divine completion of creation, especially since the Book of Exodus derives a conclusive law from it: "Six days thou shalt do thy work, and on the seventh day thou shalt rest . . ."[1] In daily life, strict compliance with this day's break in the continuity of daily labor shows the everlasting covenant established with the people of Israel.[2] Over time it becomes the identifying and differentiating sign of Jews among the nations. Between the end of the second century and the beginning of the third, the Roman historian Cassius Dio wrote of "the day called the day of Saturn, on which, among many other most peculiar observances, [Jews] undertake no serious occupation."[3] Whatever the sequential rhythms marked by the astrological landmarks of ancient societies, the way that Judaism organized the days of temporality that typify it mark a break with the rhythms of nature and the stars. Arranged by divine request, they reveal a purely mathematical order. Named by its progress, the Jewish week is called *shavua* (seven) or sometimes in ancient Hebrew, just *shabbat*, showing the numerical sequence from one seventh day to the next. This *hebdomade*[4] is arranged around the day that indicates the cyclical and recurrent vacuum granted each week to God. In so doing, it designates each day by its number, forming terraces from the first one that opens the week after Shabbat until the sixth, which precedes and prepares for it, *erev shabbat*, the "evening—or eve—of the sabbath." The Jewish week is arranged by the numerical designation of its intervals as day 1, day 2, day 3, and so on, up to the sixth day of which the "eve" opens onto Shabbat. Tradition holds that Adam personally named the days and put nights before them: "It is there [in Palestine] that the calendar began after the six days of creation. Adam, then, began to name the days," Yehudah Halevi writes in his book *The Kuzari*, composed around 1140 CE.[5]

However, designating a "day" is not enough to make its understanding clear. For if the Jewish day is distinguished by its number, it also possesses its own duration. For the ancient Egyptians, Chaldeans, Persians, and ancient Syrians, the calendar day was solar, starting at sunrise. Yet like the Chinese, the Hebrews and later the Jews, ancient Greeks, Romans, and modern Muslims begin it at sunset. Arabs of old, following Ptolemy,[6] began it at noon, while astronomers, following Chaldean precursors and, much later, Copernicus, always start it at midnight.[7] In Judaism, the interval that marks the sequence corresponding to day seems determined by the biblical account of the days of creation ("And the evening and the morning were the first day").[8] From the viewpoint of Jewish law, it organizes a temporal unity starting and ending at sunset, *m'erev ad 'erev*, according to Leviticus (23:32). This time interval is not based on a fixed scope of hours as is the case now with the twenty-four-hour system. It hinges on a concept of radiance and darkness, whose unfolding may vary from one place or country to another. One Shabbat observed between dusk and the following nightfall during December in Finland will be significantly longer than the same Shabbat celebrated in Latin America. It stems from the biblical story that God works in the daytime hours, since the text specifies "and the evening and the morning" (*boker* in Hebrew) and divine works are described as being done starting in the mornings. Days originate with darkness, but daytime unfolds in the light, so there is a visible distinction between daily temporal unity, consisting of a complete cycle of dusk and night, and the period of sunshine, of dawn and daylight. Dusk marks the end of human activity, heralding another day, and most actions described in the Bible stop when brightness ceases, especially if they began in the light of dawn. This applies to the battle between Moses and Amalek. Joshua's stopping the sun may be seen in the same way, allowing him to fight until the day was over.[9] Clear subdivisions are in keeping with the idea of a daily sequence. Mornings, there is a difference between dawn, daybreak, and the light of day. At night, dusk, darkness, and the middle of the night are separate. These temporal sections point to exact moments that serve in turn to cause actions and events. Each action is placed in a sequence included in time begun the previous night and not in an instant located in daytime.

The astrological division of the week was established around the second century BCE. Deriving from the study of planetary orbits, the names of days refer in every Western European language to the unchanging positions of Saturn—Saturday, Jupiter—Thursday (*jeudi* in French), Mars—Tuesday (*mardi* in French), and the Sun—Sunday.[10] Also Venus—Friday (*vendredi* in French), Mercury—Wednesday (*mercredi* in French), and the Moon—Monday (*la Lune—lundi* in French).[11] Cassius Dio states that after having been started by the Egyptians, this division became normal for Romans and the rest of humanity.[12] The week is used in the calendars of Trajan and the Fathers of the Church. Each of its days is symbolized by a planet, as found in frescoes unearthed at Pompeii.[13] This management of days by planets is also represented in the *Pirkei* (chapters) attributed to Rabbi Eliezer ben Hyrcanus (first–second centuries CE): "On the first day Mercury and the Sun, on the second day Jupiter and the Moon, on the third day Venus and Mars, on the fourth day Saturn and Mercury, on the fifth day the Sun and Jupiter, on the sixth day the Moon and Venus, on the seventh day Mars and Saturn."[14] This sequence, recently introduced in the Hellenistic world in his time, was doubtless rooted in Jewish law for Josephus, who writes: "What is more, even among the masses for a long time there has been much emulation of our piety, and there is not one city of the Greeks, nor a single barbarian nation, where the custom of the seventh day, on which we rest, has not permeated."[15] Striving to differentiate itself from Judaism, the Christian West sought its own temporal benchmarks, and a few centuries later, it found a way of its own to escape both pagan astrology and Jewish traditions. In the fourth century, the *Apostolic Constitutions* noted that the Church celebrated the Resurrection on Sunday, but the creation the day before.[16] The process of separation seems to have been complete by the time Saint Jerome writes: "The Lord made all the days; all the rest may belong to Jews, heretics, and pagans. Sunday [*dies dominica*], the day of Resurrection, is the day of Christians."[17]

Although Jewish temporality is embodied in the seven-day *hebdomade,* Genesis terms Jacob's seven years' labor before he marries Rachel a *shavu'a* (week),[18] showing that the order of temporality could also be fixed by other sequential series articulated by the number seven,[19] without their corresponding to days. It is not possible to evaluate them precisely prior to the Exile, but such "weeks of years" comprised six years of agricultural labor, followed by a sabbatical year called *shemittah* or *shevi'it,* a time of fallow during which all agricultural activity stopped, debts were forgiven, and slaves freed.[20] Some researchers date the observance of *shemittah* from the establishment of the sabbatical *hebdomade.* Others question whether the sabbatical year even existed, but from the building of the Second Temple until the period of the Amoraim (third century), the information is ample and exact enough to permit the study of its calendrical construction (see further on this subject the work of Benedict Zuckermann,[21] Hayyim Yehiel Bornstein,[22] and Ben Zion Wacholder,[23] among others). Such practices, which continued to be observed until the fifth century CE, strengthened the cycle of the hebdomade, which began to be counted at Yom Kippur and concluded with the completion of seven "weeks of years."

In What Year?

From week to week a continuity is established, regulated by months whose succession comprises a lunisolar year. The temporal sections are organized around the concepts of *molad* and *tekufah. Molad* (birth) is the precise moment when the new moon reappears after having been hidden in the form of a very thin crescent. This phenomenon recurs every twenty-nine days,[24] forming the lunar month and serving as a marker for the start of each month. *Tekufah* (cycle) is a solar marker, generally coinciding with a solstice or equinox. The Jewish year has four such seasons, located in the months of Tishri (September-October), Tevet (December-January), Nisan (April-May) and Tammuz (June-July). Each month opens with a new moon (Rosh Hodesh), but according to the Torah, the year starts with the first month of spring, Nisan. It is a solar year organized by lunar months that begins by accompanying the exodus from Egypt, a central historical event that leads to the injunction always to commemorate that date.[25] Yet starting the year in autumn remains linked to solar years, while doing so in the spring relates to lunar months. Paradoxically, the fixing of Rosh Ha-shanah on the first day of Tishri follows the rules of *molad*, the lunar cycle, while the cycle of seasons is adjusted by an additional month so that the spring equinox precedes the *tekufah*.

Many changes occurred in the chronological system used to count off centuries before one finally prevailed over the others. In Judaism, this progress is described by a rabbinic text from the Aggadah recalling the series of markers used since the biblical era, the first set by the exodus from Egypt, and the second by the building of the Temple of Solomon. Apart from this text, other milestones may be found by reading the books of the Bible, such as the use of the length of the reign of different kings of Judea and Israel during the time of captivity in Babylon. The books of Maccabees[26] indicate that the rededication of the Second Temple, commemorated by the holiday of Hanukkah, was also a temporal referent. Later and in various guises, other chronological models are mentioned, based on the year of the Temple's destruction. Finally, a standard is reached, the epoch of the world, *annus mundi*, as found in traditional Jewish texts as *le-yetsirah* (formation) and *beri'at 'olam* (creation of the world).[27] This fixing of a unique era of reference defines an axis of time, but does not determine a canonical use of temporality. We observe this in noting how the fluctuation in temporal stages linked to the interpretation of events can come to determine the understanding of periodizations.

A passage from Ezekiel (1-2) involving dual dating that is well known to biblical scholars may be taken as a first example: "Now it came to pass in the thirtieth year, in the fourth month, in the fifth day of the month. . . . In the fifth day of the month, which was the fifth year of king Jehoiachin's captivity." The uninformed reader might easily skip from the first mention of an era with an unknown reference— that is, the thirtieth year—to that of the fifth year of the era of "king Jehoiachin's captivity," an event dated to 586 BCE based on various references to it elsewhere. Yet only by moving the axis of time does it become possible to grasp the scale of the first dating employed, showing a twenty-five-year discrepancy with the second in terms of the moment indicated. Taking as a starting era of reference the eighteenth year of the reign of Josiah, during which the Priestly Code was found, and adding the years that his successors reigned until Nebuchadnezzar's deportation of Jehoiachin, we arrive at 592 BCE, which fits with other known deductions. In this case, the scale rises from an axis fixed by the moment of the break caused by reauthorization of the law,[28] followed by years of royal reigns whose use is determined by local covenants. The same problem is raised by the differences in dating in the account of events in the two books of Maccabees, which present a year's disparity, somehow making the second book precede the first. In the first book, Antiochus IV Epiphanes dies during a fruitless raid on Persia in the year 149 of the Seleucid era [164 BCE]. He was succeeded by his son Antiochus V Eupator [murdered 161 BCE aged 11]. In the second book, a letter recounting these events is dated to the year 148, which can be seen by juxtaposing the tales: "King Antiochus died there in the year 149"[29] states the first account, whereas the second claims: "The one hundred forty-eighth year, Dioscorinthius twenty-fourth. . . . Now that our father has gone on to the gods."[30] The discrepancy can be explained in terms of differing use of the calendar. In 1 Maccabees, the year begins on the first day of the month of Nisan ("spring"): "So Jonathan put on the sacred vestments in the seventh month of the one hundred sixtieth year, at the festival of booths."[31] In 2 Maccabees, the year starts on the first of Tishri ("autumn"). The year in the Seleucid era, further examined below, is counted here starting with two different times.[32] This is apparent from 1 Maccabees: "Thus the yoke of the heathen was taken away from Israel in the hundred and seventieth year [142 BCE]. Then the people of Israel began to write in their instruments and contracts in the first year of Simon the high priest [Judah Maccabee's brother], the governor and leader of the Jews."[33] Although brief, this era remains that of *ge'ulat yisrael*, a fleeting time of deliverance preceding that of *hurban ha-bayit*, the destruction of the Second Temple. Even though citing the Seleucid era may have been customary, other methods of calendrical reference can be found during the period.

The rabbinic literature indicates that after the death of Simon, the counting is undertaken starting with his son John: "in such a year of Johanan, the High Priest,"[34] beginning with the dates that followed the reigns of the Hasmonaean Lineage and then those of the Herodian dynasty. Most researchers who are interested in questions of eras and calendars have concluded from this that starting with this epoch, the calculation of the Seleucid era was dismissed,[35] even though it is still mentioned in the two books.

Two more examples of different temporal usages, among many other possibilities, derive from recent archaeological finds in the caves of Wadi Murabba'at near Bethlehem: "[of yea]r two of Nero Caesar . . . in this year of Release," states a borrower's note written in Aramaic; while another, from a series of fragments dated in the same way shows that "[On the twentieth of She]vat of the year two of the Redemption of Israel by Shimeon ben K[os]ba, the prince of [I]srael. . . . This land I have rented starting from you from today until the end of the eve of Shemittah, which are years full, [fi]scal years, five, of tenancy."[36] It is not essential for our subject to enter into polemics about the dating of these documents. Yet it is relevant to note that Józef Milik, the archaeologist who published it, dated the first papyrus to 13 October 55 or 12 October 56 CE.[37] It may be noted that the temporality evoked in the first document fits the standard usage of the Roman era, whereas the second is dated to the second year of "the Redemption of Israel by Shimeon ben K[os]ba," an unequivocally Jewish temporality. Starting with the Bar Kokhba revolt in 131 CE, this era is also identified by other words: "10 Adar, year 3 of the Freedom of Israel, at Kafar Bebayu, Hadar the son of Jehuda, of Kafar Bebayu, told Eleazar, registrar of the place . . ."[38]

For How Long?

Disposing of a calendar that expresses the scheduling of time for daily life is not enough to integrate the present moment into the vast dimension of time. It is still necessary to make it follow the past. The problem of elapsing time inevitably takes us back to the start of the creation of the world. Yet biblical narrative, so eloquent about divine actions, offers little evidence of historicist concerns. To try to place the history of the Jewish people in a time scale, chroniclers, sages, and rabbis had to struggle with some difficult issues posed by the scriptures. To resolve them and create a chronology, they would come to terms with the means that they had at their disposal.

Each occasional reader of the biblical text may quickly skim the signs of temporality offered by a person or series of events without noticing that their situation in a given time is a permanent challenge to modern customs. The biblical story includes genealogical descriptions that are extremely precise about the series of generations before the Flood. Adam became the father of Seth at age 130, then lived for another 800 years.[39] "In the six hundredth year of Noah's life, in the second month, the seventeenth day of the month, . . . the windows of heaven were opened. And the rain was upon the earth forty days and forty nights."[40] The Flood had a clearly reflected duration in an order of time, but which one? The six hundredth year in the life of Noah is not much of an issue, since generational continuity is given since Adam, nor is the seventeenth day, because the lunar cycles can be tracked. By contrast, the "second" month remains oddly cryptic. As mentioned, rabbis disagree over the interpretation of the annual series that this year joins—in the autumn, starting in Tishri? Then the second month would be Marcheshvan. Or the spring, beginning in Nisan? In that case, it would be Iyar.[41] The Torah indicates two different circumstances for starting a new year. "This month shall be unto you the beginning of months: it shall be the first month of the year to you," Moses and Aaron are commanded.[42] "In the seventh month, in the first day of the month, shall ye have a [great] sabbath [*shabbaton*]."[43] Clear though these verses may seem out of context, they have sparked criticism from sages and exegetes. To grasp the substance of this debate over the start of the year, we must return to the notion of an axis of time.

Was the world created in Tishri/autumn, as Rabbi Eliezer states, or Nisan/spring, as Rabbi Joshua ben Hananiah asserts? Although tradition prefers the first suggestion, after struggles between the Palestinian and Babylonian authorities over setting the months, to mark the new year is part of a double register;[44] the liturgical year is not the same as the year of public accounts. Although the celebration ordered by Moses opens the liturgical year, the second suggestion, *shabbaton*, "the great shabbat," is seen as the "renewal" of the year,[45] or the point of changing the date. So that the seasonal year, regulated by months, begins in the spring, while that of numbers and changing of the date starts in autumn. Following the exegetes, Josephus states that Moses chose the month of Nisan to mark the break caused by the exodus from Egypt in ancient ritual, but "he preserved the original order of the months as to selling and buying and other ordinary affairs."[46] These determinant elements for allocating Jewish time situate a calculation based on a point that, established in an axis, sets the choice of renewal and start of the year and its scansions. Placing itself in a larger system, it determines the fixing of a year zero or year 1, from which an era will be formed. But how was the process that leads to introducing this model of dating arrived at and imposed on the Jewish world?

Data about duration found in biblical stories do not fit in a linear unfolding of given units. They may vary from one tale to another and cannot always be usefully juxtaposed. No trace of chronological concerns can be found in the Torah, since this type of counting only began later. It turns out that when dates are indicated throughout the books of the Bible, they refer to individual lifetimes or royal reigns. For in fact, the books of the Bible are strewn with many examples of dating that show the diverse customs in surrounding societies through the different eras that existed, but none of the temporal systems mentioned echo the slightest reference to a fixed era of the world.

A linear reading of the books of the Bible shows that scribes for the Books of Kings and Chronicles count time by taking as an indicative mark the years in which the kings of Judea and Israel reigned. Apart from Ezekiel, whose dates are calculated from the captivity of King Jehoiachin, those of the Diaspora do so, however, based on the reigns of the kings of Babylon and Persia. Amos tells of the "days of Uzziah king of Judah, and in the days of Jeroboam the son of Joash king of Israel, two years before the earthquake."[47] And as we have seen, Ezekiel describes his vision "in the thirtieth year, in the fourth month, on the fifth day of the month. . . . On the fifth day of the month, which was in the fifth year of King Jehoiachin's captivity."[48]

Until When?

If the orientation of time's axis and arrow assumes a determining importance, it is because time is conceived of as the eschatological fabric par excellence. As long as time does not seem precisely defined by its limit, however, there is no need to pin an arrow on it. As soon as time is grasped as having an origin leading to an end, its linearity implies that creation—as the start of time—will surely reach an end, whether it be the messianic coming or when its flow has ceased. The content of Daniel's vision, the birthplace of calculations about waiting, is clear about its point: "Understand, O son of man: for at the time of the end shall be the vision." Or indeed: "Now I am come to make thee understand what shall befall thy people in the latter days." It is just as conclusive in justifying the attempts at a number-based approach to the future: "In the first year of his reign I Daniel understood by books the number of the years, whereof the word of the Lord came to Jeremiah the prophet, that he would accomplish seventy years in the desolations of Jerusalem." Especially as the account of temporal closure is promptly offered here: "Know therefore and understand, that from the going forth of the commandment to restore and to build Jerusalem unto the Messiah the Prince shall be seven weeks, and threescore and two weeks." It has all the more evocative strength because this revelation seems to have been confirmed by events that occurred later in the history of the Jews: "And arms shall stand on his part, and they shall pollute the sanctuary of strength, and shall take away the daily sacrifice, and they shall place the abomination that maketh desolate.. . . . And they that understand among the people shall instruct many: yet they shall fall by the sword, and by flame, by captivity, and by spoil, many days."[49] The simultaneous reinterpretation of visions, discussed in more detail below, as well as explanations that the text itself furnishes, will provide the basis for messianic conjecture. This is because they permit us to situate the end of the world in a linear duration that is already quantified in terms of evenings and mornings, days, times, and weeks. These should be enough to solve the mysteries of duration and grasp the hidden meaning.[50] The series of historical sequence of kings and four empires, which tradition gives as Babylon,

Persia, Greece, and Rome, symbolizes the ages of history. This paves the way for all speculative potential by authorizing cross-referencing between numerical, as well as mystical, temporal indications.

Between the Exodus from Egypt and Solomon's Temple

A final question must be asked: how to assess the time that has passed between the events described in Scripture and the present moment when the landmarks of time overlap and are divided around shifting points of departure? A *mekhilta*[51] indicates the use of different markers for dating. Time is calculated from the exodus from Egypt until the building of the Temple. Once the Temple was built, the count resumes from the date of its construction until its ruin. Those unable to situate themselves in these calculations must refer to kingdoms.[52] Many models for dating appear in the biblical corpus, but the reference to time data fixed according to the exodus from Egypt remains an isolated case: "And it came to pass in the four hundred and eightieth year after the children of Israel were come out of the land of Egypt," says 1 Kings,[53] which echoes Exodus: "And it came to pass at the end of the four hundred and thirty years, even the selfsame day it came to pass, that all the hosts of the Lord went out from the land of Egypt."[54] Despite the assertion of the *mekhilta* text, there is no evidence that this method of calculation was ever really used, while other circumstances that appear more often seem likelier. The same applies to dating based on the building and destruction of the Temple of Solomon, which is scarcely mentioned in the biblical texts themselves, where the scribes repeatedly refer to the reigns of the kings of Judea and Israel.[55]

Hayyim Yehiel Bornstein wonders about the assertion in this *mekhilta*. After a careful study of the progress of dating methods used in the Jewish world since ancient Israel, he concludes that if dating methods after the exodus from Egypt or the building of the Temple were standards, they would have been integrated into the texts. Scribes for the books of Kings would not have needed to pin each new reign to the preceding one.[56] Even more, had this system existed at the time of the Mishnah, which started to be written before the destruction of the Second Temple,[57] why wasn't it even mentioned? The standardization of dates on legal documents following the official form imposed by the Romans is explicable, especially for divorce decrees issued for women to remarry. Yet in chronological matters, the Mishnah only mentions dates as calculated in the Median and Greek kingdoms.[58] In fact, Persian dynasties, which Jewish authors sometimes call "Mede," or *Bet Ahinam*, are mentioned in the books of Esther, Daniel, Haggai, Zechariah, Ezra, and Nehemiah. Some of these references seem to relate to the Arsacid system of dating,[59] which begins in 64 of the Seleucid era, or 248/249 BCE. The *mekhilta* speaks of dating from the "building of the Temple until its destruction": "After the Temple was built, we began to count beginning with the construction, then the construction was no longer remembered, so we counted beginning with its destruction." This is doubtful, since measuring time based on the destruction of the Second Temple only really became the norm in the Mishnah period: "Rabbi Yose ben Halaftah states: During the Temple period, the Persian kingdom lasted 34 years, the Greek kingdom 180 years, the Hasmonean kingdom 103, and Herod's kingdom 103 years. From there and ever since, we count [from] the destruction of the Temple. In exile [*golah*] were noted the period of contracts according to . . . Greek reigns."[60]

The first chronological compendium, listing the generations before the Flood, is chapter 5 of Genesis, which gives temporal recorders an opportunity to lay the groundwork for a calculation of time starting from the origins of the world's creation, since the story states that Adam was 130 years old when his son Seth was born, and he lived another 800 years after that. Then, adding the generations with lifespans mentioned here and there, calculations can be made by adding, for example: "From Adam to the Flood, 1,656 years [elapse]. Enoch buried Adam and lived for another 57 years." Or calculations can combine jubilees—cycles of 49 years—also counted starting from the beginning of the world.[61]

Deeply rooted in Leviticus, the creation of this system is enriched by a note made in Ezekiel: "In the five and twentieth year of our captivity, in the beginning of the year [the Hebrew original uses the term Rosh Ha-shanah], in the tenth day of the month, in the fourteenth year after that the city was smitten . . ."[62] The Talmud discusses the same subject this way: "What then is the year that begins on the tenth day of the month? Jubilee year!" Which allows us to affirm that if the twenty-fifth year of exile for Jehoiachin was a jubilee year, the following calculation is possible: the destruction of the Temple, which took place in the eleventh year of Jehoiachin, was the thirty-sixth of the jubilee, the fifth of Jehoiachin was the thirtieth of the jubilee, since the eighteenth of Isaiah was the beginning of the jubilee. Going back farther in the cycles from Sennacherib to Hezekiah, we can easily date the construction of Temple to the middle of the jubilee, in the fourth year of the cycle of the "week of years."[63] Still, some troubling questions arise about the full duration. Do the "days" of creating the world mean days that begin one evening and end the next, or are they sacred "days" whose flow eludes human understanding and calculation? Finally, must the period of the Flood be inserted into a worldly continuity, or by its innate supernatural aspect be removed from the mundane's history?[64]

These questionings, which denote an eschatological idea of chronology, ask what obliges rabbis to make such calculations, and when? One response is found in apocryphal texts, pseudepigrapha, and apocalypses not retained in the Hebrew canon. The purpose of apocryphal texts and apocalypses is to add interpretations to information available in the Bible. Naturally, conjectures abound relating to chronographic processes. Examples are found in the Apocalypse of Abraham, the Book of Enoch, the Testament of Levi, the Assumption [or Testament] of Moses, and Pseudo-Philo's *Liber antiquitatum biblicarum* (Book of Biblical Antiquities), a manual of biblical history possibly written in the first or second century, as well as in Midrashic literature.[1] Written during the time of the Second Temple until after its destruction, approximately between the third century BCE and the first century CE, these works show trial and error, as messianic perspectives are opened by these chronological approaches before they become fixed.[2] The Book of Jubilees, which is not retained in the biblical canon, fully employs the method of chronological deduction by septennial cycles, supposedly periods of forty-nine years, with each year lasting exactly 364 days. Sometimes cited in medieval sources as the Apocalypse of Moses or the Little Genesis,[3] its time flow is wholly calculated by cycles. Its prologue suggests as much, with its first words, which were long used as its title: "These are the words regarding the divisions of the times of the law and of the testimony, of the events of the years, of the weeks of their jubilees throughout all the years of eternity as He related [them] to Moses on Mount Sinai when he went up to receive the stone tablets . . ." According to this system, Cain built the first city: "In the first year of the first week of the fifth jubilee [197] houses were built on the earth. Then Cain built a city and named it after his son Enoch." Jacob received the testament of his mother, Rebecca, "In the second year of this week, in this jubilee [2109]." Moses was born "during the fourth week, in its sixth year, in the forty-eighth jubilee [2330]." The narrative ends with what occurs in the fiftieth jubilee—2450 *anno mundi*—by recalling the revelation of the Passover laws and the time determination organized by Shabbat and fallow years: "For this reason I have arranged for you the weeks of years and the jubilees—49 jubilees from the time of Adam until today, and one week and two years."[4] The Book of Jubilees describes Jewish sacred history from the creation of the world to the revelation on Sinai, building or elaborating on antique narrative traditions built around Genesis that sometimes may be found in other texts. When it was written and by whom remain subjects of arduous debate. Situated between the third century and the period running until the reign of John Hyrcanus, around 135 and 105 BCE, it resembles Midrashic-style commentary on Genesis and might date from the time of writings found at Qumran, such as the Temple Scroll.[5] It comprises the oldest surviving Jewish chronology and has distinctive legal and calendrical features. These include a solar calendar and a year that has 364 days and 52 weeks (discussed below), which may imply a sectarian production community.[6] It attests to use of a form of calculation that by combining the quantifiable with the mysticism, allows for the handling of past and future chronology.

Another chronological system, rather similar to this one in its futuristic outlook, although quite different in content, was not only included in the biblical canon but inserted in the middle of the Hebrew Bible's conjectures about the coming redemption. The Book of Daniel, neither a chronicle nor a tale of the past, should be read as an outline of the future. As such, the text plays with explicit and implicit references to time. The moment of the story is precisely determined: "In the third year of the reign of Jehoiakim king of Judah came Nebuchadnezzar king of Babylon unto Jerusalem, and besieged it"; "In the third year of the reign of king Belshazzar . . ."; "In the first year of Darius . . ."; "In the third year of Cyrus king of Persia. . . ."[7] It also expresses the temporal space surrounding the numbers and key ideas of duration offered throughout the Torah. The sequence and divisions of the future are defined in terms of "evenings and mornings," "days," "time," and "half a time."[8] Visions spread over stretches of "weeks" and "thousandths," and the text widely employs allegories for the number four.[9] Nebuchadnezzar's dream, as described in chapter 2, subdivides history into eras as revealed by the king's vision of himself changing from a statue of gold to one of silver, gold, bronze, then iron, and finally of clay. This prefaces the predicting in chapter 7, which explains a vision of four dreadful animals, a lion with eagle's wings, a bear devouring itself, a leopard with bird wings and four heads, and a ram with two horns of different lengths, which "did according to his will, and became great. . . . [the] two horns are the kings of Media and Persia. And the rough goat is the king of Grecia. . . . four kingdoms shall stand up out of the nation."[10] These visions are developed in the series of chapters that follows. Including the past and future in the same revelation, this type of interpretation, perhaps begun by the Books of Enoch and Jubilees, appealed chiefly over the centuries to readers trying to decipher Daniel's mysteries.

One premise informs these two approaches and governs each of these systems: time is "counted." It is not destined to last for eternity, since it must end at a time chosen and fixed by God. Jubilee time must continue in a vaguely defined way, starting with the end of the first fifty cycles in which Israel crosses the river Jordan.[11] If so, then time in the Book of Daniel follows a cycle of seventy weeks of years, starting at a given point. The main difference between the two chronological systems is that the first offers no way to link the theophany at Sinai to the course of history that follows, unless by deciphering numeric clues. By contrast, the Book of Daniel allows thinking about the totality of history. Projecting a wide-ranging pattern in which empires and nations follow one another within a timespan fixed by the final redemption of its people, it offers an actual way to foresee the coming of the Messiah, as Josephus suggests: "But he [Daniel] also determined the time when these things would come about."[12] Doubtless this is why most eschatological conjectures include the course followed by the foretellings of Daniel.

Eight Historiographical Scansions
Between Adam and the Present Time

> For everything to do with the Greeks I have found to be recent, so
> to speak from yesterday or the day before—I mean the founding
> of cities, and matters concerning the invention of arts and the
> recording of laws; and just about the most recent of all for them is
> care in relation to the writing of histories.
>
> Josephus, *Against Apion* (1.1–2.7)[1]

The appearance of chronographies may be linked to mark a split between mythical and historical times. Temporal processes of key heroes
and events in history allow us to coordinate between past and present.
This boundary becomes clear when Eratosthenes of Cyrene, a close
contemporary of the translation of the Septuagint, says that the Trojan
War is the first "datable" event in human history. The chronography
evolving from Alexandria sought to standardize extant chronicles and
genealogies in the Greek and Eastern worlds.[2] This effort also spreads
among the Jews. By dating the pivotal events for their people, such
as the Flood, the exodus from Egypt, and building of the Temple,
they remarkably compel them to be located in history. This practice,
which follows—and sometimes coincides with—mainly eschatological
chronologies, involves a wholly different attitude about the past. Apart
from texts known for belonging to the intertestamentary corpus of the
mystical type, there are also fragments dating back to antiquity that
are attributed more or less certainly to Jewish authors. These writings are poems, sometimes epics, Apocrypha, and snippets of historical tales, some of which may be put to use here.[3] As far as is known
from surviving texts, the first Jewish chronographer was a Demetrius
who seems to have lived in Alexandria during the third century BCE.[4]
The seven odd extant fragments of his work are preserved by other
writers in quotations or excerpts. Five of them are cited by Alexander Polyhistor (ca. 85–35 BCE) in his treatise *Peri Ioudaiōn* (On the
Jews).[5] These fragments, subsequently used by Eusebius in his *Preparations for the Gospel*, form the most meaningful collection. The other
two derive from the *Stromata* (Miscellanies) by Clement of Alexandria.[6] Demetrius the Chronographer is said to have compiled a *Book*

of Kings, now lost, based on the Bible, probably the Septuagint. In it, his dating system offered a chronology of Genesis and the lives of the patriarchs, starting from the world's creation. Demetrius is thought to have belonged to an exegetical school, and his work seems to have been aimed at readers familiar with the Bible rather than a wider audience in Greece.[7]

The historian Eupolemus of Palestine is known through the same patristic channel quoting sources that exalt the venerability of Israel's history and, by extension, that of the Church that followed. He seems to be the same Eupolemus, the son of John, the son of Accos, who was sent by Judah Maccabee with Jason, son of Eleazar, to negotiate a treaty with Rome in 161–160 BCE.[8] Of his writings, also dealing with kings of Judea, five fragments survive. Used by Alexander Polyhistor, the first four were next summarized by Eusebius, while the fifth is found only in Clement of Alexandria.[9] Widely quoted in antiquity and during the Middle Ages, a first brief fragment presents Moses as the first wise man in history. The second, the longest remnant of an ancient Judaeo-Greek text before Philo, briefly covers the history of Israel from Moses to David, before focusing on the building of Solomon's Temple. In spite of his priestly ancestry and the Palestinian milieu in which he was raised, Eupolemus's chronicle contains many mistakes. Not least is that in it David is presented as the son of Saul.[10] The third fragment, only a few lines long, indicated how many years Solomon reigned, while the fourth, longer, turns to Jeremiah and describes the sack of the Temple by Nebuchadnezzar. The fifth fragment calculates the time that elapsed since Adam until what must be when the work was written, the reign of Demetrius I Soter, from 161–150 BCE.

Two other classic sources of ancient chronology related to the midrashic genre, the first canonical Jewish texts of this type, have survived in complete form, the *Seder 'olam rabbah* (Great order of the world) and *Seder 'olam zutta* (Smaller order of the world). These writings have a separate status in Judaism as part of the classic patrimony of ancient sources of chronology. To some extent they represent a Jewish chronicle of the universe. The Talmud attributes the former, widely cited in traditional texts, to Yose ben Halafta, one of the Tannaim, or rabbinic sages, who lived in the second century.[11] The latter text, obviously using the same template, is not attributed to any author and its year of composition remains disputed. It seems to date from the Middle Ages and might have been written, according to a consensus, either in the sixth century, at the time of the Savoraim, in the seventh century, based on the genealogy of Babylonian exilarchs, or in the ninth century.[12]

Between Biblical History and Exegesis: Creating a Chronology

Fragments of the book about the kings of Judea written by Demetrius, known as the Chronographer, allow us to identify the origin of these sources, in which the stretched numbers are seen as typical of the Septuagint (see the comparative table in the Appendix). The time separating the Flood from the arrival of Jacob in Egypt is 1,360 years for the Septuagint, but reduced to 580 years in the Masoretic text.[13] The Septuagint points to a period of 3,624 years between Adam and the entry of Joseph's brothers into Egypt, while the Masoretic text puts it at 2,238 years. Demetrius affirms: "And there are 3,624 years from Adam until the entry into Egypt of the relations of Joseph; and 1,360 years from the Flood to the arrival of Jacob in Egypt."[14] Seen as the first Jewish author to write in Greek, Demetrius provides evidence of the major role played by the Alexandrian translation of the Bible, which he was the first to demonstrate. Using the contemporary academic phrase "a question arises," Demetrius brings up debates that are sometimes found in the Talmud. Finally, if it is accepted that his only source was the Pentateuch, his chronicle offers exegetical input all the more striking for being critical.[15] Eupolemus adds more complexity and gives cause for more thought. As mentioned above, both Demetrius and Eupolemus produced chronologies of biblical history. Starting with the creation of man and continuing the tale up to their own eras, they also chose titles that mentioned the kings of Judea. Yet while Demetrius stays faithful to his source, Eupolemus changes the text, debating or refuting it. Doing so, the latter draws from the basis of the Aggadah or indulges in some quirks, drawing on writings by Ctesias of Cnidus[16] and Herodotus.[17] Eupolemus made the conscious literary choice to write in the Greek fluently spoken in Palestine,[18] whereas his origins might have inclined him more naturally to Aramaic or Hebrew. The Septuagint text influenced the use of some distinctive narrative items, such as Solomon's coronation at age twelve, the spelling of certain names, and technical terms used for the synagogue.[19] In contrast, other names are spelled in the Masoretic style and some terms are translated by the word adapted into Greek, such as *ulam* (Hebrew for porch, hall, or vestibule), which is simply transliterated in the Septuagint.[20] The author appears to fully grasp his sources and the different texts, which he uses appropriately. In terms of our subject, it is noteworthy that Eupolemus's analyses of time throughout his chronicle, while mostly following the tradition of the Hebrew text, sometimes offer surprising details and results.[21] However, his dating of the earth cannot be ascribed to any identified source: "All the years from Adam until the fifth year of the reign of Demetrius, in the twelfth year that Ptolemy ruled over Egypt, total 5,149. And from the time when Moses led the Jews out of Egypt to the aforesaid time [Adam's] was 2,580 years."[22] His chronology of events between the creation and the exodus from Egypt differs from every other known one. Did he do the calculations himself or glean them from an extant chronology? Should they be attributed to later authors? We cannot know whether the first number, placing the creation at 5307 BCE, was interpolated to get close to the sixth millennium during his later citations. In contrast, the second is closer to the proto-Masoretic tradition of 2,448 years than to the Septuagint, which dates the exodus from Egypt to the year 3819.[23]

The chronographer Justus of Tiberias, son of Pistus, is far less well documented. Justus is only remembered because he is mentioned in Josephus's autobiography, which presents him as a long-time rival and seeks to wrong-foot him. His personality, although only depicted negatively, comes through more than his writings. His name, like that of his father, shows Hellenistic influence, and Josephus admits that he was "well trained in the Greek sort of Education."[24] Nothing survives of his account of the war against Rome,[25] which sparked the ire of Josephus,[26] nor of his chronicle, indexed in the ninth century by Photius I, patriarch of Constantinople, under the rubric "The Kings of the Jews, Arranged in Genealogical Tables."[27] What is known of his writings amounts to a few lines. His history of the Roman-Jewish war is condemned by Josephus,[28] and his chronicle from Moses until the death of Agrippa II is termed "poor in details" by Photius. A sentence by Diogenes Laertius, writing at the start of the third century, implies that this chronicle might have begun with the creation of the world.[29] Nevertheless, modern researchers grant him the key role in aligning the history of Israel with that of other nations. Even more noteworthy, he inspired the chronographies of Sextus Julius Africanus and Eusebius.[30] The nature of his attacks on Josephus remains moot, like his chronology. Some writers have concluded that his account vanished because it was better or more accurate than the surviving one by Josephus, because the latter was prejudiced in favor of Rome.[31] This argument easily collapses. As Palestinian Jewish aristocrats, the two writers seem to share the same background, and as one-time secretary at the court of the tetrarch Agrippa II, Justus could not have been a sworn enemy of Rome. Of the various theories trying to grasp the substance of the two historians' clash over their descriptions of the Judaean war, one might have been pertinent here had it been supported by any source. In the enduring discussion about the possibility that the passage concerning Jesus and John the Baptist in Josephus's *Jewish Antiquities*[32] was a later interpolation, it has been proposed that Justus's main criticism was of Josephus's use of the Septuagint. At a time when Christianity was increasing in importance and the Jews, possibly conscious of the risks they incurred in the propagation of their Bible, were turning toward its canonization, a skillful suggestion of misinterpretation might make sense. Notwithstanding the attraction of the allegation, however, Josephus's numerous arguments in his own defense are in no way on textual or theological grounds.[33]

The World Order: Chronology in the Service of Exegesis

The version of the *Seder 'olam rabbah* that we know has three parts with ten chapters each. It makes up a chronicle of "biblical time" stretching from the beginnings until the coming of the Seleucid era, dating from the reconquest of Babylon in 312–11 BCE by Alexander the Great's former general Seleucus, who ruled much of the Near East. Its narrative starts with the creation of the world and ends with the Bar Kokhba revolt in 132 CE. Reduced to a minor portion, the post-biblical period is gathered in the final chapter. Plainly, the main point of the document is neither chronologically presenting the Second Temple period nor assessing the time elapsed between Esther and Bar Kokhba. Noting the dryness of the text,[34] historians observe the paradoxical gap between caring for a chronological ordering of the past and contradictions in historical circumstances which turn temporality into a mathematical challenge. The text offers a chronology inferred from the ages, life spans, or reigns of the people mentioned. The exception is a prefatory section about the lapse of time between Adam and the Flood. No chronological system is proposed that slices up lengths of time from one event to the next. The reader of the *Seder 'olam* arrives at a total of 420 years "between the construction of the Second Temple and its destruction," counting 34 years as passing between the Second Temple and the reign of Alexander; 180 years for the length of Hellenistic rule; 103 years between the Hasmonaean dynasty ruled by John Hyrcanus (135 BCE) and Herod; and 103 years between the reign of Herod and the destruction of the Temple.[35] Taken up by the Talmud,[36] this chronology raises some questions beyond just arithmetical problems. As we shall see below, the start of the Seleucid era being delayed by six years means the gap between its arrival in Palestine and the destruction of the Temple is sharply reduced. Herod's coronation varies by two years and the year of the destruction of the Second Temple becomes 68 CE, whereas it is currently dated at 70.[37] It seems incomprehensible that the time "between the destruction of the First Temple," which lasted for seventy years, and "that [the destruction] of the Second" could be shortened to 420 years.[38] The fact that the Second Temple had existed for more than 600 years [538 BCE–70 CE] must have been known so short a time after its destruction, especially if one accepts Chaim Milikowsky's theory that the chronology was compiled in the late first century CE during the lifetime of the last generation to have lived before the destruction of the Temple[39] Perhaps as Hayyim Bornstein suggests, a process of shunning evil made some Jews choose a false date for building the Temple, starting with the date of its destruction and adding a span of 420 years, which permits an automatic return to its first "construction."[40] These numerical wanderings may be seen in the light of another theory, seemingly derived from reading the chapter itself.[41] The author of the text supposedly tried to make his calculations jibe with the prophecies of Daniel, according to which seventy weeks of years or 490 years had to pass between the return of the exiled people and the destruction of the Temple: "Seventy weeks are attached to your people. . . . As for the city and sanctuary, the people of a leader who will come to destroy them."[42] Starting with Jeremiah's claim that the exile really lasted 70 years, the 420 years calculated between the return of the exiled people from Babylon, the rebuilding and subsequent destruction of the Temple mean a difference of 187 years with the accepted dates. This is because the return occurred in 537 BCE and the destruction of the Temple in 70 CE, or a period elapsed of 607 years and not 420. Yet in shrinking this count, exactly one thousand years passed between the exodus from Egypt and the beginning of the era of contracts (*minyan shetarot*), a count later justified by the scholar Al-Bīrūnī. Two other paths may also be opened to explain the internal logic governing the *Seder 'olam*. The sole use of biblical sources by the first Jewish chronographs of the Hellenistic period, whether Demetrius or the rabbinic sage (*tanna*) who wrote the text, may suggest a cultural horizon restricted to Jewish resources. Unlike Josephus, it may also reflect a deliberate choice to overlook the historical options in Christian chronicles. The account of *Seder 'olam* roughly confuses different Persian kings, grouping them all under the name of Artaxerxes.[43] This leads it to reduce the 204 years of Persian rule to a span of 52 or 54 years. Doing so, it constricts the period from the rebuilding of the Temple by Zerubbabel in 516 BCE to Alexander's conquest to 34 years. This makes into contemporaries such disparate people as Zerubbabel—who lived in the sixth century BCE—Haggai, Zechariah, and Malachi, all prophets of the fifth century BCE, and Simeon the Just, the High Priest who lived in the third century BCE. This contemporaneity is made random by a peculiar use of chronology, tending to make history conform with prophecy more than a quantifiable continuity.[44]

What Source for the Stories?

Jewish chronographers write the history of their people in a framework set up by Greek authors, whose perspective includes the most distant origins of humanity. The Torah presents Judaism as a younger division of humanity. Do chronographers wish to compete with age-old civilizations? Is it a question of proving the seniority of Jewish monotheism and the people of the covenant, as the writings of Josephus and Philo announce? Changing the biblical story into "ordinary" history by an approach reflecting chronology and seeking to explain exegetical problems is the same as the process that moves Greek chronographs to collect episodes of what makes up their prehistory. Ben Zion Wacholder identifies three stages in the writing of Jewish chronologies. The first tries to collect and reconcile biblical dates. The second aims at synchronizing biblical and Greek myths, and the third inserts biblical events into a world chronicle.[45] All three place the Bible at the origins of humanity. This process locates the biblical story at the center of dating processes and of chronographic activity. In this way, the source upon which the stories draw, crucial for all temporal standardization, also determines its variants.

The few surviving fragments of works written by ancient Jewish historians,[46] whether Demetrius or Eupolemos, seem to show that the estimate of time elapsed between the creation of the first humans and their day is based on numbers from the Septuagint and not according to evaluations in the *Seder ʿolam* or the Masoretic text of the Bible. It is impossible with our current knowledge to do more than guess about the discrepancies and origins of these numbers. Yet their existence and diffusion in the ancient world may be traced. Whatever the true origin of the authorship of the Greek Bible text, whether instigated by Ptolemy II Philadelphus[47] or Alexandrian Jews, as soon as it was translated, perhaps in the third century BCE, this version of the Bible was used by Jews and possibly non-Jews.[48] During ancient times and the period being studied here, the Septuagint consists only of a limited corpus of the five books of the Pentateuch. In its later extended meaning, the books of Esther, Psalms, Jeremiah, and Daniel are added, as well as Deuterocanonical and apocryphal books not accepted in the Jewish canon. The *Letter of Aristeas*, which recounts the miraculous authorship of seventy-two sages who came from Palestine, cannot be taken as a trustworthy historical account.[49] This description, whether meant as propaganda for Jews or gentiles, does not refer to writing a joint text, but a sacred book inspired by the divine breath.[50] Yet even before the writing of what is called the Septuagint, translations—possibly partial ones—of the Bible into Greek must have circulated to an extent that is impossible to know. Or so implies Aristobulus of Paneas (first half of the second century BCE), who states that Plato and Pythagoras took the "best" of Greek wisdom from Jewish sources,[51] or indeed quotations by Diodorus Siculus.[52] Since the *Hexapla* of Origen, differences have been pointed out between the Masoretic and Greek texts. These may just as well be due to literary development as to the influence of the surroundings on the text's interpretation by its readers or a translation consciously shaded by its authors. Disparities between the texts are especially visible in reducing anthropomorphism in the Bible. Plural forms assigned to the divine are changed into singular forms, going from "we" to "I." Some researchers even suggest that the Septuagint offered nuances of language such that it might be seen as an adaptation of the biblical text for a readership imbued with Hellenistic philosophical knowledge. Many points of Hebrew theology were changed, transposed into more abstract ideas, and stripped of mythology.[53] In this context, the long chronology of the Septuagint may be ascribed to the chronographic activity during the time it was written, to the desire of Jewish exegete-historians to set down their origins and laws regarding the dawn of civilization.[54]

Some fragments written by old Jewish chroniclers survived in Christian sources and theology, making it easy to suspect partisan interpolations or readings. Yet studying some excerpts of biblical chronographies over the centuries makes it possible to observe that there are two kinds of biblical sources used by Jewish authors. The lengths of time appearing in the Septuagint are found continuously in Demetrius and intermittently in Eupolemus, never in the rabbinical chronology of the *Seder 'olam*. To explain this difference, Josephus may once again be called to bear witness here. The comparative table in the Appendix (pp. 225–226) shows that he varies in his books between different numbers of which some conform to the Septuagint and others to the Masoretic text. Still others seem to be simple mistakes. When writing his various works, Josephus probably used assessments from different versions of the biblical text.[55] In the first century, these differences in biblical chronology would be conveyed by versions adopting either the Alexandrine or Hebrew tradition. The work of Eupolemus is based on this continual shifting between traditions shown from an historical point of view in Palestine by archaeological finds in caves dating from the Bar Kokhba revolt and those at Qumran.[56] In short, chronographic activity expressed throughout writings of this time might belong to historical activity traceable in the Hellenistic world as much as to Masoretic activity. For its part, the latter aimed at standardizing and stabilizing sacred texts. Hailed in the *Letter of Aristeas* and praised by Philo as " how great an undertaking it was,"[57] the translation into Greek would later be compared by rabbis to the idolatrous worship of the Golden Calf.[58] This judgment briefly summarizes the change in attitudes of Jews between the third century BCE and the second century CE. Revised translations of the Greek text that followed, by Aquila of Sinope, Theodotion, and Symmachus,[59] ended the flow of this mixed tradition,[60] thereafter considered harmful by rabbis.

In this historical context, tannaitic exegesis, which is the basis for the chronology of the *Seder 'olam*, became part of tradition, ensured by the forms of rabbinic transmission. Approaches sometimes differ slightly on the authorship of this work, but most researchers classify it as a rabbinic literary product. Its language belongs to that tradition distinctively enough for it to be assigned there. Yet its attention to chronology clashes with rabbinical output by the sages who—it is widely agreed—show little interest in history and chronography. According to Milikowsky, the *tanna* to whom the text remains traditionally attributed would be more of a "transmitter" or "courier" than literally a writer or author. He would have published it by adding or possibly rewriting some sections from an older version of biblical chronology. Milikowsky's presentation is based both on a philological study of the text and on works produced throughout the Hellenistic period. No version of a proto–*Seder 'olam* has survived, so it is difficult to prove that one existed. The theory remains no less intriguing and the analysis convincing, insofar as it puts us in view of a process of textual and historic ripening, rather than an exceptional event. The historiographical productivity of Jews during late antiquity is undisputed and remarkable. In view of the productivity that followed, biblical chronologies in all likelihood existed, given the traces found of them in apocryphal writings and in the works of ancient historians.[61] Acknowledging that the text is not self-sufficient, it can only be approached in the light of knowledge of scripture. It must be seen as a chronology related to the exegetic type of the Midrash. The main difference is that the *Seder 'olam* construes biblical data strictly, without adding details or extra lore. Like Demetrius in earlier years, rationalizing a nebulous exegetics, it employs only Jewish sources.[62] Non-biblical annals and chronicles are shown to have existed, dating back to the time of the Kings and Judges,[63] although they have vanished. This suggests that oral and written traditions about the chronology of scripture were passed on throughout antiquity, based upon which the first chronographers would have composed their writings. From Demetrius to the *Seder 'olam*, by way of Eupolemus, Justus of Tiberias, and Josephus,[64] a common thread of exegetical chronology unraveled from the patristic literature was compiled in the *Seder 'olam*. In this sense, differences seen between Greek writings (which may derive from Palestine as well as being disseminated there) and Hebrew writings also prove the diversity, if not plurality, of traditions coexisting within Judaism of the Second Temple period, before it was codified by rabbinic normalization after the Temple's destruction. This being the case, a Hebrew text such as the *Seder 'olam* allows us to document the signs of this development long before it takes place.

Nine Mathematical Scansions

In What Era?

The Seleucid Era

The Seleucid era is often mentioned in rabbinical literature, variously called the *minyan yevani* (Greek era), *malkhut yavan* (Greek kingdom), *malkhut parass* (Persian kingdom), and *minyan shetarot* (era of contracts). In the post-biblical period, Jews most commonly used its commencement as terminus a quo for dating purposes, whether alone or in tandem with other temporal constructions. Introduced after the battle of Raphia, won by Seleucus I Nicator, a general under Alexander the Great and dynastic founder, over Demetrius I of Macedon, during the spring or summer of 312 BCE, this system was gradually adopted by different countries and cities, becoming common in Asia Minor and the Near East. Introduced in the autumn of the Macedonian year in 312 BCE on the first of Dios, the commencement date was pushed back to the first of Nisan, 311. The Jews of Syria and Asia Minor adopted it starting in October 312 BCE, and those of Babylon did so in April 311 BCE, also introducing that usage in Palestine. This explains in part the diverging dates found in the books of Maccabees.[1] Although the Seleucid dynasty lasted less than 250 years, Jews of the Near East anachronistically dated from that era in rabbinical documents[2] even after it was abolished by David ben Solomon ibn Abi Zimra in Egypt in 1527.[3] The Talmud describes the passing of this style of dating, Alexandrian dating, according to this source, based not on the reign of Seleucus but of that of Alexander the Great.[4] The period the sages called the "Persian kingdom" would accordingly have existed for thirty-four years in the era of the Second Temple. Commencing with Alexander the Great's defeat of Darius III of Persia at the battle of Issus in November 333 BCE, the "Greek kingdom" had existed in Elam (ancient Iran) for six years before spreading throughout the ancient world, leading to the introduction of the system of calendrical calculation known as the "era of contracts," a Jewish eponym for the Seleucid era. The Talmud dates this to forty years after the building of the Second Temple and a millennium after the exodus from Egypt, or 3,448 years after the creation of the world.[5] "[F]rom the day Greek rule began, prophecy ceased in Israel in the year 3448 [from the creation of the world], then Haggai, Zechariah, and Malachi died. And Alexander Mokdon [the Macedonian] reigned for twelve years and four kings came after him," the *Seder 'olam zutta* says.[6] The era of contracts, calculated as commencing from the death of Alexander in June 323 BCE, thus did not begin with the six years of Greek rule in Elam. In the Near East, scholars used the system of dating shown in the Talmud and various *aggadot* disseminated there. By associating the Seleucid era with the end of prophecy, they came to merge what they saw as the Alexandrian dating system into the process that ended the biblical era. This change connected a dating era originally linked with an outside event to a specifically Jewish notion, transformed into a foundational event. The era of contracts, so named during the time of the "government of the elders," the reign of the Great Assembly convoked by Ezra, provided a link of continuity between the latter and the sages of the Mishnah.[7] "Until then [the era of Alexander], prophets had prophesied moved by the divine spirit [*ruah ha-kodesh*], but from this time on, people heeded the sages," the *Seder 'olam* says. "Bow down thine ear, and hear the words of the wise, and apply thine heart unto my knowledge" (Prov. 22:17).[8] Thus the great Babylonian master Sa'adia Ga'on was able to assert in the preface to a book that it "was written in the fourteenth year, one thousand two hundred years having elapsed since the day of the prophetic vision," whereas in fact he was referring to the Seleucid era.[9] So saying, Sa'adia Ga'on dates the cessation of prophecy from the first year of the Seleucid era, or 3448. Yet nothing contradicts the theory that he simply placed Darius's death year six years before the Seleucid era began, or in 3442, and started the Seleucid era with the death of Alexander. A copy of the Bible from Egypt, dating from 1009 CE, bears a handwritten note referring to this projection of the Seleucid era on the end of prophecy:

"Achieved in the month of Sivan of the year 4770 since the creation of the world, the year 1440 since the exile of Yehoyachin, that is the year [1]319 of Greek rule, which is the era of contracts and the end of prophecy, and the year 940 since the destruction of the Second Temple, and 399 of the reign of the little horn [the Islamic Hegira]."[10] Likewise, the author of a midrash names the Seleucid era as being the "end of prophecy in the days of Alexander."[11] The twelfth-century mathematician and astronomer Abraham bar Hiyya shows that this widely accepted confusion became traditional in writing of the Seleucid era as dating from the

> start of the rule of Alexander Mokdon (the Macedonian), called the era of contracts, because he obliged everyone to reckon [the years] under his name. . . . The era of contracts, in which vision [i.e., prophecy] ceased, was ratified in the era of Haggai, Zechariah, and Malachi, forty years after the building of the Second Temple, and it was the start [of the period] of the people of the Great Assembly. By our calculations, 3,449 full years thus passed between the creation of the world and the end of prophecy for the people of the East who count from the creation of the world starting with [the year] 3448, and between that date (and that of the exodus from Egypt) and the end of prophecy, one thousand full years passed.[12]

The Era of Destruction

Placed by Jewish chroniclers in the year 381 of the Seleucid era, corresponding to the year 3828 according to the Jewish era of the world's creation, year 1 of the era of the destruction of the Temple corresponds to year 68/69 CE. To control temporality according to different historical benchmarks, Jews have always been locating themselves with an accounting of time, whether dating from a given moment or an era bounded by an event. Owing to many local variations to which their calculation is subject, key events in Jewish history such as the exodus from Egypt and the building of the Temple are difficult to pinpoint in time. The Talmud specifies that to know how to situate oneself in time, it is advisable to combine the era of the world with the Seleucid era. Vestiges of a kind of calculation are found, indicated in the name of Rav

Papa (ca. 300–375 CE): those who did not know the year of the destruction of the Temple (*hurban*) were advised to ask a notary public, who would mark the decimal place in the common Seleucid year. Having done so, he would add the number 20 and in this way, he would find the total for the present year, counted off from the era of the *hurban*, without the thousandths and hundredths supposed to be known by all.[13] Starting with this system, if instead of adding the number 20 to the Seleucid year and finding the year counted off according to the era of the destruction of the Temple, the number 80 was simply added to the era of the *hurban*, one would find the position in the era of contracts.[14] In the name of Rav Huna, the Talmud also indicates that by adding a year to the era of the destruction of the Temple, then by dividing that date in "large numbers" of 50 years, anyone seeking the number of a year in a septennial cycle would obtain a reckoning of jubilees and fallow farm years by "small" numbers of 7. He should deduct 2 for each period of 100 years, add these 2's up, and divide the result by 7, which would indicate exactly in what year of the Sabbath cycle he was situated. Finally, when we read in the Talmud that the Seleucid era added to the number 48 results in the sum of the year of the world without the thousandths or hundredths,[15] it may be deduced that the chronological system referring to the principle of the era of the creation of the world was well-known—if not employed—before it became standard.

But how are we to understand this method of multiplying references to arrive at a date? Take, for example, this improbable formula for the Julian calendar date 9 September 1047: "[Rav Solomon bar Yehuda] is the leader of the yeshiva now, in the year 4807 of the creation, year 975 of the *hurban* and the year 1356 of the *shetarot*, the 15th of Elul."[16] This profusion of temporal parameters is also used by Maimonides: "In the year 1107 of the destruction of the Temple, 1487 of the Seleucid era, 4936 of the Creation" [or 1176 CE]."[17] It is still found in the fourteenth century in the calculations of Isaac Israeli ben Joseph: The Mishnah was completed in "the 3949th year of the era of the earth, the 500th of the era of contracts [or Seleucid era], the 120th of the destruction of the Temple."[18] Conversion of dates as shown is also a prime source of mistakes and misunderstandings.

It is sometimes hard to conceive of the inherent variations on the fact that the Seleucid era usually starts in autumn, and that of the destruction of the Temple always begins in summer. Also, that the ninth of Av, the fast day that commemorates the destruction of the two temples, is part of a year that began with New Year's Day (Rosh Ha-shanah) of the year 69. It is unsurprising that inconsistencies and temporal divergences can occur between events and their positioning in time. The lack of standard, uniform criteria and the simultaneous use of various systems of dating cited in biblical sources and ancient texts often leads to anachronisms, not only in rabbinic writings but in the work of researchers. It also produces bizarre results, especially when these calculations become the subject of disputes about exegetical readings, political rivalries, and theological clashes. Sa'adia Ga'on demonstrates this, writing:

> This year in which we find ourselves now is the year 1238 of the reign of Alexander, the year 4686 from the creation of the world according to our chronological table. Others calculate 4687 since the creation, which is unthinkable, because this calculation [of ours] is right; our forebears handed down the tradition to us through the Talmud that there was a difference of two years between the *Seder 'olam* and the reign of Alexander, and they indicated it . . ."[19]

Ten Directed Time

> The world is fated to last six thousand years. Two thousand years of chaos [*tohu*], two thousand years of Torah, two thousand years of days of the Messiah.
>
> Avodah zarah 9a[1]

A figure of thought emerges here. Arithmetical conjectures make sense within a daily scheduling that constantly plays with flow against stasis. So some Jews count, calculate, and recalculate the time elapsed between the creation and the key events of Judaism. They do so the better to integrate history into the prophesied promise of redemption, which mystical exegesis predicts must occur in the seventh millennium. Hence the importance of aligning past events in a temporal system reported in the accounts of the visions of Daniel. Perhaps this is also why tradition fixed the world order as canonical, without asking if or caring whether the numbers mentioned are correct. If the flow of centuries is to be seen in a Jewish temporal order, the point is not certified exactness in light of pinpointed events that occurred. Instead, it is rather in the aptitude that is bestowed to interrelate events and herald them in a precise numerical system. So the wholly profane event of the start of the Seleucid era, Seleucus I Nicator's reconquest of Babylon, finally demonstrates the period of the end of prophecy and "biblical times." The same applies when, without even asking about the real length of the period between the deportation of the Jews to Babylon and the rebuilding of the Temple according to dates given in the books of Ezra and Nehemiah, the *Seder 'olam* chooses to refer to seventy years as proclaimed in the Book of Daniel and repeated in the books of Isaiah and Jeremiah. The principle of this rabbinic arithmetic defying mathematical logic is also seen in the chronology in Abraham ibn Daud's twelfth-century *Sefer ha-Kabbalah* (Book of Tradition):[2] "Behold how trustworthy are the consolations of our God, blessed be His name, for the chronology of their exile corresponded to that of their redemption. Twenty-one years passed from the beginning of their exile [by Nebuchadnezzar] until the destruction of the Temple and the cessation of the monarchy [*Sedekiah*]. Similarly, twenty-one years passed from the time its rebuilding was begun until it was completed."[3] The author seems not to care that the time sequence used here lacks all resemblance to biblical indications. His statement is more about affirming hope for redemption that may be calculated than any historical probability.[4]

During the period from the start of the writing of the Mishnah to that which is seen as the completion of the Talmud, rabbinic thought was in the process of subsuming the history of humanity into a Jewish chronology. This shift, which would finally materialize with the adoption of dating by the age of the world, was still in its early stages. This style of reference is not yet seen in any official document, but it emerges here and there, mentioned sporadically, in a *baraita* or a talmudic citation not intelligible until a much later era. This change taking shape within rabbinic Judaism expands in eschatological space, which will slowly generate a belief in redemption and retribution in a world to come. Daniel's vision also illustrates this: "And many of them that sleep in the dust of the earth shall awake, some to everlasting life, and some to shame and everlasting contempt."[5] It will take almost two centuries (from around 130 BCE to 70 CE) for the Pharisees to impose these beliefs, rejected by the Sadducees who deny that a future life, divine judgment, or angelic hierarchy are ideas inherent in the ancestral religion, since they are not mentioned in the canonical writings.[6] The triumphant "world to come" (*'olam ha-ba'a*) was accordingly underwritten with a retrospective chronology based on which events could credibly be predicted. Thereafter, history was finalized. It was no longer limited to a festive annual unfolding meant to ensure the relaying of identity by carrying out the "duty of memory" of biblical events that ritual expresses in this world. Biblical events themselves were inscribed into the process of world history, which in turn dovetails with Jewish history, culminating in the vision of the world to come.

Biblical criticism acts similarly when it tries to match philological study with theological certainty. In analyzing scripture to establish the authentic sources of the religion of Israel, does it not seek foreign input to justify the New Covenant or reaffirm the prior ones?

Analysis of the observance of jubilee year provides one example. As we have seen, Leviticus is the basis for this cycle, which reemerges in Nehemiah, in the name of Ezra: "They clave to their brethren, . . . and entered into a curse, and into an oath, to walk in God's law, which was given by Moses, the servant of God . . . and that we would leave [the earth lie fallow] the seventh year, and the exaction of every debt."[7] Is resting the land the repetition of an ancient practice, neglected but still familiar, or the start of a new order taken from laws imported from Babylon? This question raises debate among historians. If, following Julius Wellhausen, we choose the second alternative, then the jubilee calendar would have been introduced at the return from the first exile, as part of a temporal order rethought by and for priests under the aegis of Ezra.[8] Located in the field of reform introduced by the cycle of Meton of Athens[9] during the fourth or the fifth century BCE, this cycle allows for seven intercalations to operate in conjunction with lunar and solar cycles. It follows the principle that 235 lunar months, or nineteen lunar years plus seven months, correspond to nineteen solar years.[10] It is clear that tradition offers an entirely different explanation, which sees in this transition the repetition of a custom observed since the week of seven days came into effect.[11] Or it might be affirming the reuse of a custom that had fallen into abeyance during exile. B. Z. Wacholder opts for the introduction of a calendar based on the system of fallow years, starting during the period of Zerubbabel, around 519–518 BCE.[12] The scholarly argument is not important. It is more pertinent to grasp the way Jewish tradition uses temporal data in its speculative framework. The emphasis on the seventh year of fallow fields is key in the perspective of building Jewish history, as confirmed by this quotation from the *Seder ʿolam,* which can be found word for word in the Talmud:

> When the Temple was destroyed for the first time, it was during the end of Shabbat, the end of the seventh year [*sheviʿit*], during the watch of Jehoiarib, on the ninth of Av. It was the same the second time [when the Second Temple was destroyed], and during this time the Levites were on duty, singing psalms. Which psalms? "And he shall bring upon them their own iniquity, and shall cut them off in their own wickedness" [Ps. 94:23].[13]

This passage perfectly illustrates talmudic customs of chronology. We saw above that to measure the time elapsed between the destruction of the two temples, the *Seder ʿolam* used the number 490 rather than the one that emerges from biblical dates, which would be 656 or 657 years. It is noteworthy that unlike the descriptions of the destruction of the Temple of Solomon in 2 Kings 25:8, which indicate that it was burned down "in the fifth month, on the seventh day of the month," Jeremiah 52:12 states that it was destroyed on the tenth day, whereas Josephus and the Taʿanit tractate date this event to the tenth of the month of Av.[14] The two conflagrations are conflated in a kind of hermeneutic program built around the vision in Daniel 9:24: "for the decision [to destroy and rebuild the Temples] was made before [the start of the] 70 years." The Mishnah relates it this way: "Five tragedies struck our forefathers on the seventeenth day of Tammuz and five more on the ninth of Av. . . . On the ninth of Av, it was decreed that our fathers would not enter the [Promised] Land, the Temple was destroyed the first and second times, Betar fortress fell, and the City [Jerusalem] was demolished."[15] Incidentally, Josephus was interested in this approach to the event: "But as for that house, God had, for certain, long ago doomed it to the fire; and now that fatal day was come, according to the revolution of ages; it was the tenth day of the month Lous [Ab], upon which it was formerly burnt by the king of Babylon."[16] Joining two destructions in the same temporal ordering, revolving around the number seven, fulfils its role. The same situation recurs in the week at the end of Shabbat, or Sunday, and during cycles, at the end of a year of fallow fields, as the Taʿanit tractate confirms. The First Temple was destroyed on the evening of the ninth of Av (*Tisha B'Av*), at the end of Shabbat, and the same is true of the Second.[17] The same desire to regroup events around pre-set symbolic dates may be found in the rabbinic argument that bases the date of the creation of the world in Tishri and not Nisan, with this assertion: "In the month of Tishri the world was created, in the month of Tishri the patriarchs were born, in the month of Tishri the patriarchs died; on Rosh Ha-shanah, God remembered Sarah, Rachel, and Hannah; on Rosh Ha-shanah, Joseph was released from jail; on Rosh Ha-shanah, slavery in Egypt ended, in the month of Nisan they were released, in the month of Tishri the deliverance of the Jews occurred."[18]

Messianism Versus Millenarianism

As Judaism sought to be more prescriptive, offering faith and laws as precepts, some of its branches broke free to pursue their own traditions. Judeo-Christians and later, in the eighth century, Karaites rejected the new teachings of oral law that the writing of ethical and legal texts would finally be fixed, driven by the Pharisees,[19] Samaritans,[20] and perhaps also the Essenes around the second century BCE. Judeo-Christians and Karaites formed dissident groups whose disputes with mainstream Judaism centered on the chronological question. These divergences are based as much on the reading of their respective versions of the biblical text as on the gaps that this reading caused in observing the liturgical calendar, as reflected by the Songs of the Sabbath Sacrifice.[21] Because biblical chronology uses a timeline considered divine, great importance is accorded it. After all, the Book of Jubilees states that "the distribution of times" was given to Moses simultaneously with the Tablets of Law. Chronology, raised to the level of the sacred, is granted the power of possessing the secret calculations for the date of the coming redemption. Like Moses, those who write the history of times past are inspired by a divine source. Incomplete surviving sources suggest that there were at least four different models of ancient chronology based on Scripture. They are named in the Septuagint, the Samaritan Pentateuch,[22] the Book of Jubilees, and the Hebrew Bible (see Appendix). There is no need to dwell on the theological trends that these systems substantiate. For now, let us note simply that the varying observance of religious formalities is accompanied by social consequences.[23] The latter grow into divergences such that the basic aspects of group worship cannot unite people within a religion that they practice simultaneously.

Conjecture about how long the world will probably exist makes up part of eschatological expectations. It plays a formative role in locating the scale of the age of the world. This chapter's talmudic epigraph is attributed to the School of Elijah. According to it, the universe will last for six thousand years, divided into two thousand years of the abyss, two thousand years of Torah, and two thousand days of the Messiah.[24] This demonstrates an ethical-mystical idea of temporal sequentiality. In circles of mystics and rabbis, there is conjecture about developing principles of calculation to match these projections with an account of human temporality. To calculate two millennia of messianic days, the moment must be specified when a line may be drawn dividing empires between the abyss and the Torah. The problem is not easy to solve, since traditions handed down from the Midrashim and Aggadah insist that the Torah, whose figures are always located in this type of text in the "narrative present," preceded the existence of the universe and assert that the Patriarchs followed its teachings, even before they were given to Moses:[25]

> In the beginning, two thousand years before the heaven and the earth, seven things were created: the Torah written with black fire on white fire, and lying in the lap of God; the Divine Throne, erected in the heaven which later was over the heads of the *Hayyot*; Paradise on the right side of God, Hell on the left side; the Celestial Sanctuary directly in front of God, having a jewel on its altar graven with the Name of the Messiah, and a Voice that cries aloud, "Return, ye children of men."[26]

> Six things preceded the creation of the world; some of them were actually created, while the creation of the others was already contemplated. The Torah and the Throne of Glory were created. . . . The creation of the Patriarchs was contemplated . . . Israel was contemplated . . . the Temple was contemplated. . . . The name of Messiah was contemplated.[27]

> Seven things were created before the world was created. They are The Torah, *Gehinnom*, the Garden of Eden, the Throne of Glory, the Temple, Repentance, and the Name of the Messiah.[28]

These quotations prove that the natural order of temporality was disrupted by conflicts between the worlds of creation and eternity. In this case, respecting the postulate of an eschatological time prior to humankind's time imposed one reading on scholars. Since the gift of the Torah transcends humanity's temporality, in order to deduce the millennia of the Messiah's reign, one needs to know how exactly those of its authority are to be calculated, based on the School of Elijah's periodization.

One path can be followed here. Although the principle has never been clearly stated, the *Seder ʿolam*'s arithmetic, which allows for a thousand years between the exodus from Egypt and the start of the era of contracts, suggests that Jewish chronology places a high symbolic value on a millennium. Taken up in the Talmud, and commented upon, as we have seen, by the twelfth-century mathematician and astronomer Abraham Bar Hiyya, this arithmetic seeks to establish a historic border between the biblical period and the era of nations:

> According to our calculation, 3,449 full years passed, then, between the creation of the world and the end of prophecy, for the people of the East who calculate the creation of the world starting from 3448, and between that date [of the exodus from Egypt] and the end of prophecy, one thousand full years went by . . . we know that the exodus from Egypt took place in 2448 of the world and between the exodus from Egypt and the start of the era of contracts, one thousand full years passed."[29]

This Jewish "millenarianism," somewhat eclipsed by the Christian version, remains to be defined.[30] Remnants of it may still be found in the Middle Ages, and it reappears to some degree with Sabbatai Zevi. Above all, it seems to have spread most during the period preceding and coinciding with the emergence of Christianity.[31] Estimates of the length of the Messiah's reign—reckoned at 6,000 or 7,000 years— have never really ceased. The period of a thousand years proclaimed by the psalmist to be in God's sight "but as yesterday when it is past, and as a watch in the night" (Ps. 90:4, the epigraph to Part II of this book) can be viewed from two perspectives, those of (a) messianic expectancy, or hope, and (b) prophetic speculation.

Hope

The messianic view blends into the kingdom of peace that precedes Judgment Day, although its duration is not always clearly mentioned: "And after that there shall be another, the eighth week, that of righteousness. . . . And after this, in the tenth week in the seventh part, There shall be the great eternal judgment"; "And His dominion will last forever until the world of corruption has ended and until the times that have been mentioned before have been fulfilled."[32] Rabbinic literature distinguishes between the "days of the Messiah" (*yemot ha-Mashiah*) and the "world to come" (*'olam ha-ba'a*), but their respective lengths are never given and the terms are sometimes interchangeable with the vague concept of the "future ahead" (*le-'atid lavo*).[33] The messianic era might just as likely last 40 years as 70, 365, 400, or even 7,000. Some say it will last a length of time equal to that which elapsed from the creation of the world to its dawning; others, the equivalent of the time from Noah to the "present moment"; while yet others claim that six earthly millennia will be followed by a seventh millennium of the messianic age.[34] The *Midrash Sefer Eliahu* (Apocalypse of Elijah) says:

> Here are the mysteries that were unveiled to Simeon ben Yohai when he was cloistered in his cave, hiding from the Prince of Edom, and prayed for forty days and forty nights, starting this way: "My Lord, how long will the prayer of your servants continue?" The secrets of the end [time] were then immediately revealed to him. . . . After two millennia the Holy One, blessed be His name, will sit on the throne of justice in the valley of Jehosaphat. Heaven and earth will instantly disintegrate and the moon will be covered with shame, and the sun with confusion [Isa. 23:24], the mountains crumble, and hills vanish [Isa. 54:10], for they remind Israel of its sins. The gates of Gehenna will open at the ford of Joshua, like the gates to the Garden of Eden to the east, on the third day, as it is written: "after two days he will have returned us to life" [Hos. 6:2], which relates to the days of the Messiah, which will last for 2,000 years. "The third day, He will have raised us, so that we may abide in Him [Hos. 6:2]," which will be Judgment Day, and woe betide those who will die on that day.[35]

This eschatological Midrash whose statements are attributed to Simeon ben Yohai—also traditionally the author of the *Zohar*, the masterwork of Kabbalah—gathers in one tale the diverse expectations of redemption found among different groups in Palestine.[36] It describes wars that supposedly will precede the coming of messianic times, heralded by three figures, a warlike messiah son of Joseph, a messiah son of Ephraim,[37] and finally the Messiah of peace, son of David. The last-mentioned is also found in the Book of Zerubbabel and the *Otot ha-mashiah* (Signs of the Messianic Age).[38] This excerpt reasserts the claim of a total duration of six thousand years for the earth. Whoever produced it, we know that its hero, probably a disciple of Rabbi Akiva, must have lived around the second century, more or less during the era of the great revolt against the Romans which ended tragically, with a bloodbath. The question of the time elapsed was being posed in terms of how many millennia had already passed in relation to those still to come. Assuming that this writer may well have been a close contemporary of the mystic Simeon ben Yohai to whom he attributes these statements, he must have lived in what he thought was the end of the fourth millennium since the creation of the world.[39] This was also a time and context in which rabbinic circles were putting the final touches on the *Seder ʿolam*'s chronology, and three new translations of Torah into Greek (by Aquila, Symmachus, and Theodotion) were made to reconcile the Septuagint as closely as possible with the Hebrew original.[40] We saw in Part I of this book that hopes of redemption reached their apogee around this time. Rabbi Akiva thought it was so close that he proclaimed the messianic status of the rebel leader Bar Kokhba. We can now see how it was that this feverish expectation was also expressed in reckonings logically founded on the hope of seeing the arrival of two millennia of messianic days as heralded. Moreover, it is not surprising to see remnants of beliefs and hopes in contemporary midrashic literature[41] that rabbinic literature was unable to take into account, being caught up then in the Masoretic process of forming a canon of texts,[42] which reveal traditions or reflect views that one might either retain or dismiss, depending on their usefulness to messianic hope.

Expecting the Messiah . . . Tomorrow or the Day After

Describing apocalyptic events to come during the divine septennial before final redemption, the tractate Sanhedrin from the Babylonian Talmud expresses the extreme backlash resulting from Jews' eschatological expectations after the destruction of the Temple in 70 and the slaughter at the fortress of Betar that followed the great revolt in 135. Taking the usual dialogue form, it brings together a range of rabbinical doctrines and teachings about eschatology. It is reprinted at length here because it collates the views that scholars take as "authorized" during the final writing of the tractate:

> "As it is written, in that day I [i.e., the Messiah] will raise up the tabernacle of David *ha-nofeleth* [that is fallen]" [Amos 9:11]. He [R. Nahman] replied, "Thus hath R. Johanan said: in the generation

when the son of David [i.e., the Messiah] will come, scholars will be few in number, and as for the rest, their eyes will fail through sorrow and grief. Multitudes of trouble and evil decrees will be promulgated anew, each new evil coming with haste before the other has ended."

Our Rabbis taught: "In the seven year cycle at the end of which the son of David will come-in the first year, this verse will be fulfilled: 'And I will cause it to rain upon one city and cause it not to rain upon another city' [Amos 4:7]; in the second, the arrows of hunger will be sent forth; in the third, a great famine, in the course of which men, women, and children, pious men and saints will die, and the Torah will be forgotten by its students; in the fourth, partial plenty; in the fifth, great plenty, when men will eat, drink and rejoice, and the Torah will return to its disciples; in the sixth, [Heavenly] sounds; in the seventh, wars; and at the conclusion of the septennate the son of David will come." R. Joseph demurred: "But so many septennates have passed, yet has he not come!"—Abaye retorted: "Were there then [Heavenly] sounds in the sixth and wars in the seventh! Moreover, have they [sc. the troubles] been in this order!"

"Wherewith thine enemies have reproached, O Lord, wherewith they have reproached the footsteps of thine anointed" [Ps. 89:52] it has been taught, R. Judah said: 'In the generation when the son of David comes, the house of assembly will be for harlots, Galilee in ruins, Gablan lie desolate, the border inhabitants wander about from city to city, receiving no hospitality, the wisdom of scribes in disfavour, God-fearing men despised, people be dog-faced [i.e., shameless], and truth entirely lacking . . ."

. . . R. Nehorai said: "In the generation when Messiah comes, young men will insult the old, and old men will stand before the young [to do them honor]; daughters will rise up against their mothers, and daughters-in-law against their mothers-in-law. The people shall be dog-faced [i.e., brazen], and a son will not be abashed in his father's presence."

It has been taught, R. Nehemiah said: "In the generation of Messiah's coming impudence will increase, esteem be perverted, the vine yield its fruit, yet shall wine be dear, and the Kingdom will be converted to heresy with none to rebuke them." This supports R. Isaac, who said: "The son of David will not come until the whole world is converted to the belief of the heretics." . . .

Our Rabbis taught: "For the Lord shall judge his people, and repent himself of his servants, when he seeth that their power is gone,
and there is none shut up, or left" [Deut. 32:36]: the son of David will
not come until denunciators are in abundance. Another interpretation
[of their power is gone]: until scholars are few. Another interpretation:
until the [last] *perutah* has gone from the purse. Yet another interpretation: until the redemption is despaired of, for it is written, "there
is none shut up or left [Deut. 32:36], as—were it possible [to say
so]—Israel had neither Supporter nor Helper. Even as R. Zera, who,
whenever he chanced upon scholars engaged thereon [i.e., in calculating the time of the Messiah's coming], would say to them: "I beg of
you, do not postpone it, for it has been taught: Three come unawares:
Messiah, a found article and a scorpion."

R. Kattina said: "Six thousand years shall the world exist, and one
[thousand, the seventh], it shall be desolate, as it is written, And the
Lord alone shall be exalted in that day" [Isa. 2:11]. Abaye said: "It
will be desolate two [thousand], as it is said, 'After two days will he
revive us: in the third day, he will raise us up, and we shall live in
his sight.'"

It has been taught in accordance with R. Kattina: "Just as the seventh year is one year of release in seven, so is the world: one thousand
years out of seven shall be fallow, as it is written, And the Lord alone
shall be exalted in that day," and it is further said, A Psalm and song
for the Sabbath day [Ps. 90:1], meaning the day that is altogether
Sabbath [i.e., the period of complete desolation; note that "day" here
means a thousand years]—and it is also said, For a thousand years in
thy sight are but as yesterday when it is past [Ps. 90].

The *Tanna debe Eliyyahu* teaches: The world is to exist six thousand years. In the first two thousand there was desolation; two thousand years the Torah flourished; and the next two thousand years is
the Messianic era, but through our many iniquities all these years have
been lost.

Elijah said to Rav Judah, the brother of R. Salia the pious: "The
world shall exist not less than eighty five jubilees, and in the last jubilee the son of David will come." He asked him, "At the beginning
or at the end?"—He replied, "I do not know." "Shall [this period] be
completed or not?"—"I do not know," he answered. R. Ashi said: He
spoke thus to him, "Before that, do not expect him; afterwards thou
mayest await him."

R. Hanan b. Tahlifa sent [word] to R. Joseph: I once met a man who possessed a scroll written in Hebrew in Assyrian characters. I said to him: "Whence has this come to thee?" He replied, "I hired myself as a mercenary in the Roman army, and found it amongst the Roman archives. In it is stated that four thousand, two hundred and ninety-one years after the creation the world will be orphaned. [As to the years following,] some of them will be spent in the war of the great sea monsters, and some in the war of Gog and Magog, and the remaining [period] will be the Messianic era, whilst the Holy One, blessed be He, will renew his world only after seven thousand years." R. Abba the son of Raba said: "The statement was after five thousand years."

It has been taught; R. Nathan said: "This verse pierces and descends to the very abyss: For the vision is yet for an appointed time, but at the end it shall speak, and not lie: though he tarry, wait for him; because it will surely come, it will not tarry" [Hab. 2:3]. Not as our Masters, who interpreted the verse, "until a time and times and the dividing of time" [Dan. 7:25]; nor as R. Simlai who expounded, "Thou feedest them with the bread of tears; and givest them tears to drink a third time" [Ps. 80:6]; nor as R. Akiba who expounded, "Yet once, it is a little while, and I will shake the heavens, and the earth" [Hag. 2:6] but the first dynasty [sc. the Hasmonean] shall last seventy years, the second [the Herodian], fifty two, and the reign of Bar Koziba two and a half years.

What is meant by "but at the end it shall speak [we-yafeah] and not lie?"—R. Samuel b. Nahmani said in the name of R. Jonathan: "Blasted be the bones of those who calculate the end." For they would say, "Since the predetermined time has arrived, and yet he has not come, he will never come." But [even so], wait for him, as it is written, "Though he tarry, wait for him." Should you say, "We look forward [to his coming] but He does not: therefore Scripture saith, And therefore will the Lord wait, that he may be gracious unto you, and therefore will he be exalted, that he may have mercy upon you" [Isa. 30:18]. But since we look forward to it, and He does likewise, what delays [his coming]?—The Attribute of Justice delays it. But since the Attribute of Justice delays it, why do we await it?—To be rewarded [for hoping], as it is written, "blessed are all they that wait for him" [Isa. 30:18]. . . .

Rab said: "All the predestined dates [for redemption] have passed, and the matter [now] depends only on repentance and good deeds." But Samuel maintained: "It is sufficient for a mourner to keep his [period of] mourning."[43]

This text offers much useful information that sheds light on our subject. First, the impact of history on messianic vision. Generally seen as peaceful, Davidic redemption here changes into redemption born of war. This revision may be related to recent events.[44] Drawing from the source of tannaitic and amoraic literature, there are numerous examples of inherent disparities in rabbinical visions of the Messiah's coming.[45] The most significant aspect of the preceding text is its counteracting any attempt at messianic fire. This is done by exploiting doom-mongering as mentioned, on the one hand, with the devastation of the world in the wars of Gog and Magog. On the other hand, there is the reminder of disaster following the revolt by Bar Kokhba, who, as elsewhere in rabbinic literature, is here unambiguously called "son of a lie."[46] There are also some commonplace elements. The reminder that, although the world's existence is foreseen to be limited in time, it remains impossible for mankind to locate itself in a divine temporal accounting. What can a thousand years mean to God? Finally, the statement that calculations about the end of the world are in vain because the matter "[now] depends only on repentance and good deeds" enshrines the principle of moving messianism into daily ritual life. Moreover, mentioning the scroll written "in Hebrew in Assyrian characters" offers precise data for dating, since the Pharisees introduced and distributed this writing.[47] We can see taking shape a concrete difference between the ideas of the second-century Tannaim and those of the Amoraim who followed them. Judah, Nehorai, and Nehemiah, who describe the conditions of the Messiah's coming "in the generation when the son of David shall come," live in the second century. Judah, brother of Rav Salia (Hasida) the Pious, who does not know whether the jubilee will reach its conclusion; Rabbi Joseph, who announces the dreadful wars of Gog and Magog; and Rav Ashi and Nathan, who state that redemption is fixed, thereby in all probability postponing messianic guarantees, date from the fourth and fifth centuries. Samuel bar Nahmani, Rabbi Zeirah, and Rav, who argue the vanity of arithmetical guesswork and insist on human responsibility for the Messiah's not coming, date from the third and fourth centuries. Yet the text shows the intense commitment of rabbis in this activity of projected calculation of the messianic coming. The date is discussed in detail and in particular; the fifth millennium marks the dividing line as in the Greek Apocalypse of Ezra, likely written in Roman Palestine at the end of the first century.[48] These explicit mentions remain exceptional in the Talmud. The fact that they are concentrated in texts from talmudic tractates that discuss chronology, Sanhedrin, cited above, and Avodah zarah 9b, shows the eschatological direction of these calculations.[49] Regarding this demonstration, it is noteworthy how the rabbis manage to achieve an eschatological balance between narrating the quantified past and future probabilities. This brings the messianic discourse to the level of "always possible," since previously done in the historical past, without having to be immediate. Between the eleventh and twelfth centuries, Rashi would extend this debate in the same spirit of overriding messianic hopes. He would resume the teaching of the School of Elijah in the Talmud, stating that although two millennia of Torah had passed, the Messiah had not come "because of our many sins."[50]

The Reckoning

The millennium may be seen from a different angle. Perhaps foreseen by Bar Hiyya, it is revealed in the writings of the Arab scholar Abū Rayhān al-Bīrūnī. A contemporary of Sherira Ga'on and Hai Ga'on, he shares their interest in calendrical chronology.[51] Yet al-Bīrūnī's curiosity goes beyond the scope of its practical elements. In the eleventh century, he describes rules for creating a calendar for every known people and notes the principles for changing eras. Regarding Judaism, he studies the literature while relying on statements by people associated with the Jewish world. The latter told him that the era of the creation of the world was delivered to the first Lawgiver. Jews devised their chronology based on the "era of Moses and David":

> "When Alexander had left Greece at the age of twenty-six years, prepared to fight with Darius, the king of the Persians, and marching upon his capital, he went down to Jerusalem, which was inhabited by the Jews; then he ordered the Jews to give up the era of Moses and David, and to use his era instead, and to adopt that very year, the twenty-seventh of his life, as the epoch of this era. The Jews obeyed his command, and accepted what he ordered; for the Rabbis allowed them such a change at the end of each millennium after Moses. And at

that time just a millennium had become complete, and their offerings and sacrifices had ceased to be practiced, as they relate."[52]

Al-Bīrūnī, while reusing their data, remains dubious about the validity of their statements, commenting:

> How little care the Jews bestow upon their chronology is shown to evidence, by the fact, that they, all of them, believe in the first instance, that between their exodus from Egypt and Alexander there is an interval of 1,000 years, corrected (i.e. made to agree with the sun or real time) by intercalation, and that they rely on this number in their computation of the qualities of the years. . . . But if we gather from their books which follow after the Thora, the years of every one of their rulers after Moses . . . , we get a sum which already at the building of Jerusalem goes beyond the millennium.[53]

Could it be that this historical structure, based on the completion of a millennium, was at the center of calculations in the *Seder 'olam*? Al-Bīrūnī knew the weak points of these calculations.[54] Yet they introduce or expand the notion that the time elapsed between the era of Moses and that of contracts was a millennium. As we have seen, the author reduced the prior periods, especially that of the Temple period and the Persian kingdom, from 607 to 420 years. In so doing, the sums performed between the exodus from Egypt and the building of the First Temple return to the 480 years mentioned in the Bible, to which he added 410 years for its construction, 70 years of exile in Babylon, and 40 years between the rebuilding of the Temple and the conquest of Palestine by Alexander.[55] Bar Hiyya confirms these calculations, as if parenthetically, without further explanation: "Between the exodus from Egypt and the start of the era of contracts, one thousand full years passed."[56] Must we conclude that somehow a millennium elapsing authorized setting the record straight with a new time? Admitting that this surmise is based on oral tradition still extant in al-Bīrūnī's day, we may take a second look at the way rabbinic arithmetic grasps chronology. The historical divisions created by the *Seder 'olam* and exegeses that are spread throughout the Talmud, even in the Passover Haggadah, suggest a periodization in which these thousand-year segments of Jewish history are meaningful. Indeed, periods of about a millennium mark specific scansions in the history of Israel. The *Seder 'olam* asserts that "from Adam to Noah, there were 1,056 years"; from the Flood to the end of Genesis, that is to say, 292 (the years between the Flood and the birth of Abraham) + 653 (from the birth of Abraham to the end of Genesis) = 945, or indeed from the exodus in Egypt to the deportation to Babylon, that is to say, 480 (Solomon builds the Temple 480 years after the exodus from Egypt) + 430 (obtained by adding together the reigns of the kings of Judea until the exile) + 70 (the length of the exile, according to Jeremiah and Zechariah) = 980 years.

Exploiting this presumption makes it possible to find this kind of calculation in Jewish literature. Although only approximately, this millennial quest may be found in Josephus. In *Jewish Antiquities*, he calculates that between the arrival of Abraham in Canaan and the destruction of the First Temple 592 + 430 years elapsed, which is to say 1,022 years.[57] Similarly, between the birth of Abraham and the destruction, 1,022 + 75, or 1,097 years passed. The history of the Jews prior to Moses ran into millennia, marking the divine transformations of its flow. As these intercessions became rarer, they might have been caused solely by human interventions that changed customary temporality. From another perspective, it can be considered that this reading only prevailed at a given time, to mark the passage from the biblical period to that of the Mishnah. The writing of the *Seder 'olam* might have indicated this move, which, as noted in Chapter 9, is described as follows: "Until then [the era of Alexander], prophets had prophesied moved by the divine spirit [*ruah ha-kodesh*], but from this time on, people heeded the sages."[58] It seems that no currently identified Jewish source attests to this millenarian idea.[59] The Talmud asks itself about the origin of this practice: "Whence do we know that we have begun to count according to the Greek kingdom? Perhaps they started to count from the exodus from Egypt and rejected the preceding millennium to adopt the new one . . ."[60]

God's Shabbat

As mentioned, the calculation of the time that had elapsed since the creation of the world also became the subject of clashes between Jewish sects, Samaritans and Karaites, as well as between Samaritans and

Christians. All of them believed that they knew the real truth, based on their own reading of the Bible. According to Al-Bīrūnī, Jews of his day counted the period between Adam being driven out of Paradise and the Flood as 1,656 years. The Samaritans reduced this number to 1,307,[61] but Christians reckoned it as 2,242 years, notably in the third-century *Chronographiai* of Sextus Julius Africanus. Yet this temporal expansion was a real breeding ground for all kinds of eschatological guesswork. It was obtained partly from the numeric variations found in the Septuagint, which routinely add one hundred years to the life spans of generations before the Flood (see Appendix).[62] Clashing in the field of the history of homiletics and hermeneutics, the two religions fought to appropriate, or conversely, to defend their chosen past.[63] Extrapolating from the 1015-year interval between the Flood and Abraham, Sextus Julius Africanus placed the death of Joseph in 3565 of the Adamic era. Adding to this count the 210 years that the Hebrews spent in Egypt, the 1,235 years that were meant to have passed between Moses and Cyrus, and the 490 years that elapsed since Cyrus, according to Daniel's prophecy, the birth of Jesus corresponded to the year 5500 of the era of the creation, at the very center of the messianic millennium.[64] Were it necessary to find out where these calculations developed, let us look at Josephus's proud statement in the first century. The history of his people he offered covers five thousand years, clearly showing that these numeric reckonings could not solely derive from clashes between Christians and Jews.[65]

"God completed his work in six days. This means that in 6000 years, God will bring each thing to completeness, since for Him, 'a day is like one thousand years.' So, my children, in six days, that is to say, in six thousand years, the universe will reach its end. 'And on the seventh day he rested.'"[66]

In the second century CE, the teaching of Pseudo-Barnabas, author of the Epistle of Barnabas, answers that of the School of Elijah transmitted by the Talmud.[67] While extolling an ardent anti-Judaism, the text uses an apocalyptic outline deeply rooted in Jewish structure, as echoed by an apocalypse found at Qumran.[68] Far from being an isolated case, the principle of six millennia, sometimes called epochs or ages, appeared in many passages of Christian literature in early centuries. In it, world chronology takes into account the beginning and end of time in a system blending chronology and eschatology:[69] "The first *parousia* of our Lord was in . . . the forty-second year of the reign of Augustus, 5,500 years after Adam," Hippolytus of Rome says. "It is necessary to reach 6,000 years before the Sabbath." In the prospect outlined by Hippolytus: "Starting with the birth of Christ, it is necessary to wait 500 more years before the end comes."[70] In 404, Saint Jerome wrote that the Petrine epistles and Psalms 89:4 were the sources of a commonly shared belief. According to it, the expression "1,000 years for a day" bolstered the belief that the world had been created in six days, and it would not last more than six thousand years, since the number seven represented the real Sabbath.[71] Since Christianity could not ignore belief in the millennium, it had to accept or fight it. Almost at the same time, Saint Augustine sought to show up this expectation as absurd, inasmuch as the City of God was not of this earth and arithmetical calculations concerning it were in vain; no historical sign could explain any event of a purely eschatological nature.[72]

The Church used extended numbers for the durations mentioned in the Septuagint, then revised and compressed them, making the world younger by several millennia in deleting the year of the world with the stroke of a pen to create the era of the Incarnation. The motivating principle is based on a simple observation. Calculating time may support the belief of the faithful, but may also be the means of their straying. Calculations of the duration of the world in the books of Isaiah and Daniel certified the proclaimed arrival of the son of man. As they were constantly overtaken by the ongoing flow of time, they could only help in leading astray.[73] Preferring the numbers of the Masoretic version to those of the Septuagint, Jerome produced a chronology making it possible to set back the end of time. The new style of calculation, built on *hebraica veritas*,[74] would finally subdue the relinquishment of the sixth millennium. Differences of opinion had always allowed polemics about the exact date of the year of the world to ignite between Christians of Alexandria, Byzantium, and elsewhere. Still, a near-consensus was reached between Jews and Christians that placed the birth of Jesus in the year 304 of the Seleucid era, or 7 BCE. Nevertheless, in the eighteenth century, the French Protestant historian Alphonse Des Vignoles could still inventory over two hundred different calculations, spanning lengths of 6,984 to 3,483 years between the creation and Christ's Nativity.[75] The Byzantines had favored the world era since the second century CE, and its use spread in documents from the tenth century on, although the Nestorian Church of the East used the Seleucid era during the Middle Ages. In contrast, starting in 816 for England, 876 in the Germanic kingdoms, around 967 for the Franks, and finally 969 for Rome, the West gradually came to choose the year of grace, recalculated by the Venerable Bede in England in the eighth century. In a few centuries, the Christian era finally imposed itself throughout the Western world. It was well established when the Hegira calendar took root in Islamic countries.[76] The Christian temporal line, after having wavered between history/chronology and eschatology, opted to dissociate these two fields. In this world, the tie between heavenly and earthly Jerusalem ceases to exist. Christian time, Western at first and universal thereafter, would remain inscribed in history. By introducing the era of the Incarnation, the Church broke the thread that tied it to Jewish eschatological sources. Spurning the exploitation of millenarianism that had enabled it to be founded, it strengthened its legitimacy.

The calculations that led to the birth of the world era were probably themselves born of the messianic expectations that flourished in Palestine during the two centuries before and after the destruction of the Temple. It is equally possible that the rabbinic system developed to vanquish world chronology, while adding it to an eschatological system that allowed Judaism—unlike the Church system—to confront historical adversity as well as messianistic defeats without crumbling. On the contrary, it permitted Judaism gradually to restore itself by invoking a future, always promised and never outdated. Messianism is thus a stable element in Judaism's historical past. It can be schematized as follows: although all the dates proposed for the arrival of redemption have come and gone, the promise remains to be realized. It is up to each one of us to fulfil it. Calculations seeking to determine the time its coming are pointless. Once traced, this temporality keeps the parallel arrows of history and eschatology in sync, so to speak, by putting the individual, as a participant in rituals, at the heart of that which is to come.

Eleven   Exercises in Rabbinic Calculation

Inscribing Oneself in Time

From epigraphic remains, it is possible to place the changes undergone over the centuries in reference to an era. Gravestones are a key source of information about calendrical customs. When they have survived the ravages of time, they indicate a date of death, allowing kinfolk to perform rituals of remembrance. For the oldest, the main problem is the condition of the inscriptions, which often causes different readings of fragments. These inscriptions are often deteriorated and subject to intense debate over interpretation. Yet to ignore them would deprive us of a rare source of information, although one to be used carefully. For Palestine, archaeology presents major signs about use of the date of the destruction of the Temple. The following three inscriptions are from Zoara, the biblical Zoar, one of the five "cities of the plain" in Genesis; Lot and his family took refuge there, thus escaping the destruction of Sodom and Gomorrah. The inscriptions, discovered and published during the twentieth century, bear witness to the intricacy of references over the course of time to the era of the destruction of the Temple and to the cycle of fallowing:

1. "May the soul of Shaul, son of . . . let rest, who died on the first of the month of Marcheshvan, in year 1 of the fallow fields; year 300 and 60 and 4 after the destruction of the house of the Temple. Peace."[1]
2. "Here [lies] the spirit of Esther, daughter of Edyo, died in the month of Shevat in year 3 of the fallow fields, year 300 of the years after the destruction of the house of the Temple. Peace. Peace."

3. May the spirit of Halifo rest, daughter of . . . died on a Tuesday, the eleventh day of the month of Elul, year [2] of the fallow fields which is the four hundredth and thirty and fifth year after the destruction of the House of the Temple, Peace be on Israel. Peace."[2]

As we have seen, Palestinian and Babylonian calculations refer differently to the Seleucid era, the former starting the year in the month of Nisan and the latter in Tishri. Also, current chronology dates the destruction of the Temple (*hurban*) and the corresponding era in a way that does not necessarily agree with previous calculations. The question thus arises of how to interpret and apply the dating in the above inscriptions, which depends as much on theory as on methodology. So how then do scholars go about analyzing these dates? The three inscriptions each give three markers of the same order: the lunar month, the year in relation to the era of the *hurban*, and the year in the cycle of fallowing.

— The first inscription names the month of Marcheshvan in the 364th year of the destruction of the Temple, which is the first year in the fallowing cycle.
— The second names the month of Shevat, year 300 of the destruction of the Temple, the third year in the fallowing cycle.
— The third names the month of Elul, year 435 of the destruction of the Temple, the seventh year in the fallowing cycle.

Synchronizing these three examples in the aforementioned systems of the era of the destruction and the cycle of fallow fields seems to pose some problems. Indeed, each inscription becomes enigmatically inconsistent with the two other datings, in view of the indicated markers. Based on the first inscription, with the year 364 the first in the sabbatical (*shemittah*) cycle, the 300th should have been the seventh, and the year 435 the second in the cycle of sabbatical years. If we accept the second inscription, with year 300 of the destruction being the third of fallow fields, then the 364th year should be the fourth, and the year 435 the fifth in the cycle of sabbatical years. The same applies to the final one, for if the third inscription is taken as a reference, the 435th year being a sabbatical year, then year 300 should have been the fifth of the cycle, and the 364th year in the cycle of sabbatical years.

To try to standardize these indications in a consistent chronology, the only conceivable solution is to correct some inscriptions to fit them together, supposing that they may have been changed over time. It is possible to alter the seventh line of the first inscription by turning the word for the number four into a five.[3] The seventh line of the second inscription may also be fixed to form the number 46 by changing the meaning of the term *min* with the letters *mem* and *vav*. Finally, it may be proposed that the start of the era of the *hurban* in the last inscription does not begin in the month of Tishri, but rather on the 9th of the month of Av.[4] Another possibility is offered by taking the "first year of the *shemittah*" in the first inscription as meaning the year before, and the sixth rather than the seventh; for the second, read year 5 instead of year 3.[5] It is hard to make these inscriptions match with jubilee cycles without engaging in conjectures about changes due to time or the engraver's oversight, which, by justifying changing the dates, make them match extant calendrical tables.[6] The argument developed by Ben Zion Wacholder suggests that the first inscription remain unchanged. Indeed, it is the only one that offers guidelines that may be cross-checked with other sources. Year 364 corresponding to the first year of *shemittah* would match year 434/435 of the Julian calendar. This epitaph would fit into the era of the creation of the world, according to the *Seder 'olam*, which states that the Temple was destroyed after a year of fallow fields. Since the number 364 is divisible by 7, it follows that the first year of the destruction was also the first year of the cycle of fallowing. It comes down to identifying the first year of the era of the destruction with the year 3830 of the creation, the year of the effective destruction of the Temple being 3829, which relates to year 4193 of the creation or 363 of the *hurban* in sabbatical years. The first inscription, mentioning the year 364 of the *hurban*, refers to the year 4194 of the creation, or the fifth century CE.[7]

From (the Era of) Destruction to (That of) Creation

The Talmud teaches that the Seleucid era precedes the era of the destruction of the Temple by three hundred and eighty full years or four hundred [years] minus twenty.[8] As we have seen, Jewish texts are full of references and calculations that trace the many temporal markers of the destruction, creation, and Seleucid eras. In addition, there is a permanent discrepancy of a year in calculations by oriental and occidental rabbis during the Middle Ages, which obliged them to adjust their arithmetic to reconcile the dating of the same event. The many disparities in dating found in ancient Jewish texts have led scholars to come up with different theories about the knowledge, if not the influence, of the world era. Ludwig Ideler believed that the sages of the talmudic era did not know about the era of the creation, since it is never mentioned in ancient texts. Indeed, only around the fifth century did it start to circulate between the East and West. To support his thesis, Ideler quotes the seventeenth-century Italian Hebraist Giulio Bartolocci, who states that the era of the creation did not spread until the time of Maimonides in the twelfth century.[9] Internal chronologies used to place the writing of the Jerusalem and Babylonian Talmuds were unaware of this system: "Rabbi Yohanan wrote the Jerusalem Talmud 300 years after the destruction"; "Between the writing of the Mishnah and the signing of the Talmud, 316 years elapsed."[10] In the sixteenth century, writing his *Me'or 'einayim* (The Light of the Eyes), the Italian Jewish humanist Azariah dei Rossi states that this calculation is not as old as it appears and dates from around the tenth century: "We are therefore in a position to state that our people began to use the anno mundi computation, so it would seem, from after the time of Rav Sherira Ga'on, less than six hundred years ago."[11] Confirming this suggestion, Eduard Mahler cites a text by Sherira Ga'on dated to the Seleucid era, leading him to accept the theory that in the eleventh century, Eastern and Palestinian Jews were still unaware of the style of dating by the era of the creation, and so based their chronology on the destruction of the Temple.[12] The argument is easy to defend. As is known, the introduction of an eschatological space of chronology in the Christian world was still in its beginnings. The era of the Incarnation was being established, but this would only come about in Europe after its introduction in the Acts of the Regensburg Concilium Germanicum in 742.[13] Then, a slow process crossed Europe from the tenth century onward, ending in the fourteenth century in Portugal. In the East, translations of the Septuagint and the work of biblical scholars featured calculations of the era of the world, and different

Christian chronologies existed and spread as well. Yet the year of the world set by these methods was not yet really known, and it was only used by some literate people in the Jewish and Christian worlds. Official Jewish documents only employ it in divorce documents, in which people from the East always refer to the Seleucid era. Westerners date based on local reigns until the eleventh century. When datings started to go by the era of the Incarnation of Christ, Jews could no longer continue to register their documents in the same system and had to switch to another one.[14] According to Mahler, this is why dating from the creation of the world, a style still almost unknown in the eleventh century, spread throughout the Jewish world during the twelfth.

This theory may seem convincing in a Western context. Yet to prove its validity, the calculation methods used by sages and rabbis must be studied. How did they place the events mentioned and dated in the Talmud and the *Seder 'olam*? As we have seen, Eastern Jews, except those living in Egypt, who long clung to the Roman system, used the Seleucid era. The *Ge'onim* in Irak were apparently unaware of any other system, even after the Hegira year appeared. Those of Palestine added the Seleucid era to the era of the destruction of the Temple. Although it is found in the ancient chronographers and the Palestinian *Seder 'olam*, dating by the era of the creation seems to have reached Jews in the West through Italy. The Seleucid era was not established in the West, but it was nonetheless known to Jews there through mentions in the Talmud,[15] writings of the *Ge'onim*, and texts in Arabic, which they read widely. It may be noted that some datings made in the West append a Seleucid era—not used by them—to dates based on the year of the world. When dates are compared, this anomaly shows that the start of the Seleucid era was calculated from either 3450 or 3449 of the era of creation, echoing the one-year difference in dating caused by starting in either 311 or 312 BCE. Interpreting this difference caused controversy between Hayyim Yehiel Bornstein and earlier researchers.[16] To grasp the issue, the calculating process used by Rabbenu Tam, a grandson of Rashi, must be studied.[17] Relying on information from the Talmud, Rabbenu Tam counts the Seleucid era in the following way: seeking to establish the year 4909 (AM, which corresponds to 1149 CE) in the seven-year cycle, he finds a relation to the year 1461 of the Seleucid era, which brings him to 1,081 years elapsed since the destruction of the Temple, mentioned in rabbinical sources as being the first of this cycle. The year 4909 coincides with the third year of the sabbatical rotation. These figures, aimed at locating the period of fallow fields, show that the Seleucid era as used by Rabbenu Tam starts in 3449 and not 3450 or 3448. Calculations of scholars whose datings by the destruction or the era of contracts were not simultaneously in effect should be compared. The exception is in Maimonides, who reckons by the Seleucid era, at a time when dating by the era of the destruction had not entirely fallen into disuse. Visibly, different systems of conversion existed between the years of the destruction and those of the world. Rabbis from Africa and Spain, on the one hand, and from Italy and France, on the other, are split between two models. As noted, Maimonides made the year 1107 of the destruction correspond with year 4936 of the creation, which places the link of the first year of the destruction at 3829, such as it is now calculated, equivalent to the year 70 CE. Nonetheless, we saw earlier that the Egyptian Pentateuch located it in the year 69. Nathan ben Jehiel of Rome, author of a talmudic lexicon from the eleventh or twelfth centuries, matches the year 1033 of the destruction with the year 4861 of the creation (1101 CE), the axis being at 3828/3829.[18] Rabbenu Tam works similarly, linking the year 1081 of the destruction of the Temple to 4909/4910 of the world (1149 CE). Isaac ben Abba Mari of Marseilles, a twelfth-century compiler of civil law, matched the year 1111 of the destruction with 4939 (1179 CE), which likewise gives 3828/3829 as the axis according to the position in the year, as we shall see below.[19]

Is this an arithmetical problem? Should the arrow of time be different oriented? From when, then, should counting from the creation of the world be set into motion? The Talmud indicates precisely that changing of dates should be undertaken in the month of Tishri. As stated, another tradition claims that the world was created before, in Nisan or Elul. Are we to start counting the first year from Tishri before the creation or the following year? Indeed, mentions of the era of the creation in terms of *le-yetsirah* or *Beri'at ha-'olam* do not match the same system of references. The narrative of Genesis relates that the world was created on the first day and man on the sixth. The gap between these two events only amounts to five days. However, it does mark a distinction between these concepts. *Barah*, the term that relates to the creation of the universe, is also used to describe God's carrying out an exceptional event in nature.[20] A different term, *yatsar*, is used for forming or fashioning animals and people.[21] Rabbinic arithmetic conveys this nuance by including a one-year discrepancy, holding that the act of creation itself, *ma'aseh be-reshit*, took place on Sunday the 25th of Elul of the year before the real emergence of the human world, *beri'at 'olam*, which occurred with the creation of Adam on Friday the first of Tishri.[22] The first year of the "creation of the universe" thus registers as the second of the "creation."[23] These distinctions seep into astronomical language, since the term "rotation" is used then to discuss the begetting of Adam, *molad Adam*, or the lunar month of Adam. Or primordial begetting, *molad Tohu*—the lunar month of chaos—which in this case, marks a virtual year. In the ninth century, Joseph the *ga'on* of Sura sought to explain this, writing: "For the earth begins to be created on the 25th of Elul, and on Friday, with the creation of Adam, the New Year begins."[24] It becomes understandable why in talmudic and medieval literature there are three different calculations, each of which claims to be made "starting with the creation." The third is the chronology in the *Seder 'olam*, which differs by two years from that currently used. In it, the destruction of the Temple is placed in year 3828 of the era of the creation, which corresponds to 68 CE. Until the tenth century, the count used most often followed talmudic indications and calculated the world's origin starting with the creation of Adam. The datings by *ge'onim* may refer to the primordial appearance.[25] By calculating the date by starting with the year after its creation, the Talmud introduces a constant discrepancy with calculations in the West, where it was determined by making it precede Adam's creation, adding a year to it. Which explains the gap of one or two years found in locating the creation of the world based on the current standard norms.

Seleucid era calculations were based on the year of the destruction of the Temple, which was just after a "year of fallow fields" (information the significance of which is now more apparent). It thus became necessary to modify chronologies to make them match. The many variations found throughout the texts may surely be due to mistakes in calculations or different use of the axis of dating. However, all show how difficult it was for the ancients to place themselves in the same framework, as well as the variations of that framework. In the twelfth century, Abraham bar Hiyya starts with the gap between calculations by people from the West and East who in Seleucid-era dating respectively took either 3449 or 3448 as the reference. He tries to find a solution allowing the three systems to match, since his goal is to permit Jews to celebrate their festivals at appropriate dates:

> If you have a date from the *Seder 'olam* by our tally and are looking for the era of contracts [date], subtract 3,449 from the *Seder 'olam* [date] and you will get the era of contracts [date]. According to people from the East, the destruction of the Second Temple occurred in [the year] 3828 of the world, and 380 years elapsed between that and the contracts; if you have the *Seder 'olam* at hand and you are looking for the destruction, subtract 3,828 from the *Seder 'olam* [date] and the remainder will be the era of the destruction [date]. If you have the era of the destruction of the Temple [date] and you are looking for the tally of the *Seder 'olam*, add 3,828 and you will obtain the era of the *Seder 'olam*. Yet if you have in mind *shetarot* [deeds dated according to the Seleucid era or the era of contracts] and want to know the era of the destruction of the Temple, subtract 380 years from contracts and the remainder will be the [era of] destruction [date]. If you are thinking of the destruction and seek the era of contracts [date], add 380 to the contracts [date] and you will get it. We know that the exodus from Egypt took place in 2448 of the world and between the exodus from Egypt and the destruction of the Temple, 1,380 years elapsed. Between the exodus from Egypt and the start of the era of contracts, one thousand full years elapsed.[26]

The sabbatical year was suspended in Roman Palestine for tax reasons and reasonably enough not observed in countries of the Diaspora. However, with its references to freeing slaves and forgiving debts, it remained a key theoretical reference point in the makeup of Jewish temporality. Aware of the complexity of an approach trying to match the different kinds of temporal markers, Bar Hiyya tried to explain the structure of the history of sabbatical and jubilee cycles. He concludes that it is impossible to correlate these cycles by simply following the year of creation or any other original base, since three major changes occurred over time. The first cycle was introduced in 2502, fourteen years after the Israelites entered Palestine in 2489 since the creation of the world. The first year of fallow fields was in 2509, reaching its jubilee year in 2552 AM. Observed continuously until the fall of Samaria in 3037, the years accumulated, forming cycles that started every fifty-one years. After the exile of "two tribes and an half tribe,"[27] these cycles were interrupted and jubilees followed one another every forty-nine years until the fall of Jerusalem in 3338. Seventy years later, during the Second Temple period, the fifty-year cycle was restored to stress the continuity between the return of the exiles and the previous occupation of the land. Yet in the absence of most of the people, this cycle counted the fiftieth year as both the end of the old and start of the new jubilee. Since the restoration occurred in the twenty-eighth year of the cycle, it began the following year and continued thus through the ages.[28]

If, like Ideler and Mahler, one focuses exclusively on the style of dating shown in official documents, one might suppose that the era of the destruction of the Temple was solely used for theological purposes. Yet the absence of any mention of the era of the destruction in divorce proceedings, for example, does not disprove the popularity of this marker, certified by many other sources in Palestine and Italy. The Babylonian Talmud only mentions it once, citing the Palestinian Amora Rabbi Hanina: "four hundred years after the destruction of the Temple." It is also only mentioned once in the Jerusalem Talmud, specifying that the length of existence of the Betar fortress was fifty-two years after the destruction of the Temple, and in a midrash.[29] The *Seder ʿolam zutta* reckons the length of time the First Temple existed according to the era of the creation of the world, and that of the Second by the Seleucid era, combined with the reigns of the Hasmonean and Herodian dynasties. The next period follows the era of the destruction, which is cited five times.[30] Many other writings powerfully show its symbolic and temporal reference value: "Ever since *Beit Hayeinu* [the House of our life] was destroyed, since a week, since a jubilee, since 777 years (and now it's already [the year] 1151)," the ninth-century Pesikta Rabbati says; in other words, all the permutations of the number seven have already gone by since the Temple was destroyed, over 777 years have elapsed.[31] "Three thousand four hundred and eight years. Since the building of the last Temple until its destruction, four hundred and twenty years. Since its destruction until now, nine hundred years," the tenth-century *Seder Eliyahu rabbah* records.[32] The author of the *piyyutim*, Eleazar Kalir, also using the date of the destruction of the Temple, adds: "900 and more . . ."[33] Another poet, Haduta (also known as Hedvata) ben Abraham, laments: "Where are your first righteous people [*hassidim*]? How long must we labor for the *admonim* [red people]? Here we are already at seven hundred and sixty-five years!"[34] As late as the eighteenth century a specimen marriage certificate entitled *ketubbah yerushalmit*, clearly translated from an Aramean text, can also be found, indicating: "On this Shabbat, this day of the month, such and such year of the creation of the month and the destruction of the holy Temple, may it be rebuilt quickly in our time and before the eyes of all Israel."[35] The era of destruction is also found cited in Karaite documents and seems to have spread widely among them, although the Seleucid era is also found cited there.[36] An Egyptian prayer ritual affirms: "I, Moshe son of Asher, I wrote this ritual . . . in the land of Maziah [Tiberias], the holy city, completed 827 years after the destruction of the Second Temple."[37]

Epitaphs and Colophons

Uncovering the range of epitaphs inscribed by Jews over the course of time displays fluctuation in framing a Jewish temporal era. Thus, epigraphy provides more accurate snapshots of dating usage at given points in time than lengthy theoretical demonstrations can. Before cemeteries attested to the adoption of the era of the world, catacombs and scattered stones reflected its gradual emergence, recording deaths for eternity. Epitaphs thus date the escape from the arithmetic of temporality more extensively than the simple register of writings by the literate. Persisting use of the era of the destruction of the Temple is found in lands where Palestinian religious authorities still held sway.[38] It can still be followed in Italy through funerary epigraphy, where it presents itself in various forms: *mi she-harav ha-bayyit*, "since the House has been destroyed," *mi-she-harav beyt ha-mikdash*, "since the house of the Temple has been destroyed"; *le-hurban ha-bayyit*, "from the destruction of the House"; *le-hurban beyt ha-mikdash*, "from the destruction of the house of the Temple"; *le-hurban beyt ha-mikdash ha-kadosh*, "from the destruction of the Holy Temple." Graziadio Isaia Ascoli published instructive epitaphs in the nineteenth century that can serve as examples, although some of them were no longer readable in his time, and he had to reproduce earlier copies of unverified texts. Ten inscriptions from the ninth century show this practice of dating, between the years 730 and 770 of the destruction of the Temple, or 4579 and 4599 of years of the creation.[39] Here are some epigraphs from Brindisi, Venosa, and Lavello:

> Here lies Lea, daughter of Yaffa Mazal. May her soul rejoin the body of the living. Deceased, from when the Temple was destroyed to her death, 764 years [832 CE], and the days of her life were 17 years . . .

> Here is buried . . . son of Yaim [*Binyamin* or *Hayyim?*], [who] died at the age of 36 in the year seven hundred and fifty-four of the destruction of the Holy Temple [822 CE]. May it be rebuilt during the days of all Israel.

> This sign marks the tomb of Notari, son of Yaim [*Binyamin* or *Hayyim?*], [who] died at the age of 25. May peace be with his eternal rest and his soul rejoin the body of the living. May his death be his pardon and atonement for all his sins. Since the Temple has been destroyed, 770 years [838 CE]. May it be rebuilt in our days and in the days of all Israel. Amen.

> May the memory of Malka be a blessing. Here lies Malka, wife of Liqhi, who left her husband, God-fearingly, at the age of 62, and this year was the seven hundred and forty-second [810 CE] from the destruction of the Temple, may it be rebuilt during the days of all Israel and may her soul rejoin the body of the living, may her soul live in peace, may her bones flourish like an herb [Isa. 66:14] . . . for an eternal life. Amen.[40]

A mixture of the eras of destruction and creation is found in the same era on the tombs of Venosa:

> Here is the resting place of Joseph, son of Benjamin, dead at 35 [or 75], in the year 4582 of the creation of the world, 753 years of the destruction of the Holy Temple [821 CE]. May it be rebuilt in our days and during the days of all Israel. Amen . . ."

> Ah, all of you who pass by again and again, lament the death of a young man! Here Caleb achieved his rest, in his sleep. Ask the mercy of He who created him for him, so that you too may gain the mercy of He who created you. For he died at the age of 23, before

fathering children, in the year 4587 of the creation of the world, 759 years of the destruction of the house of the Temple [827 CE].[41]

Some dates mentioned in the ninth-century Italian inscriptions raise a familiar conundrum. Dated for the most part by the era of the destruction, they are sometimes embellished by the era of the creation, which shows a regular gap of one year, since the era of destruction is sometimes counted from the year 3828 of the creation, and sometimes from the year 3829, that is to say, either 68 or 69 CE. To explain this discrepancy, Umberto Cassutto reasons in terms of the calendar. The "era of the *hurban*" starts two months before the end of the year, on the ninth or tenth of Av, the tenth lunar month of the Jewish year. Locating the year of the creation starting from the era of the *hurban* depends on the placement of the event that we wish to date in the course of the month. If it falls in the part of the year between Rosh Ha-shanah and the start of the month of Av, 3829 must be taken as the start of the era of the creation. But if it occurred between Tisha B'Av, the fast of the ninth of Av, and the end of the month of Elul, the years since the *hurban* must be counted only from 3828.[42] That references to the era of the destruction of the Temple were still common in the ninth century did not prevent Shabbetai Donnolo from stating in the preface to the commentary on the *Sefer Yetsirah* that he had left his birthplace on the "ninth day of the month of Tammuz in the year 4685 [925 CE] since the creation of the world that is the eleventh year of the 247th cycle" and was writing in that "unwise generation of our time in the year 4742 [982 CE] since the creation of the world, which is the eleventh year of the 250th cycle."[43] In 1881, after a trip to the Crimea, Daniel Chwolson brought back some inscriptions from the cemetery of Chufut-Kale.[44] Written entirely in Hebrew, they seemed to be well enough preserved to be dated securely. One, whose text is missing, dates to 4373 *le-yetsirah*, or 613 CE, while two others, whose epitaphs are complete, date to the fourth century:

Here is the stone which I placed at the head of the tomb of Joseph, son of Elijah, dead in 4136 of the creation [376 CE].

This is the gravestone of the tomb of Golaph, daughter of Shabbatai, who died in year 4108 of the creation [348 CE].[45]

In the absence of any indication other than the year, it is quite risky to challenge a reading and revise the numbers. If, however, these inscriptions were accurate, then they were truly the oldest known Jewish epitaphs to refer to the era of the world.[46] It remains for specialists in calculation to decide about the inscription according to *le-yetsirah*, which would seem to have followed, and not preceded as it did here, the one of *le-beri'at 'olam.*[47]

As for Italian tombs, only after the twelfth century in Benevento and Trani did they date solely by the era of the world:

The fourth day of the week, the 21 of the moon of [Kislev] of the year 4914 of the creation [9 December 1153 in the Julian calendar] rab. Jacob, son of Hezekiah, the venerable master, aged 70 . . .

Here lies Zipora, virtuous lady, daughter of master . . . , wife of . . . , died the 24 Kislev of the year [5]252 [26 November 1491 in the Julian calendar].[48]

Colophons may also turn out to be a source of the unexpected. It is scarcely surprising to find dating by the era of the destruction of the Temple in certain Italian works up to 1441. It is doubtless more so to also find Christian forms of dating in Jewish holy books.[49] As Michael Riegler notes, this singularity appeared in the fourteenth century, in an Italian colophon dated 1383, now in Paris.[50] The coexistence of Christian days and months with numbers of Jewish temporality surely bothered no rabbinic authority: "This sacred work was completed the 21st of the second month of Adar, 21 March of the year [5] 293" (i.e., 1533). Completed twenty years later, the Ferrara Bible clearly divides the dating processes according to religion. Its Judaeo-Spanish (Ladino) language version is dated 1 March 1553. The Hebrew indicates 14 Adar 5313. Whereas only the names of publisher and printer are given in Ladino, in the Hebrew version they identify themselves as Jews.[51] This rare instance of a colophon in which the year of the Christian era is conflated, all of a piece, with the era of the creation is, however, somewhat disconcerting: "Completed . . . the sixth day, 11 of the month of Nisan, the year [5]249 of the creation, which is the 16th of the month of March in the year 1489 for Christians."[52]

It may be unsound to draw conclusions based on these few scattered data. Analyzing the forty-one inscriptions published by Ascoli reveals that only thirteen of them contain dates, perhaps because of changes to them or their not being engraved on stone. Eight place themselves according to the era of the destruction of the Temple, two combine the era of the destruction with the era of the creation, and three only take account of the era of the world. Their literary form and use of first letters instead of spelled-out numbers already show classical dating, especially in instances of "small calculation," where the number of the fifth millennium is only implied.[53] The few examples cited here show the development of the general nature of such epitaphs. The oldest ones appearing in lists, engraved in Latin or Greek, note the Jewish origin of people whose first names alone are used, with a Jewish symbol or transliterated Hebrew word.[54] They gradually grow more verbose, including a Hebrew term, often *shalom* (peace), as in the Hebraic epigraphs noted in Palestine; then they mention the names of fathers and sometimes spouses, of the deceased. Starting with the seventh century, the vernacular yields to Hebrew throughout southern Italy.[55] The inscriptions that are partially translated here as examples, mainly from the ninth and twelfth centuries, are wholly written in Hebrew. Some, in a lyrical style akin to mournful Victorian verse, address the memories and emotions of passers-by.[56] As the texts are padded, the datings become more exact. In the first centuries of the common era, epitaphs in catacombs do not bear dates.[57] Later, reminders of the era of the destruction of the Temple develop. Days are added, first emerging as we have seen, in an inscription from Zoara, then months, and finally the era of the world. These additions refer precisely to the process of liturgical standardization under way in the same space-time.[58]

Arranging Temporality

One observation must be made about dating conversion. There is a regular two-year discrepancy when the usual conversion tables are used to match dates of the Jewish era converted into the common era by Ascoli for his epigraphs. However, in theory the calculation is fairly simple. It can be done in two ways, by subtracting or adding, keeping in mind that the Jewish year changes in Tishri/September, while the Christian one does so in January. The common era date can be found by deducting 3,760 for the era of the Incarnation from the year of the world. Or 240 can be added to the year of the world to find the CE date (minus the thousandth). However, in the examples presented here, when we use the year 70 as a reference for dates according to the era of the destruction of the Temple, while the era of the world is held to commence in 3830, a further discrepancy of two years occurs compared to the number for the year of the world. It then becomes impossible to make it match with the date obtained by Ascoli according to the Christian era. Let us retrace our steps. The inscription from Brindisi gives only the era of the destruction year 764, which Ascoli converts to 832 CE. Adding 764 to 70, we obtain 834. The same is true for the inscription from Venosa: to the era of the destruction year 754, we add 70, giving 824, converted by Ascoli to 822 CE. It is the same in every case. For Ascoli's dating to be exactly correct, the era of the destruction must be taken as a reference point (according to the year 3828 or 3829) as the rabbinic method provides. In this way the axis of the destruction of the Temple does not refer to 70, as in the custom of the current tables of conversion, but in the year 68, as the *Seder 'olam* affirms. We may conclude that the system used by Ascoli to match inscriptions with the common era is based on ancient Jewish arithmetic.

Incidentally, this arithmetical model is the one that should be used to place medieval Jewish datings. Datings for the following two colophons will illustrate this suggestion. They also could have supported the argument about the disparities in the systems spread across different communities in the West and East, had the explanation of the rabbinic process used in this case not been of yet another kind.

The first text is from Italy: " . . . completed the third Shabbat (in the third week) the 21st day of the moon of Elul, year five thousand and one hundred and fifty-two years from the creation and one thousand three hundred twenty-four from the destruction of the Temple. May it rapidly be rebuilt in our days . . ." The operation is then easily performed. When we subtract 1,324 (for the destruction) from 5152 (the era of the world), we obtain the axis of 3828, which places the year of the destruction of the Temple at 68. Then the date of the Christian era is Tuesday 10 September 1392 in the Julian calendar.

The second indicates: "25th day of the moon of Sivan, 1738 of the era of contracts, 5187 of the creation, 1358 of the destruction of the Second

Temple."[59] Taking 1,358 away from 5187, we get 3829 for the axis, then in converting the year 5187 to the era of the Incarnation, the date of Friday 20 June 1427 in the Julian calendar. This colophon, from Yemen, could have been dated using the Eastern axis suggested by Bar Hiyya.[60] However, it seems to use the Western axis of a destruction set in the year 69, as was the case of Rabbenu Tam.[61] Here the division between East and West would seem to be contradicted by geography. The Italian colophon follows the Eastern system of dating, whereas inversely, the Yemenite one is part of the Western system. Yet observing the position of months indicated in the Jewish year, the first colophon, written on 21 Elul, is located after 9 Av and before the end of the month of Elul. According to the previously discussed demonstration by Cassuto, it calls for 3828 as its axis, whereas the second, placed in Sivan, between Rosh Ha-shanah and the 9th of Av, requires using 3829 as axis.[62] Location in the era of the destruction of the Temple is thus based not only on position in the era of the world, but also on the calendar.

Edgar Frank analyzes another method of calculation, perceiving five systems of which three main ones overlap, helping to locate the era of the world. Noting these three major models, which he names AM1, AM2, and AM3, Frank manages to reconcile calculations of the ancients and the moderns. He establishes that the drift between the years 3828 and 3830, which is to say 68 or 70 CE, marking the destruction of the Second Temple, is simply a matter of whether one uses year zero or year one.

Called *BeHaR"D* in Jewish sources, AM1 must be understood as the transposition of numerical values of letters in Hebrew (see the table in the Appendix, p. 235): the *b*, corresponding to the number two = the second day, or Monday; *H* = 5; the fifth hour after the start of Monday = Sunday, 11 p.m.; *Resh"Daleth* = 204 = 204 fractions of hours = 11 minutes, 20 seconds. The AM1 method starts twelve months before creation and is part of the virtual chronology that precedes creation. It refers to the *molad Tohu*, and only the five last days and fourteen hours are part of the order of creation.[63]

The AM2 method, which is found in sources known as *VeY"D*, means: Vav = 6, or the sixth day = Friday; *Yod"Dalet* = 14, or 14 hours after Thursday (i.e., 6 p.m.) = Friday at 8 a.m. AM2 marks a count that is performed starting from the creation of Adam.

The new year of AM3 begins at the moment when the third year of AM1 rejoins the second year of AM2, according to the formula *G' K"B TT'V*, which is deciphered as follows: Gimmel = 3, or the third day, Tuesday; *Kaf"Bet* = 22, or 22 hours after Monday at noon, which is to say, 4 p.m on Tuesday.

TavTav'Vav = 876, or 876 fractions of hours = 48 minutes, 40 seconds. This principle of calculation refers to the year when Adam was one year old. AM3 relates to the age of humanity.[64]

The Coming of the Era of the World

In the absence of a standard uniformly spread throughout the entire Jewish world, people who lived in Islamic or Christian countries did their respective dating by observing rules of conversion. It seems that it was easily acknowledged that by the aforementioned talmudic formula, the year of the destruction formed the year 380/81 of the era of contracts. In the tenth century in North Africa, Rav Nissim Ga'on confirms that the completion of the Mishnah occurred in the year 530 of contracts, which corresponds to 150 of the destruction.[65] This agrees with the Spaniard Yehudah Halevi at about the same time: "The *Mishnah* was compiled in the year 530, according to the era of the "Documents" [Seleucid era], which corresponds to the year 150 after the destruction of the Temple, and 530 years after the termination of prophecy."[66] And when Maimonides mentions the year 1487 of contracts, stating that it corresponds to the year 1107 of the destruction, or that year 1489 of contracts is equivalent to the year 1109, he confirms the use of the interval of 380 years reported in the Talmud. A final example, drawn from the beginning of a book by Abba Mari ben Moses ben Joseph, will enable us to grasp the reasoning that rabbi's calculations used to situate temporality: "Today we count 4,939 years since the creation of the world, which corresponds to 1491 of the Seleucid era, which is 1931 of the building of the Temple and 1111 of the *hurban*—may it be rebuilt promptly in our days—and 2491 since the exodus from Egypt."[67] To understand these indications, we must follow these procedures: to arrive at dating according to the Christian era, we must first relocate the axis of destruction: 4939 minus 1111 equals 3828;

the axis is placed at 68 CE. In this way, by adding 1111 to 68, we arrive at 1179 CE. Then, to follow the data that are obtained and grasp the structure of the Seleucid era, we subtract 380 from 1491, which refers to the indication given by the era of the destruction of the Temple, namely, 1111, whose Seleucid axis (4939–1111) is 3448. The exodus from Egypt (4939–2491) is an exact match for the rabbinic date of 2448. The sum of these calculations routinely corresponds to the givens established by tradition. Only one element disrupts these operations. Placement starting with the building of the Temple (4939–1931) brings us to 3008, and the duration would be 820 years, which corresponds with nothing identifiable. However, by removing one of the two *tav* whose numerical value is 400, we return to the commonly accepted figure of 420 years. If we assume that the transcription contains a duplication, the approaches established by the *Seder ʿolam* and the Talmud are thus found together again in the twelfth century.

Standardizing dating benchmarks also emerges from the need to solve practical questions. An intriguing example, if not direct cause, is divorce legislation. The model Aramean marriage certificate still currently used then recalls the diversity of styles of dating in the Jewish world by specifying the date of the ceremony "according to the method that we use here in the city of . . . ," but writing a divorce decree required strictness. Indeed, to settle the legitimacy of a birth or remarriage, the date on a document had to match temporal criteria known everywhere. The Mishnah set the canons of validity for the decree: "written under an authority no longer in force, the kingdom of Media or Greece, starting with the building of the Temple or the destruction of the Temple, the *get* [divorce decree] is invalid; for these eras do not correspond with the views of sages who have established that in divorce decrees the era of the reign of the current king must be noted."[68] Rambam commented: "From this, it was decided to count in divorce decrees according to the country's current monarchies, to 'keep peace with the monarchy' and not by virtue of a monarchy from another country, whether in terms of the building or destruction of the Temple. . . . Israel already had the habit of citing the creation or the reign of Alexander of Macedon, which is the Seleucid era, in divorce decrees."[69] We may assume that due to variations in different indicators of "current reigns," gradually the fourteenth-century rule came into effect: "Everywhere the custom is to count beginning with the creation of the world."[70] This dating according to "the creation" had to be unified. Which is why in *Ashkenaz,* the eleventh-century ritual book *Mahzor Vitry* states: "He who writes a divorce decree, when it is a matter of a style [of dating] that we do not use here, will mention the place where the scribe is located at the time of writing as well as where the witnesses are located at the time of signing. He will also specify the place of residence of the husband and wife at the moment of writing the divorce decree."[71] After this statement intended for the scribe, the book next offers the standard format for the decree, written, it is mentioned, following the model created by Rabbi Jacob ben Meir, Rabbenu Tam: "In the week of such a parashah, which day of the month in such a moon, in this or that year of the creation of the world according to the count we use here, in such a place, by such a river . . ."[72]

Twelve Exercises in Rabbinic Thought

That the calendrical era of the creation of the world finally incorporated standard practices by medieval scribes and rabbis shows that an
"accounting" system of temporality had become rooted in concepts
and customs. This measure of time became habitual after a slow process that led to a distinction between the time of the origins of the
world [creation] and that of the history of mankind. This distinction
provides two axes of time, allowing us to differentiate between time
scales in the biblical narrative. Differentiation between different biblical times is especially detectable in the conformity of dating of the end
of the prophecy about Alexander's conquest. The mishnaic Judaization
of the Seleucid era, confirmed by the *Seder 'olam*, shows a will to impose a Jewish thread of continuity on universal chronology. We have
seen how the calculations of elapsed time, devised according to different cultural models followed by the communities of the East and
West, all aimed to create a unified model of Jewish temporality. This
conceptualization of a specifically Jewish temporality follows a school
of thought begun long before these communities emerged as rivals
for spiritual leadership of the Jewish world. How was this notion of
changing time to a Jewish temporality arranged within tradition? Studies of the case presented in this chapter shed light on historical development that began after a series of singular events, the restoration of
the kingdom and national history. This development is expressed in
determining the canon and Jewish text of the Bible in treating both
events and the calendar. These, in turn, reflect the relationship to history which underlie the building of time perceived by Jewish criteria
of understandability.

The Event: Between History and Prophecy

Setting aside specific problems linked to questions of chronology, dating, and issues of power, temporality is also based on the capacity conferred on the event to play a part in history and be situated in time. Among later books of the Bible, Maccabees and Daniel share the feature of describing a key period in the history of the Near East in general, and Jews in particular, following the Greek world's violent intrusion into its ancient civilizations. The shock that followed had significant impacts in the political, cultural, and religious realms for all the peoples involved in this conquest. Although the return under Persian rule of the exiles from Babylon concludes the Bible's account of the national history of the people of Israel, the Greek invasion awoke a strong sense of nationalism, which led to political and spiritual recovery and the reinstatement of a Jewish kingdom in Palestine. Nevertheless, this finds no place in Jewish writings, and tradition would reduce it to the establishment of a new ritual celebration. This factual lack led to it being asserted that Jews neglected history, at least that of the present, which will be tomorrow's past, to focus on eternity.

Comparing the narrative forms of the books of Maccabees and Daniel allows us to grasp the content of events described in the context of their temporality. Briefly mentioned earlier to shed light on issues of the positioning of the axis of time, the books of Maccabees indicate the difference between the calendar used in starting the year based on the Seleucid era by the Jews of Palestine and those of the Diaspora. As for the Book of Daniel, it reveals a form of eschatological structure of time. These books' treatment of historical events—typical of contemporary Judaism's approach to temporality—tells much about central elements in the evolution of prerabbinic thought.

The Books of Maccabees

Gathered under a single title, but written by two authors answering different narrative aims, these two books describe the tribulations the Jews were subjected to during the reign of the Seleucid monarch Antiochus IV Epiphanes [175–164 BCE]. The revolt that followed and the takeover by the Hasmonean dynasty provides background for the end of the Second Temple era: rivalries, conspiracies, wars, power struggles, and the process of change linked to Hellenization.

Josephus offers an account of these happenings,[1] but all historical memory of them has been erased in Jewish tradition, which retains only the celebration of the festival of Hanukkah from 25 Kislev (December) to 2 Tevet, which commemorates the purification and rededication of the Temple after its desecration. Its duration of eight days symbolizes the miracle of lamps that burned beyond their natural capacity, leaving the Jews time to produce more pure oil for the candelabrum (menorah) of the Temple.[2] Jewish tradition says nothing of the situation that led to this reconsecration, apart from its association with the Maccabean family. Since the books of Maccabees were not accepted in the biblical canon, perhaps only some vague references to these pages of history may have survived in later chroniclers, little concerned with the Hasmonean victory, had not Greek translations preserved an account of it.[3] Apart from a few dates, the Talmud contains nothing about the Maccabean revolt that might add details of a factual nature. Although the "Hasmonean house" and the high priest Mattathias are mentioned, neither Judah nor his brothers figure in it. Only Josephus reported the victorious saga, an overture to the successive wars that led to the decimation of the kingdom and the fall of the Temple. Preserved in the Septuagint, the two books of Maccabees were included in the Christian Old Testament without the story that they tell having been recorded in the patrimony of Jewish tradition. This fact alone might raise some questions. Saint Augustine writes:

> From this time, after the restoration of the temple, it was no kings who ruled in Judea but princes, down to the time of Aristobulus. The reckoning of their dates is not to be found, in the Holy Scriptures which are called "canonical", but in other documents, which include the books of the Maccabees. These are regarded as canonical by the Church, (though not by the Jews), because of the savage, the amazing sufferings endured by some of the martyrs, who, before Christ's coming in his human body, contended even unto death, for the cause of God's law, and held firm under the most appalling agonies."[4]

However, it would be false to conclude that this Christian appropriation might have had any influence on the inclusion of the Maccabees in Jewish sacred history. The canon had already been defined before-hand.[5] It might be useful to grasp the reason why the described events are not included in the Jewish tradition. The content of these stories seem up to the standards of the narration of works otherwise retained.[6]

The first book of Maccabees, originally written in Hebrew, seems to have been composed during the reign of John Hyrcanus (134–104 BCE) as an official chronicle for the dynasty.[7] The second appears to be a summary of five works written by a Jew of the Diaspora named Jason of Cyrene, about whom nothing more is known.[8] For reasons that remain unclear in the first book,[9] the Seleucid king Antiochus IV Epiphanes launched a campaign of unprecedented religious oppression, using every possible means to prevent Jews from preserving their customs, turning religious taboos into requirements and obligations into proscriptions. Circumcision and study of the Torah were banned on pain of death, houses and the Temple were desecrated, sacrifices were misappropriated, and pork became required eating. Everything seems to have been implemented to paganize the Jews of Jerusalem and Judea, but without their coreligionists in other lands being threatened in the least. The zealots revolted, managed to overcome armed troops, captured the city and cleansed it, reconsecrated the Temple, and put the Hasmonean dynasty on the throne. All Jews were ordered to celebrate 25 Kislev in memory of these happenings; one of the aims of 2 Maccabees seems, in fact, to have been the institution of the celebration of Hanukkah itself. Many historical studies have been written about all this,[10] so it is not necessary to go into detail here, but a brief summary is needed. 1 Maccabees covers a period of forty years, between the accession of Antiochus in 175 BCE and the coronation of John Hyrcanus in 134 BCE. The book is divided into three parts, each of which describes the brave deeds of the three sons of Mattathias, instigator of the revolt, whom Judah, Jonathan, and Simon followed as resistance leaders. Clearly written by a Hasmonean follower, the text does not get bogged down in subtleties. All adversaries, whether Seleucid or Pharisee, are depicted as enemies and heathen. Jews who did not support the rebellion are traitors and turncoats. The tale as a whole recounts God's triumph over idolaters and the doing of religious justice.

2 Maccabees is not intended as the continuation of the first book. Perhaps written in Palestine during the reign of Alexander Jannaeus

(103–76 BCE), it offers another account of the same events, composed in Greek for Alexandrian Jews, as one of the two letters as preamble indicates. It covers a reduced period of about fifteen years by starting the narration earlier in time, during the reign of Seleucus IV Philopator, who preceded Antiochus, and ending it with the defeat of Nicanor, before the death of Judah Maccabee. The first book is factual, narrating details of the discord and wars by the Jews against the Gentiles, without shedding light on the conditions that led to them. In contrast, the second reads into the facts from an eschatological viewpoint and is much more concerned with the edifying, rather than the bellicose, aspects of this revolt. Yet only after reading the second text does the obscurity of the situation and incidents discussed in the first become clearer. The point of the second book is to create a new festivity within the ceremonies of Judaism, and so it focuses on the religious basis. This is perhaps why most of the text describes the sanctity of the restored Temple and seeks to establish the miraculous side of the warlike upheaval that let to its reconsecration. Yet it is due to this text that it can be grasped why a Seleucid king championed a religion that he did not observe. The violent eruption into Jewish religious life of Antiochus IV Epiphanes resulted from conflicts between the partisans of Hellenism and its enemies that wracked the Jews of Jerusalem. Two millennia later, Elias Bickerman argued that Antiochus was summoned to aid aristocrats and lapsed priests who supported assimilation.[11] While each book focuses on repressive measures against observant Jews, the first emphasizes accounts of rebel battles, while the second prioritizes the martyrdom of the resistance fighters.

For historical temporality, anecdotes mean little here. Clearly, the time of the tale differs from that of the narrations of the Pentateuch. In this text, as in Esther, Daniel, and some prophets, there is no point in trying to cling to datings of scripture. The first book starts with the conquest by Alexander the Great, placing it immediately in the Seleucid era, called the "kingdom of the Greeks." The viewpoint of the recounted event remains that of the triumph of prophecy, for as the last message of Mattathias affirms: "And thus consider ye throughout all ages, that none that put their trust in him shall be overcome. Fear not then the words of a sinful man: for his glory shall be dung and worms."[12] Yet this prophecy is clearly over, referring to a hope based on past history. The use of Seleucid sources is more noteworthy, although commonplace. The author of 1 Maccabees did not try to standardize them with those applicable in Jerusalem. This is indicated by the statement that Epiphanes ascended the throne "in the hundred and thirty and seventh year of the kingdom of the Greeks" (1 Macc. 1:10), which is only plausible if the axis is restored to the Macedonian scale of autumn 312. These shiftings of axes are interesting insofar as they mainly occur when the facts described relate to events in general, blunders to be found in Josephus and many other ancient authors.[13] For them, consistency in dates, which is hard to achieve without a widespread uniform style, is not the main purpose of the accounts. Yet it may be noted that the narrative model of the first book approaches chronological precision more than the second, usually reporting years, months, and days in which incidents occur, as well as their duration. This is a basic difference between these stories and the account in the Book of Daniel, which, in chapter 11, also provides a description. While sharing the same assumption of a history with a divine leadership, the historical vision in the books of Maccabees remains more precise, less allusive, and in this way, cannot be a universal system. It remains linked to special events, taken as instruments of the divine plan. To be sure, kings are mere pawns of the punishment that God intends to mete out to his people, only to bring the faithful to see the error of their ways. This vision of the completion of the divine plan in the history of the Jews oddly recurs in the third century, written by Philostratus of Lemnos: "After Titus had taken Jerusalem . . . [he said] that it was not himself that had accomplished this exploit, but that he had merely lent his arm to God, who had so manifested his wrath."[14] So, events only have meaning from an ethico-religious viewpoint, showing the grip of God on human temporality. Time revealed here cannot be seen as "Jewish" by reason of its contents. Its flow remains that of the nations, in this case, the Seleucid Empire. Its starting point highlights a local pace that subsumes the differences that elsewhere exist between how Jews of Palestine and Babylon interpret the start of the year. With some caution, we may identify a dual aspect of time when 1 Maccabees, while stating that the year 170 is the start of the era of "Simon the High Priest," continues its tale without any narrative break, adding that Jews entered the citadel on the 23rd of the second month of the year 171.[15]

In the religious history of the Jews, the two centuries that surround the fall of the Temple, between 135 BCE and 70 CE, may be seen as ones of clashes between different streams of Judaism, typified by the fights between Sadducees and Pharisees, until the latter finally won. The books of Maccabees locate exactly this key point in the changing of beliefs. 1 Maccabees distances itself from Israel's past, bluntly proclaiming the end of the era of prophecy. No one knew what to do with the desecrated altar, it tells us, so they "pulled it down" and stored it "until there should come a prophet." A similar expression is also used about the choice of Simon, presented as valid "until there should arise a faithful prophet."[16] The rebels counted no prophet or messiah among themselves. Still, God was with them in their struggles, but these men guided their own destinies, while waiting for a sign to be disclosed. 2 Maccabees confirms the introduction of doctrines clearly dividing the domains of here below and the beyond. Biblical stories recount irreversible death and an unheard *sheol*.[17] Reading the books of Maccabees, we see the emergence of practices integrating ritual and attitudes. Judah's prayer for redeeming the souls of sinners shows that death is no longer an end.[18] Just as the focus on stories of martyrs shows that the resurrection is confidently, if not ardently, expected: "Thou . . . destroyest us out of this present life: but the King of the world will raise us up, who die for his laws, in the resurrection of eternal life."[19] This doctrine of future life, specified by the principle of retribution to come, *ba ʿolam ha-ba'a*, for deeds done here below, *ba ʿolam ha-zeh*, probably current in some Jewish circles for some time, is confirmed by the books of Daniel and Enoch, written more or less during the same era. In this way, the books of Maccabees show us the triumph of the faith in the world to come over the finiteness of the present one, specific to Sadducean beliefs still expressed in Sirach.[20] Hence, the victory of the oral law over the written law.[21] Momigliano believes that the exclusion of the Maccabees, like that of Josephus, from Hebraic Jewish literature is one of the facets of the denial of history that Jews developed after the fall of the Temple.[22] He thus supports the analyses mentioned in Part I of this book. Yet this charge is not enough to complete understanding or capture the ongoing phenomenon and process in Judaism. Possibly, if not probably, the historical nature of these narratives worked against their inclusion in the heritage, but other factors may have also taken part in this vanishing.

Daniel

The influence of Hellenistic culture throughout the Book of Daniel has already been thoroughly studied, especially in terms of the doctrine of the succession of four empires, at the origin of which is Zoroastrianism as well as Hesiod.[23] We saw above what reading this text might offer in terms of an eschatological window. Instead, we shall now read it as a form of history-making. Without ever being directly mentioned in the Book of Daniel, Antiochus IV's tyranny and abuse of the Jews are described in detail, as having to occur "till the [divine] indignation be accomplished."[24] In this way, it affirms, as do the books of Maccabees, that the Jews were punished because of evils committed against their God, and not because of a revolt against public policy. The question of when the whole text was written is vital for its analysis, but one moment will be taken into account here, located somewhere between the start of Alexander's reign and the Hasmonean victory.[25] Its author or authors are less important than the data it may convey about its relationship to history. Yet its style only allows speculative readings, so it is difficult to make a documentary source of it. Seen as an apocalyptic account of a point in history, it may offer some facts. In terms of the vision described, the surrounding world is more nightmare than paradise. The Greek Empire is depicted as a monstrous animal. If so, nothing comparable can be found in the bestiary of known creatures. The text suggests the notion of a huge divide between the past and the present time, whose destructive element is indicated in the voracious nature of the beast. Beyond any theological consideration, it is a question of social and political changes that alter the course of things by acting on daily and traditional life.

Persian rule as described in the Book of Daniel differs greatly from Macedonian rule. Unlike Eastern princes, Greek kings are inaccessible, distant, and rigid. Their iron jaws suggest impersonal, almost mechanical cruelty.[26] The description of the fourth empire that, by arising, reduces the three previous ones, while daring to "think to change times and laws," is an almost explicit reference to Alexander.[27] The Macedonian's name remains linked in passing to the Seleucid era, as we have seen. Read in this context, the Macedonian conquest creates such a violent break with the old order that the only alternative is divine intervention. As in 1 Maccabees, Antiochus extends the process begun by Alexander. Yet unlike its presentation in that book, Daniel makes of it an infernal advent. The people who inhabit this empire, who in the Maccabean books are sometimes compassionate and helpful, are here inhuman and create an evil spirit. Moreover, this story is made apocalyptic by the systematic division between the realms of good and evil, order and chaos, as well as the war between good and evil, ending in divine victory. Even more, the text takes an important step forward. Suggesting a threefold division of world history, it may be seen as prefiguring historical theology: (a) the first time of history consists of the national history of Israel, the gift of tradition; it goes from the creation of the world until the fall of the First Temple; (b) the second time is that of the four empires of the world; it inherently includes their decline and ends in persecutions; (c) the third and last time is that of the "eternal kingdom"; it follows the destruction of the world and the unholy empires.[28]

To represent time, the Book of Daniel outlines a diagram organizing a circular movement around the moment, still situated during Persian rule, at which his vision occurs. The latter unfolds in the future, while recounting events that take place in the present. The narrative is thus not meant to be descriptive but rather, as we have seen, prospective. Yet the pacts, wars, and incidents described are well enough substantiated to be easily identified.

Prophecy: Conjugating the Past at Every Time

As history-making, the Book of Daniel, like the books of Maccabees, illustrates a specific point in Hebrew literature as much as a step in the creation of Jewish opinions in this era. The end of prophecy is mourned in Maccabees, while the vision of Daniel makes it possible to see the results of this process in Jewish tradition. Indeed, Daniel does not see himself as a prophet. God never speaks through him. Even more, by nurturing predictions that were brought to bear in the past, he makes it clear that their impact in his day cannot be intelligible without channeling them through an oracle. So that as an alternative to prophecy, we deal with a decoding that resembles exegesis, which is described in visionary form. This change in discourse shows that the prophetic word is no longer seen as a living expression. It is recorded, deposited in the extant corpus. Yet divine inspiration remains vital as the only current way for mankind to grasp it. This is a possible reading of explanations scattered through the text that clarify its obscurities. They are meant to establish a new analysis of ancient revelations, especially those of Jeremiah, about the seventy years of grief promised between the destruction and rebuilding of the Temple. Better still, Daniel sets a time limit. The old prediction first came to pass with the rebuilding of the First Temple, and may occur a second time, renewed by its split into "weeks of years," if it is known how to decipher how it will happen and act accordingly to cause it to occur.[29] Based on the count of jubilees, the calculating system in the Book of Daniel suggests rethinking the freeing of the slaves, then symbolizing the exiles from Israel, in forty-nine-year cycles. The prophetic vision told to Daniel is based on the already extant revealed patrimony, left with the prophets (Isaiah, Jeremiah) and in Leviticus.[30] The sum of seventy sabbatical cycles, corresponding to a time span of 490 years, may be calculated if it is understood as being the period that elapsed between the destruction of the First Temple in 587 BCE and the desecration of the Second Temple by Antiochus IV Epiphanes between 175 and 164 BCE. (1 Maccabees states that the year 170 was the start of the era of Simon the High Priest.) This period is the one that must precede redemption. The temporal pattern, based on variations around multiples of seven and seventy, reveals how open it is to the imminence of the last sabbatical "week" where the author felt he was situated.[31]

Between exegesis and innovation there is also Daniel's confession of sins. Echoing the scourges predicted in Leviticus as punishment for the Israelites transgressing the covenant, it especially applies to laws concerning leaving the land fallow, upon which Daniel's time schedule for redemption hinges.[32] Taking over for his time the prophecy of Jeremiah and the threats of Leviticus, Daniel conveys the new idea of power granted to the nation's collective repentance. He will obtain the promised divine mercy and thereby, the resurrection. A similar concept is found in the Scroll of the Psalms found at Qumran, which must have been written at the same time.[33] So, the procedures by which the page of history as historical event is transposed in Jewish literature of this era may be grasped through these two kinds of texts. Temporality remains profane in the books of Maccabees. The story, although miraculous, expresses the reincarnation of a dynasty. The books of Maccabees suggest a growing gap in the divine word, or in other words, the silence of God. In response, the Book of Daniel affirms the abiding validity of the ancient words. Moving the scene of the action toward exegesis, the story shows that prophecy uttered in the past may also occur now, becoming a kind of ideally modern revelation. The principle developed by the sages, according to which the biblical story expresses a divine word rather than a human one, is reflected here. The permanence of the tale of Daniel confronts the fleetingness of that of the Maccabees. This might be what led to the expulsion of the Maccabees from this patrimony. For of the profusion of prophecies thundered daily during the Second Temple era, it was decided that only those useful in the present and future would be retranscribed. In rejecting those that only referred to events, the sages gambled on the future.[34]

The Calendar and the Sects: Between Time and History

When for a short century the Hasmoneans reestablished the sovereignty of Israel, sects blossomed, including the Dead Sea Sect. How to grasp the sudden emergence of these breakaways from within a triumphant Judaism? Most researchers remain cautious in theorizing about any correlation between these two phenomena, of which the accounts by Philo and Josephus and documents such as the Scroll of the Temple and many fragments of copies of the Books of Enoch and Jubilees found on the scene cannot be ignored.[35] Historical analysis of sects usually employs two typologies. The first gathers the sects with a revolutionary agenda, seeking to expunge the past. By contrast, the other unites those that aim to maintain ancient traditions threatened by change. The Dead Sea Sect, insofar as one existed, would fall into the second category. The conservative nature of laws governing the Qumran community emphasizes the singular nature of the break in the order of time represented by their calendar. Examining the reasons that might have led these "ultra-conservatives" to adopt a drastic reform of the Law, researchers offer theories mobilizing the overall vision of society of that time.[36] They mention an annual solar celebratory rhythm, clearly asynchronous with the lunisolar one directed from the Jerusalem Temple.[37] Perhaps they summarize the attitudes of a group worried about the authenticity of its religious practices, to the point of predicting the worst for any person who strayed, if only for a day, in observing a "fixed period" for a biblical celebration. If such is the case, how to grasp this rigidity about a calendar that was not anchored in tradition? The problem of calendrical differences is central in the questions raised by analyzing the documents that came to light at the Qumran site. All by itself, it may cast doubt on the general approach to the ancient Israelite world. As we have seen, calendars and documents referring to it, discovered in the vicinity of the site, demonstrate the existence of an annual solar calendar, whereas most ancient sources and rabbinic literature refer to the lunisolar calendrical system as still currently in use. In this annual cycle, the meeting of lunar months and solar seasons works by the periodic insertion of an extra month. This breach of extant knowledge led researchers pursuing the scientific logic of "known facts" to analyze the phenomenon in the context of the overall rejection by these groups of customs applicable to Jerusalem. Establishing the solar calendar, seen as a "radical innovation," may have played a role "decisive in the isolation of the sect in terms of the Judaism of its era."[38] Yet this presumption of innovation has been called into question by subsequent research. The Jerusalem Talmud states that Johanan bar Nappaha counted twenty-four groups with different mandates in Judaism just before the fall of the Temple.[39] This proliferation makes it difficult to imagine such isolation, resulting more from a general phenomenon of increase than cultist exclusion. Now long-scattered findings seem to corroborate each other in disputing the coherence of this reading, which seems increasingly less clear. Adding to the complexity of the historical time line for the Second Temple period, "Qumran-ist" researchers extend enquiries central to our history of time by deepening them. Some of their theories shed new light on some aspects of the plurality of temporalities that we have observed here. Yet as we have constantly seen, guidance for dating provided by biblical sources poses technical and philological problems. The interpretation of data is impacted, remaining speculative.

1, 2, 3 . . . Sun![40]

Documentary research has shown possible use of the solar calendar before the Second Temple period. Signs of this solar calendar appear in the Bible in Priestly Source (P) and the books of Ezekiel, Haggai, and Zechariah.[41] Deepening this rereading, Michael Chyutin has devised a theory based on the fact that the Hebrews originally used an ancient calendar, which employed basic principles to determine agricultural life. It worked within an unchanging cycle of festive celebrations linked to seasons and likely established in local solar traditions from Canaan, emanating from Egyptian rule over the area since the era of the Patriarchs. According to Chyutin, the formal establishment of this calendar dates back to King Solomon's time, a point when the institution of the kingdom and its operating principles were solidifying. This calendar dictated the pace of religious life for the Israelites despite conquests and repeated regional power struggles that might have altered it. So the calendrical aspects that reappear in the Qumran texts were the remnants of a "war of the calendars" experienced by Hebrew history, divided between simultaneous economic and cultural influences from Egypt and Babylon, from the First Temple until the Second.[42]

Daniel's vision of the fourth empire claiming to "change times and laws" may reasonably be related to a calendrical upheaval.[43] It is the link that structures the orders of time and the laws that govern it. Brought back to the inauguration of the Seleucid era imposed at the time of Antiochus IV Epiphanes, this change could also relate to the annual calendrical cycle in effect until then, which remains largely unknown.[44] The Greco-Macedonian administrative calendar competed with the cultural calendar at the time, leading the Jews to start living by a system of double temporality. To the cultural time set by the Temple, and based on the ancient Egyptian solar system, was juxtaposed profane time that governed relationships to the state, established by the Greek and Babylonian lunisolar model.[45] On the basis of chronologies of various kings listed in the Bible, von Rad guessed, to some outrage, that different temporalities existed between the kingdoms of Judea and Israel.[46] Before him, Wellhausen had noted that a change of the Hebrew calendar was made in the Priestly Code. The change of year, which at the time of the kings occurred in autumn, according to Wellhausen, while remaining located at the same point in time, was thereafter situated in the "seventh months," which meant moving the new year to springtime.[47] The reason was subsequently understood. Wellhausen was certain that the introduction of a double calendar should be seen here, governing religious life from autumn festivals—remnants of an ancient tradition— and civil life from spring festivals. As additional proof, in writings of the time of the Babylonian Exile, months started to be called by numbers, replacing the "former Hebrew names *Aviv, Ziv, Bul, Eitanim*, etc.," at the same time that the vernal year was introduced.[48] Josephus, seeking to date the Flood, also encountered the problem of biblical double datings, which he tried to resolve:

> This calamity happened in the six hundredth year of Noah's government [age], in the second month, called by the Macedonians *Dius*, but by the Hebrews *Marchesvan*: for so did they order their year in Egypt. But Moses appointed that *Nisan*, which is the same with *Xanthicus*, should be the first month for their festivals, because he brought them out of Egypt in that month: so that this month began the year as to all the solemnities they observed to the honor of God, although he preserved the original order of the months as to selling and buying, and other ordinary affairs.[49]

Did the "new order" reported by Josephus correspond to an ancient calendar used since the already distant Mosaic period? Or was it due to more recent changes that were nonetheless attributed to Moses? Making it even more difficult to decide, the Babylonian calendar also contains the same traces of a calendrical change. Jean Bottéro notes that the name of Tesrit, the month corresponding to the Hebrew Tishri, means "beginnings" in Akkadian, whereas Nisan marks the start of the year.[50] The question is not merely rhetorical; Julius Caesar's annual solar calendar was introduced in 45 BCE, not long before Josephus tried to master the great variety of eras and calendars that confronted him.[51] For Palestine, the Mishnah states that during the first-century struggles between different currents of spiritual power in Yavneh and the rest of the country, Rabban Gamaliel I compelled Rabbi Joshua ben Hananiah to visit Yavneh, bearing a staff and monetary payment on the day that according to Rabbi Joshua's calculations should be Yom Kippur.[52] In this way, this act of surrender settled the decision-making authority of the academy over all the people. Does fixing the day for celebrating Yom Kippur on a date different from the one sought by the ancient tradition of Jerusalem, represented by Rabbi Joshua ben Hananiah, fit the framework of a Roman reform inflicted on a conquered region? Does it mark the victory of one calendrical style over another? Or does it express a simple difference of opinion linked to inherent problems in observing an astronomical cycle still imperfectly governed by calculations?[53]

The Sun Has a Date with the Moon

Basing himself on a remark by the tenth-century Karaite dogmatist Al-Qirqasani, Michael Chyutin proposes a solution to these relatively insoluble problems.[54] The first schism in the history of Israel, under the iron rule of Rehoboam, which led to the separation of the two kingdoms and the building of the temples at Bethel and Dan, was evidently accompanied by the establishment of a new calendar. In a mainly agricultural society, it would be apter for the climate of the northern seasons than the solar calendar directed from Jerusalem. The emergence of Samaritan dissent after the conquest of Samaria by Babylon having confirmed Rehoboam's lunisolar system, biblical festivals and ceremonies no longer fell on the same days in Judea—the source of spiritual leadership for Jerusalem—and in Galilee, part of the northern kingdom.[55] After the destruction of the First Temple and the return of the Jews from Babylon, two currents—Babylonian and Palestinian, both cultural and religious—developed within Judaism. The oral law, the Mishnah, the Talmud, and rabbinic literature in general demonstrate this, preserving remnants of debates from the Second Temple era about calendrical differences, especially about determining the days of the new moon that underpin the new year.[56] Against rabbinic tradition and Josephus, who suggest moving the new year from autumn to spring, Chyutin suggests that the changeover in seasons should be inverted. Recognizing that in the First Temple era the ancient calendar was solar, because linked to the one found in Egypt and rooted in local cultural traditions, the new year had to be celebrated in Nisan, in spring, he believes. For him it was only at the change of rulership during the Babylonian conquest or later, after the Hasmonean victory, that the new year would be set to the autumn month of Tishri, in effect for the Seleucids.[57] Using a solar day of the Egyptian kind, the start of the day was calculated beginning with the morning during the First Temple era. During the Second Temple era, it was first noted in the evening, according to Babylonian custom based on the appearance of the moon. Chyutin justifies using names for the months following the numerical system after the return of the Jews from Babylon, as substantiated in the Talmud, in terms of the introduction of the lunisolar calendar. The lunisolar system of intercalation forces the "doubling" of a month, while the solar calendar, less subject to human changes and mistakes because it does not require observation of the stars or introduce an extra day, does not necessitate them.[58] Wellhausen noted this change and located it in the same chronology. Yet he attributed it to the establishment of the new calendrical year, starting with Nisan, "under the influence of the Babylonians."[59] Both agreed on the calendrical changes that occurred in Judaism under Babylonian influence, but their theories differed about the shifting of the new year from spring to autumn, or inversely from autumn to spring.

This puzzle may be partly resolved by apocryphal and pseudoepigraphical texts found at Qumran that remained outside the canon. 1 Enoch bases its legitimacy on its age. Its name implies that it was written by an author from before the Flood (see Appendix for a table of biblical genealogy). The astronomic tract it contains is regarded as the oldest surviving one, since the text supposedly dates back to the third century BCE.[60] Four copies of it were recovered at Qumran. The calendar surely describes a solar system, which it maintains was revealed to Enoch by the archangel Uriel: "And the sun and the stars bring in all the years exactly, so that they do not advance or delay their position by a single day unto eternity; but complete the years with perfect justice in 364 days."[61] The daily unit is also directed by this star, with the year starting in spring because "during this period the day becomes daily longer and the night nightly shorter to the thirtieth morning."[62] It is odd that this calendar is fully aware of the calendar using the lunar system, which it presents with the faults of a year defective by ten years over the sun, and which seems to be blamed in the rest of the text: "And in the days of the sinners the years shall be shortened. . . . And the rain shall be kept back . . . the fruits of the earth shall be backward, And shall not grow in their time, . . . And the moon shall alter her order."[63]

Fifteen or sixteen fragments from different copies of the Book of Jubilees were found at Qumran.[64] The work is in line with heavenly revelations: the organization of time was first revealed to Enoch and then transmitted to Moses. This pre-Flood patronage that he refers to should ensure its continuity: "And he was the first among men that are born on earth who learnt writing and knowledge and wisdom and who wrote down the signs of heaven according to the order of their months in a book, that men might know the seasons of the years according to the order of their separate months. . . . [He] recounted the weeks of the jubilees, and made known to them the days of the years, and set in order the months and recounted the Sabbaths of the years as we made (them), known to him."[65] Basing its legitimacy on that of Enoch, the Book of the Jubilees presents itself with the strictness of a revealed calendar: "Thus it is engraven and ordained on the heavenly tablets." As such, it endures no change: "And command thou the children of Israel that they observe the years according to this reckoning—three hundred and sixty-four days, and (these) will constitute a complete year."[66] The solar system is described in a more detailed way in the Book of Jubilees than in the Book of Enoch, since it includes festivals in its structure. The incantatory nature of its statements on the original authenticity of its calendar likely played a major role in the link established by researchers between the appearance of the sect and the Book of Jubilees. For the book's distribution is demonstrated by other discovered fragments, including the so-called Damascus Document Scroll,[67] which clearly specifies: "Behold, it is exactly explained in the Book of the Divisions of the Seasons" (16:1).[68] The "Rule of the Community" alludes to years of "emancipation" and of "weeks of years,"[69] and "Thanksgiving Hymns" (*Hodayot*) expand the eternal aspect of the revelation: "Constantly, in all the origins of Time, the basic divisions of duration and the seasonal cycle, at their determined hour, by their signs for all their subjugation, at the sure and determined hour because it is from the mouth of God . . . for the God of knowledge created it."[70] The Temple Scroll decrees the engagement of the date for the new year: "[On the] fourteenth of the first month . . . they will declare Passover for Yahweh" (17:6).[71] One of the pseudo-Davidian psalms describes the succession for that year: "He writes psalms . . . for all the days of the year, 364; and for the sabbath offerings, fifty-two chants; and for the offering at the start of the months . . . thirty chants" (27:5–9).[72] This annual arrangement is found again in the Songs of the Sabbath Sacrifice, also referred to as the Angelic Liturgy.[73]

The solar nature of the calendar included in these texts is undoubted. Yet nothing suggests that it would persist from the era of the Patriarchs and King Solomon until the Second Temple, if only among sectarian groups. Indeed, researchers have even doubted the solar calendar's use in practice, theorizing that, far from being representative of a sectarian calendar, these Qumran texts were the work of supporters of the traditional division of time, which was threatened by the infiltration of a secular, civil calendar into the religious calendar used in Temple service. If so, rather than challenging Jerusalemite tradition, these groups may actually have been defending its distinctiveness, which was at the risk of being coalesced into the Hellenistic world.[74]

Calendrical Matters

Let us return to the history that begins to be detectable in this theory. The first calendar designed to bind the administrative grid and Temple service dates back to the building of the Temple by King Solomon. The fact that the Temple faces east, like ancient and Egyptian temples, possibly indicates its solar positioning.[75] The calendar of biblical festivals shows an archaic agricultural rhythm—explicitly declared in the Book of Enoch—that does not require specific astronomical or scientific knowledge, as does observing the lunar cycle. This calendar, taken as solar, conflates religious and secular time. The first schism soon introduced the use of a lunisolar calendar that had both religious—it was used in the cults of Dan and Bethel—and secular administrative applications. These two uses betray the Egyptian and Mesopotamian areas of influence to which the Jewish kingdoms were subject. The rise in cultural influence of the Babylonian empire is seen in writings from the times of the conquest, deportation, and return. Names for months follow numbers, duplications emerge in computations and chronologies, datings differ between the Greek and Hebrew versions of the Bible. Two kinds of calendars were used simultaneously after the return of the Jews from Babylon. One was civil, lunisolar and matching the timetables of the conquerors; the other was religious and solar, used in Palestine until it was finally overwhelmed by the growing authority of Babylonian Jews in the promulgation of laws. Among other things, establishing a canonical Masoretic text of the Bible aimed at resolving the divergence in solar and lunar dates by the new introduction of the lunisolar calendar. Traces of this synchronizing process can be seen in scripture: "The word that came to Jeremiah concerning all the people of Judah, in the fourth year of Jehoiakim the son of Josiah king of Judah, that was the first year of Nebuchadnezzar king of Babylon. . . . From the thirteenth year of Josiah the son of Amon king of Judah, even unto this day, that is the three and twentieth year, the word of the Lord hath come unto me . . .";[76] "In the four and twentieth day of the sixth month, in the second year of Darius the king . . ."[77]

These two examples show the process of fitting ancient dates to new criteria and the coexistence of a dual system as found in Aramean papyri in Egypt.[78] The first example integrates the eras of Judea and Babylon and the second, the numerical system for naming months with the Persian era. More revealing is the evidence written on *ostraca* from the Egyptian Jewish military colony of Elephantine, dating from the start of the fifth century BCE. The oldest of these fragments of pottery asks fellow Jews: "When do you celebrate Passover?" An official document dated 419–418 BCE also shows the importance given to the date of that celebration: "And now, this year, year 5 of Darius the king, from the king it has been sent to Arsame: now you thus count fourteen days of Nisan and on the 14th at twilight the Passover observe and from day 15 until day 21 of [Nisan]. . . . Seven days unleavened bread eat . . . be pure and take heed . . . from day 14 of Nisan at sunset until day 21st of Nisan . . . to my brothers, Jedanya and his colleagues, the Jewish Troop, your brother Hanania."[79] This fragment indicates that it was a decree determining that the festival must be celebrated according to the fixed date in the Persian calendar and not observed because of the germination of firstfruits or the Egyptian solar calendar. The celebration had to start on the evening of the Persian lunisolar calendar and not the morning of the Egyptian solar calendar.[80] These epistolary exchanges occurred between the appearance of Ezra around 458 BCE and the destruction of the Temple of Elephantine in 411–410 BCE. Is Hanania the brother of Nehemiah, come to Egypt to uphold the decisions of the scribes? Or the head of the citadel of Jerusalem? No matter. The influence of the Babylonian-led Great Assembly seems evident. Whether this calendrical diversity continued throughout the Second Temple era remains unsure. Yet the books of Maccabees contain some indications that support this theory. "Now on the five and twentieth day of the ninth month, which is called the month Casleu [*kislev*], in the hundred forty and eighth year, they rose up betimes in the morning," 1 Macc. 4:52 says; "in the hundred threescore and seventeenth year, in the eleventh month, called Sabat [*shevat*]" (16:14). "And they ordained all with a common decree in no case to let that day pass without solemnity, but to celebrate the thirtieth day of the twelfth month, which in the Syrian tongue is called *Adar*, the day before Mardocheus's day," 2 Macc. 15:36 notes. Here the numerical designations of months from the Seleucid era are still used. Yet the names of months, given with an insistence that suggests that Alexandrian Jews might be unaware of them, leaves no room for doubt. If the year started with the month of Tishri, then Kislev would be the third month, Shevat the fifth, and Adar the sixth. By contrast, if the annual cycle were organized starting with the month of Nisan, then Kislev would be the ninth month, Shevat the eleventh, and Adar the twelfth, as the texts suggest (see the table indicating the order of appearance of the months, pp. 195–196).

The exact date when these books were written is unknown. A temporal range of between 134 and 76 BCE would be indicated if they were written under the respective reigns of John Hyrcanus and Alexander Jannaeus. It follows that the numerical designation of months was still the current standard, intelligible to all, whereas in Palestine the custom of calling them by names had recently been introduced, while still referring to their number in order to identify them. The Talmud states that these names were imported from Babylon and sheds light on their meaning.[81] Some are mentioned in postexilic biblical literature: in Zechariah, Kislev is the ninth month and Shevat the eleventh;[82] in Nehemiah, Kislev, Nisan, and Elul appear;[83] Esther cites Nisan, Sivan, Tevet, and the twelfth month, Adar.[84] The months of Tishri, Heshvan/Marcheshvan, Iyyar, Tammuz, and Av do not appear in scripture. Incidentally, when the text indicates the month by its number, it is called *hodesh*, which may refer to a period of thirty days,[85] whereas when it is named, the term *yareah* (moon) is used instead, indicating a unit varying from twenty-nine to thirty days. The preexilic corpus indicates names that later vanish. The exodus from Egypt occurs "in the month of Aviv," which can be translated as the month of the "ripe head of grain."[86] The others only appear in Kings, and describe the building of the Temple by Solomon. Defined are the "month (*hodesh*) Ziv, which is the second month," which can be translated literally as the month of splendor or brilliance, but which is also called the "moon of Ziv"; the "moon of Bul, the eighth month," is the rainy moon; and the moon of "Eitanim is the seventh month" or the month of the powerful.[87] This mixture of names between the solar number and lunar month leads to the recognition of a dual calendar, not yet standardized, in the sources. In the ninth century, the Karaite master Benjamin Nahawandi noted this coexistence in scripture.[88] Successive chapters date Haggai's prophetic vision differently: "In the four and twentieth day of the sixth month, in the second year of Darius the king. In the seventh month, in the one and twentieth day of the month . . ."[89] Sa'adia Ga'on declares that Nahawandi stressed at the time, "I had in my hands . . . the month [the date] counted by the sun and the month by the moon, and its prophecy took place on the day to which two dates are given, the 24th of the month of Elul and the 21st of Tishri."[90]

Another source of data likely to shed light on this debate is the *Megillat Ta'anit* (The Scroll of Fasting), attributed by the Talmud to followers of Eleazar ben Hanina ben Hizkiah ben Garon,[91] whom Josephus accuses of having led the revolt against the Romans.[92] Its text is based in the tannaitic and Pharisaic tradition from just before the fall of the Second Temple. This extracanonical list of dates was published for the first time along with the *Seder 'olam*. It belongs to the singular corpus that Jewish tradition holds to be historical[93] and is probably the oldest surviving Jewish legal text, dating from the era of the revolt against the Romans (66–70), or, at latest, that of Bar Kokhba. The scroll compiles a list of thirty-five days of celebrations observed during the Second Temple era, all linked to events not mentioned in scripture and during which it is forbidden to fast or grieve. In spite of the brevity of the explanations given, it becomes apparent that most of these holidays celebrate military victories of the Hasmonean era. Some recall the Pharisaic success in legal matters over the Sadducees. Few reiterate past events, and some are placed in the Roman era. No incident can be dated after 66/67. All these commemorations were abandoned after the destruction of the Temple, apart from the festivals of Purim and Hanukkah. The list forms an annual scheduling, which is distributed starting with the month of Nisan. This contradicts the statement in the Mishnah that the month of Nisan is only "New Year's day for kings and pilgrimages."[94] Yet it matches Josephus's observation that since Moses, this month has led the annual rhythm of the divine service. It may be logically established that in the Second Temple era, and until its fall, a calendrical system existed in which the religious year began in the spring. Admittedly, dissident groups may have escaped to the desert, and the texts found at Qumran may reflect different trends contending within Judaism. These observations in no way negate the theory that the solar system, inherent to this structure, formed the religious calendar of the Jews at some time.

The Hasmonean saga can now be read in a different light. The recovery of autonomy and sovereignty may have set off a messianic fervor, as seen in texts from this time, which all seem convinced of the imminent end of time. This turmoil may have been followed by a return to the sources of biblical Judaism, jeopardized by the imposition of foreign laws after the successive Persian and Greek conquests.[95] Fighting between different currents of Hellenophilic or Hellenophobic, and pro- or anti-Hasmonean, Judaism united these trends within groups made up of different registers of temporality. To defend their view of Judaism, some favored a temporality of origins, revealed and transmitted by Enoch and Moses. Others favored Greek temporality. Between the messianic nature of the Hasmonean victory and the chagrin that the Messiah had not come, there developed a wide movement of strictness, marked by Pharisianism and the rendering of the oral law into writing.[96] Its spread is also seen in the Temple Scroll and the "Manual of Discipline" (also called the "Rule of the Community"). Over time, the Hellenophilic leaning won out, as the attitudes of the last Hasmonean sovereigns show. These groups of Jews sought to defend antique traditions and oppose dual calendrical systems and changing the profane calendar into a calendar of Temple services. Aside from a brief revival during Bar Kokhba's "liberation of Israel," such conflicts were submerged in the general bringing to heel of the population after the Temple was destroyed.

With the eclipse of the notion that the solar calendar of the Qumran sects caused radical break, the evolution of a dual temporal system, anchored since biblical times in the different versions of scripture circulating throughout Palestine and the Diaspora, becomes completely plausible as a vector of difference.[97] Origen, who as a resident of third-century Alexandria must have known the background of these debates, already believed this.[98] So the task of fixing, and choosing a canon of, biblical texts was born or resulted from the dialectic between these circles of influence and this turn toward strictness. The aim was a kind of pacification that allowed for cultural unity, balancing the loss of political unity, assuming it had ever existed. Developing a strictly Jewish temporal system was the best way of doing so. The coexistence in biblical sources of different dating systems can likewise be explained. Instead of erasing all traces of the different registers of temporality, it unites them, just as rabbinic texts marshal the different opinions of the sages on halakhic issues.

The Hebrew Months and Their Order

- Order of appearance of the Hebrew months by the lunisolar calendar, starting the year in Tishri/autumn:
  Tishri, Heshvan, Kislev, Tevet, Shevat, Adar, Nisan, Iyyar, Sivan, Tammuz, Av, Elul

1	2	3	4	5	6
Tishri	Heshvan	Kislev	Tevet	Shevat	Adar
7	8	9	10	11	12
Nisan	Iyyar	Sivan	Tammuz	Av	Elul

- Order of appearance of the months by the solar calendar, starting the year in Nisan/spring:
  Nisan, Iyyar, Sivan, Tammuz, Av, Elul, Tishri, Heshvan, Kislev, Tevet, Shevat, Adar

1	2	3	4	5	6
Nisan	Iyyar	Sivan	Tammuz	Av	Elul
7	8	9	10	11	12
Tishri	Heshvan	Kislev	Tevet	Shevat	Adar

- Ancient months:
  Aviv = Nisan; Ziv = Iyyar; Bul = Heshvan; Eitanim = Tishri

1	2	3	4	5	6
Aviv Nisan	Ziv Iyyar				
7	8	9	10	11	12
Eitanim Tishri	Bul Heshvan				

The Perpetual Calendar

From this calendar war, Jewish tradition only retained the tale of a fight between the stars, dating back to the creation of the universe. Jewish legends tell of the original creation of two twin stars, the sun and the moon. The latter was diminished owing to its arrogance. Still, the moon was assigned the sharing out of the world to come granted to Israel, while the sun obtained the right to rule over the nations in the world below. So that the diurnal and nocturnal stars were both emblematic of relationships between the nations and Israel. For the Midrash, the sun symbolizes Esau, who represented the color red of Rome and by extension, the nations. While the moon, which never dies, is the emblem of Jacob, or Israel.[99] Nothing is known about the way in which the alleged Hillel II replaced the uncertain calendar based only on the observation of the sky and germination in 359–360 with a fixed, perpetual calendar that employed scholarly calculations.[100] The previous system had granted the patriarch of Palestine, who publicly announced the calendar for the year based on his assessment of nature's progression, complete freedom to intercalate as he saw fit. Patriarch Judah the Prince took advantage of this, it seems, when he proclaimed nine months defective one year.[101] Tradition holds that Hillel II for the first time worked out the precise junction between the respective rates of the lunar months and solar seasons by creating a recurrent model with intercalations, which relies on introducing seven intercalary years (with a thirteenth month) into the Metonic cycle of nineteen years that the Talmud sanctions by the formula created by Rav Adda bar Ahavah.[102] The very first writing of a complete astronomical system close to this one is reported in a later text, entitled the *Baraita of Samuel*.[103] Describing how in the year 4536, or 776 CE, the exact conjunction of the lunar and solar cycles occurred, so that all calendrical cycles coincided, the author comes up with astronomical calculations reconciling all Jewish markers: seasons, sabbatical cycles, and lunar months. Let us leave aside the technical aspects of this system, since invalidated. The text, as the first to locate itself both in the era of the creation and in an astronomical system, is also unusual in that it avoids any mystical discourse. It pretends to no revelation nor to any handing down by tradition. It simply aims to explain to readers the cryptic scientific system upon which the Jewish calendar rests, based solely on the point of view of astronomical observation.[104] The unknown author of this *baraita* may thus be seen as a precursor of the illustrious medieval Jewish astronomers.

The Last (Calendrical) War

To determine temporality, questions about time do not come down simply to problems in dating. Adjusting the calendar also reflects key power struggles, as we see in cases such as the conflict over the proclamation of the new year that broke out in the year 921 CE and led to a temporary schism between the academies of Babylon and Palestine. The quarrel was not about using the era of the *hurban* or divergences over calculating the era of the world, but it nevertheless affected these two ways of perceiving time in Jewish tradition. This dispute ended the hegemony of Jewish spiritual authority in the Holy Land in law-making, affirming the supremacy in the field of halakhic law of the authorities of Sura and Pumbedita over those of Jerusalem.[105] As Palestinian spiritual domination gradually declined, Diaspora academies were strengthened. Until then, declaring new moons and setting the day for the festival of Passover, the basis for all annual celebrations, had fallen within the jurisdiction of the religious administration in Jerusalem, which accorded itself the exclusive right to regulate intercalations governing the annual cycle. Signs by which nature indicated the coming of spring were only seen as acceptable from a legal point of view when they emerged from the land of Israel.[106] On the authority of an ancient tradition affirming that the world had been created in Nisan, Palestinians calculated the annual calendar on the basis of the new moon, while Babylonians took the month of Tishri as a point of departure. Jerusalem announced that Passover of the year 922, 4682 of the creation, would be celebrated on a Sunday, and the new year would therefore fall on a Tuesday. This declaration was based on the observation that the day of the new moon of Tishri 4684 (September 923) would occur fourteen minutes after noon. The son of Aaron Ben Meir, the leader of the Palestinians, proposed that the entry into this new year not be delayed, but that the year 4682 be shortened by making the months of Heshvan and Kislev defective, reducing their length to twenty-nine days. The Babylonians, based on the creation in Tishri, estimated that by adding suitable intervals to the first of Nisan, the accepted limit for the visibility of the first day of the new moon could be pushed back.[107] Unlike Ben Meir's son, Sa'adia ben Yosef, who was not yet appointed a *ga'on*, insisted that the year 4682 be augmented by allotting thirty days to Heshvan and Kislev. In this case, Passover fell on a Tuesday, which put the new year on a Thursday. Babylonians and Palestinians were violently opposed, brandishing their respective calculations and conclusions.[108] Although conceding that the representative from Jerusalem had respected the forms stipulated by law for such a proclamation, the Babylonian *ga'on* resisted, and the absolute right of Palestinians to legislate on the calendar and Rosh Hodesh (first day of the new moon) was withdrawn.

It was already contested, as one of the letters written at the height of the controversy shows:

> For several years, emissaries from Babylon had gone up to Palestine and closely investigated the mysteries of intercalation together with the Palestinian sages. They had studied it so attentively that for many years past they have been proclaiming new moons in Babylonia on their own. The Palestinian sages for their part likewise calculated and set new moons. During all these years, these respective calculations led them to the same results, and no difference arose between them. In this way the computation was staunchly upheld, and the holidays have uniformly been observed at the same time."[109]

How this schism was resolved remains as obscure as the technicalities that fueled it. The Nestorian Elias of Nisibis says that in "[t]he year 309 of the Hegira, beginning Saturday 12th of Iyar [May] of the year 1232 of the Greeks [921] . . . [there] befell a division/disagreement (*pùlàgà*) between the Jews of the West and the Jews of the East concerning the calculation of their festivals. And the Jews who are in the West made the beginning (*rèsà*) of their year Tuesday and those of the East (made it) Thursday."[110] So the Jews of Palestine and Egypt celebrated the new year 4683 [922] on Tuesday, while those of Babylon observed it on Thursday, which was felt by that generation, Ben Meir writes, as a "subject of shame among the Gentiles and derision among the sectarians [Karaites]."[111] As we have seen, a few years later, in 926, Sa'adia returned to the debate to explain the calculating mistakes by the Westerners—those "others"—who refused to admit the accuracy of the Babylonian tradition, conveyed by the Talmud, of fixing the calendar.[112]

This defeat of Palestinian power came at the end of a decline evident in the long-standing disparity in power relations between the Jews of Palestine and the Diaspora, which only remained in balance owing to the holiness conceded to the land of Israel. This may have played a role in the fact that the era of the *destruction*, although used to date all letters sent from Palestine during this dispute, could not compete with the era of contracts, more widespread in the Near East as a dating system. Although it never vanished entirely, the era of the *destruction* was never dominant either.[113] The era of the *hurban* would remain latent and judging by the statement by Maimonides, limited to the observance of the seven-year cycle, itself relatively neglected since the Diaspora and the end of Jewish agricultural life in Palestine.[114] Favoring the abandonment of indicators of temporality linked to the land of Israel and the specific history of the Temple, the new calendar was based on the conjunction of principles, using the pace of celebrations required by the Bible to reconcile arithmetical and astronomic calculations. It culminated in the development of a ritual agenda relatively detached from the seasons in Palestine.

Thirteen   A Fleeting Conclusion

At this stage of the investigation, it may be useful to recall the stakes and restate the problems. After considering the most widely received notions of "time," Part I of this book roughed out an outline of the construction of a "Jewish time." One broad consensus, epitomized by the German Jewish historian Heinrich Graetz (1817–1891), was that after their dispersal from the Holy Land, the Jews cared about neither history nor the moment, and their religion was based more in the future than in the present.[1] Behind this lay another unreasonable, although legitimate, question: if, as suggested by philosophers and historians, the notion of human interdependence with history is taken to be a Christian one, is it valid in the Jewish world? Long experience of the Jewish society known as "traditional," because Jews were not integrated into civil society from a juridical perspective and were ruled by their own laws and traditions before their emancipation, led to other questions on historiography. How to summarize the inner developments of a society that claims to be prescriptive, and denies all value to innovation, without going to the sources of this attitude? How to grasp changes in beliefs and attitudes when the first principle is: "The thing that hath been, it is that which shall be; and that which is done is that which shall be done: and there is no new thing under the sun"?[2] The path I sought to open followed the progress of the dual ideas of a "world to come" and "in this world here" (*ba-olam ha-ba'* / *le-'atid lavo* versus *ba-'olam ha-zeh*), which should permit grasping their impact on the inclusion of Jews in the present of their history. Only a study of temporality could achieve this. Yet before even thinking of grasping the least experience of time, many pitfalls appeared, owing to the number of research tasks, each more theological than the next, involved in analyzing the relationship of the Jews and the Bible, the Bible and time, and Jews and the writing of history. The logic of research led me to the emergence of these ideas. Part II then strove to grasp the framework of the creation of rabbinic thought, following the work done over several centuries on the eschatological concept of the world to come and the emergence of the concept of the era of the world into history.

It was foreseeable that the documents discussed up to this point have not routed the hordes of historians, biblical scholars, and specialists in antiquity who, with individual nuances, express the same certainties as the Hellenist Martin Hengel: "The Torah became an essentially ahistorical entity";[3] "The moment the Rabbinate achieved its final rule over Palestinian Judaism after Jabne, the almost thousand-year-old tradition of Israelite and Jewish history writing came to an end. . . . Under the guidance of the Rabbis, the pious Jew found his satisfaction in preoccupation with what for him was the unfathomable Torah, unfathomable because it encompassed God's very wisdom itself."[4]

The texts used in the writing of this book were selected for their narrative and interpretative nature. As narrative sources, they present a view of time past and history; as interpretive sources, they reveal a hermeneutic vision of the future at work in biblical readings. Analysis of the data clearly outlined some aspects of the ideas of temporality specific to the Jewish world between the end of the Second Temple and the development of the rabbinic period. The books of Maccabees and Daniel show us how history and historical events were transposed into Jewish literature at the end of the Second Temple era. In the books of Maccabees, temporality remained secular, while events were inscribed into a "Jewish" course of time. In Daniel, the principle was affirmed that the event only has meaning when it helps to shape the future by reinterpreting the past in eschatological time. Rereading the history of the biblical calendar in the light of the Qumran texts showed the continuing use of dual temporality, rooted as much in history as in the very approach of time.

The writings of the earliest chronographers show that despite the Talmud's wording, the writing of the *Seder ʿolam* does not seem to be the work of an isolated individual, single-handedly compiling a biblical chronology inspired by unforeseen historiographical curiosity. The inclusion of the *Seder ʿolam* in the later rabbinic corpus shows the simultaneity of a dual development, which finds completion during the second century. Chronographers tend to record Jewish chronology parallel to that of other nations, while the *Seder 'olam* ignores other nations. If some chronologies based on the text of the Septuagint make allegorical use of the Bible with a universal mission, they in any case show the existence of exegetical historical activity, of which the most literal version has by itself penetrated tradition, perhaps ousting other writings that are now lost. Without the Christian appropriation of ancient Jewish authors, we would know nothing about these chronographers today. Only they, along with the finds from the Cairo Genizah and Qumran, show that until they were eclipsed by the inclusion of the "universal" chronology of the *Seder 'olam* in the rabbinic corpus, figures with millenarian import are found in the Jewish representational space before the fall of the Temple. The simultaneity in talmudic texts of debates over the date of the coming of the Messiah and chronology shed light on the eschatological orientation of this activity from the outset.[5]

At the start of the eleventh century, when Al-Bīrūnī wrote his work, the memory of polemics between Christians and Jews about the previous millennium was still fresh, but an opaque veil was drawn—on both sides, it seems—over what mathematics may have contributed in the expectations of Jews. He comments:

> The Jews and Christians differ widely on this subject; for, according to the doctrine of the Jews, the time between Adam and Alexander is 3,448 years, whilst, according to the Christian doctrine, it is 5,180 years. The Christians reproach the Jews with having diminished the number of years with the view of making the appearance of Jesus fall into the fourth millennium in the middle of the seven millennia, which are, according to their view, the time of the duration of the world, so as not to coincide with that time at which, as the prophets after Moses had prophesied, the birth of Jesus from a pure virgin at the end of time, was to take place.[6]

The process leading to the production of history called "linear" owes much to the invention of a national religious narrative. The encounter between chronology and eschatology allowed the historical tale to rise to the universal by expanding its territory to the whole of the past and future of humanity, henceforth situated between creation and the end of time. Ascribing the invention of this kind of history to Christian historians of the fourth century CE, as Philippe Ariès does, for example, leads to ignoring the movement that simultaneously embraces developments in the extension of the past found in both Judaism and Christianity.[7] This movement emerged in the Hellenistic world around the fifth century BCE. So when G. E. R. Lloyd asserts: "There is no such thing as *the* Greek view of time," he means that in the approaches of the Greeks, many different concepts of time are mixed.[8] This plurality is rediscovered at the source of different elements that create the perception of time in every culture. It may therefore be affirmed that crystallization around a singular approach to time worked by using a kind of common heritage to which were joined dissimilar forms dictated by cultural and religious differences that societies had developed.

Judaism's Three "Times"

The texts mentioned in these chapters place a Jewish axis in time. Each in its own way expresses registers usable by the Jewish world. The books of Maccabees, although suggesting the establishment of a specific register, remain in Seleucid temporality. The Book of Daniel adds a prophetic register to Persian temporality. Yet it introduces to the Jewish patrimony a universal rereading of history, suitable for apocalypses. The Apocalypses and the Book of the Jubilees only discuss eschatological time. The *Seder ʻolam* develops a temporality that deliberately excludes any outside contamination. In creating a strictly Jewish biblical chronology, and deliberately removing itself from any cross-checking with outside sources, it is a historical outlier, but it nevertheless records biblical chronology in linear fashion. Just as the late third-century BCE Jewish chronographer Demetrius referred his history back to the creation of the world, although locating his story in the secular time of Ptolemy IV Philopator I, the *Seder ʻolam* does not use the era it creates to place its story in past centuries.[9] The temporality specific to this Jewish chronology in no way resembles historical temporality. Nevertheless, through this temporality of Jewish chronology, the era "of the world" finally takes its place in the historical inscription of time. To achieve this, all kinds of arithmetical and astronomical reckonings had to be done, of which we have traced the trials and errors. It would take several more centuries for the establishment of the era of the world, inferred from exegeses, to create the historical temporality of the Jews.

The biblical chronologies briefly studied here add motion between the structures of world history and distinctly Jewish history. At times, they aim at recording the incidents of Jewish history in the light of the reigns of sovereigns whose existence is documented in historical sources, and at others, they locate their stories entirely in the temporality of their surroundings, as Josephus does in his *Jewish War*. Moreover, they signal that the era of the world, still unknown as such in their time, was nonetheless already being used in reconstructions by chronographers. In some ways, its later use may be compared to that of the prophetic Word. The year of the world is contained in the biblical account, and long before it is seen as an era of reference, it may serve as an essential clue for those who know how to use the exegeses. Its Christian users took advantage of this. Appropriation of the historical past went hand in hand with religious conversion, and the proselyte won over to a new faith acquired the whole of its history. Like most of the texts surveyed thus far, the Epistle of Barnabas shows that calculating elapsed millennia was a practice that originally arose in a Jewish context. Christianity thus emerged from a branch of messianic Judaism that followed its own path. It is in the dialectic between messianism and its neutralization that we should seek the reason for demise of diverse biblical exegetical traditions (including the writing of Apocalypses).

An overview of the political conditions of the history of Israel shows that the Jews lost all national autonomy after the return from Babylonian exile, the rise of priestly religion, and the assembling of the biblical canon. The outline of the rabbinic concept of history, introduced in the Book of Daniel, is found again in the break caused by the fall of the First Temple and the end of prophecy.[10] The Jewish entry into world history (or the end of the national history of Israel) shows itself under Ptolemaic, Seleucid, Greek, and Roman rule. It is marked by the blossoming of many eschatological, gnostic, historical, and in short, Hellenistic concepts during the Second Temple era. Offset during the Hasmonean and Herodian kingdoms by a rise in messianic hope, these diverse elaborations blended into the evolving academic rabbinic Judaism of Palestine and Babylon after the destruction of the Temple, notably introducing a binary notion of time into rabbinic thought.

These historical developments directly impacted concepts of time. Sources presented here show that three forms of the inscription of dating exist, using Jewish points of reference. They are, in order of age: (1) the jubilee/fallow fields system; (2) the destruction of the Temple system; and (3) the creation of the world era system. Yet a conceptual chronology required that this order be inverted to arrive at a logical sequence, resulting in: (1) creation; (2) jubilee/fallow fields; (3) destruction. The historical structure of these models is nonetheless explicable.

(1) The jubilee/fallowing system apparently accompanied the return of the exiles from Babylon.[11] Perhaps from a cosmic perspective identifying people with their land, it conceives of a "space-time" uniting human temporality with that of the earth, and by extension, calls for forgiveness of debts and the manumitting of slaves. The sanctification of the land (and those who dwell there) remains shaped by the geographic scope imposed by the presence of the Temple, without the national independence of the Israelites being required.

(2) The system of dating from the destruction of the Temple marks the end of the mutuality between Jews and their land. This date sets a first limiting point in time for linking rites to a place, even if the process had already begun earlier with the geographical spread of Jews throughout the Roman Empire. The suspension of rituals linked with the Temple strengthened the institution of human government, defined by establishing the biblical canon (the divine Word was thereafter debarred) and documenting the oral law. Introducing a reminder of an historical event as a temporal marker also meant that Jews had acceded to a linear conception of history.

(3) The dating system starting with the creation of the world amounts to a wholly different approach. From now on, the deed is done. Jews are dispersed among the nations; they have neither a national territory nor a Temple assuring sanctity and the divine Presence among them. Their history, which began at the start of the world, continues in a universal framework. The records of temporality surrounding them have changed. Time is presently guided by a religious content. The Christian West substitutes the Church's linear historical

itinerary for secular temporality defined by royal reigns. Time is no longer divided by the lifetimes of princes; it multiplies years in an infinite course. It may reasonably be supposed that the Jewish reference to the era of the world became commonly used during the High Middle Ages in Europe. Between the ninth and tenth centuries, contemporaneously with the introduction as markers of the Hegira in the East and the Incarnation in the West, as Christianity and Islam broke away from the temporality of the Hebrew Bible, epitaphs dating in terms of the era of creation proliferated. Christians, perhaps weary of revising the counts, left the era of the world to scholarly conjecture, but Jews made it a distinguishing standard. So the use of the era of the world occurred naturally. It was already present and only needed to be sought "in the words of the sages."

Without any authority deemed supreme in Judaism, it is impossible to find any rabbinic decree from any time or place stating that the dates should henceforth be standardized. Yet it may be noted that calculations of the era of the world slowly become less arbitrary and seem to merge somewhat, notwithstanding that Yemenite Jews would continue to count from the era of the destruction of the Temple until the twentieth century, and Egyptian Jews referenced the Seleucid era until the sixteenth century.[12] Without seeking to return to arguments by different researchers, who for more than a century have held that dating by the era of the world was gradually imposed around the twelfth century, some aspects have nonetheless developed to support pushing this theory back by two or three centuries. To be sure, the development of the mathematical sciences and astronomy played a role in stabilizing arithmetical counts and chronologies. However, factors such as the spread of sects, the triumph of Christianity, and mystical expectations contributed to this as well, as I hope I have shown.

In practices noted over the centuries, it may be seen that while Jews preserved the markers of creation and destruction, that of fallow fields, limited to abstract rabbinic calculations, had only regained meaning recently in the State of Israel, owing to the reunion of the Jews with their land. Although the markers of creation and destruction may be seen as historical, that of jubilee is not of the same style. Although serving as a temporal marker, it is cyclic and remains ahistorical, since it recalls no event apart from the divine act of creation, which cannot be localized. Dating from the era of the world is part of systematization that aspires to be universal. The world belongs to all its inhabitants, but the destruction of the Temple can only serve as a marker for Jews. The same is true of the jubilee cycle, which only concerns them, unlike all other landowners. The cycle of fallow fields is a direct reminder of the seventh day granted the Jews and, like Shabbat, it is law only for them. Of these three Jewish temporal indicators, one is universal and the other two are strictly Jewish. "Jewish time" would therefore be one made of a universal and specific mixture, likely to change and level out differently, according to the era. This mixture echoes the "three times" of Rosenzweig, composed of the ideas of creation, revelation, and redemption, but reverses the proportion granted to the universal and singular.[13] Here, creation and redemption are universal, while revelation applies only to Jews. However, Jewish time's register of temporality enables it to recreate a "space-time" that is uniquely its own anywhere.[14]

Awareness of Time, Sense of History (Continued)

Finally, it is worth noting the relationship established by the Jews to history in this era, in which the sages stress that the divine Word had ceased to be uttered, "when the last prophets, Haggai, Zechariah and Malachi, died, the Holy Spirit left Israel."[15] The *Seder ʿolam* registers this phenomenon in a process of transposing the divine Word into human words: "Until then [the era of Alexander], prophets made prophecies impelled by the spirit of holiness [*ruah ha-kodesh*], but starting with this time, the words of the sages were heeded."[16] In this way, via the Great Assembly, about which almost nothing is known, divine inspiration passes into the "words of the sages," many of which have survived through the writing of the Mishnah and later, the Talmud.[17] Breaking with the old order of things, which occurred around the time of Ezra, or with the rebuilding of the Temple, assisted in the reinterpretation of the laws that followed the return from Babylon. Paradoxically, these statements are made during the era of the end of the Second Temple, at a time of intense prophetic activity and uncontrolled growth of Jewish sects in Palestine: "one [prophet] in the morning, one at twilight," as Rabbi Juda ha-Nassi observed laconically.[18] Yet tradition asserts that the end of prophecy is less tied to internal development than to an event, the conquest of the Holy Land by Alexander the Great. Seen from this angle, this retiring of the Word is a purely historical circumstance, and its insertion into Jewish chronology becomes one of the wheels of sequentiality that the latter establishes. Now dividing the history of the world into periods, the era of prophecy marked a turning point in the different stages of human-ity. It created a transition between the supernatural and natural, divine and human, realms, in other words between creation and history. To be sure, components of the historical process may be mythical. For all that, they still represent the basis of the world in which dwell hu-mans, whose social laws must, by following the stage of prophecies, determine relationships and conduct. In this way, the law—because decreed by the human voice—has a historical nature, while prophecy remains eschatological.[19] One might find in the dismissal of prophecy to bygone days the aforementioned Christian dichotomy reflecting the break introduced in the arithmetic of temporality between the architectures of the heavenly and the earthly Jerusalem. One might also resort to the eternal problem of the long-lost golden age to ex-plain the phenomenon. Indeed, apart from Josephus and apparently Justus of Tiberias, starting with the first century and for a long time, works wholly devoted to the history of the Jews were written by non-Jewish or spurious authors, such as the *Josippon*.[20] By asserting the end of prophecy, Jews thereby entered human history. This un-fathomed paradox was revealed while the Jews had given up writing about the unfolding of their history in order to restrict themselves to writing the law. Perhaps they were opting for a different vision of what history might be. Is it truly surprising that this phenomenon followed a period of historical emphasis during which recent events were systematically integrated into the liturgical calendar, as seen by the introduction of the historic festivals of Purim and Hanukkah and the writing of the Scroll of Fasting? Military or theological victories seen as likely to strengthen the messianic aspect of Jewish temporal-ity become purely anecdotal—and therefore unnecessary—within the framework of the turnaround after the crackdown on the last revolt against the Romans. Woven from a blend of historical events grasped in terms of eschatology, the time of history developed by the rabbis is located beyond the continuity of a linear tale. So while the Scroll of Fasting, in direct contact with historical events that it returns to the annual calendar, is excluded from tradition, texts such as the books of Esther and Daniel, which describe the present, are displayed like voices transmitting promises to come from the depths of time. From then on, it is understandable that the time of history must leave an imprint, like a lesson from the resurfaced past, in the present that it penetrates and shapes.[21] The origins of this form of accession to history have taken shape on these pages. It validates a hermetic partition between holy, prophetic history—that of yesterday and tomorrow—and the secular human history of today.

Here we need to pass over some centuries at a bound. Noteworthy things happened in the interval, but it would be unfortunate to ignore the way in which the process that led to the creation of Jewish temporality reversed itself in modern times. This is also an occasion to revisit, via the history of the reading of the *Seder 'olam*, the dispute that has divided historians of the Jewish world into partisans either of memory or of history.[22] Between these two opposite poles, where is the Jewish concept of temporality situated? The debate over the adversarial relationship between memory and history mentioned at the start of this book cannot be easily resolved. To be sure, Jewish tradition uses the prophetic principle as an archetype. In this way, it consolidates the collective memory of a dispersed people whose scriptures are the proof of unity. Yet the oral law and its constant redesign in every Jewish place and time mark a history which is not monolithic. Lessons remain always valid, but are nonetheless grasped and reread in the light of today's concerns. Listing Jews in a dual registry of temporality makes it possible to proceed between awareness of history and the contrivance of memory. These different registers, like messianic hopes, are likely to be activated or neutralized based on the present.

The debate about the dominance of memory over history in Jewish society hinged on one theme: the lack of historical accounts in the Jewish world. This was held to be true from the closing of the biblical canon until the nineteenth century, with the exception of the sixteenth century, when several Jewish historical chronicles emerged simultaneously. Much research has settled the debate by showing that, based on texts, a narrative continuity in Judaism must be recognized for the whole medieval period.[23] Different chronicles appeared in the sixteenth century that, each in its own way, aimed to reestablish the historical chain of the Jewish past, while making it part of the history of nations.[24] They show that a specific phenomenon was developing at that time. Joseph ha-Kohen (1496–ca. 1575) proudly announces that "since Josippon"—whom he mistakes for Josephus—no one apart from himself had written the history of his people.[25] Gershom Scholem related this phenomenon to the effects of the expulsion from Spain. After Scholem, historians linked this renewal of historical writing to a process of messianic awakening of which it was the expression. Two sixteenth-century authors from this group, Azariah dei Rossi and David Gans, enlighten the debate opened with the *Seder 'olam*.

When the humanist dei Rossi published *Me'or 'einayim* (*The Light of the Eyes*) on 18 November 1573,[26] the book sent shock waves through the Jewish world. This was neither because dei Rossi used data from Christian sources in tracing the history of the Jews—other Jewish chronicles do this as well—nor because he draws on Greek philosophers and historians to do so. Rather, his account was rejected because, in contrast to contemporary Jewish historians, he questions the chronology of the beginning. His book, which is both innovative and conformist, provoked disproportionately violent reactions.[27] Classified among books "not to read" or have in one's library, *Me'or 'einayim* was anathematized, and only the death of Joseph ben Ephraim Karo, the codifier of the *Shulhan 'arukh*, saved it from being burned.[28] The subversiveness of dei Rossi's criticisms is clear from Judah Loew ben Betsalel's *Be'er ha-golah* (Well of exile):[29]

> In his [chapter] "Yemei 'olam" [Days of the world], he started to move away from the norm and flatly to deny all our traditions on subjects accepted by all the sages of Israel in the Babylon and Jerusalem Talmuds, as well as all the *midrashim*, as if it isn't common sense that the First Temple lasted 410 years and the Second 420. . . . [30] This had never happened in Israel before: "Remember the days of old, consider the years of many generations."[31]

In defense of Jewish memory, in the name of generations of sages who had succeeded one another since the time of the prophets, the rabbi of Prague cried infidelity, afraid that the chronology transmitted by their intervention might be challenged and fall into ignorant hands. Yet this reaction, which is only one among others, also shows a clash that is worth trying to understand to its full extent. Shortly before his death, to answer the charges raised by his work, dei Rossi published an additional text meant to "refute the objections to the chapter 'Yemei 'olam,'" intensifying and justifying his approach.[32] Evidently, dei Rossi's challenge to rabbinic arithmetic could indeed have graver results than a simple scholarly row. Firstly, it revived the old-age dispute about the calendar, for dei Rossi states that the system of intercalations, upon which the Jewish religious cycle depended, had been invented by the sages and not revealed to Moses. As such, this system was comparable with those of other nations, which might have inspired it. Secondly, based on the dispute between Rabbi Joshua and Rabbi Eliezer, as related in different passages of the Talmud, dei Rossi states that the world was created on the first of Nisan, concluding that its attribution to Rosh Ha-shanah in the month of Tishri was merely a late addition, dating to the time when the liturgy was laid down.[33] Finally, as noted, dei Rossi simply questioned everything about the introduction of the era of the world, highlighting the relatively recent origin of the custom, which was so rooted in the system of beliefs of his day that it might have been included among the "laws revealed at Sinai."[34]

Was dei Rossi aware that he was presenting a challenge to the historical system created by rabbinic thought, based on the chronology of the *Seder 'olam?* By recalculating durations established since the beginning of the world, inevitably he found flaws in the chronology of creation. A certain number of years are missing, which means that the "present moment" is no longer in its right place. It should be located a few centuries later. To be sure, it can be quite destabilizing that the count does not add up. How much more so, with all the more reason, to assume that if the chronological system is inadequate, the calendar that governs celebrations is too. In this case, Jewish temporality in its entirety is found wanting. This rereading of the event provoked by the *Me'or 'einayim* is clearly perceived by some of his contemporaries. The reaction of the Prague historian and astronomer David Gans (1541–1613)—the first Ashkenazi chronographer and the last chronicler of his century—who appeals for traditional chronology, shows this

in no uncertain terms.[35] Without getting into the ban decreed by his
teacher, the MaHaRaL, throughout his chronology Gans resumes the
debate with dei Rossi over the length of the years of the world. He
shows clearly that the real question is not exactly how many years have
elapsed, but to which system this chronology belongs:

> The children of Israel left Egypt after 430 years. . . . All this occurred
> in the year 2448 of creation, for as it is written in the parashah of *Bo*,
> "and this was at the end of 430 years." We count the 430 years starting
> with the seventieth year of Abraham. . . . And from there, 400 until
> the exodus from Egypt, and all that put together brings us to the year
> 2448 and this is specified in the *Seder ʿolam rabbah*, chapter 3, and in
> the *Mekhilta debo el-Paro, Exodus rabbah*, and *Tanhuma de-shemot*.
>
> In spite of this, the author of *Meh'or ʿeinayim*, chapter 35, reports
> the opinion of the latest codifiers that another calculation exists. . . .
> Therefore, from these five greats of the world,[36] . . . who agree to
> count 430 years starting with the birth of Isaac, in the year 48 of the
> third millennium, the exodus from Egypt having occurred, based on
> their statements, thirty years after the calculation of 448, namely, in
> the year 478. . . . The opinion of the author of *Me'or ʿeinayim* in his
> chapter 35, casts doubt on the years of the creation in three places.
> Before transmitting his statements, I would like to offer the count of
> years according to our custom of counting today. . . . Between the
> exodus from Egypt and the building of the Temple by King Solomon,
> it is said in the verse of 1 Kings 6: "And it came to pass in the four
> hundred and eightieth year after the children of Israel were come out
> of the land of Egypt that the Temple was built." From the start of
> the building of the First Temple until its destruction, we count 410
> years, according to the *Seder ʿolam rabbah*. Yet Rashi, the RaBaD,
> and David Kimhi[37] differed there too . . . and this is the second place
> that disrupts the calculations of the years of the creation. Between
> the destruction of the First Temple and the building of the Second,
> in the second year of Darius, there are seventy years, which are also
> mentioned in a verse of Jeremiah 25 and 29, as well as in Zechariah 1
> and Daniel 9. Between the building of the Second Temple and Greek
> rule, we calculate according to our teachers, may their memory be
> blessed, thirty-four, which also raised many suspicions, as we saw with
> the year 3448, and this is the place of the third calling into question.
> Between the start of the Greek kingdom until today, which is the year
> 5352 [1592] according to the opinion of all exegetes and codifiers, there

are 1,904 years, as shown by the era of contracts of the year 448 of the fourth millennium. . . . When all the numbers match, we arrive at 5352 [1592]. . . . If we add or subtract even one of these numbers, then we must add or subtract that of the years [elapsed] since creation, and because the five greats of this world . . . agree that 430 years were fully counted starting with the birth of Isaac, which gave them for the exile in Egypt a surplus on the count of 210, of thirty years, and it follows that this year which is the year 5352 [1592] would be the year [5]382 [1622], thirty years later. And this is the opinion of *Me'or 'einayim* such as it appears in chapters 35 and 40 of his book.[38]

Here David Gans argues in favor of a historical combination, transmitted by tradition, that includes chronology as well as the calendar that governs temporality. In bringing the contentious issues raised by dei Rossi to the attention of the reader, Gans does not dismiss them lightly. He explains why, even if it is conceivable that this chronographic method is wrong, it cannot undermine the totality that it controls. Gans does not base his defense on the grounds of exactness, but in accordance with logic. He relies on historical data reported and interpreted by tradition, but not as Rabbi Loew did, in the name of sacred history, or as Ibn Daud did, in the name of inherent promises. Gans sometimes justifies the validity of the traditional approach, in spite of its clear chronographic deficiency, in a quasi-acrobatic way. Not seeking to sidestep pitfalls, he faces them modestly. For example, he notes that not everyone in the Great Assembly was of the same generation.[39] Conceding to dei Rossi that it is unthinkable that Persian rule only lasted fifty-two years, he takes the mistake to be a printer's error that replaced the number 200 with 2.[40]

In this way, his defense of the traditional system expresses a clear historical conscience. It is based on an analysis that rests on the quantitative method, but also considers its consequences in the realm of temporality. The sixteenth-century questioning of durations established by the *Seder 'olam* is part of a reflection that discerns among them the historical elements relating to the sacred and the profane. From then on, it can be seen that the process that took hold during antiquity and the pre-rabbinic era is being inverted. It was a matter of conceiving a strictly Jewish temporality—and therefore holy—by integrating all the historical and temporal data within the same framework to the exclusion of any source apart from biblical information. Which the sages did, starting with the *Seder 'olam*. A history system resulted that, by standardizing the chronological agency to the course of the stars, created a perfect fit between celebrations and in representing divinely conceived time, which leaves nothing to chance and governs daily life. When after more than a millennium had elapsed historians sought to remake history by retracing a temporal line that simultaneously described the time of nations and of Israel, they faced the inherent contradictions in this convergence. For this history, deployed as a model of temporality, polished by the sages, codifiers, thinkers, and philosophers who followed one another over the centuries, cannot be challenged without exploding the whole system. So piety is not the only reason that Gans refutes the possibility that dei Rossi's calculations might result in a general reappraisal of the Jewish calendar, rather than the calculations themselves. The temporal wire stretched since antiquity by the chronological exegesis of the *Seder 'olam*, whose expression is perfectly developed here, is suddenly stretched thin. If the dual temporality inherent in this system permitted navigating smoothly between (holy) Jewish temporality and (profane) external temporality, how to consider this internal differentiation within Jewish temporality? For what is sketched by dei Rossi and Gans, and doubtless before them, is now the possibility of grasping a Jewish history that refers as much to the sacred as to the profane. Are these two analysts of the Jewish world ready to accept the consequences of their studies? "In any event, regardless of whatever increases or subtractions that will be made to aera mundi computations, we shall always retain it: the custom of the ancestors of Israel has the status of Torah as bygone days," dei Rossi declares. "Opposition to anything related to the laws of the Torah is far from the object of this investigation, nor will anything be proposed that would mar the honor of our rabbis, may they rest in peace."[41] Gans offers the guarantee: "There is no mistake in our use of the calculation of the years of creation that might result in rejecting a law or Commandment; even in terms of the tally of *BeHaR"D*, no solemnity will be added to or subtracted from the set date.[42] And nothing will be moved amid the calculation of the *molad* [birth / new moon] as long as the world lasts."[43] It is impossible this time to cast doubt on their adhesion to the memory of the sages and the transmission of the laws. Is memory pitted against history? From now on, it seems that the question is irrelevant, since rather than competing, they strengthen each other.

Despite the general consensus about the messianic nature of sixteenth-century historiographical creations, we are nonetheless unlikely to find in the two works invoked here any expectation more intense than that of the decorum required of any Jewish author. Indeed, dei Rossi writes: "I observe the band of sons of prophets who expect the year 335 [1575] to be a day of the Lord in which He shall effect a joyous salvation for his people that will last forever."[44] In a way, he does so the better to stress the futility of conjecture based on a mistaken sum. For he states at the outset, even before going on to shed light on this reckoning, that the disparity between the years elapsed between creation and the traditional calculation is not a matter of a few figures, but of some decades. It is well known that scholars in the Jewish world still calculated the coming of the Messiah and persisted in examining the omens of Daniel, talmudic debates, and the *Seder Eliyahu*.[45] The talmudic system of chronology was enhanced over the centuries by reckonings by rabbis keen on astronomy and astrology who all through the Middle Ages sought to determine the probability of His coming by casting learned horoscopes.[46] Dei Rossi—like Gans—rejects astrology. He adds some examples of customs involving *gematria* [Assyro-Babylonian numerology] as a speculative matter. Yet it is unlikely that dei Rossi went in for calculating probabilities or forecasting, and he does not lead his readers along this path. Which does not keep him from mentioning, among the motives for his research, that he hopes to shed light on some basic principles of messianic time, "which, according to many respected opinions, is very close now."[47] It seems that the quest for rational historic truth matters more to dei Rossi than waiting for the Messiah who, according to him, is in the control of the order of things, and will appear when He chooses and in good time.

Gans's case is more complex.[48] A modern astronomer in his century, apologist for the traditionally transmitted chronology, and chronicler of events, he notes everything relating to the phenomenal, whether it be comets or legends. He does not necessarily criticize his sources—that was not the point of his work—but he does not hesitate to indicate and reject, if need be, statements that defy logic or cannot be supported by rabbinic sources. The influence of his German contemporaries is tangible in his work, which scrupulously cites the origins of his information.[49] He also cites other Jewish chroniclers insofar as he accepts their statements. So he draws copiously on dei Rossi, sometimes following his proofs by quoting his explanations word for word.[50] If Gans does not shrink from a messianic reading of incidents that he describes, it is nonetheless impossible to link his expectation with the consequences of the expulsion from Spain, sparking an outburst of hope, as Scholem would have it. The events in question occurred for the moment outside the Jewish world. The stress that Gans places on the description of the history of Christians and their trials and tribulations remains unprecedented in the Jewish world. Dividing his account into two distinct parts, between the history of the Jews and the Christians, he nevertheless combines them in a narrative that often contradicts the theoretical approach. Yet if dei Rossi is immersed in the Italy of mysticism and the Renaissance, Gans is steeped in the atmosphere of Prague, a city as mystical as it was humanist, with a very different political, cultural, and religious context. After centuries of endless wars, for the moment, diverse religions and cultures, businesspeople, and scientists from across the spectrum coexist. Reform is accompanied by the implicit recognition of sects, and millenarianism proliferates in an apocalyptic atmosphere.[51] Sustained by allusions to Isaiah and Daniel, generations of visionaries followed one another in predicting the imminence of the end. From Jan Hus to Philipp Melanchthon, and including Nicholas of Cusa and Guillaume Postel, conjectures on the probable duration of the universe made in the Christian world put into perspective the force of those in the Jewish world.[52] The times were saturated with expectations of redemption. The messianic coming might therefore seem near in the reign of Holy Roman Emperor Rudolf II. The situation of the Jews and Christians, like the relationships between them, was very unusual. This turbulent intellectual landscape cannot be overlooked, and no one can say to what extent this chronicle directly results from the convergence of these hopes.

The debate about the passage of time was just as vigorous in the sixteenth century as it must have been formerly in antiquity. The fundamental difference lies in the approach, which, this time, far from seeking to establish a doctrine, sought to justify its basis. Indeed, for the first time, and possibly the last, the years of the Jewish era of the world were discussed from a scientific point of view.[53] The editions of the *Seder 'olam* that follow one another, starting with that of Jacob Emden, show that the debate has shifted within the Jewish world.[54] From now on, Jewish temporality will be an implicit part of conflicts between partisans of the Enlightenment and those of Orthodoxy. And when nineteenth-century scholars exhume the *Me'or 'Einayim* from the libraries to which it had been relegated, it will no longer be a subject of dispute, other instruments of dating having been deployed. The work will be a philological support, allowing further research. Scholars will no longer feel obliged to finish each presentation with an edifying catchphrase, as dei Rossi did. From this point forward, the breakthrough in the separation of science and religion by dei Rossi and Gans allows mistakes to be noted without being sacrilegious.[55] Finally, in the meantime, the very concept of time, which had become relative under the impetus of discoveries by Newton and George Berkeley and the philosophy of Immanuel Kant, will be transformed.

The history of the traditional reading of the *Seder 'olam* shows a world ruled by its own laws. Born of the meeting of an exegetical movement and the desire to find the probable date of the coming of the Messiah, the calculation of time elapsed since the creation served these two causes over the centuries. From the time of biblical Judaism until the sixteenth century, then, it seems that the "providential" history prized by theologians was replaced by the order of the world, established as a historical system, without much opposition. Integrated into tradition, this system contained both the spark and the limits of messianism. It calculates but cannot count, measures the present based on the past, but cannot situate it. Supported jointly by memory and history, this order of the world appeals like all the rest, alternatively to this side and that. And like hours measured by a clepsydra, whose fill varies according to whether they are diurnal or nocturnal, memory and history are not always weighed by the same measure, but together they constitute the beam of the scale.

Let us hasten through further centuries to get a brief glimpse of further developments of this adventure. In the eighteenth and nineteenth centuries, rediscovering Hellenism and biblical criticism, Jewish scholars of the Enlightenment sought to return to the source of the roots of

Judaism. As this book draws to a close, we see that they followed the path of those who, at the start of the era, had supported the revealed calendar subject to criticism from astronomers. Yet unlike those who once fought the intrusion of the "time of nations" into Jewish temporality, they sought a return to the diversity and variety of temporal registers to let them resume a dialogue, which they felt had been disrupted for centuries, with the rest of the world. By reinventing a Judaism that was universalist and devoid of any nationalism, perhaps seen in the light of the works of Philo of Alexandria, they thought to preserve the Jews from a history of withdrawal.[56] This withdrawal was established during the talmudic era, as Marcel Simon, among other historians, defined it.[57] Perhaps they put aside the balance between the world of tomorrow and that of today as established by the categories of thought about Judaism devised by the rabbis, a balance that the sages constructed at the same time that they created a guarantee of the resurrection, shortly after the Maccabee era. The introduction of a temporality in "this world below" achieved by the rabbis over the centuries kept Judaism from disintegrating and allowed it to carry on within nations, while participating in a dual temporal register. Once the sacred was separated from the profane at the center of Jewish temporality, an imbalance appeared. The narrative could continue with the philosophy of history. Once again, Jewish scholars like Nachman Krochmal[58] and Heinrich Graetz found in the past of tradition the tools to construct a history that they defined as being essentially turned toward the future.[59] From now on, between science and orthodoxy, the question of temporality hung suspended between the future and the past. As for the present, the Orthodox German rabbi Samson Raphael Hirsch (1808–1888) summed up its ambivalence in a phrase: "The catechism of the Jew consists of his calendar."[60] But all that belongs to the rest of the story.

Afterword to the English Translation

The perception and understanding of time are endless matters. They constantly soar beyond classical approaches to astronomy, mathematics, and physics, reaching the cognitive realm. In the human and social sciences, they make up one of the ways in which groups forge social ties, express their special features, and structure their collective awareness. Our relationship to time is also one of the primary forms of knowledge. In brief, time and its corollary, temporality, are the central components of human experience. Studying the construction of a Jewish temporality amounts in some respects to grasping a basic element of the dynamics that allowed Jews to continue as a distinct group in the midst of the Islamic and Christian societies they have been living in.

About twenty years ago, when I began this project, almost no scholarly work had been done on the link Jews developed with time, apart from studies by theologians, often based on a Christian reading of the Bible. Unconcerned about the meaning of temporality established by "real" Jews, they basically perceived Judaism as detached from any mooring in historical time. Since then, obviously, times have changed. This book proves it in many ways. Working in a then little known field, it progressed by seeking landmarks, historical moorings for questions that the historiography of Jewish studies had hitherto scarcely asked. Meanwhile some studies of the calendar and almanacs (by Sacha Stern,[1] Michael Chyutin,[2] and Elisheva Carlebach,[3] among others) added other input to what had been a preliminary introduction to questions of time, later developed in a more concrete way in the second volume to my study.[4] Moreover, it became possible to gauge how technological advances changed the perception of time itself. Once "digital," time became virtual. Doing so, it changed the task of the researcher, who thereafter could annul time and space by flying with a mere click through sources and references without even moving a chair or consulting a timepiece. Sources and references also evolved, growing exponentially at the speed of light. Updating this work would have multiplied its length tenfold, while also perhaps leading it to other approaches. Thanks to Benyamin Wattenberg's invaluable comments, however, I have only corrected some textual errors and details in this English translation and added some essential new references to the notes and bibliography. These reveal the vital progress in research in Jewish studies in recent years. In all the areas discussed here, research has expanded so greatly that the question of time that I have tried to grasp, and that of the temporality of the reader for whom this book is intended, are astonishingly relevant to what lies at the heart of my project, rooted as it is in a temporality located and replayed between past and present.

I am pleased to express my gratitude to those who made it possible for this book to be presented to a new readership: Steven Zipperstein and Aron Rodrigue, editors of the Stanford University Press's Stanford Studies in Jewish History and Culture series; Eric Brandt and Mariana Raykov, the Stanford editorial team; Benjamin Ivry, whose skills were applied to this text, putting it into lively English; the copy editor, Peter Dreyer, for his precious *akribeia*; Hélène Monsacré, who took care of the publication from the start; and, last but not least, the institutions that provided the financial support without which the book would not have appeared, the Fondation pour la mémoire de la Shoah, the Centre national du livre, the Jewish Federation of Greater Hartford, and the Centre de recherches historiques at the École des hautes études en sciences sociales.

I am dedicating this book to the memory of Alex Derczanski (1924–2014), Z"l.

SYLVIE ANNE GOLDBERG

Reference Matter

Appendix

The tables below, based on biblical calculations of time and their theological interpretations, which reflect the practices both of the rabbis and of the Fathers of the Church, may serve to clarify the chronological calculations found in ancient and medieval Jewish literature.

According to Genesis 5:

Adam fathered Seth at the age of 130, then lived 800 more years =	930 years.
Seth lived 105 years and after having begot Enos lived another 807 years =	912 years.
Enos lived 90 years and after having begot Cainan lived another 815 years =	905 years.
Cainan lived 70 years, and after begetting Mahalalel, lived another 840 years =	910 years.
Mahalalel lived 65 years and after begetting Jared lived another 830 years =	895 years.
Jared lived 162 years and after begetting Enoch lived another 800 years =	962 years.
Enoch lived 65 years and after begetting Methuselah,	
Enoch walked with God for 300 years =	365 years.
Methuselah lived 187 years and after begetting Lamech lived another 782 years =	969 years.
Lamech lived 182 years and after begetting Noah lived another 595 years =	777 years.

Noah was 500 years old when he begat Shem, Ham, and Japheth.

The following table gives the numbers found in Genesis 5:3–31, Masoretic texts (MT), the Samaritan text (ST), Septuagint, and Josephus's *Jewish Antiquities* (*JA*), showing ages at the time of the birth of the eldest son and their lifespans:

Gen. 5	MT	ST	Septuagint	JA	lifespan
Adam	130	130	230	230	930
	800	800	700	700	
Seth	105	105	205	205	912
	807	807	707	707	
Enos	90	090	190	190	930
	840	840	740	740	

Cainan	70 840	70 840	170 740	170 740	910
Mahalalel	65 830	65 830	165 730	165 730	895
Jared	162 800	62 847	162 800	162 965	962
Enoch	65 300	065 300	165 200	165 200	365
Methuselah	187 782	067 720	167 802	187 782	969
Lamech	182 595	053 600	188 565	082 625	777; 653; 753; 707
Noah	600 350	600 350	600 350	600 350	950
Total = Flood	1,656	1,307	2,242	2,656	

From the Flood to the Birth of Abraham:

Gen. 11:10–26 J, *JA* 1: 149

MT	ST	Septuagint	J
292	942	1072	(292) 993

Data from the Seder 'olam rabbah:

From Adam to the Flood, 1,656 years elapsed. Enoch buried Adam and lived for 57 years after him.

Between the Flood and the birth of Peleg ("division") [Gen. 10:25: "for in his days the earth was divided"], there was an interval of 340 years.

Abraham was 48 years old at the time of the division, was 99 years old when he was circumcised, and died at the age of 175.

Isaac died at the age of 180, and Jacob at 147.

Joseph died at 110.

Thus:	*Anno Mundi* (*AM*)
Birth of Abraham	1948
Arrival in Canaan	2023
Birth of Ishmael	2034
Birth of Isaac	2048
Death of Sarah	2085

Marriage of Isaac	2088
Birth of Jacob	2108
Death of Abraham	2123
Birth of Joseph	2199
Sale of Joseph	2216
Death of Isaac	2228
Descent to Egypt	2238
Death of Jacob	2255
Death of Joseph	2309
Birth of Moses	2368
Exodus from Egypt	2448
Crossing the Jordan, death of Moses	2488

However, the numbers are not regarded as reliable data, inasmuch as Exodus 12:41 tells us: "And it came to pass at the end of the four hundred and thirty years, even the selfsame day it came to pass, that all the hosts of the Lord went out from the land of Egypt."

— God predicts 400 years' slavery in Egypt (Gen. 15:13–14);
— the stay in Egypt lasts 430 years (Exod. 12:40);
— tradition teaches that the actual stay was 210 years;
— the rabbis reduced it to 86 years.

Rabbinic exegesis explains that:

— the count of 400 years starts with the birth of Isaac;
— Isaac begat Jacob at the age of 60;
— Jacob left for Egypt at the age of 130: 60 + 130 = 190.

The number of years of Egyptian bondage traditionally accepted is 210 (400–190). Exodus 12:40 tells us, however: "Now the sojourning of the children of Israel, who dwelt in Egypt, was four hundred and thirty years"; to arrive at this number, the 30 years before the birth of Isaac must be added to the 400 of God's prediction.

The *Seder 'olam* states that the real enslavement began after a change of pharaohs, and only after the birth of Miriam, and lasted 86 years. Tradition interprets this in numeric form as follows:

86 = 1/5 of 430 of the Exodus = 4 cups of wine, representing the reprieve, 4/5, granted to the Hebrews, since the term for cup, *koss*, has a numerical value of 86.

Results:

From the Flood to the birth of Abraham: 292 years.
From the birth of Abraham to the end of Genesis: 361 years = 653 years.
Solomon builds the temple in the 480th year after the exodus from Egypt
(1 Kings 6:1) and finishes it in 20 years = 500 years after the exodus from Egypt.

The First Temple lasts for 480 years.

The cumulative reigns of the Kings of Judea add up to 430 years, until the Babylonian Exile.

Jeremiah and Zechariah state that the exile lasted 70 years until the return.

From the exodus to the deportation to Babylon = 480+430+70 = 980 (or almost 1,000 years).

In Josephus:

Consecrated in 3102 *AM* (*JA*, 8:61), or 612/592 years after the exodus from Egypt, 1,440 years after the Flood, and 3,572 (?) years after creation, the Temple of Solomon is destroyed after standing for 470 years.

Chronology based on the Seder 'olam *(ed. Weinstock):*

- Destruction of the First Temple by Nebuchadnezzar: 3338 *AM*
      Evil-Merodach (reigned 22 years):   3364 *AM*
      Belshazzar: 3386 *AM*
      Died in: 3389 *AM*
      Koresh the Persian (Cyrus the Great):   3390 *AM*
      Ahasuerus and Esther: 3392 *AM*
      Darius (their son):   3409 *AM*
- Construction of the Second Temple in   3408 *AM*
      Remains standing: 70 years
      Persian kingdom lasts: 34 years
      Alexander the Great born: 3423 *AM*
      Arrives in Palestine at aged nineteen in: 3442 *AM*
      So-called Greek kingdom lasts: 180 years
      Hasmonean dynasty lasts: 103 years
      Herodian dynasty lasts: 103 years
- Total of reigns until the destruction of the Second Temple = 420 years

- Destruction of the Second Temple: 3828 *AM*
      Between the exodus from Egypt and the building of the First Temple 480 years elapsed. The Temple was built over 410 years.
      Between the destruction and the reign of Darius: 52 years
      Between Koresh and Darius: 18 years
      Between the building of the Second Temple and the fall of the Persians 34 years elapsed.
      From the conquest of Elam to the Greek kingdom: 6 years
- Total between the exodus from Egypt and the Greek kingdom =
                                                           around 1,000 years

Septuagint (third century BCE):

From Adam to the Flood:	2242 *AM*
Elapsed until the birth of Peleg (Gen.10:25):	3,000 years
Abraham:	3314 *AM*
Entry into Egypt:	3604 *AM*
Exodus:	3819 *AM*
Founding of the Temple:	4259 *AM*
Destruction of the Temple:	4689 *AM*

Why?

— "For a thousand years in thy sight are but as yesterday when it is past"
(Ps. 90:4)

— 7 days of creation = 6 × 1,000 + 1,000 years of Shabbat = divine Advent, or
end of time

— Daniel 8:14: 2,300 evenings and mornings = 1,150 days = 3 years, 3 months
= period of Antiochus IV Epiphanes

— Daniel 9: 70 shemittot cycles between the oracle of Jeremiah and the
repopulation of Jerusalem = 70 fallow years = 490 years

— coming of the Messiah after 6,000 years = 2240 CE

— from Peleg to Jesus, Sextus Julius Africanus (third century) calculates
5,499 years, birth of Jesus = 5500 or 5503 *AM*

— for the Christians of Alexandria = 5493

— for the Christians of Byzantium = 5509

— 6,000 years elapsed = death of Jesus

• Note: the year 1 according to the era of the destruction of the Temple = 381
of the Seleucid Era = 3830 *AM*

Era of the Incarnation = 3760 *AM*

Approximate Chronology

Before the Christian Era

2000–1500 (about):	the Middle Bronze Age
1700:	Hammurabi
1650–1500:	Epoch of the Patriarchs
1500–1200:	Israel in Egypt
1300:	Exodus from Egypt
1225–1020:	Period of the Judges
1029–1004:	Saul
1004–965:	David (for Judah 1004–998)
965–926:	Solomon
967–800:	Amos, Hosea, Isaiah, Micah
872–852:	Elijah (under the kingship of Jehoshaphat)
721:	Capture of Samaria
663 or 586:	Founding of the military colony of Elephantine in Egypt
639–609:	Josiah
621:	Deuteronomic reform (Jeremiah)
598:	Babylonians invade the kingdom of Judah (Jeremiah)
608–593:	Jehoiakim (Jeremiah)
587:	Second invasion of Nebuchadnezzar (Jeremiah + Ezekiel)
586:	Capture of Jerusalem (Jeremiah + Ezekiel)
586–516 (538):	Babylonian Captivity (Ezekiel)
538:	The Edict of Cyrus the Great authorizing the return of exiled people (Deutero-Isaiah)
522–486:	Darius I
520–516:	Zerubbabel completes the Second Temple (Haggai)
Around 500:	Malachi
486–465:	Xerxes I or Ahasuerus
458 (397):	Ezra, second return (Great Assembly)

445–433:	Nehemiah, governor of Judah (Great Assembly)
411–410:	Destruction of the temple of Elephantine (Great Assembly)
336–323:	Alexander the Great (332 in Palestine); Simeon the Just; Samaritan schism (Great Assembly)
312–311:	Battle of Gaza; Egyptian rule over Palestine; start of the Seleucid era
200–100:	Letter of Aristeas; beginning of the Septuagint
200–198:	Charter of Antiochus
Around 180:	Ben Sira (Ecclesiasticus or Sirach)
160:	Start of the Maccabean revolt
160:	Rededication of the Temple, Chanukah
160:	Death of Judah Maccabee
Around 160:	Temple at Leontopolis founded by Onias IV
143–134:	Simon Maccabeus, declared a prince in 141/143; order to the Jewish communities in Egypt to celebrate Chanukah
140–139:	Rome recognizes the independence of Judea; expulsion of the Jews from Rome
63:	Conquest of Jerusalem by Pompey
54:	Sack of the Temple by Crassus
39–34:	Herod rebuilds the Temple (era of the academies of Hillel and Shammai)

The Christian Era

4–6:	Partition of Judea; administrative supervision by Roman procurators
14–37:	Tiberius; ministry of John the Baptist and Jesus
29–30:	Crucifixion of Jesus
37–41:	Caligula; riots in Alexandria (39); Philo in Rome
66–70:	Jewish-Roman wars; Josephus; burning of the Second Temple
69–79:	Yohanan ben Zakkai founds the academy at Yavneh
73:	Closure of the Temple at Leontopolis
81–96:	Domitian; Gamaliel the Elder (in Rome in 95)
117–138:	Hadrian; Rabbi Akiva starts the Mishnah, later compiled by Judah ha-Nassi (the Prince)
132–135:	Bar Kokhba revolt; death of Rabbi Akiva
138–161:	Antoninus Pius; rebuilding of the Sanhedrin at Osha; Simeon ben Gamliel, patriarch; Simeon bar Yochai, Rabbi Meir, Yose ben Halafta (author of the *Seder ʿolam*); Jose the Galilean

170–217:	Judah the Prince, patriarch; completion of the Mishnah
219–247:	Sura, Nehardea, and ben Lakish Academies in Tiberias
230:	Rabbi Yohanan bar Nappah starts to compile the Jerusalem Talmud
254–299:	Pumbedita Academy
313:	Victory of Christianity
320–365:	Hillel II
321:	Constantine the Great, edict to the Cologne community
358–359:	Hillel II proclaims the perpetual calendar
375–427:	Rav Ashi of Sura starts compiling the Babylonian Talmud
385:	Completion of the Jerusalem Talmud under Rabbi Gamaliel ben Yehudah, or according to other, in 415 under the Patriarchate
400–429:	Gamaliel the Elder; suppression of the patriarchy in Palestine; the Palestinian Talmud is doubtless finished, around 415 or 385 according to some
474–499:	Ravina II closes the Babylonian Talmud
500:	Theoderic the Great, king of the Ostrogoths, confirms the Jews' privileges

The Alphabet and Numerical Values of Letters

aleph (a)	= 1	א
bet (b)	= 2	ב
gimel (g)	= 3	ג
dalet (d)	= 4	ד
he (h)	= 5	ה
vav (v)	= 6	ו
zayin (z)	= 7	ז
het (c)	= 8	ח
tet (e)	= 9	ט
yod (y)	= 10	י
kaf (k)	= 20	כ
lamed (l)	= 30	ל
mem (m)	= 40	מ
nun (n)	= 50	נ
samekh (s)	= 60	ס
ayin (i)	= 70	ע
pe (p)	= 80	פ
tsadi (x)	= 90	צ
qof (q)	= 100	ק
resh (r)	= 200	ר
shin (s)	= 300	ש
tav (t)	= 400	ת

Notes

Abbreviations

Annales HSS	Annales: Histoire, Sciences Sociales
BT	Babylonian Talmud
CBQ	Catholic Biblical Quarterly
EJ	Encyclopaedia Judaica, ed. Cecil Roth et al., 16 vols. (Jerusalem: Keter; New York: Macmillan, 1971–1972)
HTR	Harvard Theological Review
HUCA	Hebrew Union College Annual
JE	The Jewish Encyclopedia, ed. Isidore Singer et al., 12 vols. (New York: Funk & Wagnalls, 1901–1906)
JPS	Jewish Publication Society of America
JQR	Jewish Quarterly Review
JSJ	Journal for the Study of Judaism
JSOT	Journal for the Study of the Old Testament
JT	Jerusalem Talmud
MGWJ	Monatsschrift für Geschichte und Wissenschaft des Judentums
REJ	Revue des études juives
RQ	Revue de Qumran
Sanh.	Sanhedrin
VT	Vetus Testamentum
VTS	Vetus Testamentum Supplementae (Leiden)

Preface

1. Ned. 28a; Git. 10b; Babba Qamma 113a; BB 54b, 55b. This decision has major importance for the relationship between Jews and their surroundings. See Philip Biberfeld, *Dina de-malkhuta dina* (Berlin: Hebräischer Verlag "Menorah," 1925); Shmuel Shilo, *Dina de-malkhuta dina* [The Law of the State Is Law] (Jerusalem: Academic Press, 1974; in Hebrew); Michael Walzer et al., eds., *The Jewish Political Tradition*, vol. 1: *Authority* (New Haven, CT: Yale University Press, 2000). And

see also Sylvie Anne Goldberg, "Common Law and Jewish Law: The Diasporic Principle of *Dina de-malkuta dina*," *Behemoth* 2 (2008): 39–53.

2. Salo W. Baron, *History and Jewish Historians* (Philadelphia: JPS, 1964), 90.

Introduction

1. Starting in 1582, the Gregorian calendar was gradually introduced as a refinement to the Julian calendar, initiated by Julius Caesar in 46 BCE as a reform of the Roman calendar. It was intended to correct the length of the year, especially to make Easter coincide with the time of year agreed upon at the First Council of Nicaea in 325. See Francesco Maiello, *Histoire du calendrier de la liturgie à l'agenda* (Paris: Seuil, 1993), and E. G. Richard, *Mapping Time: The Calendar and Its History* (Oxford: Oxford University Press, 1998).

2. Shavuot, the Feast of Weeks, is a Jewish holiday that occurs on the sixth day of the Hebrew month of Sivan (late May or early June), commemorating the anniversary of the day God gave the Torah to the nation of Israel on Mount Sinai after the exodus from Egypt. It coincides with Pentecost in the Christian calendar.

3. According to tradition, the first and second Jerusalem Temples were destroyed in the month of Av, the Comforter (July–August), so named because, as the month in which the preordained destruction had occurred, it also had to be the month of consolation; for redemption would occur: just as the first part of God's promise had been kept, the second part would be too.

4. The year of the world, *annus mundi*, is based on chronologies compiled from genealogies in the Bible.

5. In present-day social life, the degrees of observance and affiliation with Jewish traditions are infinitely variable. They may range from a simple reminder of identity to strict observance of the whole of the Law, including the observance to different extents of holidays, dietary laws, and the use of the Jewish calendar during times of cyclic transitions in life, such as circumcisions, bar mitsvot and bat mitsvot (marking the entry of young people into the community), marriages, and anniversaries of bereavements. There is also a total diversity of community affiliations, more or less Orthodox or Reform, just as there are an infinite number of identifications with Judaism.

6. See Eviatar Zerubavel, *The Seven Day Circle: The History and Meaning of the Week* (New York: Macmillan, 1985), and id., *Hidden Rhythms: Schedules and Calendars in Social Life* (Chicago: University of Chicago Press, 1981).

7. On the day of redemption, the "remnant of the people of Israel," or *She'erit Yisrael*, would consist of those who had stayed faithful to the divine covenant. The idea appears in the prophetic books, notably in Isa. 46:3, Jer. 31:6–7, Ezra 11:13, and Mic. 5:5–7, and is mentioned in Lev. 26:36–45, where their return from exile is forecast.

8. The Babylonian Exile, also termed the First Exile, dates to around 597–538 BCE. It is widely held that the Hebrews brought back with them from Babylon significant portions of their calendar, the names of months in particular.

9. The development of the cycle of ritual life is traced in Part II of this book. See also Salo W. Baron, *A Social and Religious History of the Jews*, vol. 8: *High Middle Ages* (New York: Columbia University Press, 1958), "Scientific Exploration," pp. 175–211.

10. In referring to "traditional society" I seek to distinguish between the Jewish social practices that preceded and those that followed the Jewish Emancipation— society governed by the laws of Jewish tradition versus society governed by the laws of citizenship. In judging them in terms of their structural dynamics, we may note the establishment of a kind of continuity in the emergence of Jewish communities in central and eastern Europe during the Middle Ages (eleventh–twelfth centuries) until their modern breakout in the eighteenth–twentieth centuries.

11. "Privileges" granted by kings, princes, lords, and so on were charters and forms of legal contracts that, in return for agreed-upon financial conditions, authorized Jews to live in certain countries, cities, or regions according to a system of communal autonomy allowing them to be governed by their own laws and to practice their religion. See Julius Aronius, *Regesten zur Geschichte der Juden im fränkischen und deutschen Reiche bis zum Jahre 1273* (Berlin: Nathansen & Lamm, 1887–1902; repr., Hildesheim: Olms, 1970), no. 168, and Louis Finkelstein, *Jewish Self-Government in the Middle Ages* (New York: Feldheim, 1924). These charters were part of a continuity of specific laws granted to Jews in antiquity, from those mentioned in the books of Ezra and Maccabees to Theodoric's charter confirming the privileges of Jews in the year 500 CE.

12. Norbert Elias, *Über die Zeit* (Frankfurt am Main: Suhrkamp, 1984); translated as *Time: An Essay* (Oxford: Blackwell, 1992) and as *An Essay on Time*, in *The Collected Works of Norbert Elias*, vol. 9 (Dublin: University College Dublin Press, 2007).

13. Alban Bensa, "De la micro histoire vers une anthropologie critique," in *Jeux d'échelles: La microanalyse à l'expérience*, ed. Jacques Revel, pp. 54–55 (Paris: Seuil, 1996).

14. Paul Ricoeur, *Time and Narrative*, vol. 1, trans. Kathleen McLaughlin and David Pellauer (Chicago: University of Chicago Press, 1984). See the first chapter, "The Aporia of the Experience of Time: Book II of Augustine's *Confessions*."

15. Although Jews employed a ritual calendar arranged in exact cycles, using chronologies and computing the date of the creation of the world posed different problems, expressed both in Messianic estimations and the establishment of "long" cycles. For this reason there are chronologies in many writings, especially those found at Qumran, long associated with what is currently called the Dead Sea Sect. See Roger T. Beckwith, "Daniel 9 and the Date of the Messiah's Coming in Essene, Hellenistic, Pharisaic, Zealot and Early Christian Communities," *RQ* 10, no. 4 [40] (1981): 521–542; L. A. Reznikoff, "Jewish Calendar Calculations," *Scripta Mathematica* 9 (1943): 191–195, 274–277; Hayyim Yehiel Bornstein, "Ta'arikhei Yisrael," *Ha-tekufah* 8 (1920): 281–338; 9 (1921): 202–264. The oldest surviving Hebrew chronology, apart from the one in the Book of Jubilees, is in *Seder 'olam*, which after the twelfth century was called *Seder 'olam rabbah* to

differentiate it from *Seder 'olam zutta*. A first edition appeared in Mantua in 1514, followed by many more. The corpus of ancient and medieval Hebrew chronologies is collected in Adolf Neubauer, ed., *Medieval Jewish Chronicles and Chronological Notes* (Oxford: Clarendon Press, 1887–1895; 2nd ed., Jerusalem: n.p., 1967). We shall return to this subject at length in Part II of this book.

16. Alphonse Dupront, *Du sacré: Croisades et pèlerinages, images et langages* (Paris: Gallimard, 1987), p. 309.

17. Marc Bloch, *Apologie pour l'histoire ou Métier d'historien* (1949), trans. Peter Putnam as *The Historian's Craft* (New York: Knopf, 1953), p. 28.

18. Krzysztof Pomian, *L'ordre du temps* (Paris: Gallimard, 1984), p. ix.

19. Ibid.: chronometry, through the use of calendars and measuring instruments; chronographies, through the entries in records and changes in them; chronologies, through series of names and dates showing the sequence of eras and their subdivisions until today; and chronosophy, which discovers references to time in animal and human bodies, in the movement of the stars, and in documents, monuments, and texts just as much as in scientific data.

20. Philippe Ariès, *Le temps de l'histoire* (Paris: Seuil, 1954; repr. with an introduction by Roger Chartier, 1986), p. 96.

21. Graziadio Isaia Ascoli, *Iscrizioni inedite o mal note greche, latine, ebraiche, di antichi sepolcri giudaici del Napolitano* (Turin: E. Loescher, 1880). For a brief history of the establishment of the Jewish cemetery, see Sylvie Anne Goldberg, *Crossing the Jabbok: Illness and Death in Ashkenazi Judaism in Sixteenth- Through Nineteenth-Century Prague* (Berkeley: University of California Press, 1996); these principles and dating practices are analyzed in Part II of this book.

22. See the epitaphs in Léon Kahn, *Histoire de la communauté israélite de Paris: Le Comité de bienfaisance, l'hôpital, l'orphelinat et les cimetières* (Paris: A. Durlacher, 1886); Gérard Nahon, "La nation juive portugaise en France, XVIe–XVIIIe siècles: Espaces et pouvoirs," *REJ* 153 (1994): 353–382; Bernard Blumenkranz, ed., *Les juifs et la Révolution française* (Toulouse: Privat, 1976); Sylvie Anne Goldberg, "La tolérance des Juifs en France: Cimetières et émancipation," in *Louis XVI: Du serment du Sacre à l'Édit de tolérance de 1787* (exhibition catalogue), pp. 55–67 (Paris: Bibliothèque, 1988). I developed this point in "Temporality as Paradox: The Jewish Time," in *Jewish Studies in a New Europe: Proceedings of the Fifth Congress of Jewish Studies in Copenhagen 1994 under the Auspices of the European Association for Jewish Studies*, ed. Ulf Haxen, Hanne Trautner-Kromann, and Karen Lisa Goldschmidt Salamon, pp. 284–293 (Copenhagen: Det Kongelige Bibliotek, 1998).

23. Bloch, *Historian's Craft*, p. 28.

24. Wissenschaft des Judentums produced the first historiographical studies of Jewish history. See *La religion comme science: La Wissenschaft des Judentums*, special issue, *Pardès*, 19–20 (1994); Sylvie Anne Goldberg, "L'étude du judaïsme: Science historique ou religieuse?" *Préfaces*, 19 (June–September 1990): 88–95; id., introduction to *Histoire juive, histoire des Juifs: D'autres approaches*, special issue, *Annales HSS* 5 (1994): 1019–1029.

25. Jewish emancipation occurred gradually between the Habsburg emperor Joseph II's 1782 Edict of Tolerance and the Russian Revolution in 1917. Historians of the Wissenschaft believed that the Middle Ages should be extended until the French Revolution in Jewish history.

26. The religious Jewish patrimony of lawmaking consists of responsa, which cover all of Jewish life from the completion of the Talmud to the present day.

27. Mircea Eliade, *The Myth of the Eternal Return:* or, *Cosmos and History*, trans. Willard R. Trask (New York: Harper, 1959, 2012); Aron Gurevich, *Categories of Medieval Culture*, trans. G. L. Campbell (London: Routledge & Kegan Paul, 1985).

28. Efraim Shmueli, *Seven Jewish Cultures: A Reinterpretation of Jewish History and Thought*, trans. Gila Shmueli (Cambridge: Cambridge University Press, 1990).

29. The concept of the resurrection of the body is based on Ezekiel's Vision (Ezek. 37: 1–14); it is sometimes replaced by belief in the immortality of the soul. Generally, it is seen as a belief of Pharisaic origin, whose arguments are presented in 2 Macc. 7:9–36; 12:43–44; see also the Book of Jubilees, 23:30. Rabbinic arguments in favor of resurrection are found in Sanh. 90b–92b; Hul. 142a; Ber. 16b; Gen. R. 20:26; Lev. R. 27:4.

30. Ta'an 2a; Sanh. 113a.

31. Mosheh ben Maimon (1135/1138–1204), known by the acronym RaMBaM, was a multifaceted personality: doctor, philosopher, theologian, codifier, and astronomer. He made immense contributions to Judaism in the field of codification, as well as in exegesis and philosophy, and also wrote medical treatises and astronomical studies. His Mishneh Torah constitutes a "second Torah" and his *Guide of the Perplexed* is a philosophical masterwork of Jewish Aristotelianism. His positions, sometimes considered close to heresy, caused violent controversy during his lifetime and afterwards. See Amos Funkenstein, *Maimonides: His Nature, History and Messianic Beliefs* (Tel Aviv: MOD Books, 1997); Yeshayahu Leibowitz, *Faith of Maimonides* (Tel Aviv: MOD Books, 1996); Moshe Idel, *Maïmonide et la mystique juive* (Paris: Cerf, 1991); *Maimonides and the Jewish Mystic* (Cluj-Napoca: Dacia, 2001); Leo Strauss, *Leo Strauss on Maimonides: The Complete Writings* (Chicago: University of Chicago Press, 2013); the introduction by Shlomo Pines preceded by a preface by Leo Strauss in Maimonides, *Guide of the Perplexed* (Chicago: University of Chicago Press, 1963), and one by Isadore Twersky to *Introduction to the Code of Maimonides* (*Mishneh Torah*) (New Haven, CT: Yale University Press, 1980); Shlomo Pines, "Les sources philosophiques du Guide des perplexes," in *La liberté de philosopher de Maïmonide à Spinoza*, trans. Rémi Brague (Paris: Desclée de Brouwer, 1997); Fred Rosner, *Moses Maimonides' Treatise "On Resurrection"* (Jerusalem: Ktav, 1982); and Moshe Halbertal, *Maimonides: Life and Thought*, trans. Joel Linsider (Princeton, NJ: Princeton University Press, 2014).

32. The method of biblical criticism has widely fueled contemporary theological disputes. By refuting the Mosaic authenticity of the Pentateuch and analyzing it philologically, it has to some extent introduced the critical examination of literature.

33. Such "intratemporality" deriving from Jewish tradition tallies with "world time" in the Heideggerian sense.

Chapter One. Ad tempus universale . . . *A Time for Everyone?*

1. Daniel Shabetaï Milo, *Trahir le temps: Histoire* (Paris: Les Belles Lettres, 1991), shows that simply by changing the dates of the start of centuries, semantics are also altered.

2. Pomian, *L'ordre du temps*, p. 233.

3. Ibid., p. 234, quoting Plato, *Timaeus* 38b, trans. A. Rivaud (Paris: Les Belles Lettres, 1970).

4. Ibid., quoting *Timaeus* 37e.

5. Ibid., p. 235, quoting Aristotle, *Physics* 12.220b5; cf. 14.223b11.

6. Ibid., quoting Aristotle, *On the Heavens* 2.1283b26–29.

7. Ibid., p. 235.

8. Ibid., quoting 14.223a5–8.

9. Ibid., quoting Aristotle, *Physics* 4.223b24–29.

10. Ibid., citing Plotinus, *The Six Enneads* 7.7–10.

11. Ibid., p. 243.

12. Gurevich, *Categories of Medieval Culture*, pp. 94–151.

13. Ibid., p. 94.

14. Ibid., p. 94.

15. Ibid., p. 98.

16. Ibid., p. 103.

17. Except for candles, shavings, hourglasses, solar calendars, and clepsydras, which are not precise instruments, but measure approximate and highly variable time.

18. See Alain Corbin, *Village Bells: Sound and Meaning in the Nineteenth-Century French Countryside*, trans. Martin Thom (New York: Columbia University Press, 1998; London: Macmillan, 1999).

19. Hervé Barreau, "La construction de la notion de temps" (doctoral thesis, Université Paris X, 1982), vol. 1, "Genèse de la notion," p. 281. I am grateful to Tony Lévy for pointing out this work to me.

20. Eliade, *Myth of the Eternal Return.*

21. "Parousia" is from the Greek for presence, arrival, or official visit.—Trans.

22. Pierre Vidal-Naquet, "Temps des dieux, temps des hommes," *Revue de l'histoire des religions* 157 (1960): 55–80; repr. in id., *The Black Hunter: Forms of Thought and Forms of Society in the Greek World* (Baltimore: Johns Hopkins University Press, 1986). Cf. the title of Chapter Four in the present volume, "God's Time, Humanity's Time." Also see the clarification by Geoffrey E. R. Lloyd, "Views on Time in Greek Thought," in Louis Gardet et al., *Cultures and Time* (Paris: UNESCO, 1976), pp. 117–148.

23. Lionel Kochan, *The Jew and His History* (New York: Macmillan, 1977; repr., Chico, CA: Scholars Press, 1985).

24. Yosef Hayim Yerushalmi, *Zakhor: Jewish History and Jewish Memory* (Seattle:

University of Washington Press, 1982, repr. 1989). Yerushalmi's study inspired a response by Amos Funkenstein, "Collective Memory and Historical Consciousness," *History and Memory* 1 (1989): 5–26.

25. Manès Sperber, *Like a Tear in the Ocean: A Trilogy*, trans. Constantine Fitzgibbon (New York: Holmes & Meier, 1988).

26. Amos Funkenstein, *Perceptions of Jewish History* (Berkeley: University of California Press, 1993).

27. Abraham Joshua Heschel, *The Sabbath: Its Meaning for Modern Man* (New York: Farrar, Straus & Young, 1951).

28. Funkenstein "Collective Memory."

29. Abraham Joshua Heschel, *God in Search of Man: A Philosophy of Judaism* (New York: Farrar, Straus & Cudahy, 1955).

30. Heschel, *Sabbath*.

31. On the twists and turns of memory and related practices, see Lucette Valensi, *Les fables de la mémoire: La glorieuse bataille des trois rois* (Paris: Seuil, 1992).

32. See, e.g., Pierre Nora, "Le retour de l'événement," in *Faire de l'histoire*, ed. Jacques Le Goff and Pierre Nora (Paris: Gallimard, 1974; repr., 1986), 1: 210–228, versus Paul Ricoeur, "Événement et sens," in *L'événement en perspective*, ed. Jean Luc Petit (Paris: Éditions de l'École des hautes études en sciences sociales, 1991), pp. 41–56.

33. See Arnaldo Momigliano, "Vico's Scienza Nuova: Roman 'Bestioni' and Roman 'Eroi,'" in id., *Essays in Ancient and Modern Historiography* (Chicago: University of Chicago Press, 2012).

34. Oscar Cullmann, *Christ and Time*, trans. F. V. Filson (Philadelphia: Westminster Press, 1950), cited by Jacques Le Goff, *Time, Work, and Culture in the Middle Ages* (Chicago: University of Chicago Press, 1980), p. 39. Also useful is the "Postscript and Retrospect (1969)" that James Barr added to the 1969 edition of his *Biblical Words for Time* (1962; London: SCM Press, 1969), pp. 170–207, in which he presents and discusses various positions on the idea of time that arose between the first and second editions; on Cullmann, see pp. 179–181.

35. Jacques Le Goff, *History and Memory*, trans. Steven Rendall and Elizabeth Claman (New York: Columbia University Press, 1992; repr. 1996), Preface, p. xv.

Chapter Two. Where Does Time Come From?

1. Gerhard von Rad, *Theologie des Alten Testament* (2 vols.; 1957; Munich: Kaiser, 1980), trans. D. M. G. Stalker as *Old Testament Theology* (London: Oliver & Boyd, 1962–1965). Von Rad, one of the last representatives of the "biblical theology" school, returns in a sense to a chronological arrangement that abandons the internal unity of the material.

2. Plato, *Timaeus* 37e.

3. Augustine, *Confessions*, bk. 9.

4. A reference to the philosopher Plotinus (ca. 204/5–270 CE).—Trans.

5. Ricoeur, *Time and Narrative*, 1: 22–30.

6. Rashi (1040–1105) was born in Troyes and studied at Worms and Mainz before founding his own school in his native city. Both in quantity and in quality, his writings are monumental. He not only wrote responsa and liturgical poems but was an authoritative jurist, and his commentaries on the Tanakh and Talmud have accompanied editions of these since the fifteenth century. To restore the meaning of certain words, he went back to the translation into Aramaic of the Targum Onkelos and found their equivalent (*le'azim*) in the French of his day, which he transliterated in Hebrew characters. His work explaining and illuminating the Talmud was followed by his disciples, the Tosafists, who represent the great school of medieval French-German exegesis.

7. The so-called Women's Bible compiled by Rabbi Jacob ben Isaac Ashkenazi of Janów in Poland (1550–1625), trans. in 2 vols. by Miriam Stark Zakon as *The Weekly Midrash: Tz'enah Ur'enah: The Classic Anthology of Torah Lore and Midrashic Commentary* (Brooklyn, NY: Mesorah, 1983, 2007), provides a fairly precise idea of such renderings.

8. Ricoeur, *Time and Narrative*, 1: 63; and see p. 59n1 for the notion of "the other of time which more than anything, intensifies the experience of time."

9. Moreover, Paul Veyne, *Writing History: Essay on Epistemology*, trans. Mina Moore-Rinvolucri (Middletown, CT: Wesleyan University Press, 1984), claims that "time is not essential to history" (p. 65).

10. Thomas Mann, *The Magic Mountain*, trans. John E. Woods (London: Everyman's Library, 2005), Foreword, p. xi.

11. Thus Jonah Fraenkel, "Time and Its Role in the Aggadic Story," in *Binah: Studies in Jewish Thought*, vol. 2, ed. Joseph Dan, 31–56 (New York: Praeger, 1989).

12. The Tanakh differs in its arrangement from Christian bibles. Cf., e.g., the order of the books in the King James Version with that in *Tanakh: A New Translation of the Holy Scriptures According to the Traditional Hebrew text: Torah, Nevi'im, Kethuvim* (Philadelphia: Jewish Publication Society of America, 1985).

13. There is no need here to describe the level of quarrels that have divided archaeologists and biblical scholars over the past century, which are constantly being revived by current political conflicts. It suffices to outline the basis of the debate around the emergence of Israelite monotheism. Was it an import linked to the return from the Babylonian Exile that crystallized around the editing or proto-canonization of the biblical texts, and thus of much later emergence than is described in biblical narrative, or rather a phenomenon rooted in the history of origins? The critical analysis of texts and their dating is also a basis for clashes over theological and scientific interpretation. If indeed there was no "conquest" of Palestine by a monotheistic people, but rather a progressive tribal development of Semitic beliefs in the region toward monotheism, calling it into question transcends the idea of religious revelation and becomes political. A glance at these debates over the historicity of biblical narratives in recent publications would be burdensome, but see Sarah Japhet, "In Search of Ancient Israel: Revisionism at All Costs," in *The Jewish Past Revisited: Reflections on Modern Jewish Historians,* ed.

David N. Myers and David B. Ruderman (New Haven, CT: Yale University Press, 1998), pp. 212–233.

14. Conflicts over the era in which Ezra and Nehemiah lived have long divided different schools. Archaeology may have resolved these matters. See William Foxwell Albright, "The Biblical Period," in *The Jews: Their History, Culture, and Religion,* ed. Louis Finkelstein (New York: Harper & Brothers, 1949), 1: 3–69.

15. After the fall of Samaria in 722 BCE, the inhabitants of the Northern Kingdom continued to worship in Shechem, whose inhabitants were among those later called Samaritans. After having refused to accept the centralization of worship in Jerusalem by claiming the greater holiness of their temple on Mount Gerizim, they repudiated the prophetic books extolling Jerusalem, favoring instead only the Torah and the Book of Joshua. It is impossible to date the Samaritan schism with any precision. Opinions ascribe it to a variety of centuries, some to the time of the rebuilding of the First Temple, while others opt for 432, or even 320, during the reign of Alexander the Great. It probably occurred during the canonizing of the books of the Tanakh, with the Samaritan Torah being written in the second century BCE as a by product. See Léon Poliakov, *Les Samaritains* (Paris: Seuil, 1991); George Foot Moore, *Judaism in the First Centuries of the Christian Era: The Age of the Tannaim* (2 vols; Cambridge, MA: Harvard University Press, 1950); and *Samaritan Documents: Relating to Their History, Religion and Life*, trans. and ed. John Bowman (Pittsburgh: Pickwick Press, 1977).

16. All Bible quotations are from the King James Version—Trans.

17. Elias J. Bickermann, "The Historical Foundations of Postbiblical Judaism," in *The Jews: Their History, Culture, and Religion*, ed. Louis Finkelstein (New York: Harper & Brothers, 1949), 1: 70–115.

18. To understand the difficulty of offering a summary chronology, see the overt differences of opinion in Max Margolis, *The Hebrew Scriptures in the Making* (Philadelphia: Jewish Publication Society of America, 1922); Salo W. Baron, *Social and Religious History of the Jews,* vol. 2: *Ancient Times to the Beginning of the Christian Era: The First Five Centuries* (New York: Columbia University Press, 1952); and André Lemaire, "Israël," in *Dictionnaire encyclopédique du Judaïsme: Esquisse de l'histoire du peuple juif,* ed. Sylvie Anne Goldberg (Paris: Cerf, 1993), pp. 1241–1260.

19. The narrative of the Book of Daniel is set during the Babylonian Exile, after the fall of the First Temple during the reign of Nebuchadnezzar II, around 545–535 BCE, but researchers date its final composition to the era of the anti-Jewish decrees issued by Antiochus IV between 1686 and 165 BCE. They see it as a current tale about the years 538–164 BCE, or from Cyrus to Antiochus. Arnaldo Momigliano notes: "The Book of Daniel has some authentic details about the fall of Babylon, such as Belshazzar's banquet and the very name of Belshazzar, though Daniel mistakenly takes him to be the son of Nebuchadnezzar, not the son and co-ruler of Nabonidus" (Momigliano, *The Classical Foundations of Modern Historiography* [Berkeley: University of California Press, 1990], p. 11).

20. Although the Book of Esther is quite popular in Jewish society, specialists have rarely been convinced of the authenticity of its narrative, given lack of confirmation from other sources. On this subject, Momigliano states that even if the story is absurd, it contains many details about court life that "ring true" (ibid.).

21. A *baraita* is a brief explanation or addition that is not found in the text of the Mishnah. It is considered of less legal importance, but may lead to controversy or add further information to a text to which it pertains.

22. BB 14b.

23. BB 14b and 15a.

24. Lazare Wogue, *Histoire de la Bible et de l'exégèse biblique jusqu'à nos jours* (Paris: Imprimerie nationale, 1881), p. 19.

25. The talmudic collection representing the oral law consists of the Mishnah, Gemara, Tosefta, Aggadah, and Midrash. The Mishnah (study by repetition), attributed to Hillel the Elder (the Talmud sometimes refers to him as "Hillel the Babylonian"), patriarch of the Sanhedrin in 30 BCE, is the oldest level of commentaries and was chiefly redacted between 180 and 220 CE by Rabbi Yehudah ha-Nassi. The Tosefta ("supplement" or "addition") is a tannaitic collection completing the Mishnah, but much more widely developed. The Gemara ("study" or "learning by tradition") written by *amoraim* (spokesmen) starting in the third century, tries to explain and interpret the laws of the Mishnah, whose poorly attributed sources it meticulously hunts down. It also contains developments on the Midrash, namely, discussions of the biblical text, and the Aggadah, homiletic tales about biblical characters and events. The two Talmuds, written separately in Palestine and Babylon, are the result of work done in the academies of the two communities to coordinate and reconcile all the legislative, legal, exegetical, and other texts. They also convey unusual sets of texts such as *baraita*, teachings on specific issues written over different times, which are duly discussed, as we have seen for the biblical canon. In case of differences of opinion between the two Talmuds, the Babylonian Talmud is usually given precedence over the Jerusalem Talmud. The two compilations were made successively. The Jerusalem Talmud began under Roman rule, under the direction of Rabbi Johanan bar Nappaha around 230 and was perhaps completed under the guidance of Gamaliel III (Rabban Gamaliel ben Yehudah) around 385 or, according to other views, around 415, at the end of the Palestinian Patriarchate. The Babylonian Talmud, completed later, was begun under Neo-Persian rule during the first half of the third century, with the teachings of Abba Arikha (known as Rav) and Samuel bar Abba, and finished around the year 500, under the leadership of Rav Ashi and his pupil, Ravina II. See H. L. Strack and G. Stemberger, *Introduction to the Talmud and Midrash*, trans. M. Bockmuehl (Edinburgh: T. & T. Clark, 1991).

26. According to the Mishnah *Avot*, the scribes (*soferim*) of the Great Assembly (*Knesset ha-gedolah*), also known as the Great Synagogue, received the Holy Word and oral law directly from the Prophets. There are no sources about the exact dates or duration of this assembly or its members. Tradition claims that it was first summoned around 444 BCE by Ezra and Nehemiah and had 120 mem-

bers, including 83 prophets and *zkenim* (ancients: community leaders, clergy, and Levites). See Neh. 10. Wogue, *Histoire de la Bible*, p. 181, believes that they were active for around 150 years, from the era of Ezra to that of Simeon the Just, a contemporary of Alexander the Great.

27. Scholars now view this very differently; see e.g., Shaye J. D. Cohen, "The Significance of Yavneh: Pharisees, Rabbis, and the End of Jewish Sectarianism," *HUCA* 55, no. 1 (1984): 27–29; Jack P. Lewis, "What Do We Mean by Jabneh?" *Journal of Bible and Religion* 32, no. 2 (April 1964): 125–132; and id., "Jamnia Revisited," in *The Canon Debate*, ed. Lee McDonald and James Sanders (Peabody, MA: Hendrickson, 2002), pp. 146–162.

28. The term *kane* is found with the meaning of "ruler" or "standard," *kane ha-midah*, in Ezra 40:3, 5, as well as in Josephus's *Against Apion* 2.17. See Josephus, *Against Apion*, translation and commentary by John M. G. Barclay (Leiden: Brill, 2007), and Sanh. 10:1.

29. The term *genizah* derives from *ganuz*, "hidden" or "concealed." Damaged texts, or those considered unusable, which contain God's name and so cannot be destroyed, must be buried. Before this, they are placed in a synagogue storeroom or side hall. In 1896, the Cairo Genizah was uncovered in the attic of the ancient Ezra Synagogue in Fostat. The attic contained abundant ancient documents and fragments from Palestine and Babylon. The work of identifying them continues. They include Hebrew fragments of such Apocryphal texts as "The Book of the All-Virtuous Wisdom of Joshua ben Sira" (commonly called the Wisdom of Sirach or the Book of Ecclesiasticus), the Testament of Levi from the Pseudepigrapha, the Jerusalem Talmud, passages from unknown midrashim, responsa from the time of the Geonim, Karaite writings, liturgical and poetic texts, and even halakhic fragments from the Academy of Tiberias, letters in the hand of Maimonides, and Yiddish texts and letters.

30. When the Book of Ruth was written remains uncertain. Opinions differ on this point, ranging from the time of Judges (around 1045 BCE) to that of Ezra and Nehemiah (around 584 BCE).

31. Ernst Jenni, "Das Wort 'olam' im Alten Testament," *Zeitschrift für die Alttestamentliche Wissenschaft* 64 (1952): 197–248; 65 (1953): 1–35.

32. See, e.g., N. Ph. Sander and I. Trenel, *Dictionnaire hébreu-français* (Paris, 1859, repr., Geneva: Slatkine, 1982); *Theological Lexicon of the Old Testament*, ed. Ernst Jenni and Claus Westermann, trans. Mark E. Biddle (Peabody, MA: Hendrickson, 1997), 2: 852–862; *Theological Dictionary of the Old Testament*, ed. G. Johannes Botterweck and Helmer Ringgren (Grand Rapids, MI: Eerdmans, 1999), vol. 10 (1999), trans. Douglas W. Stott, 530–545.

33. Gen. 21:33.

34. Deut. 32:7.

35. Marcus Jastrow, *A Dictionary of the Targumim, the Talmud Babli and Yerushalmi, and the Midrashic Literature* (Philadelphia: Pardes, 1886–1903).

36. Barr, *Biblical Words for Time*; id., *Old and New Interpretation: A Study of*

the Two Testaments (London: SCM Press, 1966); id., *Semantics of Biblical Language* (Oxford: Oxford University Press, 1961). Thanks to Yosef Hayim Yerushalmi for having drawn my attention to this author and helping by his critiques to expand my thought.

37. Von Rad, *Old Testament Theology*, 1: 139.

38. Gershom Scholem, "Revelation and Tradition as Religious Categories in Judaism," in id., *The Messianic Idea in Judaism and Other Essays on Jewish Spirituality* (New York: Schocken Books, 1971), pp. 282–303, 289.

39. Gen. 17:9–11.

40. Exod. 20:19.

41. 2 Kings 23:2.

42. Neh. 8:1.

43. United Monarchy: the kingdom of Israel and Judea during the reigns of Saul, David, and Solomon, usually dated from 1020 to 930 BCE.—Trans.

44. Margolis, *Hebrew Scriptures*.

45. See Ruth Reichelberg, *L'Aventure prophétique: Jonas menteur de vérité* (Paris: Albin Michel, 1995).

46. See Yehezkel Kaufmann, *Toledot ha-'emunah ha-yisraelit* (Tel Aviv: Dvir, 1936–1956), abridged and trans. Moshe Greenberg as *The Religion of Israel: From the Beginnings to the Babylonian Exile* (Chicago: University of Chicago Press, 1960; repr. New York: Schocken Books, 1972). The book's third section is about prophesying.

47. Ibid., 157–158.

48. Martin Heidegger, *Being and Time*, trans. John MacQuarrie and Edward Robinson (New York: Harper, 1962); originally published in German in 1927 under the title *Sein und Zeit*. Since the 1930s, many Heideggerian themes have become widely familiar.

49. See Joan Stambaugh, "Existential Time in Kierkegaard and Heidegger," in Anindita Niyogi Balslev and J. N. Mohanty, *Religion and Time* (Leiden: Brill, 1993), pp. 46–60, esp. p. 54.

50. Biblical criticism that rejects Mosaic authorship of the Torah, a school of thought that began with the *Critica sacra* of Joseph Justus Scaliger (1540–1609), appeared gradually in the Western world during the early modern era. It developed starting in the seventeenth century from critiques by Baruch Spinoza in his *Tractatus Theologico-Politicus* (1670) and Richard Simon in *Histoire critique du Vieux Testament* (1678). In the Jewish world, it sprang from the critical exegeses of Ibn Ezra (1092–1167), Ibn Yahya (1515–1548), and Samuel Luzzato (1800–1865). Then it developed in the aftermath of the Haskalah until it broadly imposed itself—outside of synagogues and churches—with Julius Wellhausen (1844–1918), who applied the principles laid down by the historians Jacob Burckhardt and Theodor Mommsen to biblical study. He prepared his sources in cultural sequences, interpreted as momentary steps in religious evolution, giving rise to the so-called documentary hypothesis. On critical studies of the Old Testament, see Adolphe Lods, *Histoire de la littérature hébraïque et juive, depuis les origines*

jusqu'à la ruine de l'État juif, 135 après J.-C. (Paris: Payot, 1950), and Baruch Halpern, *The First Historians: The Hebrew Bible and History* (San Francisco: Harper & Row, 1988).

51. The discussion is in texts by the *tannaim* and *amoraim*; see Yad. 3:5; Meg. 7a.

52. See Sanh. 100b and Tos Yad 2:5.

53. Wellhausen's documentary hypothesis revolutionized the approach to sacred texts, already subject to historical criticism since the days of Erasmus and Spinoza. Between 1876 and 1878, he published articles that formed the basis of *Die Composition des Hexateuchs und der historischen Bücher des Alten Testaments* (Berlin: G. Reimer, 1899), in which he definitively rejected the idea of a single author of the Torah. See Julius Wellhausen, *Geschichte Israels*, vol. 1 (Berlin: G. Reimer, 1878); id., *Prolegomena zur Geschichte Israels* (1883), trans. as *Prolegomena to the History of Ancient Israel* (New York: Meridian Library, 1957). And see also Wellhausen's main detractors, such as Benno Jacob, *Das Erste Buch der Tora* (Berlin: Schocken, 1934), who totally refutes the documentary hypothesis, and those who partially accept it, such as Kaufmann, in *Religion of Israel*, and Umberto Cassuto, *The Documentary Hypothesis and the Composition of the Pentateuch*, trans. Israel Abrahams (Jerusalem: Magnes Press, 1983). See, too, the critique of William F. Albright, based on archaeological research, *From the Stone Age to Christianity: Monotheism and the Historical Process* (2nd ed., Baltimore: Johns Hopkins University Press, 1967), and Frederick Greenspahn, *New Insights and Scholarship in Hebrew Bible* (New York: New York University Press, 2008).

54. Margolis, *Hebrew Scriptures*, p. 47.

55. See Heinrich Graetz "Die allerneueste Bibelkritik: Wellhausen-Renan," in *MGWJ* 35 (1886): 193–204, 233–251. On the process, or the narrative of the Bible reworked, see Michael Fishbane, *Biblical Interpretation in Ancient Israel* (Oxford: Clarendon Press, 1988). And see Yaacov Shavit and Mordechai Eran, *The Hebrew Bible Reborn: From Holy Scripture to the Book of Books. A History of Biblical Culture and the Battles over the Bible in Modern Judaism*, trans. from the Hebrew by Chaya Naor (Berlin: Walter de Gruyter, 2007), pp. 133–139.

56. See, on this subject, Jacques Briend, "La composition du Pentateuque entre hier et aujourd'hui," in *Naissance de la méthode critique* (Paris: Cerf, 1992), pp. 197–204, and *Le canon de l'Ancien Testament: Sa formation, son histoire*, ed. J. D. Kaestli and O. Wermelinger (Geneva: Labor et Fides, 1984).

57. The JE sources are in Exod. 12:21–27; 13:1–16; the Ten Commandments, 20:2–14; the Law of the Great Union, 20:19–23, ending with verse 20–33; the Small Union, 34:17–26, whose prologue is found in verses 10–16. The laws of P contain the rest of the legal material in Exodus and all the codifying material in Leviticus and Numbers, as well as the laws in Gen. 9:1–7; 17:10–14. Deut. 12–27 contains all the laws of D, although there is a version of the Ten Commandments in chapter 5. See Kaufmann, *Religion of Israel*, p. 166n4.

58. Ziony Zevit, "Converging Lines of Evidence Bearing on the Date of P," *Zeitschrift für die Altestamententliche Wissenschaft* 94 (1982): 481–511.

59. Ta'an 2a.

60. Of the "rejoicing at the place of the water-drawing," we ultimately do not know much, except that it is a ritual accompanying the start of a new annual liturgical cycle, beginning during the Feast of Tabernacles. It is mentioned in Isa. 12:3. Robert Graves and Raphael Patai, in *The Hebrew Myths: The Book of Genesis* (Garden City, NY: Doubleday, 1964), understood this ritual as a rite of reiteration of the act of creation. See also Hans Gottlieb, in Benedickt Otzen, Hans Gottlieb, and Knud Jeppesen, *Myths in the Old Testament* (London: SCM Press, 1980), p. 66.

61. These ceremonies are described in Pss. 81:13–14; 99:6–8; 114:1–4; 66:5–6.

62. See Graves and Patai, *Hebrew Myths*; Jean Bottéro, *Babylone et la Bible: Entretiens avec Hélène Monsacré* (Paris: Les Belles Lettres, 1994); Pierre Gibert, *Bible, mythes et récits de commencement* (Paris: Seuil, 1986).

63. Sir James G. Frazer, *Folklore in the Old Testament: Studies in Comparative Religion, Legend, and Law* (London: Macmillan, 1918), 1: 4.

64. Wellhausen, *Prolegomena*, p. 307.

65. See n. 6 above.

66. Rashi: "'Eyn ha-miqra ha-zeh omer 'ela darshoni," i.e., this biblical verse raises more questions than it provides answers to.

67. Graves and Patai, *Hebrew Myths*, pp. 41–48.

68. Gen. 2:1–2.

69. Ta'anit is a tractate of the Mishnah, Tosefta, and Talmud concerning religious observance.

70. *Judah Hallevi's Kitab al Khazari*, trans. from the Arabic by Hartwig Hirschfeld (London: Routledge, 1905), 2.50, p. 114 [originally titled *The Book of Refutation and Proof on Behalf of the Despised Religion*—Trans.]. For new insights, scholarship, and bibliography, see Diana Lobel, *Between Mysticism and Philosophy: Sufi Langage and Religious Experience in Judah Halevi's Kuzari* (Albany: State University of New York Press, 2000), and Adam Shear, *The Kuzari and the Shaping of Jewish Identity 1167–1900* (Cambridge: Cambridge University Press, 2008).

71. Gen. 2:17.

72. During the forty days that Moses spent on Mt. Sinai (Exod. 34:28), he studied the Torah "in all its dimensions," even with all the interpretation that would come in the future; see *Midrash Tanhuma*, ed. Solomon Buber (Vilno [Vilnius], 1885), 2, 60a; 58b, and Gershom Scholem, "Revelation and Tradition as Religious Categories in Judaism," in id., *Messianic Idea in Judaism*, p. 283.

73. Deut. 5:2–3.

74. Deut. 29:9–14.

75. Von Rad, *Old Testament Theology*; P. Steensgaard, "Time in Judaism" in Anindita Niyogi Balslev and J. N. Mohanty, *Religion and Time* (Leiden: Brill, 1993), pp. 63–108.

76. Rashi on Gen. 2:1–2.

77. Ricoeur, *Time and Narrative*, 1: 84–85.

Chapter Three. Where Is Time Going?

1. Midrash Rabbah: Genesis, 9:5. This commentary ascribed to Rabbi Meir Ba'al Ha-Nes (Rabbi Meir the miracle maker), one of the most renowned *tannaim* (rabbinic sages quoted in the Mishnah), detaches death, as a factor in the order of things, from the idea of sin attached to the episode of the serpent. See Ephraim E. Urbach, *The Sages: Their Concepts and Beliefs*, trans. Israel Abrahams (1975; Jerusalem: Magnes Press, 1987), 1: 429. For Rabbi Meir's influence on the *amoraim* (spokesmen), see p. 279.

2. Rabbi Simeon Singer, *The Authorised Daily Prayer Book of the United Hebrew Congregations of the British Empire* (London: Eyre & Spottiswoode, 1890). The hymn *Adon 'olam*, "Lord of the Universe," is often tentatively attributed to the eleventh-century poet Solomon ibn Gabirol, because of its metrics, or to Rav Hai Gaon (939–1038). It first appears in German Ashkenazi liturgy around the fourteenth century, and by the following century, it had become part of Jewish ritual everywhere. See Abraham Zebi Idelsohn, *Jewish Liturgy and Its Developments* (1932; repr., New York: Schocken Books, 1967).

3. Singer, *Authorised Daily Prayer Book*.

4. See Ismar Elbogen, *Der Jüdische Gottesdienst in seiner geschichtlichen Entwicklung* (Leipzig: Fock, 1913), trans. Raymond P. Scheindlin as *Jewish Liturgy: A Comprehensive History* (Philadelphia: JPS, 1993).

5. Franz Rosenzweig, *The Star of Redemption*, trans. Barbara E. Galli (Madison: University of Wisconsin Press, 2005).

6. Ibid., p. 268.

7. Ibid., p. 443.

8. Crescas occupied a central place in medieval Jewish philosophy, especially for his determination that Jews remain observant. To this end, he repudiated both Christian dogma and the philosophy of Maimonides, whom he regarded as a threat.

9. The philosopher, mathematician, astronomer, and talmudist Gersonides, also known as RaLBaG, an acronym for Rabbi Levi Ben Gershom, was a thinker in the Aristotelian tradition of Maimonides. His philosophical positions, especially his rejection of the idea of creation ex nihilo, caused his weighty biblical commentary to be banned in the fifteenth century; see the reconstruction of the "affair" in the preface by Robert Bonfil to the facsimile of the first edition (Mantua, 1475) of Judah ben Jehiel's *Nofet tsufim* (Jerusalem: National Library, 1981), pp. 7–69. His commentaries on Aristotle and Averroes, published in 1319, were translated into Latin as *Liber syllogismi recti*, and a chapter of his commentary on Averroes appeared in a printing of Aristotle's works in Venice in 1550–1552. His scientific works focused on arithmetic, geometry, trigonometry, and astronomy. Translations into English include the *Commentary of Levi ben Gerson on the Book of Job*, trans. Abraham L. Lassen (New York: Bloch, 1946); *Creation of the World According to Gersonides*, trans. Jacob Staub (Chico, CA: Scholars Press, 1982); *The Wars of the Lord*, trans. Seymour Feldman (Philadelphia: JPS, 1984–1999); and *Commentary on*

Song of Songs, trans. and ed. Menachem Kellner (New Haven, CT: Yale University Press, 1998). For different views of his approach, see esp. *Studies on Gersonides: A Fourteenth-Century Jewish Philosopher-Scientist*, ed. Gad Freudenthal (Leiden: Brill, 1992); Bernard R. Goldstein, *The Astronomy of Levi Ben Gerson, 1288–1344: A Critical Edition of Chapters 1–20* (New York: Springer, 1985); id., "Levi Ben Gerson's Astrology in Historical Perspective," in *Gersonide en son temps: Science et philosophie médiévales*, ed. Gilbert Dahan (Louvain: Peeters, 1991); and Charles Touati, *La pensée philosophique et théologique de Gersonide* (Paris: Gallimard, 1992).

10. See Julius Guttmann, *Philosophies of Judaism: The History of Jewish Philosophy from Biblical Times to Franz Rosenzweig*, trans. David W. Silverman (New York: Holt, Rinehart & Winston, 1964), pp. 240–242.

11. Avicenna's influence on Jewish thinkers remains to be explored in depth. His works circulated widely in the Jewish world in Arabic and Hebrew translations, notably through the *Sefer ha-Shamayim ve-ha-ʿolam* (*De caelo et mundo*) and *Maqasid al-falasifa* (Intentions of the philosophers) by Abu Hamid al-Ghazali (1058–1111), a Hebrew translation of which was available during the Middle Ages.

12. With respect to a "natural theology," see Avital Wohlman, *Thomas d'Aquin et Maïmonide: Un dialogue exemplaire* (Paris: Cerf, 1988).

13. Guttmann, *Philosophies of Judaism*, p. 259.

14. Which did not prevent Maimonides, following Aristotle, from adopting the principle that "time is composed of instants." See Maimonides, *The Guide of the Perplexed*, vol. 1, trans. Shlomo Pines (Chicago: University of Chicago Press, 1979), 1.73, p. 194. Here the metaphor was doubtless more precise than the archetype. See Harry Austryn Wolfson, *Crescas' Critique of Aristotle: Problems of Aristotle's Physics in Jewish and Arabic Philosophy* (Cambridge, MA: Harvard University Press, 1929), pp. 200–201 (Wolfson argues that Crescas had developed the Maimonidian theory of the process of the infinite, but it would seem from his work that he somehow missed the radical aspects of Crescas's critique). See further also Warren Z. Harvey, "A Third Approach to Maimonides' Cosmogony-Prophetology Puzzle," *Harvard Theological Review* 74 (1981), p. 296n36, and id., *Physics and Metaphysics in Hasdai Crescas* (Amsterdam: J. G. Gieben, 1998). Israel Efros, *The Problem of Space in Jewish Medieval Philosophy* (New York: Columbia University Press, 1917), pp. 88–109, insists on the "vision of the infinite of medieval Jewish philosophers" and traces this concept from Maimonides through the Catalan philosopher Moses of Narbonne (Narboni), Gersonides, and Crescas.

15. I am indebted to W. Zeev Harvey for his judicious comment about Maimonides beginning all his books with the words *be-shem ha-shem el ʿolam*: "In the name of God, God of the universe / of time," and above all for the considerable help he provided in this philosophical discussion.

16. Joseph Albo reportedly took part in the Disputation of Tortosa, a religious debate between Christians and Jews, in 1413–1414. Albo's philosophical approach can be seen in his *Sefer ha-ʿIkkarim: Book of Principles*, ed. Isaac Husik (Philadelphia: JPS, 1929–1930; repr., 1946).

17. See Guttmann, *Philosophies of Judaism*, p. 281.

18. Warren Z. Harvey, "Albo's Discussion on Time," *JQR* 70 (1980): 215. On the characteristics attributed to time by Jewish thinkers in the Middle Ages, see Shlomo Pines, notably *Nouvelles études sur Awḥad al-Zamân Abu-l-Barakât al-Baghdâdî* (Paris: Durlacher, 1955), and *The Collected Works of Shlomo Pines*, vol. 1: *Studies in Abu'l-Barakāt Al-Baghdādī: Physics and Metaphysics* (Jerusalem: Magnes Press; Leiden: Brill, 1979).

19. Emmanuel Lévinas, *Time and the Other*, trans. Richard A. Cohen (Pittsburgh, PA: Duquesne University Press, 1987), p. 79.

20. Guttmann, *Philosophies of Judaism*, p. 12.

21. The *unio mystica* is the divine union that the individual human soul forges with the Godhead.—Trans.

22. Guttmann, *Philosophies of Judaism*, pp. 8–10.

23. See the discussion led by Karl Löwith, *Meaning in History: The Theological Implications of the Philosophy of History* (Chicago: University of Chicago Press, 1949), esp. pp. 182–207.

24. Guttmann, *Philosophies of Judaism*, p. 12.

25. Also see Erwin Panofsky, *Studies in Iconology: Humanistic Themes in the Art of the Renaissance* (1939; repr., New York: Harper & Row, 1972), notably the difference between the metaphors of Kairos in ancient Greek art, able to balance on a razor's edge, and Aion in Iranian art, the eternal and inexhaustible creative principle that allows us to follow the transformation of the Greek metaphor of Chronos to that of the Roman Kronos, "father of all things" (p. 74).

26. André Néher, "The View on Time and History in Jewish Culture," in Louis Gardet et al., *Cultures and Time* (Paris: UNESCO, 1976), pp. 149–168.

27. Ibid.

28. See Gen. 1:2–3.

29. Deut. 32:7.

30. Ibid.

31. Gen. 1:4.

32. Gen. 1:14.

33. Gen. 49:1; also Num. 24:14; Deut. 4:30, 31:29.

34. See Scholem, "Redemption Through Sin," in id., *Messianic Idea in Judaism*, pp. 132–133.

35. In Num. 24:14.

36. Eliade, *Myth of the Eternal Return*, p. 22.

37. The theological concept of *imitatio dei* conveys the obligation of humans to imitate God, as instructed in Lev. 19:2, Deut. 10:12, and elsewhere.—Trans.

38. Gen. 2:1.

39. Eliade, *Myth of the Eternal Return*, p. 35.

40. Eliade applies the Latin *illud tempus* (that time) to a "time out of time" that he describes as unchanging and belonging to eternity.—Trans.

41. Gershom Scholem, "The Crisis of Tradition in Jewish Messianism," in id.,

Messianic Idea in Judaism, pp. 49–77. On profane time, see Sylvie Anne Goldberg, "Categories of Time: Scales and Values in Ashkenazi Culture," *Jewish Studies* 39 (1999): 87–96, and "Les jeux du temps dans la culture ashkénaze," *REJ* 160, nos. 1–2 (January–June 2001): 155–168.

42. See Rosenzweig, *Star of Redemption*, esp. pp. 402, 418.

43. Scholem, "The Crisis of Tradition in Jewish Messianism" in id., *Messianic Idea in Judaism*, pp. 61, 70.

44. See von Rad, *Old Testament Theology*, 2: 99–125.

45. *Gilgul* (cycle), pl. *gilgulim*, is a kabbalistic progress of transmigration of souls, reincarnation, or metempsychosis, not mentioned in the Bible but much discussed in later Judaism.—Trans.

46. See A. J. Gurevich, "Time as a Problem of Cultural History," in Louis Gardet et al., *Cultures and Time* (Paris: UNESCO, 1976), pp. 229–245.

47. Ibid., p. 243.

Chapter Four. God's Time, Humanity's Time

1. Von Rad, *Old Testament Theology*, 2: 99.

2. A point-by-point refutation of the conclusions by von Rad and other theologians who followed him in his findings that created a distinction between the concepts of Greek or Indo-European time and that of Israelites or Semites, whether cyclic or linear, based mostly on a philological analysis of Hebraic syntax that overlooks any difference between present or future time, can be found in Arnaldo Momigliano, "Time in Ancient Historiography," *History and Theory* 6, suppl. 6 (1966): 1–23, and id., *Essays in Ancient and Modern Historiography* (Middletown, CT: Wesleyan University Press, 1977; repr., Chicago: Chicago University Press 2012), pp. 179 –204. This supposedly led to the ancient Hebrews' failure to develop "a proper historical sense, and therefore a historiography." However, if this were true, Momigliano suggests wittily, "it was really for the Jews to have a Herodotus, and for the Greeks to hope in the Messiah," since the lack of "a clear notion of the future" should hinder rather than encourage messianic expectations (*Essays in Ancient and Modern Historiography*, p. 183).

3. James Barr, *Comparative Philology and the Text of the Old Testament* (Oxford: Oxford University Press, 1968). See also id., "Story and History in Biblical Theology: The Third Nuveen Lecture," *The Journal of Religion* 56, no. 1 (January 1976): 1–17), repr. in *Bible and Interpretation: The Collected Essays of James Barr*, ed. John Barton (Oxford: Oxford University Press, 2013), 1: 233–248.

4. For example, taking as point of departure the semi-evolutionist linguistic argument of the anthropologist E. E. Evans-Pritchard about the Nuers' lacking a word for time, Sacha Stern, *Time and Process in Ancient Judaism* (Portland, OR: Littman Library of Jewish Civilization, 2003), proceeds to claim that since there is no single word in ancient Hebrew for "true" time in the Greek sense, the very notion of time itself must have been nonexistent in ancient Judaism. See also Sylvie Anne Goldberg, "De la Bible et des notions d'espace et de temps: Essai sur l'usage

des catégories dans le monde achkénaze du Moyen Âge à l'époque moderne," *Annales HSS* 5 (September–October 1997): 987–1015.

5. "There is no rigorous order for before or after in the Torah," Rashi affirms, clarifying a difficult text (Exod. 4:20) that employs a verb in the past tense (he took) to indicate an action in the future. See Uriel Simon, "Time and Space in Biblical Thinking" (PhD diss., Hebrew University of Jerusalem, 1961; in Hebrew), which is largely based on the philological studies in vogue during the 1960s (Böman, Cullman, von Rad, et al.), which Simon attempts, with only partial success, to shift from their context to play down the apologetics. And see also Mordechai Akiva Friedman, "On Linguistic Chronology in Rabbinic Literature," *Sidra: A Journal for the Study of Rabbinic Literature* 1 (1985): 59–68 (in Hebrew).

6. Heschel, *Sabbath*, "Prologue: Architecture of Time," pp. 2–10, esp. p. 8.

7. Rosh Hodesh (lit., head of the month), once a meaningful festival associated with the new moon, marks the first day of each month in the Hebrew calendar.—Trans.

8. Gen. 1:3.

9. Von Rad, *Old Testament Theology*, 1: 106.

10. Ibid., pp. 111–115.

11. The term "deuterocanonical" refers to writings identified by the Catholic Church and Eastern Christianity as scripture, but not accepted as part of the Hebrew Bible.—Trans.

12. Von Rad, *Old Testament Theology*, 1: 118–121. This "salvation history" approach is sharply criticized by Thomas L. Thompson, in *The Historicity of the Patriarchal Narratives: The Quest for the Historical Abraham* (Berlin: Walter de Gruyter, 1974; repr., Harrisburg, PA: Trinity Press International, 2002), p. 328.

13. Von Rad, *Old Testament Theology*, 1: 128.

14. Moreover, von Rad relies on different chronologies for the kings of Judea and Israel, concluding that the kingdoms of Israel and Judea constituted separate realms of temporality (ibid., 2: 99–119). This deduction outraged Barr, *Biblical Words for Time*, p. 32, and Momigliano, "Time in Ancient Historiography," p. 6. A wholly different blueprint might also have existed, fixing numerical sums of symbolic duration. Such chronologies and regimes of temporality are further considered in Part II.

15. Judg. 9:56–57, 10:1–6 passim.

16. 2 Kings 15:23–26. This mention, among many others, of the "annals of the kings of Israel" shows the existence in ancient Israel of old chronicles upon which the authors of the Bible doubtless based their work, especially Kings. Josephus, *Against Apion* 1.1, affirms this too. Also see Momigliano, "Time in Ancient Historiography," p. 18.

17. 2 Kings 15:32–36.

18. 2 Kings 25:27.

19. 1 Kings 1:6, 1:17.

20. 1 Kings 13:2; 2 Kings 23:16–18.

21. 2 Sam. 7.

22. Isa. 9:3; Jer. 30:8.

23. Isa. 9:5; 55:3.

24. Isa. 13:23; Jer. 46–51.

25. Isa. 43:5, 14; Jer. 33:18.

26. Isa. 54:11.

27. Isa. 1:24–28.

28. Isa. 4:20; 30:23.

29. Isa. 45:14; *Zech.* 8:20–23.

30. Isa. 11:6–9. See Steensgaard, "Time in Judaism," in Balslev and Mohanty, *Religion and Time*, p. 85.

31. Carlo Ginzburg, *Myths, Emblems, Clues*, trans. John and Anne C. Tedeschi (Baltimore: Johns Hopkins University Press, 1989; repr., 2013), p. 98.

32. Helmer Ringgren, *Israelitische Religion* (Stuttgart: W. Kohlhammer, 1963), trans. David E. Green as *Israelite Religion* (Philadelphia: Fortress Press, 1966).

33. On this subject, see the discussion against the approaches of Christian theologians led by Kaufmann in *Religion of Israel*, pp. 400–409.

34. Jer. 31:7; 31:31.

35. Isa. 56–66, 65:4; 57:3–10; 65:3–7.

36. See Isa. 56:1–8; 58:13; Jer. 17:19–27; Ezra 4:12–15; 22:26–44. On circumcision, see Lawrence A. Hoffman, *Covenant of Blood: Circumcision and Gender in Rabbinic Judaism* (Chicago: University of Chicago Press, 1996).

37. See Ezra 8. Much less documented than Nehemiah, the personality of Ezra remains enigmatic; some researchers see in the description of Ezra as a "scribe, being very ready in the law of Moses, that was given by the God of Israel" an indication that he was a Persian civil servant in charge of Jewish affairs, like Nehemiah; see Momigliano, *Classical Foundations*, pp. 10–11. As for Nehemiah, Arnaldo Momigliano, *Alien Wisdom: The Limits of Hellenization* (Cambridge: Cambridge University Press, 1975), p. 81, describes him as a "tyrant imposed by the Persians" in the Greek meaning of the term.

38. The books of Maccabees date to the second century BCE, and Josephus puts the Samaritan schism in the fourth century BCE. See Chapter Two, n. 15, above.

39. Jer. 32:40. See also, starting with Jer. 30, Jeremiah's description of the "end of days."

40. See the in-depth study of the books of Maccabees by Elias J. Bickerman, *Der Gott der Makkabäer: Untersuchungen über Sinn und Ursprung der Makkabäischen Erhebung* (Berlin: Schocken, 1937), translated as *The God of the Maccabees: Studies on the Meaning and Origin of the Maccabean Revolt* (Leiden: Brill, 1979).

41. See Chapter Two, n. 25, above.

42. For an overview of studies on Flavius Josephus, as well as a glimpse of hypotheses about and analyses of his works, see Louis H. Feldman, *Josephus and Modern Scholarship (1937–1980)* (Berlin: Walter de Gruyter, 1984). See also Tessa Rajak, *Josephus: The Historian and His Society* (London: Duckworth, 1983; 2nd ed., 2002).

43. See the preface by Pierre Vidal-Naquet, "Du bon usage de la trahison," in *La guerre des Juifs*, trans. P. Savinel (Paris: Minuit, 1977), and Arnaldo Momigliano, *Essays on Ancient and Modern Judaism*, trans. S. Berti (Chicago: University of Chicago Press, 1994), pp. 67–87. In Jewish historiography, the place granted to Josephus is often revealing of ideological positions. Although lack of space prevents a full account of studies of his character and meaning for the history of the Jews, see nevertheless D. R. Schwartz, "On Abraham Shalit, Herod, Josephus, the Holocaust, Horst R. Moehring, and the Study of Ancient Jewish History," *Jewish History* 2, no. 2 (Autumn 1987): 7–28; id., *Studies in the Jewish Background of Christianity* (Tübingen: Mohr Siebeck, 1992); Shaye J. D. Cohen, "History and Historiography in the *Against Apion* of Josephus," in *Essays in Jewish Historiography: History and Theory*, ed. Ada Rapoport-Albert, suppl. 27, no. 4 (Middletown, CT: Wesleyan University Press, 1988), pp. 1–11; and *Early Judaism and Its Modern Interpreters*, ed. Robert Kraft and Georges W. E. Nickelsburg (Atlanta: Scholars Press, 1986).

44. See Heinz Schreckenberg, *Die Flavius-Josephus Tradition in Antike und Mittellater*, Arbeiten zur Literatur und Geschichte des hellenistischen Judentums 5 (Leiden: Brill, 1972); id., *Rezeptionsgeschichte und Textkritische Untersuchungen zu Flavius Josephus*, ibid., 10 (1977); L. H. Feldman, *Josephus: A Supplementary Bibliography* (London: Garland, 1986); id., *Josephus and Modern Scholarship*; and Menahem Mor and Uriel Rappaport, "The World of the Historical Bibliographer," *Jewish History* 1, no. 2 (Autumn 1986): 65–78.

45. Many examples of the dialectic of punishments and rewards are scattered thoroughout Josephus's works. See, e.g., his Preface to *Jewish War*, trans. H. S. J. Thackeray (Cambridge, MA: Harvard University Press, 1928), 1.4.10, 5.9.399–404, and 7.8.328 in *The New Complete Works of Josephus*, trans. William Whiston (Grand Rapids, MI: Kregel, 1999). And see further the Bibliography for editions of his writings.

46. "God is fled out of his sanctuary, and stands on the side of those against whom you fight." Josephus, *Jewish War* 5.9.412 (quoted from Whiston).

47. Ibid., 5.9.387. Isa. 7:3–9; 14:28–32; 30:1–7; 31:1, 3.

48. Num. 23:23.

49. Josephus, *Jewish Antiquities*, trans. H. S. J. Thackeray (Cambridge, MA: Harvard University Press, 1998), 4.6.125 (quoted from Whiston).

Chapter Five. The Time to Come

1. For an English translation, see *Midrash Rabbah*, ed. Harry Freedman and Maurice Simon (London: Soncino Press, 1992), 1: 9.

2. See Panofsky, *Studies in Iconology*, pp. 75–78.

3. Adopting the analyses of Gershom Scholem in *Messianic Idea in Judaism* and *Sabbatai Sevi: The Mystical Messiah, 1626–1676* (Princeton, NJ: Princeton University Press, 1973), and those of Jonathan Frankel in *Prophecy and Politics: Socialism, Nationalism, and the Russian Jews, 1862–1917* (Cambridge: Cambridge

University Press, 1981); also Zalman Shazar (Rubashov), "The Messiah Scribe," *Ha-Shiloah* 29 (1913): 36–47; repr., Jerusalem: Mosad Bialik, 1970 (in Hebrew).

4. On phenomenology, see Maurice Merleau-Ponty, *Phénoménologie de la perception* (Paris: Gallimard, 1945), trans. Colin Smith as *Phenomenology of Perception* (London: Routledge, 1962).

5. This shift occurs two or three centuries after the time of wisdom literature, according to Jenni, "Wort," 65 (1953), §§ 24, 25.

6. Kohelet 12:5. Variously translated as "a house of eternal life" or "the grave," this term for cemetery transcends time. It can be found in the commentaries Kohelet Rabbah 10:9; Targum Isaiah 40:11; Mo'ed Katan 80b, as well as the Yiddish *besoylm*. See Goldberg, *Crossing*, p. 21.

7. In philosophy, an "aporia" is an expression of confusion or doubt, from the Greek for difficulty or perplexity.—Trans.

8. Hans-Georg Gadamer, *Truth and Method*, trans. Joel Weinsheimer and Donald G. Marshall (London: Continuum, 2004); on this subject, see Françoise Dastur, *Dire le temps: Esquisse d'une chronologie phénoménologique* (Paris: Encre Marine, 1994), p. 41n47.

9. The pioneer in terminological analysis of words referring to time in the Old Testament is Conrad von Orelli, *Die hebräischen Synonyma der Zeit und Ewigkeit, genetisch und sprachvergleichend dargestellt* (Leipzig: A. Lorentz, 1871), who provided a philological basis for the theological analyses of his successors.

10. See p. 38.

11. Kohelet 3:1–2, which to be exact should be provided with the Hebrew term "'et," as we shall see later in this chapter.

12. The *Birkat ha-mazon* or Blessing on Nourishment.

13. Est. 9:27; 9:31.

14. Neh. 2:6; 13:31.

15. Dan. 3:7–8; 2:16.

16. Exod. 9:5.

17. This frequently occurs, as in Exod. 27:21; 28:43; 30:15; we find the same meaning in the writings called Qumranian, where the term *mo'ed* appears in the Community Rule (1QS) and the Damascus Document Scroll (4Q271Df); see J. Licht, "Time and Eschatology in Apocalyptic Literature and in Qumran," *Journal of Jewish Studies* 16 (1965): 177–182.

18. Gen. 1:14; see p. 49 for its use in the account of the creation.

19. Lev. 23:44.

20. Dan. 7:25.

21. Isa. 1:13.

22. Students of the philosophy of Martin Heidegger translate his phrase *immer schon* as "always already"; see, e.g., *The Cambridge Companion to Heidegger's "Being and Time,"* ed. Mark A. Wrathall (Cambridge: Cambridge University Press, 2013), p. 92.—Trans.

23. See Bernard Dupuy, "Temps et eschatologie dans le judaïsme," in *Temps*

et eschatologie: Données bibliques et problématiques contemporaines, ed. Jean-Louis Leuba (Paris: Cerf, 1994), pp. 39–53.

24. Gen. 21:22.

25. Kohelet 3:1–2. On the complexities of this text, see the doctoral dissertation of H.-J. Blieffert, *Weltanschauung und Gottesglaube im Buch Kohelet. Darstellung und Kritik* (Rostock: R. Beckmann, 1938), p. 25, and George A. Barton, *A Critical and Exegetical Commentary on the Book of Ecclesiastes* (Edinburgh: T. & T. Clark, 1908).

26. Hag. 1–2.

27. In *Der Ursprung der israelitisch-jüdischen Eschatologie* (Göttingen: Vandenhoeck & Ruprecht, 1905), Hugo Gressmann notes the coexistence of two contradictory types of eschatology in Jewish texts: that of tragedy and destruction, *Unheilseschatologie,* goes hand in hand with that of joy and salvation, *Heilseschatologie.* See the review by Marcel Mauss in *Oeuvres* (Paris: Minuit, 1974), 2: 582–585.

28. In his thirteen articles of faith, Maimonides affirms belief in the Messiah, whom he personifies only in "The Epistle to Yemen": "As to the place where the Messiah will make his first appearance, Scripture intimates that he will first present himself only in the Land of Israel, as we read, 'He will suddenly appear in His Temple' (Malachi 3:1)." *Moses Maimonides' Epistle to Yemen: The Arabic Original and the Three Hebrew Versions,* ed. Abraham S. Halkin, trans. Boaz Cohen (New York: American Academy for Jewish Research, 1952), p. xvii; repr. in *Crisis and Leadership: Epistles of Maimonides,* trans. Abraham S. Halkin, ed. id. and David Hartman (Philadelphia: JPS, 1985; repr., 1992), p. 125.

29. Sanh. 98a.

30. As the Mishneh Torah explicitly states. See Halbertal, *Maimonides: Life and Thought,* esp. p. 224.

31. The Messiah from the house of David appears in the prophecy of Jer. 30:9 and Ezra 34:23 as a "second David." The *Amidah,* or daily prayer of eighteen blessings (*Shmoneh Esreh*), dating to the Mishnaic period before and after the destruction of the Temple, mentions this Messiah in the fourteenth and fifteenth blessings.

32. The first mention of the Messiah son of Joseph is in the Babylonian Talmud, Sukkah 52a, where Rabbi Hanina ben Dosa (first century CE) is cited. This Messiah would become part of apocalypses and *midrashim* in later centuries. He is mentioned by Sa'adia Ga'on (*Emunot ve-De'ot,* 8) and Hai Ga'on (*Ta'am Zkenim*).

33. See David Flusser, *Judaism and the Origins of Christianity* (Jerusalem: Magnes, 1988), esp. pp. 246–279; also Nahmanides, *The Disputation at Barcelona,* trans. Charles B. Chavel (New York: Shilo, 1983).

34. See Maimonides, "Epistle to Yemen" and "Treatise on Resurrection," in id., *Crisis and Leadership,* trans. and ed. Halkin and Hartman; new ed., trans. and ed. Fred Rosner (New York: Ktav, 1982).

35. The advance of Pharisaic doctrine may be seen in the works of Josephus, who at the end of his life, in his last writings, declared himself to be a Pharisee.

See Steve Mason, *Flavius Josephus on the Pharisees: A Composition-Critical Study* (Leiden: Brill, 1991). On resurrection, see Goldberg, *Crossing*; on messianism in general, see Gershom Scholem, esp. *Messianic Idea in Judaism*; for a critique of his approach, see Moshe Idel, *Kabbalah: New Perspectives* (New Haven, CT: Yale University Press, 1988).

36. Two traditions about Bar Kokhba coexist. The first is positive: he is one of the great emblematic figures of revolt against the Romans, even though his name only appears in Christian sources. He died in the year 135 and his name (son of a star) suggests, according to the reading in Num. 24:17, that he was also one of the messianic figures of his time. His death is embroidered with legends and the tale of the massacre at Betar fortress, where he took refuge, recounts fierce fighting (Git. 56a–b; Shir ha-Shirim Rabbah 2:17; Midrash Eikhah Rabbah 2:2,4; Rabbi Nathan et al., *Aboth de Rabbi Nathan*, ed. S. Schecter (New Haven, CT: Feldheim), 138:115). The memory of the fall of Betar as well as his battle are commemorated by the fast on the 9th of Av, as well as by counting the *'omer*. [The counting of the *'omer* enumerates the forty-nine days between Passover and Shavuot as indicated in Lev.23:15–16. *'Omer*, a sacrifice containing a measure (*'omer*) of barley, was offered in the Temple in Jerusalem, until wheat was offered at the Temple on Shavuot. The measure *'omer* was used in the Jerusalem Temple era for grains and other dry materials. *Lag Ba'Omer*, celebrated on the thirty-third day of the counting of the *'omer*, falls on the eighteenth day of the month of Iyar. In modern-day Israel, *Lag Ba'Omer* was recast as a commemoration of the Bar Kokhba revolt (it had previously celebrated Rabbi Shimon bar Yochai and the *Zohar*).—Trans.]

The other tradition is negative, since in Jewish sources he is called Bar Kozibah (son of the lie); there is a medieval tale that a dynasty of that name existed. After the death of its first ruler, his son Rufus succeeded him, followed in turn by Rufus's son Romulus. See "R. Abraham ben David's Chronicle" (in Hebrew), in *Medieval Jewish Chronicles*, ed. Neubauer, 1: 47–82; see also Peter Schäfer, *History of the Jews in Antiquity: The Jews of Palestine from Alexander the Great to the Arab Conquest* (London: Routledge, 1995). A substantial bibliography recounts the changes caused by the event in Jewish tradition, enriched by archaeological discoveries from the past century; see Brook W. R. Pearson, "The Book of the Twelve, Aqiba's Messianic Interpretations, and the Refuge Caves of the Second Jewish War," in *The Scrolls and the Scriptures: Qumran Fifty Years After*, ed. S. E. Porter and C. A. Evans (Sheffield, UK: Sheffield Academic Press, 1997), pp. 221–239; B. W. R. Pearson, "Dry Bones in the Judean Desert: The Messiah of Ephraim, Ezekiel 37, and the Post-Revolutionary Followers of Bar Kokhba," *JSJ* 29, no. 2 (May 1998): 192–201. Recent approaches are summed up in Mathew V. Novenson, "Why Does R. Akiba Acclaim Bar Kokhba as Messiah?" *JSJ* 40, no. 4 (2009): 551–572.

37. Von Rad, *Old Testament Theology*, 1: 80.

38. Zech. 7. On the penitential rituals of the era, see Hans-Eberhard von Waldow, "Anlaß und Hintergrund der Verkündigung des Deuterojesaja" (diss., Bonn, 1953), p. 112, cited by von Rad, *Old Testament Theology*, 1: 81.

39. Von Rad, *Old Testament Theology*, 1: 82.

40. See esp. the deuterocanonical Letter of Jeremiah, 29.

41. Hag. 2:20; Zech. 4:14.

42. Von Rad, *Old Testament Theology*, 1: 90.

43. Ibid., p. 90.

44. This change has been studied in depth by Old Testament specialists such as Martin Noth, *Amt und Berufung im Alten Testament* (Bonn: Hanstein, 1958).

45. See Jacob Neusner, *A History of the Jews in Babylonia*, vol 1: *The Parthian Period*; vol. 2: *The Early Sasanian Period* (Leiden: Brill, 1965–1966); Josephus, *Jewish War* 5.9.412 (quoted from Whiston).

46. Jacob Neusner, "The Religious Uses of History: Judaism in First Century A.D. Palestine and Third-Century Babylonia," *History and Theory* 5 (1966): 153–171.

47. Urbach, *Sages*, 1: 593–603. According to talmudic sources, the Academy of Hillel's disputes over lawmaking with the followers of the rival Shammai Academy turned deadly. Shammai won out because of the large number of zealots associated with it. See JT Shab. 1, 4; Shab. 13a; 17a; *Mekhilta de-Rabbi Ishmael*, 229; Aggadat Shir ha Shirim, n. 33; Josephus, *Jewish War*, Anthony J. Saldarini, "Johanan ben Zakkai's Escape from Jerusalem: Origin and Development of a Rabbinic Story," *JSJ* 6 (1975): 189–204.

48. Also see Jacob Neusner, *A Life of Rabban Yohanan ben Zakkai: ca. 1–80 CE* (Leiden: Brill, 1962), and Urbach, *Sages*, 1: 596–599.

49. See n. 36 above.

50. As expressed in the apocalyptic books 4 Ezra and Baruch.

51. Apocalyptic 4 Ezra 10–11, 26–20; 5 Ezra 4–5; 6 Ezra 55–56.

52. Bar. 4:17–23; 4:25–30.

53. Rabbi Nathan et al., *The Fathers According to Rabbi Nathan* (*Abot de Rabbi Nathan*) *Version B: A Translation and Commentary*, trans. and ed. Anthony J. Saldarini (Leiden: Brill, 1975), B 31, p. 182. In Hebrew in *Aboth de Rabbi Nathan*, p. 67.

54. Rabbi Nathan et al., *Aboth de Rabbi Nathan 4*, in *The Fathers According to Rabbi Nathan*, trans. and ed. Judah Goldin (New Haven, CT: Yale University Press, 1956), p. 34; in *Fathers*, trans. and ed. Saldarini, p. 75; Hebrew, *Aboth de Rabbi Nathan*, ed. Schechter, p. 21; commentaries on Deut. 28–47 in Ket. 66b.

55. BB 60 b. See also Neusner, *Life of Rabban Yohanan ben Zakkai*, p. 192.

56. During the reign of Peroz I, eighteenth king of the Sassanid Empire (457–484).

57. During the reign of Hormizd IV (579–590).

58. Abba Arikha ("Rav") and Samuel of Nehardea (Mar Samuel Yarhina'ah) were leading first-generation third-century Babylonian *amoraim*. Rav opened the Sura rabbinical school in 219, and his contemporary Samuel succeeded his father at the Nehardea academy. These were the most prestigious Babylonian rabbinical schools of their time.

59. Neusner, "Religious Uses of History," p. 162.

60. JT, RH, 3, 8.

61. Sukkah, 29b.

62. Sanh. 97b. We shall return in greater depth to this text in Part II of this book.

63. Ibid. The two discussions are presented together, the second being based on the first. In the Book of Esther, Haman plots to kill all the Jews in ancient Persia. He is finally defeated by Mordecai, and his fall is feted during Purim, the Feast of Lots.

64. Pes. 68a; Shab. 63a, on Deut. 15:11, and Ber. 34b.

65. Pes. 68a.

66. See Exod. 24:11, Ber. 17a.

67. Neusner, "Religious Uses of History," p. 165.

68. Menahot 98a.

69. Shmueli, *Seven Jewish Cultures*, p. 149.

70. "The view of linear time that predominates in the Bible underwent a change, and the rabbinic writings evince what Lévi-Strauss refers to as a totemic time view," Nissan Rubin and Admiel Kosman say in "The Clothing of the Primordial Adam as a Symbol of Apocalyptic Time in the Midrashic Sources," *HTR* 90, no. 2 1997, p. 157; cf. the idea of "playing memory against the present time" in Horst Günther, *Zeit der Geschichte: Welterfahrung und Zeitkategorien in der Geschichtsphilosophie* (Frankfurt am Main: Fischer Taschenbuch, 1993).

71. As in Menahot 29b.

72. "The Greek historian was always aware of being in danger of saying something that was not true or even probable. Not that he invariably cared to avoid the danger. But the choice between what is true and untrue, or at least what is probable and improbable, was inherent in the profession of the historian" (Momigliano, *Classical Foundations*, p. 19).

73. Neusner, "Religious Uses of History," p. 167.

74. For more detailed criticism of the school of Gershom Scholem's approach to messianism, see David Biale, *Gershom Scholem: Kabbalah and Counter-History* (Cambridge, MA: Harvard University Press, 1979), and esp. Moshe Idel, *Kabbalah* (1988) and "Mystique juive et histoire juive," special issue of *Annales HSS* 5 (1994): 1223–1240.

75. Maimonides, commentary on Mishnah Sanh. 10.1.

76. Neusner, "Religious Uses of History," p. 167.

77. Yerushalmi, *Zakhor*, p. 24.

78. Sanh. 97b, as cited ibid., pp. 24–25.

79. Studies of Hellenism are an important area of research in their own right. The number of works on the subject make mere references seem trivial. Nevertheless, see the following classics: Johann Gustav Droysen, *Geschichte des Hellenismus*, vols. 1–2 (Hamburg: F. Perthes, 1836–1843); on Hellenistic Judaism, Emil Schürer, *Geschichte des Jüdischen Volkes im Zeitalter Jesu Christi* (Leipzig: J. C.

Hinrichs, 1886–1890; 4th ed., 1901–1909), trans. T. A. Burkill et al. in 3 vols., rev. and ed. Géza Vermes and Fergus Millar as *The History of the Jewish People in the Age of Jesus Christ* (Edinburgh: T. & T. Clark, 1973–1987); Saul Lieberman, *Greek in Jewish Palestine: Studies in the Life and Manners of Jewish Palestine in the II–IV Centuries C.E.* (New York: Jewish Theological Seminary of America, 1942); id., *Hellenism in Jewish Palestine: Studies in the Literary Transmission, Beliefs and Manners of Palestine in the I Century B.C.E–IV Century C.E.* (New York: Jewish Theological Seminary of America, 1950); Elias J. Bickerman, *Institutions des Séleucides* (Paris: P. Geuthner, 1938); id., *From Ezra to the Last of the Maccabees: Foundation of Post-Biblical Judaism* (New York: Schocken Books, 1978); id., *The Jews in the Greek Age* (New York: JTS, 1988); Schäfer, *History of the Jews in Antiquity.* On methodological problems, see Momigliano, *Essays, Classical Foundations,* and *Alien Wisdom;* C. Saulnier and C. Perrot, *Histoire d'Israël: De la conquête d'Alexandre à la destruction du Temple* (Paris: Cerf, 1985), esp. for maps and diagrams.

80. See Victor Tcherikover, *Hellenistic Civilization and the Jews,* trans. S. Applebaum (Philadelphia: JPS, 1966). For the Christian point of view, see Martin Hengel, *Judentum und Hellenismus: Studien zu ihrer Begegnung unter Berücksichtigung Palästinas bis zur Mitte des 2. Jhs. v. Chr.* (Tübingen: Mohr, 1973), trans. J. Bowden as *Judaism and Hellenism: Studies in Their Encounter in Palestine During the Early Hellenistic Period* (2 vols.; London: SCM Press, 1974); Marie-Françoise Baslez, *Bible et histoire: Judaïsme, hellénisme, christianisme* (Paris: Fayard, 1998); and *The Jewish Apocalyptic Heritage in Early Christianity,* ed. James C. VanderKam and William Adler (Assen: Van Gorcum; Minneapolis: Fortress Press, 1996).

81. Momigliano, "Time in Ancient Historiography."

82. Many works by Philo were preserved by the Church in the original Greek or Armenian, among them historico-apologetic texts, including *Apology for the Jews; Life of Moses; In Flaccum,* written against Flaccus, the governor who had encouraged the anti-Jewish uprising in Alexandria; and *Legatio ad Caium,* the story of his mission to Caligula, as well as the philosophical works *Quod omnis probus liber sit* (including data about the Essenes); *De aeternitate mundi; De Providentiae;* and the only surviving description of the Therapeute sect in *De vita contemplativa.* Most of his work consists of exegetical commentary on the Pentateuch and explanations of Jewish Law, such as *De opificio mundi* (On the creation of the world); *De Abrahamo* (On Abraham); *De Decalogo* (On the Ten Commandments); and *De specialibus legibus* (On specific legislation). He also wrote a *Legum allegoriae,* comprising eighteen allegorical interpretive treatises on the seventeen chapters of Genesis, as well as *Quaestiones et solutiones in Exodum,* "questions and answers" about the books of Genesis and Exodus. The standard edition of his work was assembled by L. Cohn and P. Wendland, *Philonis Alexandrini opera quae supersunt,* vols. 1–7 (Berlin: G. Reimer, 1896–1930). For the complete works in English, see *The Works of Philo: Complete and Unabridged,* trans. Charles D. Yonge (Peabody,

MA: Hendrickson, 1995); *The Works of Philo* (Cambridge, MA: Harvard University Press; London: William Heinemann, 1929–1953), vols. 1–10, trans. and ed. F. H. Colson and G. H. Whitaker, and vols. 10–12, ed. Ralph Marcus. There are also translations and commentaries on individual works such as Pieter W. van der Horst, *Philo's Flaccus: The First Pogrom* (Leiden: Brill, 2003). On Philo's life and work, see H. A. Wolfson, *Philo: Foundations of Religious Philosophy in Judaism, Christianity, and Islam* (Cambridge, MA: Harvard University Press, 1947), vols. 1–2.

83. Isa. 11:6–9.

84. See Wolfson, *Philo*, esp. 2: 411; Philo, *In Flaccum* 5.25–11.96, and *Legatio ad Caium* 18.120 and 20.135.

85. Philo, *Quaestiones et solutiones in Exodum*, "On Rewards and Punishments," 8.4.171, in id., *Works*, trans. Colson and Whitaker, p. 421.

86. Ezra 8:11–12.

87. Lev. 26:40.

88. Deut. 30:2.

89. "Yet through Divine mercy and their own merits they escaped safely" (Sanh.12a).

90. Isa. 2:2–4; Mic. 4:1–2.

91. Sibylline Oracles 3.702–722.

92. Wolfson, *Philo*, 2: 415.

93. Ibid., p. 419. This harks back to Plutarch's wording in *De Alexandri magni fortuna aut virtute* 1.6.

94. The Fathers of the Church emphasized this aspect of Philo's thought.

95. Robert Louis Wilken, *Judaism and the Early Christian Mind: A Study of Cyril of Alexandria's Exegesis and Theology* (New Haven, CT: Yale University Press, 1971), p. 43, quoting Alexander Fuks and Victor Tcherikover, *Corpus Papyrorum judaicarum* (Cambridge, MA: Harvard University Press for the Magnes Press, Hebrew University, 1957–1964), p. 1178.

96. Nahum Norbert Glatzer, *Untersuchungen zur Geschichtslehrer der Tannaiten* (Berlin: Schocken, 1933), pp. 10–31, partly reprinted as "The *Tannaim* and History," in *The Christian and Judaic Invention of History*, ed. Jacob Neusner (Atlanta: Scholars Press, 1990), pp. 125–142 (see esp. p. 126).

97. Heinrich Graetz, *The Structure of Jewish History, and Other Essays*, trans. and ed. Ismar Schorsch (New York: Jewish Theological Seminary of America, 1975), p. 72.

98. F. W. J. von Schelling, *The Ages of the World*, trans. Frederick de Wolfe Bolman, Jr. (New York: Columbia University Press, 1942), p. 83.

Part II: The Course of Eras and Calculations of Time

1. Issues related to the question of continuity between pre-rabbinic and rabbinic Judaism have been analyzed by Francis Schmidt in his introduction to *How the Temple Thinks: Identity and Social Cohesion in Ancient Judaism* (Sheffield, UK: Sheffield Academic Press, 2001). Véronique Gillet-Didier carefully distinguishes the concepts inherent in names for periods, such as the use of the terms

"Hellenistic," "Second Temple," and "intertestamentary." See her Introduction to "Temps de Dieu, temps des hommes: Généalogie, calendrier et tradition dans le judaïsme de l'époque hellénistique et romaine" (PhD diss., École pratique des hautes études, Paris, 1997), pp. 8–12. Many thanks to her for sending this to me.

2. The Cairo Genizah is a vast trove of fragmentary Jewish documents discovered in a synagogue there. See Chapter Two, n. 29.

3. See Lev. 25:8: "And thou shalt number seven sabbaths of years unto thee, seven times seven years; and the space of the seven sabbaths of years shall be unto thee forty and nine years."—Trans.

Chapter Six. Temporal Scansions

1. Exod. 23:12; 34:21.

2. Exod. 31:13, 16.

3. Cassius Dio, *Roman History* 37.17, in *Dio's Roman History*, trans. Earnest Cary (9 vols.; Cambridge, MA: Harvard University Press; London: W. Heinemann, 1914–1927).

4. [The ablative singular of the Latin word *hebdomas*, meaning the number seven; a week or seven days; or the seventh day. Trans.] The term *hebdomad* is used in the Septuagint of Lev. 25:8 to indicate a seven-year period, when the Hebrew has "seven sabbaths of years," meaning forty-nine years.

5. Yehudah Halevi, *The Kuzari*, bk. 2, 20, p. 94. See Sanh. 38b, where he names the animals.

6. Claudius Ptolemy was a Greco-Egyptian astronomer and geographer in Alexandria during the middle of the second century CE.—Trans.

7. Venance Grumel, *Traité d'études byzantines*, vol. 1: *La chronologie* (Paris: Presses universitaires de France, 1958). [See also Roger S. Bagnall and Klaas A. Worp, *Chronological Systems of Byzantine Egypt* (Leiden: Brill, 2004).—Trans.]

8. Gen. 1:5.

9. Exod. 17:12; Josh. 10:13. See Moïse Sibony, *Le jour dans le judaïsme: Son histoire et ses moments significatifs* (Tours: Moïse Sibony and Centre national de la recherche scientifique, 1986), p. 28.

10. The German equivalent, *Sonntag*, is likewise the day of the sun; the French and Italian names, however, derive from the Latin term *dominica*, the Lord's Day, rather than *dies solis*.

11. Auguste Bouché-Leclercq, *L'astrologie grecque* (Paris: E. Leroux, 1899; repr., Brussels: Culture et Civilisation, 1963); Emil Schürer, "Die Siebentägige Woche im Gebrauche der christlichen Kirche der ersten Jahrhunderte," *Zeitschriften für die Neutestamentliche Wissenschaft* 6 (1905): 18–19; Francis H. Colson, *The Week* (Cambridge: Cambridge University Press, 1926), pp. 31–33; Charles Pietri, "Le temps de la semaine à Rome et dans l'Italie," in *Le temps chrétien de la fin de l'Antiquité au Moyen âge, IIIe–XIIIe siècles: [Colloque,] Paris, 9–12 mars 1981* (Paris: Éditions du CNRS, 1984), pp. 63–97.

12. Cassius Dio, *Roman History* 37.18.

13. Colson, *Week*, p. 32; Solomon Gandz, "The Origin of the Planetary Week, or the Planetary Week in Hebrew Literature," *Proceedings of the American Academy for Jewish Research* 18 (1948–1949): 213–254.

14. Eliezer ben Hyrcanus, *Pirkê de Rabbi Eliezer*, trans. and ed. Gerald Friedlander (London: Kegan Paul, Trench, Trubner; New York: Bloch, 1916; repr., New York: Hermon Press, 1965), chap. 6, p. 32. Friedlander says in his introduction that this collection, probably compiled around 830 and first published in Constantinople in 1514, is composed of three major parts, dealing with: (1) the ten divine descents; (2) the *Ma'aseh Be-reshit* (Work of creation) and *Ma'aseh Merkabah* (Works of the chariot), as well as secrets of the calendar and redemption; and (3) *Shemoneh Esrei*, the prayer of eighteen blessings. These parts no longer exist in this form, but calendrical elements are found in chapters 6–8. See also the edition and commentary of Rabbi David ben Yehuda Luria (RaDaL; 1798–1855), *Sefer pirḳei Rabi Eli'ezer im Bi'ur* (Warsaw: H. E. Bamberg, 1852; repr., New York: Om, 1946; Jerusalem, 1969; in Hebrew); *Pirke de-Rabbi Eliezer: Nach der Edition Venedig 1544 unter Berücksichtigung der Edition Warschau 1852*, trans. and ed. Dagmar Börner-Klein (Frankfurt: Peter Lang, 2004); and *Pirkei de-Rabbi Eliezer: Text, Redaction and a Sample Synopsis*, ed. Eliezer Treitl (Jerusalem: Yad Yitshak Ben Tsevi, 2012; in Hebrew). And see, too, Steven Daniel Sacks, *Midrash and Multiplicity: Pirke de-Rabbi Eliezer and the Renewal of Rabbinic Interpretive Culture* (Berlin: Walter de Gruyter, 2009), and Rachel Adelman, *The Return of the Repressed: Pirke de-Rabbi Eliezer and the Pseudepigrapha* (Leiden: Brill, 2009).

15. See Josephus, *Against Apion* 2.282; *Flavius Josephus: Translation and Commentary*, ed. Steve Mason (Leiden: Brill), 10: 327–328. F. H. Colson (*Week*, p. 9) seems to agree: "We measure our time in cycles of seven days primarily because the Jews, at the time of our era, had come to attach vast importance to the religious observance of one day of seven."

16. Pietri, "Temps de la semaine à Rome," p. 71. [*Constitutiones Apostolorum*, eight treatises, possibly written in Syria, on morality and liturgy from around 375–380 CE.—Trans.]

17. "Dies Dominica," *Corpus Christianorum: Series Latina*, in 2 parts (Turnholt, Belgium: Brepols, 1954), 78, p. 546. Also see Pierre Grelot, "Du sabbat juif au dimanche chrétien," *La maison Dieu* 123 (1975): 79–107; 124 (1976): 15–124.

18. Gen. 29:27.

19. See André Caquot and Arnaud Sérandour, "La périodisation: De la Bible à l'Apocalyptique," in *Proche-Orient ancien: Temps vécu, temps pensé*, ed. Françoise Briquel-Chatonnet and Hélène Lozachmeur (Paris: J. Maisonneuve, 1998), pp. 83–98.

20. Deut. 15:12.

21. Benedict Zuckermann, "Über Sabbatjahrcyclus und Jobelperiode: Ein Beitrag zur Archäologie und Chronologie der vor- und nachexilischen Zeit, mit einer angehängten Sabbatjahrtafel," in *Jahresbericht des jüdisch-theologischen Seminars 'Fraenckelscher Stiftung'* (Breslau: Korn, 1857), trans. A. Löwy as *A Treatise of the Sabbatical Cycle and the Jubilee: A Contribution to the Archaeology and Chronology*

of the Time Anterior and Subsequent to the Captivity. Accompanied by a Table of Sabbatical Years (New York: Hermon Press, 1974).

22. Hayyim Yehiel Bornstein, "Heshbon shemitim ve-yovelot," *Ha-tekufah* 11 (1921): 238–260; 14–15 (1923): 321–372; 16 (1924): 228–292.

23. Ben Zion Wacholder, "The Calendar of Sabbatical Cycles During the Second Temple and the Early Rabbinic Period," *HUCA* 44 (1973): 153–196, tried to show that the jubilee chronology established by Zuckermann in "Über Sabbatjahrcyclus" and relied upon by authorities such as Emil Schürer in "Siebentägige Woche," F. K. Ginzel in *Handbuch der mathematischen und technischen Chronologie: Das Zeitrechnungswesen der Völker*, vol. 2: *Zeitrechnung der Juden, der Naturvölker, der Römer und Griechen, sowie Nachtrage zum I. Bande* (Leipzig: J. C. Hinrichs, 1906–1914), and Solomon Zeitlin in *Megillat Taʻanit as a Source for Jewish Chronology and History in the Hellenistic and Roman Periods* (Philadelphia: Dropsie College for Hebrew and Cognate Learning, 1922) was obsolete in the light of recent studies based on archaeological discoveries.

24. Or more exactly, every 29 days, 12 hours, and 793 *halakim* (portions). See Chapter 12, n. 102 for the explanation.

25. Exod. 12:2; 12:18.

26. However, as we have seen, the books of Maccabees remained outside the Jewish biblical canon.

27. Internal variations may also be noted in calculating different eras that form variants within the same count and often lead to mistakes in dating by rabbis and researchers. As we shall see later, the Seleucid era, the destruction of the second Temple, and the calendrical year all gave rise to variant chronologies. See Edgar Frank, *Talmudic and Rabbinical Chronology: The System of Counting Years in Jewish Literature* (New York: Philip Feldheim, 1956).

28. See Chapter Two, pp. 33 and 40; see also and Eduard Mahler, *Handbuch der Jüdischen Chronologie* (Leipzig: Fock, 1916; repr., Hildesheim: Georg Olms, 1967).

29. 1 Macc. 6:16.

30. 2 Macc. 11:21, 23ff.

31. 1 Macc. 10:21. Sukkot, the Feast of Booths or Feast of Tabernacles, is celebrated between the 15th and the 21st of Tishrei. By mentioning the "seventh month," the writer shows that the year is counted starting from the month of Nisan. See the table of months, pp. 195–196.

32. Mahler, *Handbuch*, pp. 140–145.

33. 1 Macc. 13:41–42. The date is confirmed by Josephus, *Jewish Antiquities* 13.6.7.213, who without any possible doubt refers to the Seleucid era when mentioning that the tribute paid by Israel was lifted on the year 170 of the Assyrian reign, begun under Seleucus I Nicator.

34. *Meg. Taʻan*, 7, *Medieval Jewish Chronicles*, ed. Neubauer, 2: 12–13; RH 18b.

35. Schürer, *History of the Jewish People*, rev. ed., 1: 190; Hugo Winckler, in Eberhard Schrader, *Die Keilinschriften und das Alte Testament*, 3rd ed. rev. Heinrich Zimmern and Hugo Winckler (Berlin: Reuther & Reichard, 1903), pp. 308, 324;

Ludwig Ideler, *Handbuch der mathematischen und technischen Chronologie* (Berlin: A. Rücker, 1825–1826), 1: 135; Ginzel, *Handbuch*, 2: 61; Mahler, *Handbuch*, p. 147.

36. Wacholder, "Calendar of Sabbatical Cycles," § 7, pp. 169–171; § 9, pp. 176–179, quoting Pierre Benoît, Józef Milik, and Roland de Vaux, *Les grottes de Murabbaât* (Oxford: Clarendon Press, 1961), vol. 2, no. 18, pp. 100–104, 122– 134. Hearty thanks to Marc Bregman, who generously provided much bibliographic information about questions of dating.

37. Archaeologists differ in their translations of one of the terms involving the year of fallow land. Milik translates it as "even if it is a year of fallow land," whereas Elisabeth Koffmahn, in her translation into German included in *Die Doppelurkunden aus der Wüste Juda: Recht und Praxis der jüdischen Papyri des 1. und 2. Jahrhunderts n. Chr. samt Übertragung der Texte und deutscher Übersetzung* (Leiden: Brill, 1968) renders it as "in this year of fallow fields" (p. 81). They also differ on the dating to be given in 54/55. See Manfred R. Lehman, "Studies in the Murabba'at and Nahal Hever Documents," *Revue de Qumran* 4, no. 13 (1963): 53– 81; Koffmahn, *Doppelurkunden*, p. 41. Wacholder, "Calendar of Sabbatical Cycles," although mainly concerned with his subject, also discusses suggested datings.

38. On Bar Kokhba, see Chapter Five, n. 36. Contract for the sale of a house, Émile Puech, "L'acte de vente d'une maison à Kafar-Bébayu en 135 de notre ère," *RQ* 34, no. 9 (July 1977): 213–221, after Józef Milik, "Un contrat juif de l'an 134 après J.-C.," *Revue biblique* 61 (1954): 182–190, and "Deux Documents inédits du désert de Juda," *Biblica* 38 (1957): 264–268.

39. See Gen. 5, which begins: "This is the book of the generations of Adam."

40. Gen. 7:11–12.

41. See Rashi, ad loc.; RH 11b.

42. Exod. 12:2.

43. Lev. 23:24; and see too Num. 29:1.

44. "One day in the year will count for a whole year" (RH 2b), meaning that on that day, the change of date will be noted.

45. Exod. 34:22. The Hebrew term *tekufah* means a cyclic period, since it marks an end as well as a start, or, putting it more simply, regeneration.

46. Josephus, *Jewish Antiquities* 1.3.3.81. "On the first of Nisan, the new year for the kings and for the festivals," says Mishnah RH 1:1. The Rosh Ha-shanah [RH] tractate in the Babylonian Talmud and Jerusalem Talmud gives full details about rites during the era of the Temple and after its destruction, but also shows the importance of localizing this holiday for dating and calendrical questions.

47. Amos 1:1.

48. Ezek. 1:1–2.

49. Dan. 8:17; 10:14; 9:2; 9:25; 11:31, 33; the last quotation describes the events that led to the Maccabean revolt and that occurred during the profanation of the Temple by Antiochus IV Epiphanes.

50. From Dan. 9 to the end of the book. We shall return to the Book of Daniel and its implications along the way.

51. The term *mekhilta* derives from the Aramaic for "measure" or "rule," offering rules of interpretation in a halakhic midrash.—Trans.

52. *Mekhilta* of R. Ishmael, *massekhet Yitro*, "in the third month."

53. 1 Kings 6:1.

54. Exod. 12:41.

55. Dating from the building of Solomon's Temple, 1 Kings 9:10, and from its destruction, mentioned as "our exile," Ezek. 40:1. Sincere thanks to Binyamin Wattenberg for this and many other valuable notes.

56. Bornstein, "Ta'arikhei Yisrael," *Ha-tekufah* 8 (1920): 285.

57. See Chapter Two, n. 25.

58. See *mishnahGit.* 8:5.

59. Arsaces I of Parthia, "the king of Persia and Media," is mentioned in 1 Macc. 14:2. The Arsacid dynasty began when Arsaces freed himself from Seleucid control and founded the Parthian empire around 250 BCE, according to Grumel, *Traité d'études byzantines*, 1: 210.

60. *Seder 'olam rabbah*, chap. 30, also in the Talmud, Avoda Zara 9a. See, too, *Medieval Jewish Chronicles*, ed. Neubauer, 2: 65–67, and *Seder 'olam: Mahadurah mada'it, perush u-mavo: Critical Edition, Commentary and Introduction*, ed. Chaim Milikowsky (Jerusalem: Yad ben Zvi, 2013; in Hebrew), 1: 323.

61. *Seder 'olam rabbah* (Vilna [Vilnius], 1845), chap. 1; *Seder 'olam: Mahadurah . . .* , ed. Milikowsky, 1: 219. I have used the CD-ROM of responsa published by Bar Ilan University (2009), offering the editions by Jeruchem Meir Leiner and Milikowsky, as well as reprints by Dov Baer Ratner, *Midrash Seder 'olam* (Vilna [Vilnius], 1897), by Shemuel Mirski (1966; repr., Jerusalem, 1988); and *Seder 'olam rabba ha-shalem . . .* , ed. Yossef Menahem Weinstock (Jerusalem: Hotsa'at Metivta Torat Ḥesed, 1956; repr., Bnei Brak: Mishor, 1990); and see also the bilingual (Hebrew/English) edition by Henrich W. Guggenheimer, *Seder 'olam: The Rabbinic View of Biblical Chronology* (Northvale, NJ: J. Aronson, 1998), p. 3. The two texts are also published in *Medieval Jewish Chronicles*, ed. Neubauer, 2: 26–88.

62. Lev. 25; Ezek. 40:1.

63. Arakh. 12a, 12b.

64. Since the stars were frozen during the Flood, the year was shortened and is not taken into account in calculations (Gen. R. 32).

Chapter Seven. Eschatological Scansions

1. On Pseudo-Philo, see Howard Jacobson, *A Commentary on Pseudo-Philo's Liber Antiquitatum Biblicarum, with Latin Text and English Translation* (Leiden: Brill 1996); *La Bible: Écrits intertestamentaires*, ed. A. Dupont-Sommer and M. Philonenko (Paris: Gallimard, 1987); Adolf Jellinek, *Bet ha-Midrash* (6 vols.; Leipzig: C. W. Vollrath, 1853–1878; repr. Jerusalem: Wahrmann Books, 1967). On apocrypha in general, see Abraham Kahana, *Ha-Sefarim ha-hitsonim: La-Torah la-Nevi'im la-Ketuvim u-she'ar sefarim hitsonim* (2 vols. [1931 or 1932]; Tel Aviv: Otsa'at Mekorot, 1956; in Hebrew), and Elia Samuele Artom, *Ha-Sefarim ha-hitsonim*

(1958; 3rd ed., Tel Aviv: Yavneh, 1967; in Hebrew). This is not meant to be an exhaustive list.

2. See Beckwith, "Daniel 9 and the Date of the Messiah's Coming."

3. It is known from fragments found at Qumran that the text was originally written in Hebrew. James C. VanderKam, *Textual and Historical Studies in the Book of Jubilees* (Missoula, MT: Scholars Press, 1977). Only an Ethiopian version translated from the Greek has survived, however.

4. Jub. 4:9; 25:1; 47:1; 48:1; 50:4, quoting from *The Book of Jubilees: A Translation*, ed. and trans. James C. VanderKam (Louvain: Peeters, 1989). See also Géza G. Xeravits, Tobias Niklas, and Isaac Halimi, *Scriptural Authority in Early Judaism and Ancient Christianity* (Berlin: Walter de Gruyter, 2013).

5. Seemingly echoes, and even similarities, may be found between this text and the Midrash Tadshe as well as the *Pirkei de-Rabbi Eliezer*. For the likenesses between the texts, see A. Epstein, "Le livre des Jubilés, Philon et le Midrasch Tadsché," *REJ* 21 (1890): 1– 25; 22 (1891): 80–97, also the articles by K. Kohler, "Jubilees, Book of," *JE* 7 (1901): 301–304, and Y. M. Grintz, "Jubilees, Book of," in *EJ*, 10: 324–325. The time of its writing is much debated, starting with the end of the second century BCE, according to Schürer, *History of the Jewish People in the Age of Jesus Christ*, rev. ed., and *The Ethiopic Version of the Hebrew Book of Jubilees*, ed. Robert Henry Charles (Oxford: Clarendon Press, 1895); in *From the Stone Age to Christianity*, Albright even places its composition in the third century BCE, based on arguments developed by Solomon Zeitlin, asserting that the work predates the fights between second-century Sadducees and Pharisees. Bickerman, *Jews in the Greek Age*, places its writing between 250 and 175 BCE; he insists on the parallels between this text and apocryphal Aramean Genesis discovered at the Qumran site, stressing the diversity and richness of exegetical traditions around the Bible in the ancient Jewish world (p. 211). *The Book of Jubilees*, ed. and trans. J. C. VanderKam, places it more precisely around 160 BCE. On the dispute that divides researchers over the Essenian theory, see the case file by Francis Schmidt, "L'étranger, le Temple et la Loi dans le judaïsme ancien," and especially Devorah Dimant, "Signification et importance des manuscrits de la mer Morte: L'état actuel des études qoumraniennes," *Annales HSS* 5 (1996): 975–1004. Albert I. Baumgarten's clarification in the introduction to *The Flourishing of Jewish Sects in the Maccabean Era: An Interpretation* (Leiden: Brill, 1997), p. 1, n. 1, shows that the trend has changed to attributing these texts to a Dead Sea "sect," whose profile remains vague, instead of to the Essenes. Norman Golb's virulent critique in *Who Wrote the Dead Sea Scrolls? The Search for the Secret of Qumran* (New York: Scribner, 1995) focuses on the presumed sectarianism of the site's inhabitants. Seeing Qumran as a military fortress more than the home of a religious brotherhood, he concludes that the provenance of the texts must be an attempt to salvage the libraries of Jerusalem in wartime. Yet, this view was advanced immediately after the discoveries were made by the archaeologist André Parrot, who supported the theory "that all these documents were sheltered at the time of the revolt (between

67 and 70 CE), precisely in a region solidly controlled by Jewish formations and where doubtless it was hoped that the Romans would never arrive." See the addendum entitled "Les manuscrits du désert de Juda" (The manuscripts from the Judean desert) that Parrot wrote for Adolphe Lods's posthumously published *Histoire de la littérature hébraïque et juive*, p. 1031.

6. Most researchers agree that the text closely follows the Halakhah, never straying from it, which makes it doubtful that the author belonged to a specific sect. A similar calendar is found in the Ethiopic Book of Enoch; Jub. 6:29–38; and Enoch 76:14 and 82:1–8. See G. F. Moore, *Judaism*, 1: 193–199; Bickerman, *Jews in the Greek Age*, p. 215; and Gene L. Davenport, *The Eschatology of the Book of Jubilees* (Leiden: Brill, 1971).

7. Dan. 1:1; 8:1; 9:1; 10:1.

8. Dan. 7:25. The term for "time" used in the text, *'idan*, is Aramaic. According to Sander and Trenel, *Dictionnaire hébreu-français*, it means the "time of the hour." Barr, *Biblical Words for Time*, p. 87, sees it as a translation of the term *et*, or simply one that conveys the idea of "time." See the discussion of terminology in Part 1 of this book. On the text of the Book of Daniel, see André LaCocque, *Daniel et son temps: Recherches sur le mouvement apocalyptique juif au IIe siècle avant Jésus-Christ* (Geneva: Labor et Fides, 1983), pp. 45–50.

9. Jewish and Semitic traditions grant powerful symbolism to the number four, which represents the four cardinal points of the earth, the four "winds," and the four species (Lev. 23:40) of Sukkot; see Isa. 11:12; Ezek. 7:2; Zech. 2:1–4; 6:1. Also see Yehezkel Kaufmann, *Toledot ha-'emunah ha-yisraelit*, 8: 235–258. Four is a divine number, because the tetragram has four letters, and contains mystical spells and numerology. See L. Finkelstein, "The Sources of the Tannaitic Midrashim," *JQR*, n.s., 21 (1941): 225; I. Zeligman, *The Treasury of Numbers* (New York: Shulsinger, 1942; in Hebrew); and Adela Yarbro Collins, *Cosmology and Eschatology in Jewish and Christian Apocalyptism* (Leiden: Brill, 1996), pp. 55–138: "The numbers which occur most frequently in this [apocalyptic] activity are seven, four, twelve and ten" (p. 89).

10. Dan. 8:4, 20–22.

11. From the text itself, nothing apparently allows us to conclude that the author believed in establishing 100 jubilees of forty-nine years, each containing seven weeks of years, or 4,900 years, as claimed in the preface to *La Bible: Écrits intertestamentaires*, ed. Dupont-Sommer and Philonenko; see also ibid., p. 808n4, more reasonable in this respect. A comparable pattern is found in the Apocalypse of Weeks of the Book of Enoch, based on an end of time set for the tenth "week," which takes 490 years, according to Devorah Dimant in "The Seventy Weeks Chronology (Dan 9, 24–27) in the Light of New Qumranic Texts," in *The Book of Daniel in the Light of New Findings*, ed. Adam S. van der Woude, pp. 57–76 (Leuven: Leuven University Press, 1993). Inasmuch as the latter text supports the same solar calendar, based on a year of 364 days and expressed by jubilees, and fragments of both documents were found at Qumran, researchers suggest that

they share the same eschatological viewpoint. On the structure of this time as a "jubilee of jubilees," see Roger T. Beckwith, "The Significance of the Calendar for Interpreting Essene Chronology and Eschatology," *RQ* 10 (1980): 167– 202, esp. pp. 185–187 (I thank Olivier Munnich for sending me this).

12. Josephus, *Jewish Antiquities* 10.11.7.267.

Chapter Eight. Historiographical Scansions

1. Josephus, *Against Apion* 1.1–2.7, trans. Barclay, ed. Mason, pp. 13–14.

2. See *History and Historians in Late Antiquity*, ed. Brian Croke and Alanna M. Emmett (Sydney: Pergamon Press, 1983).

3. For an overview of the literature of this time, also including the books of Maccabees, Philo, and Josephus, and an analysis of studies of them, see Harold W. Attridge, "Jewish Historiography," in *Early Judaism*, ed. Kraft and Nickelsburg, pp. 311–343. Also, John R. Bartlett, *Jews in the Hellenistic World: Josephus, Aristeas, The Sibylline Oracles, Eupolemus* (Cambridge: Cambridge University Press, 1985).

4. Demetrius is mentioned in the lists of Josephus and Clement of Alexandria, possibly during the reign of Ptolemy IV Philopator (221–204 BCE). See Jacob Freudenthal, *Alexander Polyhistor und die von ihm erhaltenen Reste judäischer und samaritanischer Geschichtswerke* (Breslau: H. Skutsch, 1874), vol. 1: *Hellenistische Studien*, pp. 35–82. In fact, we know nothing precise about him as a person. His situation in time is deduced by his mention of Ptolemy IV Philopator, just as his use of the Ptolemaic era suggests that he lived in Alexandria. See, too, E. J. Bickerman, "The Jewish Historian Demetrios," in *Christianity, Judaism, and Other Greco-Roman Cults*, ed. Jacob Neusner (Leiden: Brill, 1975), vol. 3: *Judaism Before 70*, pp. 72–84, and Moses Gaster, "Demetrius und Seder 'olam: Ein Problem der hellenistischen Literatur," in *Festskrift i anledning af professor David Simonsens 70-aarige fødselsdag* (Copenhagen: Hertz's Bogtrykkeri, 1923), pp. 243–252. B. Z. Wacholder, *Eupolemus: A Study of Judaeo-Greek Literature* (Cincinnati: Hebrew Union College–Jewish Institute of Religion, 1974 [i.e., 1975]), pp. 280–282, suggested that he might have lived in Palestine under Egyptian rule. Also see James E. Crouch, *Demetrius the Chronographer and the Beginnings of Hellenistic Jewish Historiography* (Nishinomiya, Japan: Kwansei Gakuin University, 1981).

5. The grammarian Alexander Polyhistor wrote historico-geographical monographs. His treatise on the Jews was used by Josephus, Clement of Alexandria, and Eusebius, who all transmit fragments of it. See *Fragmenta historicum graecorum*, ed. K. Müller (Paris: A. F. Didot, 1841–1870); Felix Jacoby, *Die Fragmente der griechischen Historiker* (Berlin: Weidmann, 1923–1955); Freudenthal, *Alexander Polyhistor*; Eusebius of Caesarea, *Preparations for the Gospel*, trans. E. H. Gifford (Oxford: Clarendon Press, 1903; repr., Eugene, OR: Wipf & Stock, 2002), bk. 9. Thanks to François Hartog for having drawn my attention to Alden A. Mosshammer, *The Chronicle of Eusebius and Greek Chronographic Tradition* (Lewisburg, PA: Bucknell University Press, 1979). There is a rich bibliography about Eusebius

and his rapport with Judaism; see *Eusebius, Christianity and Judaism*, ed. H. W. Attridge and Gohei Hata (Detroit: Wayne State University Press, 1992); Robert M. Grant, *Eusebius as Church Historian* (Oxford: Clarendon Press, 1980).

6. See *The Writings of Clement of Alexandria*, ed. William Wilson (Edinburgh: T. & T. Clark, 1867–1872); Clement of Alexandria, *Miscellanies [Stromata]*, Book 7, ed. and trans. Fenton John Anthony Hort and Joseph Bickersteth Mayor (London: Macmillan, 1902; repr., Cambridge: Cambridge University Press. 2010); and see also *The Seventh Book of the Stromateis: Proceedings of the Colloquium on Clement of Alexandria (Olomouc* [Czech Republic], *October 21–23, 2010)*, ed. Matyáš Havrda, Vít Hušek, and Jana Plátová (Leiden: Brill, 2012).

7. A. Schalit, "Demetrius," in *EJ*, 5: 1490–1491; Hengel, *Judaism and Hellenism*; Carl R. Holladay, *Fragments from Hellenistic Jewish Authors*, vol. 1: *Historians* (Chico, CA: Scholars Press, 1983), pp. 51–91; John Hanson, "Demetrius the Chronographer," in *The Old Testament Pseudepigrapha* (Garden City, NY: Doubleday, 1983), ed. J. H. Charlesworth, 2: 843–854. On the possible Greek readership of the Bible, see this chapter, n. 48; Momigliano's harsh judgment of these chronographers in *Alien Wisdom*, pp. 92–93; and Tessa Rajak, *Translation and Survival: The Greek Bible of the Ancient Jewish Diaspora* (Oxford: Oxford University Press, 2009).

8. 1 Mac. 8:17–32; also see his father, cited in 2 Mac. 4:11. The second ambassador would have been the noted Jason of Cyrene, whose work, now lost, is said to have formed the basis of 2 Mac. See Arnaldo Momigliano, "The Romans and the Maccabees," in *Jewish History: Essays in Honour of Chimen Abramsky*, ed. Ada Rapoport-Albert and Steven Zipperstein (London: Peter Halban, 1988), p. 236.

9. Eusebius, *Preparations for the Gospel* 1.9; Clement of Alexandria, *Miscellanies* 1.21.

10. "Saul was chosen as king by Samuel and reigned. . . . Next, David his son ascended the throne" (Eusebius, *Preparations for the Gospel* 30.2–3, p. 311). See Wacholder, *Eupolemus*, pp. 2, 131; id., "Eupolemus," in *EJ*, 6: 964–965; Holladay, *Fragments*, 1: 93–156.

11. Yev. 82b; Nid. 46b; *Seder 'olam rabbah* is also mentioned in Shab. 88a; Sanh. 86a. Printed for the first time in Mantua in 1514, with the *Seder 'olam Zutta*, the *Seder* [or *Sefer*] *ha-Kabbalah* by Abraham ibn Daud, and the *Megillat Ta'anit*, the *Seder 'olam* was reprinted many times. It appeared, accompanied by the *Seder 'olam zutta* translated into Latin by Gilbert Génébrard in Paris in 1577, and with a Latin translation in Amsterdam in 1699, with an introduction and notes by John Meyer. Jacob Emden (Hamburg, 1757) and Elijah ben Shlomo Zalman Kremer, the Vilna Ga'on (Shklov [Škłoŭ, Belarus], 1801) among others, wrote commentaries, which were printed alongside the text in some editions. On the writing of the *Seder 'olam*, see Leopold Zunz, *Die gottesdienstlichen Vorträge der Juden historisch entwickelt: Ein Beitrag zur Alterthumskunde und biblischen Kritik, zur Literatur- und Religionsgeschichte* (1832; Piscataway, NJ: Gorgias Press, 2003); *Ha-derashot be-Yisrael*, trans. Leopold Zunz and Chanoch Albeck (Jerusalem: Mosad Bialik,

1954); and *Seder ʿolam: Critical Edition, Commentary and Introduction*, ed. Chaim Milikowsky (2 vols.; Jerusalem: Yad ben Zvi, 2013; in Hebrew).

12. See Chaim Tykocinsky, "Bustenai rosh ha-golah [Bustanay the exilarch]," *Dvir* 1 (1923): 145–179; Alexander D. Goode, "The Exilarchate in the Eastern Caliphate, 637–1258," *JQR*, n.s., 31 (1940/1941): 149–169; *Seder ʿolam rabbah ha-shalem*, ed. Weinstock. The theory that it was written in the sixth century is doubtful, since its chronology goes up to the eighth century.

13. The Masoretic text was established by scribes who ensured the final transmission (*massar*) of the Torah text. The Masoretic process of setting the text and its pointing extended between the Second Temple and the tenth century. On the *baraita* relating to the order of the biblical canon, see Part I, pp. 34–35 and Chapter Two, n. 22.

14. Eusebius, *Preparations for the Gospel*, 9.21.18, p. 253; Holladay, *Fragments*, 1: 73.

15. In citing Gen. 35: 16, Demetrius signals his use of the Greek version, which differs from the Masoretic text, especially in its singular subject, which is plural in the Hebrew. In addition to the excerpts in Eusebius, *Preparations for the Gospel*, cited above, see Holladay, *Fragments*, 1: 51–54.

16. Ctesias of Cnidus (fifth century BCE) wrote a history of Assyria and Persia.—Trans.

17. Identified by Wacholder, *Eupolemus*, p. 13, in fragments 1:2 § 30 and 4, § 4. On the reworking of Jewish history in a Greek guise, see Erich Gruen, *Heritage and Hellenism: The Reinvention of Jewish Tradition* (Berkeley: University of California Press, 1998).

18. Freudenthal describes Eupolemus as a "Jewish author who only superficially draws in the spirit of Greek literature" (*Alexander Polyhistor*, 1: 109–110), adding that his style "is as faulty and as tasteless as it is false, the vocabulary very limited, the sentence structure clumsy and confusing, almost incomprehensible." Felix Jacoby is just as severe: "His style is indigent, vocabulary impoverished, and sentence structure gauche" ("Eupolemus," in von Pauly, *Paulys Realencyclopädie der classischen Altertumswissenschaft . . . Ephoros bis Eutychos*, 6: 1229 [Stuttgart: Metzler, 1907]). Wacholder finds his vocabulary "narrow and his syntax atrocious" and concludes that "only the presumed existence of a distinct Judaeo-Greek dialect renders Eupolemus' Greek tolerable" (*Eupolemus*, p. 257).

19. Holladay, *Fragments*, 1, frg. 2, pp. 115–119, although the coronation of Solomon at the age of twelve is also found in *Seder ʿolam* 14. See also Freudenthal, *Alexander Polyhistor*, 1: 119; Holladay, *Fragments*, 1, frg. 2, pp. 100–101.

20. Holladay, *Fragments*, 1, frg. 2b, § 30.4, § 33.1; § 34.1; § 34.4 on 1 Kings 6:3, p.101n15; Freudenthal, *Alexander Polyhistor*, 1: 108, 209.

21. See Holladay, *Fragments*, 1, frg. 2, § 30.1, p. 115: Moses prophesied for forty years, Joshua for thirty, and so on, but Saul's twenty-one-year reign does not tally with anything traceable, just as the indication that "his son David succeeded him" is difficult to source. However, the statement that Solomon lived for fifty-two years

and reigned peacefully for forty is based on a proto-Masoretic text, albeit in regard to a lifespan about which no data exist. Josephus, *Jewish Antiquities* 8.211 offers a comparable figure: Solomon reigned for eighty years and lived to be ninety-four.

22. Holladay, *Fragments*, 1, frg. 5, §§ 4–5, p. 135, quoting Clement of Alexandria, *Miscellanies*, bk. 1, chap. 21.

23. See the theories for both collected by Holladay, *Fragments*, 1: 155–156nn119–121; also Alfred von Gutschmid, "Zeit und Zeitrechnung der jüdischen Historiker Demetrios und Eupolemos," in *Kleine Schriften*, ed. Franz Rühl (Leipzig: Teubner, 1890), 2: 186–195. Jeremy Hughes offers yet another theory, that Eupolemus would have followed a plan based on the number 1,580. Correcting the number 2, assumed to derive from a scribe's mistake, 576 years passed between the death of Moses and Solomon's coronation, plus forty years in the desert, to which he adds four years of Solomon's reign, arriving at 620 years for the time from Exodus to the building of the Temple. This leaves 960 years between the building of the Temple and the fifth year of the reign of Demetrius, and 960 divides neatly into two equal periods of 480 years. This number pattern is also found in the priestly chronology and the *Seder 'olam*. See Hughes, *Secrets of the Times: Myth and History in Biblical Chronology* (Sheffield, UK: *JSOT*, 1990), pp. 243–244.

24. *Life of Josephus* 9.40, ed. Mason, 9: 45; Tessa Rajak, "Justus of Tiberius," *Classical Quarterly* 23 (1973): 345–368; and id., *The Jewish Dialogue with Greece and Rome: Studies in Cultural and Social Interaction* (Leiden: Brill, 2002), pp. 161–194.

25. Apparently most writers who referred to Justus's book subsequently came to it via their reading of Josephus. See Holladay, *Fragments*, 1: 372.

26. Richard Laqueur suggested that *Against Apion* 1.46–56 was only written to refute charges by Justus of Tiberias against Josephus. See Laqueur, *Der jüdische Historiker Flavius Josephus: Ein biographischer Versuch auf neuer quellenkritischer Grundlage* (Rome: "L'Erma" di Bretschneider, 1970), pp. 6–23. This theory is refuted by Théodore Reinach in his edition of *Contre Apion*, trans. Léon Blum (Paris: Les Belles Lettres, 1930), p. 11n1.

27. Photius, *Bibliothèque*, ed. René Henry (Paris: Les Belles Lettres, 1959–1991), frg. 33; see also id., *The Bibliotheca: A Selection*, ed. Nigel Guy Wilson (London: Duckworth, 1994).

28. *Life of Josephus*, "Digression Against Justus," 65.336–367; ed. Mason, pp. 135–150.

29. See Schürer, *History of the Jewish People*, 1: 35; and again the fragment in *Life of Josephus*, p. 225, where Photius says that "his idiom is very concise" and adds that "he preserved no memory whatsoever."

30. Simple mentions are collected in Holladay, *Fragments*, 1: 371–389; Jacoby, *Fragmente*, 3C, pp. 695, 734; id., "Iustus," in von Pauly, *Paulys Realencyclopädie der classischen Altertumswissenschaft . . . Ius liberorum bis Katochos* (Stuttgart: Metzler, 1919), 10: 1341–1346. See also Schürer, *History of the Jewish People*, 1: 34–37; von Gutschmid, *Kleine Schriften* (cited n. 23 above), 2: 196–203; Heinrich Gelzer,

Sextus Julius Africanus und die byzantinische Chronographie (Leipzig: Teubner, 1880; repr., New York: B. Franklin, 1967), 1: 19–21; 264–265. Wacholder, *Eupolemus*, pp. 106–128, claims that a chronology synchronizing biblical narrative and general history already existed in the first century; see the refutation by Milikowsky, "*Seder 'olam* and Jewish Chronography," in *Proceedings of the American Academy for Jewish Research* 52 (1995), p. 130n26.

31. See the diverse discussions among scholars on this subject in Feldman, *Josephus and Modern Scholarship*, pp. 673–725, esp. p. 692, and "Selective Critical Bibliography," in *Josephus, the Bible, and History*, ed. Feldman and Hata (Leiden: Brill, 1989), pp. 343–344.

32. Josephus, *Jewish Antiquities* 18.5.116–119; 20, 9.1. 200.

33. Laqueur, *Der jüdische Historiker Flavius Josephus*, pp. 274–278; L. H. Feldman in *Josephus, the Bible, and History*, p. 432.

34. See esp. Baron, *Social and Religious History of the Jews*, vol. 2: *Ancient Times*, p.141: "On the whole, this chronicle is dry as dust."

35. *Seder 'olam*, chap. 30, *Critical Edition*, ed. Chaim Milikowsky, 1: 323.

36. AZ 9a with Rashi's explanation, 10a.

37. Oddly, Franz Rühl, "Der Ursprung der jüdischen Weltära," *Deutsche Zeitschrift für Geschichtswissenschaft*, n.s., 2 (1898): 185–203, uses data in the *Seder 'olam* to place the sack of Jerusalem in 80 CE (p. 192).

38. *Seder 'olam*, chap. 28: "70 for its destruction and 420 its rebuilding." *Critical Edition*, ed. Chaim Milikowsky, 1: 317.

39. See Milikowsky's preface to his edition of the *Seder 'olam*, p. 17. Special thanks to Professor Milikowsky for giving me his manuscript, a text that opens a window on the creation of the rabbinical mind in past centuries.

40. Bornstein, "Ta'arikhei Yisrael," *Ha-tekufah* 8 (1920): 288.

41. See Isidore Loeb, "Notes sur l'histoire des Juifs: La chronologie juive," *REJ* 19 (1889): 202–205.

42. Dan. 9:24, 26; also Joseph Jacobs, "Chronology," in *JE*, 4: 64–75. Ibn Daud's reading of this chronology proposed in the twelfth century leaves no doubt about a decision to insert these numbers in the prophetic outline of Daniel as expressed by Jeremiah and Isaiah (see Chapter Two, n. 44) and his biblical chronology, discussed further (see Chapter Ten, n. 2).

43. "All of this [Persian] royalty is named Artaxerxes" (*Seder 'olam*, ed. Milikowsky 30.5, 1: 321).

44. Ibid., esp. chap. 20, 1: 279–285.

45. B. Z. Wacholder, "Biblical Chronology in the Hellenistic World Chronicles," *HTR* 61 (1968): 451–481.

46. These ancient historians do not always present themselves as Jews, but Eusebius of Caesarea's *Preparations for the Gospel* identifies them as such by grouping them. Neither Josephus nor Demetrius nor Eupolemus identify as Jews. Nor does Philo the Elder (of whom it is only known that he is not Philo of Alexandria, but the author of an epic text about Jerusalem, of which twenty-four lines sur-

vive). The three fragments imply that he might have written a biblical chronology to be placed between Demetrius and Eupolemos, which he possibly gleaned from Polyhistor. See *Contre Apion*, trans. Blum, ed. Reinach, Introduction, p. 27; also Momigliano, *Alien Wisdom*, p. 91; Schürer, *History of the Jewish People*, 3: 555–556.

47. Ptolemy II Philadelphus reigned in Egypt from 283 BCE to 246 BCE. —Trans.

48. However, Momigliano affirms that only Jews and people of Jewish origin read the Bible: "It was indeed, very difficult to find somebody non-Jewish reading the Bible in Greek, even when it was made available in that language" (*Alien Wisdom*, p. 8); "The Bible was no literature for pagans. . . . If we find a pagan who had a slight acquaintance with the Bible, . . . we suspect direct Jewish influence" ("Pagan and Christian Historiography in the Fourth Century A.D.," in id., *Essays in Ancient and Modern Historiography*, p. 109). And see Rajak, *Translation and Survival*, chap. 8.

49. Although he presents himself as a Greek worshiper of Zeus, Aristeas was an Alexandrian Jew, according to researchers. His letter addressed to his brother describes the translation of the Bible by seventy-two Palestinian scholars—six from each tribe—at the request of Ptolemy, who wished to add it to the Library of Alexandria. Completed in seventy-two days, it was accepted as "law coming from God." The date of its writing, between the third century BCE and the first century CE, remains debated. Insofar as it is quoted by Josephus, however, it cannot postdate him. See *Aristeas to Philocrates* (*Letters of Aristeas*), ed. and trans. Moses Hadas (New York: Harper, 1951; repr., New York: Ktav, 1973); André Pelletier, *La lettre d'Aristée à Philocrate* (Paris: Cerf, 1962); L. Hermann, "La lettre d'Aristée à Philocrate et l'empereur Titus," *Latomus* 25 (1966): 58–77; Victor Tcherikover, "The Ideology of the Letter of Aristeas," *HTR* 51 (1958): 59–85; id., "Jewish Apologetic Literature Reconsidered," *Eos* 48, no. 3 (1956): 169–193; Rajak, *Translation and Survival*, pp. 259–261.

50. "They would prophesy as if God had taken possession of their spirits, not with different words, but all with the same words and same turn of phrase, each one as if taking dictation from an invisible prompter" (Philo, *On the Life of Moses*, 2.37, in *The Works of Philo*, trans. Charles D. Yonge).

51. "It is evident that Plato closely followed our legislation, and has carefully studied the several precepts contained in it . . . it is manifest that many things have been borrowed by the aforesaid philosopher, for he is very learned: as also Pythagoras transferred many of our precepts and inserted them in his own system of doctrines. But the entire translation of all the contents of our law was made in the time of the king surnamed Philadelphus" (Eusebius of Caesarea, *Praeparatio Evangelica*, bks. 12–13). Philo (*De prov.* 2.91; *De vita Mosis* 1.6.29) and Josephus also held that the Bible influenced Greek thinkers: "These notions of God are the sentiments of the wisest among the Grecians, and how they were taught them upon the principles that he afforded them. However, they testify, with great assurance, that these notions are just, and agreeable to the nature of God, and to his majesty;

for Pythagoras, and Anaxagoras, and Plato, and the Stoic philosophers that succeeded them, and almost all the rest, are of the same sentiments, and had the same
notions of the nature of God" (Josephus, *Against Apion* 2.168).

52. Diodorus Siculus citing Hecataeus of Abdera (end of the fourth century
BCE), who despite many mistakes about Mosaic law itself shows a certain knowledge of the text, *Bibliotheca historica*, 40, cited by Photius in the ninth century
in his *Codex*, 244. See the annotated document and its presentation by Holladay,
"Pseudo-Hecateus," in *Fragments*, 1: 277–297; and Menahem Stern, "Diodorus,"
in *Greek and Latin Authors on Jews and Judaism* (Jerusalem: Israel Academy of
Sciences and Humanities, 1974), 1: 167–189.

53. C. Rabin, "The Translation Process and the Character of the Septuagint,"
Textus 6 (1968): 1–26; Hengel, *Judaism and Hellenism*; André Néher, "La pensée
judéo-Alexandrine," in *Histoire de la philosophie: Encyclopédie de la Pléiade* (Paris:
Gallimard, 1969), 1: 69–71; R. Marcus, "Jewish and Greek Elements in the Septuagint," in *Louis Ginzberg Jubilee Volume on the Occasion of His Seventieth Birthday*
(New York: American Academy for Jewish Research, 1945), pp. 227–245. There are
some examples of "updating" of the religious meaning of certain terms by translating them into Greek in Baslez, *Bible et histoire: Judaïsme, hellénisme, christianisme*,
pp. 23–26. On "linguistic communication" and theological choices determined by
the content of translated words, see Barr, *Biblical Words for Time*, esp. pp. 110–134.

54. Wacholder, "Biblical Chronology," p. 457n19, suggests inconclusively that
Demetrius may have been a translator of the Septuagint. And see Bickerman,
"Jewish Historian Demetrios," pp. 75–76; E. Preuss, *Die Zeitrechnung der Septua-
ginta* (Berlin: L. Dehmigke, 1859).

55. Josephus states (*Jewish Antiquities* 1.15.17; *Against Apion* 1.10:54) that he
used a Hebrew text, possibly from the Temple archives. Confessing to inadequate
Greek, he says that he wrote the *Jewish War* in the "language of his fathers," that is
to say, Aramaic (*Jewish War*, Preface, 1.3). On his knowledge of languages, see Rajak
Josephus: The Historian and His Society, esp. pp. 230–232. Still, Josephus seems to
have owned a version of the Bible closer to the Septuagint than the Masoretic text
as it is known today. See Étienne Nodet's detailed study, *Le Pentateuque de Flavius Josèphe* (Paris: Cerf, 1996). Researchers agree that in counting the generations
before the Flood, Josephus follows the Septuagint; Wacholder, "Biblical Chronology," believes that for those after the Flood, he relies on the Hebrew version.

56. See the Greek fragments published in Maurice Baillet, Joseph Thadée
Milik, and Roland de Vaux, *Les "petites grottes" de Qumran: Exploration de la fal-
aise, les grottes 2Q, 3Q, 5Q, 6Q, 7Q 10Q, le rouleau de cuivre* (Oxford: Clarendon
Press, 1962); P. W. Skehan, "The Biblical Scrolls from Qumran and the Text of the
Old Testament," *Biblical Archaeologist* 28, no. 3 (1965): 87.

57. Philo, *De vita Mosis* 2.34, in id., *Works*, ed. Colson, 6: 465.

58. Megillah 9a describes the translators' work as done under divine influence,
only for it to be rejected later in Soferim 1.7 and Sefer Torah 1.8, showing the rabbis'
change of opinion. On the reactions of rabbis to the Septuagint, see the analysis

by Karlheinz Müller, "Die rabbinischen Nachrichten über die Anfänge der Septuaginta," in *Wort, Lied und Gottespruch: Festschrift für Joseph Ziegler* (Würzburg: Echter Verlag, Katholisches Bibelwerk, 1972), 1: 73–93; Daniel Barthélemy, *Les devanciers d'Aquila* (Leiden: Brill, 1963); id., "Eusèbe, la LXX et les autres," in *La Bible et les Pères: Colloque de Strasbourg* (Paris: Presses universitaires de France, 1971), pp. 51–65; also Feldman, *Josephus and Modern Scholarship*, p. 209.

59. There was long-standing disagreement over the identification of Aquila with Onkelos, who produced the Targum Onkelos, the Aramaic translation of the Torah. Both were proselytes, and some researchers used to believe that they might be the same person, although now consensus agrees that the Targum Onkelos must be dated from the Byzantine era. See B. J. Roberts, *The Old Testament: Text and Versions* (Cardiff: University of Wales Press, 1951), as opposed to A. E. Silverstone, *Aquila and Onkelos* (Manchester, UK: Manchester University Press, 1931; repr., 1970); review and summary in Johannes Petrus Maria van der Ploeg, "Recente Pesittà-Studies (sind 1927)," *Jaarbericht Ex Oriente Lux* 10, no. 3 (1944–1948): 392–399; Lieberman, *Greek in Jewish Palestine*, p. 17; Dominique Barthélemy, "Qui est Symmaque?" (1974), repr. in *Études d'histoire du texte de l'Ancien Testament*, ed. Dominique Barthélemy, 307–321 (Fribourg: Éditions universitaires; Göttingen: Vandenhoeck & Ruprecht, 1978).

60. Unmentioned here so far are the internal distinctions between cultures called, simply for the sake of convenience, "Greek" and "Palestinian." Yet researchers distinguish variants between different cultures (including Jewish ones) in Egypt, Palestine, and the Near East in general. See Aryeh Kasher, *Jews in Hellenistic and Roman Egypt: The Struggle for Equal Rights* (Tübingen: J. C. B. Mohr, 1985).

61. See Wacholder, "Biblical Chronology"; *Seder 'olam: Critical Edition . . .* , ed. Milikowsky; and Milikowsky, "*Seder 'olam* and Jewish Chronography."

62. Bickerman, "Jewish Historian Demetrios."

63. See mentions in Part I of this book of the existence of annals in the Books of Kings; also Hughes, *Secrets of the Times*.

64. On these writings, see Holladay, *Fragments*, vol. 1; Wacholder, *Eupolemos*; Freudenthal, *Alexander Polyhistor*; Hengel, *Judaism and Hellenism*; *Seder 'olam: Critical Edition . . .* , ed. Milikowsky, 1: 3–17.

Chapter Nine. Mathematical Scansions

1. 1 Macc. 1:10. See the correlation tables with Julian dates in P. V. Neugebauer, *Hilfstafeln zur technischen Chronologie* (Kiel: Verlag der Astronomischen Nachrichten, 1937), p. 45.

2. This was sometimes done as late as the twentieth century, as by Yemenite Jews.

3. Ibn Zimra, called RaDBaZ, was born in Spain around 1479 and died in Safed in either 1574 or 1589. See Máttis Kantor, *Codex Judaica: Chronological Index of Jewish History* (New York: Zichron Press, 2005), p. 210; Mahler, *Handbuch*, pp. 134–136. "He cancelled the era of contracts, which had been counted off since the time of

Alexander"; in J. H. Mikhael, *Or Ha-Hayyim* (Frankfurt am Main, 1881), no. 779, pp. 347–348, cited by Michael Riegler in "Colophons of Medieval Hebrew Manuscripts as Historical Sources" (PhD diss., Hebrew University of Jerusalem, 1995; in Hebrew), p. 319n14, whom I thank for making his research available to me.

4. There were several "Alexandrian eras," notably one in Babylon that started on the first of Nisan, 330 BCE, which Jews must have used before moving on to the Seleucid era. This must surely play a part in the muddled calculations of terms and equivalences.

5. AZ 9a; 10a.

6. *Seder ʿolam zutta*, in *Medieval Jewish Chronicles*, ed. Neubauer, 2: 74; also Bornstein, "Taʾarikhei Yisrael," *Ha-tekufah* 8 (1920): 292. The text of *Seder ʿolam rabba ha-shalem* edited by Weinstock differs somewhat: "During his era Greek rule took hold, in the year of Media and Persia. Haggai, Zechariah, and Malachi died. At the same time, prophecy ended in Israel. This was the year 3442 after the creation of the world" (pp. 84–86).

7. On the Great Assembly and the time of writing the Mishnah, see Chapter Two, nn. 25–26.

8. *Seder ʿolam rabbah*, chap. 30. See *Medieval Jewish Chronicles*, ed. Neubauer, 2: 65–67; *Seder ʿolam*, ed. Milikowsky, 1: 322; *Seder ʿolam*, trans. Guggenheimer, p. 260.

9. The Egyptian-born scientist and defender of orthodoxy Saʿadia ben Yosef Gaʾon (882/892–942), director of the academies of Pumbedita and later Sura, is one of the most outstanding figures of the Geonic period. His first book, *Sefer ha-Agron*, was a Hebrew dictionary (913). This was followed by works of exegesis (his *Tafsir al-Sabʾina Lafzah* remains the great classic for Arabists), liturgy (*Siddur*), lawmaking, and responsa. He also wrote the first philosophical introduction to Judaism (933), *Sefer ʾemunoth ve-deʿoth*, trans. from Arabic by Judah ben Saul ibn Tibbon (1186; Constantinople, 1562), trans. Samuel Rosenblatt as *The Book of Beliefs and Opinions* (New Haven, CT: Yale University Press, 1948). He became known above all for his fight against deviation, especially Karaism, and during his famous debate with Palestinian rulers about establishing the calendar. See H. Y. Bornstein, "Mahloket RaSaG u-ben Meir," in *Sefer ha-yovel: Huval shai li-khevod Nahum Sokolow be-yom melot hamesh ve-ʿesrim shanah la-ʿavodato ha-sifrutit* [Jubilee volume for Nahum Sokolov], 19–189 (Warsaw: Bi-Defus Shuldberg, 1904), p. 72; *Sefer ha-Agron*, in A. E. Harkavy's *Zikhron le-rishonim*, 8, 5 (St. Petersburg: Mekitsei Nirdamim, 1891); Bornstein, "Taʾarikhei Yisrael," *Ha-tekufah* 8 (1920): 293. Among his numerous biographies, see Henri Malter, *Saadia Gaon: His Life and Work* (Philadelphia: JPS, 1921; repr., 2009). See also Robert Brody, *Saʿadyah Gaon*, trans. Betsy Rosenberg (Oxford: Littman Library of Jewish Civilization, 2013), and Sylvie Anne Goldberg, *La clepsydre II: Temps de Jérusalem, temps de Babylone* (Paris: Albin Michel, 2004).

10. A. E. Harkavy and H. L. Strack, *Catalog der hebräischen Bibelhandschriften der Kaiserlichen öffentlichen Bibliothek* (St. Petersburg: C. Ricker; Leipzig: J. C. Hinrichs, 1875), pt. 2, codex B19a, p. 265.

11. Tobiah ben Eliezer, *Midrash Lekah tov: ʿal hamisha humshei Tora = Lekach-tob*,

ed. Salomon Buber (Vilna [Vilnius]: Romm, 1884); *Parashah Shelah*, cited by Bornstein, "Ta'arikhei Yisrael," *Ha-tekufah* 8 (1920): 293.

12. Abraham bar Hiyya Savasorda, *Sefer ha-'Ibbur* (written in 1122), ed. Herschell E. Filipowsky (London: Longman, Brown, Green & Longmans 1851), 3.8, p. 99. The Spanish philosopher, mathematician, and astronomer Abraham bar Hiyya ha-Nassi (1070–1136 or 1145) wrote what may be taken as the first Hebrew encyclopaedia, *Yesodei ha-tevunah u-migdal ha-'emunah*, published by M. Steinschneider under the title "Die Encyklopädie des Abraham bar Chijja" in the journal *Hebräische Bibliographie (Ha-mazkir)* 7 (Berlin: A. Asher, 1864), pp. 84–95; and see Mercedes Rubio, "The First Hebrew Encyclopedia of Science: Abraham bar Hiyya's *Yesodei ha-Tevunah u-Migdal ha-Emunah*," in *The Medieval Hebrew Encyclopedias of Science and Philosophy*, ed. Steven Harvey (Dordrecht: Kluwer, 2000), pp. 140–153. He also introduced Arabic trigonometry to the West with his Latin translation of *Hibbur ha-Meshihah ve-ha-Tishboret* by Plato Tiburtinus in 1145 (*Liber Embadorum*). His astronomical, astrological, and philosophical works include *Sefer hegyon ha-nefesh: 'u sefer ha-musar* (Leipzig: C. W. Vollrath, 1860) and *The Meditation of the Sad Soul*, trans. Geoffrey Wigoder (New York: Schocken Books, 1969). See also Hannu Töyrylä, *Abraham Bar Hiyya on Time, History, Exile and Redemption: An Analysis of Megillat ha-Megalleh* (Leiden: Brill, 2014).

13. AZ 9a.

14. Frank, *Talmudic and Rabbinical Chronology*, p. 37.

15. AZ 9b.

16. *Seder 'olam zutta ve-seder tannayim ve-amorayim*, anonymous fragment of a text attributed to Nathan the Babylonian (tenth century) or Yom Tov of Joigny (France, eleventh century); see *Medieval Jewish Chronicles*, ed. Neubauer, 2: 178. There must be a problem of reading or transcription of the manuscript, since this date poses a problem of consistency. If signs of the destruction of the Temple and the era of contracts may overlap one another, they still do not correspond with that of the creation, revealing a gap of three or four years. For the system to agree, 4807 must be corrected to 4804, which means reading the letter *zayin* as *dalet* (see table of numerical values of Hebrew letters, p. 235).

17. Mishneh Torah on Shemittah 10: 4.

18. Isaac Israeli ben Joseph, *Sefer yesod 'olam* (ca. 1310), fol. 84b, ed. Jacob Shklover (Berlin, 1777); ed. Dov Beer Goldberg and Ariyeh Leib Rozenkranz, *Liber Jesod Olam seu fundamentum mundi: opus astronomicum celeberrimum* (2 vols.; Berlin: Kornaggi, 1844–1846), 2, part 4, 18, p. 34b.

19. Here Sa'adia Ga'on tackles the Western chronological table based on Palestinian tradition. Cited by Abraham bar Hiyya, *Sefer ha-'Ibbur*, ed. Filipowsky, 3.7, p. 97; Benjamin Menashe Lewin, *'Otsar ha-ge'onim* [Otzar ha-Geonim: Thesaurus of the Gaonic Responsa and Commentaries Following the Order of the Talmudic Tractates] (13 vols.; Haifa: N. Warhaftig, 1928; Jerusalem: Mosad ha-Rav Kuk, 1928–1943), 5, 1.3, p. 15; Frank, *Talmudic and Rabbinical Chronology*, p. 36; H. Y. Bornstein, "Ta'arikhei Yisrael," *Ha-tekufah* 9 (1921): 223.

Chapter Ten. Directed Time

1. Chapter epigraph: AZ 9a.

2. Abraham ibn Daud, known as Rabad I (ca. 1110–1180), *Sefer ha-Kabbalah* (Book of Tradition), written ca. 1160–1161, pub. 1514, ed. Gerson D. Cohen (Philadelphia: Jewish Publication Society of America, 1967). Cohen rejects the idea that ibn Daud directly used the *Seder 'olam rabbah* or *Seder 'olam zutta*, despite the major intellectual similarities that seem to make this notion obvious (see pp. 164–169).

3. Ibid., English, p. 10; Hebrew, p. 6.

4. See G. D. Cohen, "The Story of the Four Captives," *Proceedings of the American Academy for Jewish Research* 29 (1960– 1961): 55–131nn135–137.

5. Dan. 12:2–3. Also see Goldberg, *Crossing*.

6. The importance of the process of the Hellenization of Judaism through this movement is stressed by Louis Finkelstein, *The Pharisees: The Sociological Background of Their Faith* (1938; repr., Philadelphia: JPS, 1946). For an analysis of the exegetical methods established, see Samuel Rosenblatt, *The Interpretation of the Bible in the Mishnah* (Baltimore: Johns Hopkins University Press, 1935); also Moore, *Judaism*, 1: 56–71, and Anthony J. Saldarini, *Pharisees, Scribes and Sadducees in Palestinian Society* (Grand Rapids, MI: Eerdmans, 2001). On the development of the Rabbinic movement and about Pharisees, see Hayim Lapin, *Rabbis as Romans: The Rabbinic Movement in Palestine, 100–400 CE* (Oxford: Oxford University Press, 2012), and Seth Schwartz, *The Ancient Jews from Alexander to Muhammad* (Cambridge: Cambridge University Press, 2014).

7. Neh. 10:29–31.

8. Wellhausen, *Prolegomena*, pp. 115–120; H. H. Rowley, "The Chronological Order of Ezra and Nehemiah," in *The Servant of the Lord and Other Essays on the Old Testament*, 2nd ed. rev. (Oxford: B. Blackwell, 1965).

9. Almost nothing is known about Meton of Athens (not even if he was really an Athenian, an astrometer, or a geometer) apart from the fact that his name is linked to the eponymous system of insertions and the nineteen-year cycle. One of the sources is Diodorus Siculus 12.36.1–2: "In the archonship of Apseudes in Athens . . . Meton, the son of Pausanias, distinguished in astronomy, published the so-called 19-year cycle, making the beginning from the 13th of the month Skirophorion in Athens." See Robert Hannah, *Time in Antiquity* (London: Routledge, 2009).

10. See Caquot and Sérandour, "Périodisation," nn. 24–25.

11. Jeffrey H. Tigay has shown how difficult it is to argue for the existence in the biblical era itself of the seven-day Jewish week as described here. Ezra evidently introduced the Sabbath shutdown (see Neh. 13:19), and the numbering of the days themselves seems to have emerged from the last Second Temple period. See Tigay, "Notes on the Development of the Jewish Week," *Erets Yisrael* 14 (1978): 111–121; Michael Chyutin, *The War of the Calendars in the Period of the Second Temple and the Redaction of the Psalms According to the Calendar* (Tel Aviv: Moden, 1993; in Hebrew), p. 52; and id., *The Role of the Solar and Lunar Calendars in the Redac-*

tion of the Psalms (Lewiston, NY: Edwin Mellen Press, 2002). H. and J. Lewy, "The Origins of the Week and the Oldest Asiatic Calendar," *HUCA* 17 (1942–1943): 8–18, support the idea of a four-day cycle preceding the seven-day one, which replaced it because of the sanctity of the time of the creation.

12. Wacholder, "Calendar of Sabbatical Cycles," p. 158.

13. *Seder 'olam rabbah*, chap. 30; Ta'anit 29a.

14. Josephus, *The Judean War*, in id., *New Complete Works*, trans. Whiston, 6.4.249. The Talmud explains that the ninth is preferred to the tenth as a day of fasting because the fire was set on the evening of the ninth (Ta'anit 29a). Also see Chaim Milikowsky, "The Date of the Destruction of the First Temple According to the *Seder 'olam*, the Tossefta and the Babylonian Talmud: Studies in the Development of a Tradition," *Tarbiz* 62, no. 4 (July–September 1993): 485–500 (in Hebrew).

15. JT, Ta'anit, 4: 4; cf. *Seder 'olam rabbah: Critical Edition*, ed. Milikowsky, chap. 28, 38–40, p. 317.

16. Josephus, *Judean War*, trans. Whiston, 6.4.5.249; in the French edition, Josephus, *La guerre des Juifs* (Paris: Minuit, 1977), 6.4.5, p. 495, P. Savinel refers in n. 3 to 30 August 70, specifying that it is the 9th of Av, but the 30th of August would be the 5th of Elul. In contrast, by taking the date of the 10th of Av, a Sunday, we end up back at 5 August 70 of the Julian calendar; the 9th of Av, falling on 4 August, was a Shabbat. The mention of the Roman month *Lous* adds to the complexity of the dating. Is it a Tyrian month, which would begin on 20 August and invalidate the day imposed by tradition, or is it a simple transposition of the Hebrew month's name meant to be understood by Roman readers? Naturally, researchers disagree on this subject. Zeitlin, *Megillat Ta'anit*, advises dissociating the calendrical systems used by Josephus in *Judean War* and *Jewish Antiquities* by accepting the most commonly held view that that dates in *Jewish Antiquities* are directly taken from Jewish sources and transposed into Syriac designation of the Tyrian calendar. Nisan corresponds with *Xanthic* and Av with *Lous*, but it must be admitted that to match the dates mentioned in *Judean War*, taken from extant sources in the Roman world, it is necessary to refer to the Tyrian calendar. It might be relevant to consider that Josephus simply shifts from one transposition of the date of a Hebrew month to a Syriac month, and then to a Tyrian date, according to the event being described. See the different opinions of Heinrich Graetz, *Geschichte der Juden von den ältesten Zeiten bis auf die Gegenwart* (Leipzig: Leiner, 1900), 3: 574– 576; Ideler, *Handbuch*, 1: 400–402; Schürer, *History of the Jewish People*, rev. ed., 1: 506 n115, discussion, pp. 596–599; also Henrico Noris, *Annus et epochae Syromacedonum in vetustis urbium Syriae nummis præsertim mediceis expositæ* (Florence: Typis sereniss. magni Ducis, 1689; Leipzig: Fritsch, 1696), p. 14; Henry Fynes Clinton, *Fasti Hellenici* (Oxford: Oxford University Press, 1895), vol. 3, app. 4. Joseph Justus Scaliger, *Opus de emendatione temporum*, vol. 1 (Geneva, 1629), and James Ussher, *Annales Veteris et Novi Testamenti* (London, 1654), 2,

even suggest that Josephus used the Roman/Julian calendar in *The Judean War*, which makes any intelligible matching of the dates impossible.

17. Ta'anit 26a, 29a. Also see Yerushalmi, *Zakhor*, p. 131n22.

18. RH 10b–11a.

19. Josephus describes the existence of four groups of "philosophers," including three sects, which he tried out one after another before finally settling on Pharisaism. The theological options for Jews in Palestine of his day were shared by the Pharisees, Sadducees, and Essenes. See *Life of Flavius Josephus* 2.10–12; *Jewish Antiquities* 18.1.2–6, Greek 11–25. A social history of why sects flourished is found in Baumgarten, *Flourishing of Jewish Sects*. And see also Mason, *Flavius Josephus on the Pharisees*.

20. See Chapter Two, n. 15.

21. John Strugnell, "The Angelic Liturgy at Qumran: 4Q Serek Shirot 'Olat Hassabbat," in International Organization of Old Testament Scholars, *Congress Volume: Oxford, 1959*, VTS, 7 (Leiden: Brill, 1960), pp. 318–345, identified in the fragments found at Qumran of the Songs of the Sabbath Sacrifice, also called the Angelic Liturgy, a calendar of twelve months with thirty days each, as in the Book of Jubilees. Also see *Angelic Liturgy: Songs of the Sabbath Sacrifice*, ed. James Hamilton Charlesworth and Carol A. Newsom (Tübingen: Mohr Siebeck; Louisville, KY: Westminster John Knox Press, 1999), and Carol A. Newsom, *Songs of the Sabbath Sacrifice: A Critical Edition* (Atlanta: Scholars Press, 1985).

22. Called *kutim* in the Talmud, the Samaritans descended from tribes that converted to Judaism. They followed the Pentateuch but rejected the rest of the Hebrew Bible, as well as the oral law. The Samaritan Pentateuch differs slightly from the Jewish text, above all in its references to Mount Gerizim.

23. See Moore, *Judaism*, 1: 194.

24. This talmudic pronouncement is fully developed in the *midrash* Seder Eliahu Rabbah, which contains several mentions of the era of the destruction of the Temple, as well as a chronological system based on six series or principles governing the universe between (1) divine law, (2) Gehenna, (3) Paradise, (4) the divine throne, (5) the name of the Messiah or the restoring of the world, and (6) the Temple. This text has not been satisfactorily dated by researchers, who also remain divided over its identification with mentions in the Babylonian Talmud. Written between the third and fourth centuries, its first version, possibly dating back to the era of the Tannaim, might have been embellished with later additions. See *Seder Eliyahu rabba ve-zutta*, ed. Meir (Ish Shalom) Friedmann (Vienna, 1902; repr., Jerusalem: Wahrmann Books, 1969), preface; also *Tanna Devei: Eliyyahu* [The Lore of the School of Elijah], trans. William Gershon, Zev Braude, and Israel J. Kapstein (Philadelphia: JPS, 1981); *Ha-derashot be-Yisrael*, trans. Zunz and Albeck, pp. 55–57, 292–298; S. Y. Rapoport, "Toledot rabbenu Nathan ish romi," in *Bikkurei ha-'Ittim* 10 (1829): 144; Mordecai Margalioth, "Le-be'aiat kadmuto shel sefer Seder Eliahu," in *Sefer Assaf*, ed. M. D. Cassuto, J. Klauzner, and Y. Colman (Jerusalem: Mossad ha-Rav Kook, 1953), pp. 370–390, and the critique by E. E. Urbach,

"Li –she'elat leshono u-mekoretav shel Sefer Seder Eliahu," *Leshonenu* 21 (1957): 183–197. All theories other than that of a single medieval author have been called into question by Ulrich Berzbach, "The Varieties of Literal Devices in a Medieval Midrash: Seder Eliyahu Rabba, Chapter 18," in *Jewish Studies at the Turn of the Twentieth Century: Proceedings of the 6th EAJS Congress, Toledo, July 1998*, ed. Judit Targarona Borrás and Ángel Sáenz-Badillos (Leiden: Brill, 1999), 1: 384–391.

25. M. Bregman, "Past and Present in Midrashic Literature," *Hebrew Annual Review* 2 (1978): 45–59; Yonah Frenkel, *Darkei ha-aggadah ve-ha-midrash* (2 vols.; Givatayyim, Israel: Masada, 1991).

26. Louis Ginzberg, *The Legends of the Jews*, vol. 1: *Bible Times and Characters from the Creation to Jacob* (Philadelphia: JPS, 1968), p. 3.

27. Gen. R. 1:4, quoted from *Midrash Rabbah: Translated into English with Notes, Glossary and Indices*, ed. Harry Freedman and Maurice Simon (London: Soncino Press, 1939; 3rd ed. 1983), vol. 1: *Genesis*, p. 6.

28. Eliezer ben Hyrcanus, *Pirkê de Rabbi Eliezer*, trans. and ed. Friedlander, pp. 10–11.

29. Bar Hiyya, *Sefer ha-'Ibbur*, 3.8, p. 99.

30. Venançe Grumel's *Traité d'études byzantines*, vol. 1: *La Chronologie*, p. 3, mentions three elements that may cause the start of global eras, the first of these being the mystical idea: "Therefore the world must last for 6,000 years, after which comes the Sabbath rest of eternity; this idea is ancient in Christianity." Stephen Jay Gould affirms that millenarianism is a Christian invention in *Questioning the Millennium: A Rationalist's Guide to a Precisely Arbitrary Countdown* (New York: Harmony Books, 1997). And, finally, see A. Biram, "Millennium" in the *Jewish Encyclopaedia* (1901), 8: 593, which was not updated and reprinted in the 1971–1972 *Encyclopaedia Judaica*, dooming it to obscurity.

31. Josephus demonstrates this for the period before the fall of the Temple (*Jewish Antiquities* 17.2.4.42–44; 20.5.1.97; 20.8.6.167–170; *Judean War* 2.13.4.259). And see Abba Hillel Silver, *A History of Messianic Speculation in Israel: From the First to the Seventeenth Centuries* (New York: Macmillan, 1927).

32. 1 Enoch, "Apocalypse of the Weeks," 93:10–17; 2 Bar. 40:3; see also 4 Ezra 7:26–31.

33. Shab. 113b; Pes. 68a; Ber. 34b; Sanh. 91b; 99a; Shab. 63a; 151b; Zevahim 118b.

34. Sanh. 99a; Yal. 806; Sanh. 97a, repeating AZ 9a.

35. *Midrash Sefer Eliahu ve-pirkei mashiah ve-nistarot de-rabbi Shimon ben Yohai* [The Apocalypse of Elijah, Maxims of the Messiah, the Mysteries of Rabbi Simeon ben Yohai], in *Bet ha-Midrash*, ed. Jellinek, 3: 65–82; pp. 78–80, 81 quoted.

36. A. J. Saldarini, "Apocalyptic and Rabbinic Literature," *Catholic Biblical Quarterly* 37 (1975): 348–58; id., "The Uses of Apocalyptic in the *Mishna* and the Tosefta," *CBQ* 39 (1977): 396–409. See also *Early Judaism*, ed. Kraft and Nickelsburg, esp. Gary G. Porton, "Diversity in Postbiblical Judaism," pp. 57–80.

37. The son of Ephraim is seen as a "secondary" messianic figure, close to the Joseph figure, and they are often confused. Yet two traditions always present him

in the form of a warrior messiah. In the first, he is a victorious warrior, and in the other he dies in battle. Here his own person illustrates one of the three ages of messianic troubles, and some researchers find it in pre-Christian and apocryphal apocalyptic writings. Joseph Heinemann showed in "The Messiah of Ephraim and the Premature Exodus of the Tribe of Ephraim," *HTR* 68 (1975): 1–15, that Bar Kokhba was identified with the messianic figure of Ephraim both before and after his defeat, and the changes made to tradition were due to the ensuing defeat. See also discussion of this by David Berger, "Three Typological Themes in Early Jewish Messianism: Messiah Son of Joseph, Rabbinic Calculations, and the Figure of Armilus," *Association for Jewish Studies Review* 10, no. 2 (1985): 141–164, subsequently called into question by Joseph Dan, "Armilus: The Jewish Antichrist and the Origins and Dating of the Sefer Zerubbavel," in *Toward the Millennium: Messianic Expectations from the Bible to Waco*, ed. Peter Schäfer and Mark R. Cohen (Leiden: Brill, 1998), pp. 73–104, esp. nn. 4 and 44.

38. Reproduced in *Bet ha-midrash*, ed. Jellinek, 3: 54–63.

39. Here I have not considered the time spent writing this belated midrash, probably from various ancient sources, just before the Muslim conquest, perhaps during the brief Persian conquest at the very start of the seventh century. See Dan, "Armilus"; Martha Himmelfarb, "Sefer Zerubbabel" in *Rabbinic Fantasies: Imaginative Narratives from Classical Hebrew Literature*, ed. D. Stern and M. J. Mirsky (New Haven, CT: Yale University Press, 1998), pp. 67–90; id., *The Apocalypse: A Brief History* (Chichester, UK: Wiley-Blackwell, 2010), pp. 118–124.

40. For a review of approaches and historical and textual theories about the emergence of the Septuagint, prototypes, and features, see Marguerite Harl, Gilles Dorival, and Olivier Munnich, *La Bible grecque des Septante: Du Judaïsme hellénistique au Christianisme ancien* (Paris: Cerf, 1994), with well-documented bibliographies for each chapter. Also, on the finalizing of the biblical text, Moshe Greenberg, *Studies in the Bible and Jewish Thought* (Philadelphia: JPS, 1995), pp. 191–208; Emmanuel Tov, *Textual Criticism of the Hebrew Bible* (Minneapolis: Fortress Press, 1992); id., "Jewish Greek Scripture," in *Early Judaism*, ed. Kraft and Nickelsburg, pp. 221–238.

41. For an approach, see Moritz Steinschneider, *Jewish Literature from the Eighth to the Eighteenth Century, with an Introduction on Talmud and Midrash* (London: Longman, Brown, Green, Longmans, & Roberts, 1857; repr., New York, Hermon Press, 1970); Yehudah Even Shemuel [Kaufman], *Midreshei Geullah*, 2nd ed. (Jerusalem: Mosad Bialik, 1954); Jacob Neusner, *Messiah in Context* (Philadelphia: Fortress Press, 1984), esp. presentation of Sanh. 96a–97b, pp. 169–177.

42. On the importance of establishing scriptural texts, see pp. 42–43.

43. Babylonian Talmud, Sanh. 97a–b, slightly modified from *Sanhedrin Translated into English*, ed. I. Epstein (London: Soncino Press, 1935).

44. See n. 37 above in this chapter; Urbach, *Sages*, 1: 655, with the description of Josephic and Davidic messianic figures, p. 130nn3–4; Heinemann, "Messiah of Ephraim"; Pearson, "Dry Bones."

45. For diverse views and objections, see Urbach, *Sages*. For the texts themselves, see *Bet ha-midrash*, ed. Jellinek. And see, too, Even Shemuel, *Midreshei Geullah*, with a wealth of information; *The Messiah Texts*, ed. Raphael Patai (Detroit: Wayne University Press, 1979); Peter Schäfer, "Diversity and Interaction: Messiahs in Early Judaism," and John G. Gager, "Messiahs and Their Followers," both in *Toward the Millennium*, ed. Schäfer and Cohen, pp. 15–46.

46. See Chapter Five, n. 36. The Fathers of the Church stress the rabbinic disparagement of Bar Kokhba, accusing him of having persecuted Christians. Eusebius calls him a "murderous bandit" in his *Church History* 4.6; see John Collins, *The Scepter and the Star: The Messiahs of the Dead Sea Scrolls and Other Ancient Literature* (New York: Doubleday, 1995), p. 202.

47. During the time of the Pharisees, the square or Assyrian script, also called the Ashuri alphabet, was a calligraphic form of the Aramaic alphabet, replacing the Paleo-Hebrew alphabet, preserved by the Samaritans. This is a further reminder of the role of the Pharisees in spreading these doctrines. See Colette Sirat, "Les lettres hébraïques: Leur existence idéale et matérielle," in *Perspectives on Jewish Thought and Mysticism*, ed. Alfred L. Ivry, Elliot R. Wolfson, and Allan Arkush, pp. 237–256, esp. p. 247 (Amsterdam: Harwood, 1998); J. P. Siegel, "The Employment of Palaeo-Hebrew Characters for the Divine Names at Qumran in the Light of Tannaitic Sources," *HUCA* 42 (1971): 159–172.

48. 4 Ezra 14:48. On the dating of this text, see Schürer, *History of the Jewish People*, 3,1: 297–301.

49. Avodah zarah 9b says, e.g.: "From the year four hundred after the destruction onwards, if one says unto you, 'Buy a field that is worth one thousand denarii for one denar'—do not buy it"; "From the year four thousand two hundred and thirty-one of the Creation of the World onward, if one says unto you, "Buy thee a field that is worth a thousand denarii for one denar,' do not buy it" (http://halak hah.com/pdf/nezikin/Avodah_Zarah.pdf). For analysis of these dates as well as those in Sanh. 97, see Silver, *History of Messianic Speculation*, and Berger, "Three Typological Themes," pp. 149–155.

50. Rashi, AZ 9a.

51. See the preface and chronological chart of *ge'onim* in Brody, *Sa'adyah Gaon*, pp. 341–345.

52. Al-Bīrūnī (973–1048), *Chronology of Ancient Nations*, trans. and ed. Carl Edward Sachau (London: W. H. Allen, 1879; repr., Frankfurt am Main: Minerva, 1969); quotation from p. 32. On the debate between Jews and Christians about elapsed time, see p. 18. In presenting the author, Sachau's introduction notes that al-Bīrūnī was the first, before Maimonides and Bar Hiyya, to study the Jewish calendar systematically and scientifically (p. 12).

53. Ibid., p. 86.

54. Al-Bīrūnī notes (ibid., pp. 87, 90) that Seder 'olam "contains a less[er] sum of years than that of *the books which follow after the Thora*" (i.e., the books of the Prophets, including the two books of Kings).

55. See *Seder ʿolam*, chap. 30.

56. See Bar Hiyya, *Sefer ha-ʿIbbur*; also Chapter Nine, n. 12.

57. Rashi corrects the traditional numbers (see Appendix, p. 227), explaining that between the destruction of the First Temple and the entry into Canaan, only 850 years elapsed; Git. 88b, Sanh. 38a.

58. *Seder ʿolam*, chap. 30.

59. Writing in the *Kalender und Jahrbuch für Israeliten auf das Jahr 5605* ("Uber die Chroniken oder Erinnerungstaflen in den israelitischen Kalendern") (Vienna, 1844–1845), pp. 247–254, S. J. Rapoport contended that Jews linked the Seleucid era, starting with spring 311 BCE, with the era of the exodus from Egypt, since the former took place just 1,000 years after the latter, and the two eras thus shared the same numbers, minus the thousands. See also id., *Sefer ʾErech millin* (Prague: M. ha-L. Landau, 1852; 2nd ed. Warsaw: Ha-sefirah, 1914), 1: 73– 76.

60. AZ 10a; also see Rashi, ad loc., who disputes the length of the elapsed millennium, creating a chronology postulating 1,380 years between the exodus from Egypt and the destruction of the Temple, from which must be subtracted the 382 years of the Seleucid era. In other words, there is a surplus of two years, which prevents us from arriving at the round number of "precisely 1,000 years."

61. Al-Bīrūnī, *Chronology*, p. 25.

62. See the reading of these disparities by Augustine, *City of God* 2:15, who tries to reduce them by aligning them.

63. Henrich Graetz, "Fälschungen in dem Texte der Septuaginta von christlicher Hand zu dogmatischen Zwecken," *MGWJ* 2 (1853): 432–436, mentions that the Fathers of the Church charged that the rabbis had faked the numbers used to date the creation; he cites a text by a Christian Father of the seventh or eighth century claiming to have "rediscovered" in a Hebrew text the same numbers as those in the Septuagint (p. 433). However, Graetz suggests that these numbers were "inflated" by the first Christians to better record the Savior in the chronology announced by divine voice. Later, numbers in Josephus would likewise have readily been standardized. Nonetheless, these are unlikely to be interpolated, since these numbers apparently spread before Christianity appeared.

64. *Ex libris chronographiae*, in *Patrologiæ cursus completus. Series græca*, ed. Jacques-Paul Migne (Paris: Migne, 1857–1866), 10: 63–94.

65. Josephus, *Against Apion* 1.1.1; *Jewish Antiquities* 1.1.13.

66. The Epistle of Barnabas 15:4a–5a, in *The Apostolic Fathers*, Volume II, ed. and trans. Bart D. Ehrman, p. 69; Robert Kraft, *Barnabas and the Didache,* vol. 3 of *The Apostolic Fathers: A New Translation and Commentary*, ed. Robert M. Grant (New York: Nelson, 1965). A product of Judeo-Christian Palestine, the Barnabas Epistle advocates abandoning Jewish ritual, despite being based on its original doctrine. Researchers believe that the author incorporated, not to say copied, the *Duae viae*, a treatise in Jewish morality. The time of its writing is naturally discussed as being between the end of the first and the beginning of the second centuries. Frédéric Manns, "Les rapports Synagogue-Église au début du IIe siècle

après J.-C. en Palestine," *Liber annuus* 31 (1981): 125–146, places it in the second century, based on likenesses between the exegetical technique of its author and the Tannaim.

67. David Flusser, *Judaism and the Origins of Christianity* (Jerusalem: Magnes Press, 1988), calls the Epistle of Barnabas one of the most virulent ancient Christian texts against Mosaic law (p. 633). See also ibid., n. 22, citing Hans Windisch, "Der Barnabasbrief" in *Handbuch zum Neuen Testament. Ergänzungsband: Die Apostolischen Väter* (Tübingen: Mohr Siebeck, 1920), 3: 393–395, praised as one of the best critiques of this text by Simon C. Mimouni, *Le Judéo-Christianisme ancien: Essais historiques* (Paris: Cerf, 1998), p. 235.

68. Devorah Dimant and John Strugnell, "4Q Second Ezechiel," *RQ* 13 (1988): 45–58, and "The Merkabah Vision in Second Ezechiel (4Q 385 4)," *RQ* 14 (1990): 331–348.

69. Arnaldo Momigliano, "Pagan and Christian Historiography in the Fourth Century A.D.," in id., *Essays in Ancient and Modern Historiography*, pp. 110–111.

70. Hippolytus of Rome, "In Danielem," in *Die griechischen christlichen Schriftsteller der ersten Jahrhunderte* (Leipzig: J. C. Hinrichs, 1897), 4: 23–24.

71. Saint Jerome, Epistle, 140:8, in *Patrologiæ cursus completus, Series latina*, ed. Migne, 22: col. 1172 (Paris: Migne, 1857–1866). See here Auguste Luneau, *L'histoire du salut chez les pères de l'Église: La doctrine des âges du monde* (Paris: Beauchesne, 1964), p. 267.

72. Saint Augustine on Ps. 89:4, in *Patrologiæ cursus completus, Series latina*, ed. Migne, 37: c.1142f.; id., *The City of God* 3.20–21, perhaps echoing the teaching of Ticonius on the "two cities." See Johannes van Oort, *Jerusalem and Babylon: A Study of Augustine's City of God and the Sources of His Doctrine of the Two Cities* (Leiden: Brill, 1991; repr., 2013).

73. See Richard Landes, "Lest the Millennium Be Fulfilled: Apocalyptic Expectations and the Pattern of Western Chronography, 100–800 C.E.," in *The Use and Abuse of Eschatology in the Middle Ages*, ed. W. Verberke, D. Verhelst, and A. Welkenhuysen (Leuven: Leuven University Press, 1988), pp. 137–212.

74. *Hebraica veritas* is an expression used in the Middle Ages to refer to Jerome's translation of the Bible into Latin directly from the Hebrew; see *Hebraica veritas? Christian Hebraists and the Study of Judaism in Early Modern Europe*, ed. Allison P. Coudert and Jeffrey S. Shoulson (Philadelphia: University of Pennsylvania Press, 2004).—Trans.

75. Alphonse Des Vignoles, *Chronologie de l'histoire sainte et des histoires étrangères qui la concernent, depuis la sortie d'Égypte jusqu'à la captivité de Babylone* (Berlin: Chez Ambroise Haude, 1738), p. 6. [Des Vignoles (1649–1744), a French historian, served as director of the Kurfürstlich-Brandenburgische Societät der Wissenschaften.—Trans.]

76. *Hegira* means "departure" and refers to Muhammad's flight from Mecca to Medina in 622, the year with which the Muslim Hegira era begins. See Louis Bazin, "Les calendriers turcs anciens et médiévaux" (PhD diss., Université de

Lille, 1974); Grumel, *Traité d'études byzantines*, vol. 1: *La chronologie*. And see also Milo, *Trahir le temps*, p. 122, who postulates a cultural overlap involved in the simultaneous appearance of the Hegira year and other eras.

Chapter Eleven. Exercises in Rabbinic Calculation

1. A. Cowley, "A Jewish Tombstone," *Palestine Exploration Fund Quarterly Statement* 57, no. 4 (October 1925): 207–210.

2. E. L. Sukenik, "*Matsevot yehudiot me-Tsoar*" (Jewish Tombs from Zoar), *Kedem* 2 (1945): 83–88. These three inscriptions are also cited in Wacholder, "Calendar of Sabbatical Cycles," § 10.

3. See the Hebrew text on pp. 180–181 of Wacholder, "Calendar of Sabbatical Cycles."

4. Moshe David Cassutto, "Ha-ta'arikhim she-beketuvot Tsoar" [Dates of the inscriptions from Zoar], *Kedem* 2 (1945): 90.

5. Akavia, "Arakhan shel ketuvot Tsoar le-Khronologia" [Chronological order of the inscriptions from Zoar], *Kedem* 2 (1945): 92–98.

6. The two researchers mentioned above base their work on the jubilee tables proposed by Benedict Zuckermann (see Chapter Six, n. 21).

7. Many works have been published on these archeological discoveries in the past few decades, adding much material, especially about this system of dating. For the inscriptions from Zoar, see Yael Wilfand, "Aramaic Tombstones from Zoar and Jewish Conceptions of the Afterlife," *JSJ* 40, nos. 4–5 (September 2009): 510–539.

8. AZ 9a.

9. Ideler, *Handbuch* 1: 568; Giulio Bartolocci, *Bibliotheca Magna Rabbinica . . . de scriptoribus et scriptis hebraicis, ordine alphabetico hebraice et latine digestis* (4 vols.; Rome, 1675–1693), S, 430. On Bartolocci, cf. Moritz Steinschneider, "Christiche Hebraisten," *Zeitschrift für die hebraische Bibliographie* 2 (1897): 51n 99.

10. Isaac Israeli, *Sefer yesod 'olam*, fol. 84b, 85b (Toledo, 1310), ed. Shklover; ed. Dov Beer Goldberg and Ariyeh Leib Rozenkranz, *Liber Jesod Olam seu Fundamentum Mundi: opus astronomicum celeberrimum* (2 vols.; Berlin: Kornaggi, 1844–1846).

11. Azariah ben Moses dei Rossi, *Me'or 'einayim* (Mantua, 1573), ed. David Cassel (Vilna [Vilnius]: 1864–1866), and *Imrei binah* [Words of understanding], chap. 25, p. 257, quoted from dei Rossi, *The Light of the Eyes*, trans. Joanna Weinberg (New Haven, CT: Yale University Press, 2001), p. 373.

12. Mahler, *Handbuch*, pp. 155–158. Another example of this ignorance is the dating in *Seder . . . tannayim ve-amorayim* cited in Chapter Nine, n. 16.

13. The Regensburg Concilium was the first important Church synod in the eastern parts of the Frankish kingdoms; its exact date (742/743) and location (long thought to be Ratisbon/Regensburg) are uncertain.—Trans.

14. For this argument, see Lajos Blau, *Die jüdische Ehescheidung und der jüdische Scheidebrief: Eine historische Untersuchung* (Strassburg: K. J. Trübner, 1911–1912).

15. AZ 9b.

16. Especially with Solomon Yehuda Rapoport, *SHiR* (1790–1867), whose find-

ings in his talmudic encyclopaedia *Sefer 'Erech milin* are fiercely debated; this may be seen by comparing the corpus to archaeological and historical sources.

17. Rabbenu Tam, *Sefer ha-yashar le-rabbenu Tam*, ed. Shraga Fish Rosenthal (Berlin: T. H. Ittskovski, 1898), 43, 2, pp. 76–77. Born Meir ben Jacob in north-central France, Rabbenu Tam (1100–1171), a grandson of Rashi, was a leading French Tosafist and halakhic authority.

18. Nathan ben Jehiel of Rome (ca. 1035–1106), known as Ba'al he-'Arukh, after the title of this lexicon, the *'Arukh*, whose first edition likely appeared around 1477, although it is unsure in what city. See S. Y. Rapoport, "Toledat rabbenu Nathan ish romi," in *Bikkurei ha-'ittim* 11 (1830): 7–79. See also *Sefer he-'Arukh: Hebero Natan Bar Yehiel ve-'alav sefer musaf ha-'arukh me-ha-hakham Binyamin Mosfiya* (Tel Aviv: Beyt Refael, 1968).

19. Isaac ben Abba Mari of Marseilles (ca. 1122–ca. 1193), *Sefer ha-'Ittur* (Venice, 1608; repr., New York: Sepher-Hermon Press, 1979); Bornstein, "Ta'arikhei Yisrael," *Ha-tekufah* 8 (1920): 325, infers a calculation made from 3829, but if 3829 is added to the count of years of destruction, a year higher by one number than the one indicated is consistently obtained. However, since it depends on the placement of the month in the year, this is resolvable; following AZ 9, a year can be added to 3828, which also gives 3829.

20. The Book of Genesis opens with the phrase "Be-reshit barah Elohim et ha-shamayim . . . ," translated as "In the beginning God created the heaven . . ."; the same verb is used in Numbers: "ve-im beri'ah yivareh ha-shem," meaning "But if the Lord make a new thing," followed by the words "and the earth open her mouth, and swallow them up" (Num. 16:30).

21. Gen. 2:7: "Va-yitsar ha-Shem Elohim et-ha-adam," or "And the Lord God formed man."

22. Sanh. 38b.

23. Maimonides, *Hilkhot Shemittah*, 10.2: "In the year . . . of the creation according to the birth of the first Adam, which was the second of Creation . . . where jubilee cycles began to be calculated."

24. Joseph ha-Ga'on, in Benjamin M. Lewin, *Otsar ha-ge'onim*, vol. 5, pt. 3, no. 15; Baron, *Social and Religious History of the Jews*, 8: 203.

25. Joseph ben Ephraim Karo, *Kesef Mishneh* (Venice, 1574–1575), glosses on Maimonides' *Mishneh Torah*, on *hilkhot shemittah*, 10.3.

26. Bar Hiyya, *Sefer ha-'Ibbur*, 3.8, p. 99; Bornstein, "Ta'arikhei Yisrael," *Ha-tekufah* 8 (1920): 326. See also Ilana Wartenberg, "The Hebrew Calendrical Bookshelf of the Early Twelfth Century: The Case of Abraham Bar Hiyya and Jacob bar Samson," in *Time, Astronomy, and Calendars in the Jewish Tradition*, ed. Sacha Stern and Charles Burnett (Leiden: Brill, 2013), pp. 97–112.

27. Josh. 14:3: "For Moses had given [the children of Israel] the inheritance of two tribes and an half tribe on the other side of the Jordan."—Trans.

28. Bar Hiyya, *Sefer ha-'Ibbur*, 3.6, p. 95; Baron, *Social and Religious History of the Jews*, 8: 209–210. In *The Interpreter's Dictionary of the Bible*, ed. George Arthur

Buttrick et al. (Nashville, TN: Abingdon Press, 1962), 2: 1002, "Jubilee, Year of," Julian Morgenstern shows the difference between the sabbatical cycle indicated in the Book of Jubilees, followed during the Maccabean period and after, based on forty-nine years, and that of the Pentateuch, based on fifty years.

29. AZ 9b; JT, Ta'anit 4, 5; Midrash Eikhah R., 2.2.

30. *Seder 'olam zutta*, in *Medieval Jewish Chronicles*, ed. Neubauer, 2: 68–88.

31. *Pesikta Rabbati*, ed. M. Friedman (1880; Tel Aviv: n.p., 1963), 1. Since the work is dated 845, the interpolated reference to 1151 must have been inserted by a later copyist. See also *Ha-derashot be-Yisrael*, trans. Zunz and Albeck, p. 379n18.

32. *Seder Eliyahu rabbah*, ed. Meir Friedmann, p. 163.

33. Eleazar Kallir, *Kerovot*, in *Jubelschrift zum neunzigsten Geburtstag des Dr. L. Zunz* (Berlin: Louis Gerschel, 1884), cited by Bornstein, "Ta'arikhei Yisrael," *Ha-tekufah* 8 (1920): 322: the total of nine hundred years is disputed, seen as a copyist's interpolation according to Ezra Fleischer, *Shirat ha-kodesh ha-ivrit be-yemei ha-benayim* (Jerusalem: Keter, 1975), p. 126n4.

34. Ezra Fleischer, "Haduta, Birebi Avraham, rishon le-payyetanei Italia," *Italia* 2 (1980): 17. The year 765 of the destruction of the Temple corresponds to 833 of the Christian era, making the former year 68 CE. The term *admonim* is unclear. It means "red," the color of the people of Esau, but may refer to "people of Edom," i.e., Romans or Byzantines as in Gen. R. 6:3.

35. *Kovetz al-yad, Mekitsei nirdamim*, year 9, cited by Bornstein, "Ta'arikhei Yisrael," *Ha-tekufah* 8 (1920): 322. See also Mordechai Akiva Friedman, "Ha-ketubot ha'arets-yisraeliot mi-tekufat ha-ge'onim," *Te'uda* 1 (Tel Aviv, 1980): 57–82, and id., *Jewish Marriage in Palestine: A Cairo Geniza Study* (2 vols.; Tel Aviv: Tel Aviv University, 1980), vol. 1: *The Ketubba Tradition*; the *ketubbah yerushalmit* appears in the *mahzor Roma* (Roman ritual of prayers) (Cassalmaggiore, 1486).

36. See Jacob Leveen, Supplementary Volume (vol. 4; London, 1935) to George Margoliouth, *Catalogue of the Hebrew and Samaritan Manuscripts in the British Museum* (London: British Museum, 1899–1915), p. 520a, reproducing a petition for divorce written in 635 (4996 AM), noting that it must mention: "days x, of the week x, of the month x, of the year x of the destruction, in the city of . . ." followed by "May Jerusalem be rebuilt," cited by Bornstein, "Ta'arikhei Yisrael" *Ha-tekufah* 8 (1920): 323. Also see the texts, which the scholarly community sees as doubtful, published by the Karaite leader Abraham Firkowitsch, *Sefer abne zikkaron* (Vilna [Vilnius]: S. J. Fin & A. G. Rozenkranc, 1872); also the Karaite colophon to the *Book of the Four Prophets*, written in 1300 of the Seleucid era in Jerusalem, 989 CE, published in *Corpus inscriptionum hebraicarum, enthaltend Grabschriften aus der Krim und andere Grab- und Inschriften in alter hebräischer Quadratschrift . . .* , ed. Daniel Chwolson (St. Petersburg: H. Schmitzdorff, 1882; repr., Hildesheim: Georg Olms, 1974), p. 217.

37. In Jacob Saphir, *Even Sapir* (2 vols.; Lyck [Ełk, Poland]: Mekitsei Nirdamim, 1866–1874; repr., Jerusalem: R. Kohen, 1998), 8a, 1: 14n2; also Aaron ben Moses ben Asher, *Sefer Dikdukei ha Te'amim* 10, *JQR*, 1908, p. 639, cited by Bornstein, "Ta'arikhei Yisrael," *Ha-tekufah* 8 (1920): 323.

38. On the spread of culture by Babylonian authorities, notably with the introduction of the Babylonian Talmud in northern European communities, see Robert (Reuven) Bonfil, "Bein Erets Yisrael le-beyn Bavel" (Between Israel and Babylon), *Shalem* 5 (1987): 1–30; id., "Le savoir et le pouvoir: Pour une histoire du rabbinat à l'époque pré-moderne," in *La Société juive à travers l'histoire*, ed. Shmuel Trigano (4 vols.; Paris: Fayard, 1992), 1: 115–195.

39. Ascoli, "Iscrizioni inedite," pp. 90–91; Umberto Cassuto, "Seforan shel shetei matsevot min ha-me'a ha-teshi'it be-derom Italia," in *Yehudim be-italia: Mehkarim = Jews in Italy: Studies Dedicated to the Memory of U. Cassuto, on the 100th Anniversary of His Birth*, ed. Haim Beinart (Jerusalem: Magnes Press, 1988), p. 5: "in the year 778 of the destruction of the Holy Temple"; p. 15: "since the Temple has been destroyed, 770 years."

40. Ascoli, "Iscrizioni inedite," no. 24, p. 66; no. 27, p. 73; no. 32, p. 77; no. 33, p. 78. See also David Noy, *Jewish Inscriptions of Western Europe* (2 vols.; Cambridge: Cambridge University Press, 1993–1995).

41. Ascoli, "Iscrizioni inedite." The first inscription, no. 25, p. 70, has been changed and there have been slightly different readings; the second, no. 31, p. 75, was already no longer extant.

42. Umberto Cassutto, "Ha-ketubot ha-ivriot shel ha-me'a ha-teshi'it be-Vinossa" (Ninth-century Hebraic inscriptions in Ventosa), *Kedem* 2 (1945): 99–120; Ascoli, "Iscrizioni inedite"; Bornstein, "Ta'arikhei Yisrael," *Ha-tekufah* 8 (1920): 328.

43. Shabbetai Donnolo (913–ca. 982), *Sefer hakhmoni*, in *Il commento di Sabbatai Donnolo sul libro della creazione pubblicato per la prima volta nel testo ebraico*, ed. David Castelli (Florence: Tip. dei successori Le Monnier, 1880; repr., in *Sefer Yetsirah* [Warsaw, 1884], pp. 121–148). This "eleventh year" is part of the nineteen-year cycle related to the ancient Greek Metonic cycle that Jewish tradition understands as the formula of *Rav Adda* bar Ahavah, see Chapter 12, n. 102; see Adolf Neubauer, "Un chapitre inédit de Sabbataï Donnolo," *REJ* 22 (1891): 213–218, esp. p. 215, and Adolf Jellinek, *Der Mensch als Gottes Ebenbild* (Leipzig: J. Rosenberg, 1854), preface published in Abraham Geiger, *Melo hofnayim: Likutim shonim mikitvei hakhmei kadmonei 'amenu* (Berlin: Ze'ev Vulf Viltsig, 1839), p. 29; Andrew Sharf, *The Universe of Shabbetai Donnolo* (Warminster, UK: Aris & Phillips, 1976), p. 9, quoted here from Piergabriele Mancuso, *Shabbetai Donnolo's Sefer Hakhmoni* (Leiden: Brill, 2010), pp. 224–225; p. 241.

44. Chufut-Kale was a medieval fortress city in the Crimea; its name in the Crimean Tatar language means "Jewish Fortress."—Trans.

45. *Corpus inscriptionum hebraicarum*, ed. Chwolson, pp. 247, 249, 313.

46. Daniel Siderski, "L'origine de l'ère juive de la création du monde," *Journal asiatique* 227 (1935): 325–329.

47. See the discussion led by Chwolson on the datings of Firkowitsch, *Sefer abne zikkaron*, using comparisons between parashiot and years when they are given, or the remnants of letters, to revise numbers upwards; also Harkavy and Ascoli's discussion of the oldest method used to indicate the era of the world, *yetsirah*

or *beriah*, in Chwolson's *Corpus inscriptionum hebraicarum*, pp. 267–282; p. 248. Abraham Elija Harkavy, *Altjüdische Denkmäler aus der Krim* (St. Petersburg: Académie impériale des sciences, 1876), pp. 132, 160.

48. Ascoli, "Iscrizioni inedite," no. 37, p. 81; no. 41, p. 87. There is a disparity in dates here. My calculations differ by one year from those of Ascoli, who gives the years 1154 and 1492. As the Christian year only begins in January, these two dates are in the total number of the previous year, in which the fourth day—Wednesday—indeed falls on December 9.

49. Riegler, "Colophons of Medieval Hebrew Manuscripts," p. 320n34.

50. BN heb. 1234, copy made at Lugo, Italy, ibid., p. 178.

51. The Ferrara Bible, possibly meant for two distinct readerships, Christians and Jews, was a collaboration between the Spanish Marrano Jerónimo de Vargas (Yom-Tob ben Levi Athias) for typography and the Portuguese Jew Duarte Pinhel (Abraham ben Salomon Usque) for translation. The Ladino edition, dedicated to Ercole II d'Este, duke of Ferrara, could be safely read by compulsory converts who had not yet "returned" to Judaism. Those who no longer feared the clutches of the Inquisition could read a separate Hebrew edition dedicated to Doña Gracia Nasi—Gracia Mendes Nasi (1510–1569), a member of a wealthy banking family, who organized an escape network to rescue conversos from the Inquisition.

52. Oxford, Bodleian Library, 452, Opp. Add. 8vo, copy from Montemayor, Spain, in Riegler, "Colophons of Medieval Hebrew Manuscripts," p. 178; my tables give an equivalent date of March 13 using the Julian calendar, as the 16th falls on a Monday and not on the sixth day, Friday.

53. The initial letters are on the inscription cited, no. 37; the absence of the 5, on no. 41. On the methods of dating, see Bornstein, "Ta'arikhei Yisrael," *Hatekufah* 9 (1921): 245–249; see also on the introduction of the numerical value of letters instead of Egyptian numbers in the Jewish world of the Tannaim around the first century, S. Lieberman, *Hellenism in Jewish Palestine*, p. 73n211; Gershom Scholem, "Gematria," in *Encyclopaedia Judaica*, ed. Cecil Roth et al. (Jerusalem: Keter, 1971–1972), 7: 369–374; the basics of numeric dating are clearly explained by Georges Ifrah, *The Universal History of Numbers: From Prehistory to the Invention of the Computer* (New York: J. Wiley, 2000). See also Sirat, "Les lettres hébraïques," in *Perspectives on Jewish Thought*.

54. See Jean-Baptiste Frey, *Corpus inscriptionum Iudaicarum: Recueil des inscriptions juives qui vont du IIIe siècle avant Jésus-Christ au VIIe siècle de notre ère* (Vatican City: Pontificio istituto di archeologia cristiana, 1936–1952), vol. 1: *Europe*, trans. as *Corpus of Jewish Inscriptions: Jewish Inscriptions from the Third Century B.C. to the Seventh Century A.D.* (New York: Ktav, 1975); also Moïse Schwab, *Rapport sur les inscriptions hébraïques de la France* (Paris: Impr. nationale, 1904); Joseph I. Derenbourg, "Les anciennes épitaphes des Juifs dans l'Italie méridionale," *REJ* 2 (1881): 131–134.

55. Frey, *Corpus inscriptionum Iudaicarum*, p. 453.

56. Especially epitaph no. 31 in the Ascoli collection.

57. See David Noy, *Jewish Inscriptions of Western Europe.*

58. Goldberg, *Crossing.*

59. Riegler, "Colophons of Medieval Hebrew Manuscripts," pp. 176–177.

60. See this chapter, n. 50.

61. When Rabbenu Tam expounded on the seven-year cycle; see this chapter, n. 17.

62. See this chapter, n. 26.

63. See this chapter, n. 23.

64. Frank, *Talmudic and Rabbinical Chronology,* pp. 14–20; also see his explanation of the operations of dating the destruction of the Second Temple, p. 13 and chap. 4, pp. 20–24. To create his outline, he notably draws from the commentary on Maimonides' *Hilkhot kiddush ha-hodesh,* 6, 8 by Rabbi Ovadya (born in 1325), as well as on the talmudic and midrashic encyclopaedia by Menaphem Kasher, *Torah Shelemah* (Jerusalem: Torah Shelema Institute, 1927–1967), 13: 110, trans. as *Encyclopedia of Biblical Interpretation,* ed. Harry Freedman (New York: American Biblical Encyclopedia Society, 1953–1979).

65. Nissim ben Jacob ben Nissim ibn Shahin (ca. 990–1062), *Sefer Mafte'ah manulei ha-Talmud* (Vienna, 1847).

66. Yehuda Halevi (ca. 1075–1141), bk. 3, 67, cited in *Judah Hallevi's Kitab al Khazari,* p. 191.

67. *Sefer ha-'Ittur* (first article =) *Ma'amar rishon: Zman* (Warsaw, 1801), p. 12.

68. *mishnahGit.,* 8:4–5.

69. *Hilkhot gerushin* (The Laws of Divorce), 1.27. See Maimonides, *Hilchot gerushin = The Laws of Divorce: A New Translation with Commentary, Diagrams, and Notes,* trans. Eliyahu Touger (Brooklyn, NY: Moznaim, 1995).

70. Jacob ben Asher, *Tur, Halakhot Gittin,* 10, 127. Jacob ben Asher (ca. 1269–ca. 1343), probably born in Cologne, moved to the kingdom of Castile where he became one of the great codifiers of Jewish law. By not keeping laws about—or deriving from—the Temple, he created a strictly rabbinic base out of the Diaspora for his codification. His main work, the *Arba'ah Turim,* published in Piove di Sacco, Italy, in 1475, served as infrastructure for later codification by Joseph Karo and Moses Isserles.

71. See Simhah ben Samuel of Vitry, *Mahzor Vitry: Nach der Handschrift im British Museum,* ed. Simon Hurwitz (Nuremberg: Bulka, 1889; repr., Jerusalem, 1988). Simhah ben Samuel (d. 1105) was a disciple of Rashi, and this work mixes law and liturgy. And see also *Hilkhot Gittin,* vol. 2, § 135, p. 780.

72. *Mahzor Vitry,* on *Sefer ha-yashar* vol. 2, § 542, *Get,* p. 783; and Rabbenu Tam, *Sefer ha-yashar le-rabbenu Tam,* ed. Shraga Fish Rosenthal, 16, p. 28.

Chapter Twelve. Exercises in Rabbinic Thought

1. Josephus, *Jewish Antiquities* 12.7.7. 323–325; *Jewish War* 1.1.

2. Hanukkah is mentioned in Meg. Ta'anit, 9, Shab 22b; 23a; JT Suk 3: 4; 53d.

3. Ancient authors other than Josephus who mention the Maccabees' military

feats include Diodorus Siculus, *Bibliotheca historica*, bk. 34, citing Posidonius of Apameia (ca. 135–151 BCE?); Tacitus, *The Histories* 5.8, trans. C. H. Moore (London: W. Heinemann, 1925–1937); and Porphyry of Tyre (234?–305? CE) in *Against the Christians*, trans. Robert M. Berchman (Leiden: Brill, 2005). See M. Stern, *Greek and Latin Authors on Jews and Judaism*, 1: 141–147, 183; 2: 423–483.

4. Saint Augustine, *The City of God* 3.18.36, trans. Henry Bettenson (rev. ed., London: Penguin Classics, 2003), pp. 810–811.

5. Josephus notes the twenty-two holy books of Judaism, a number that corresponds to the Greek division of Scripture, adding: "It is true, our history since Artaxerxes has also been written very particularly, but has not been esteemed of the like authority with the former by our forefathers, because there are not been an exact succession of prophets since that time" (*Against Apion* 1.8.38–41).

6. Hengel, *Judaism and Hellenism*, p. 99, sees a direct continuity with Kings and Chronicles in the style and content of 1 Macc.

7. See Diego Arenhoevel, *Die Theokratie nach dem 1. und 2. Makkabäerbucher* (Mainz: Grünewald, 1967).

8. See Jonathan A. Goldstein, *II Maccabees: A New Translation with Introduction and Commentary* (Garden City, NY: Doubleday, 1983; repr. New Haven, CT: Yale University Press, 2011), on Jason of Cyrene's date and Alexandrian context. For an overview of the theories about him, see Hengel, *Judaism and Hellenism*, pp. 96–98 and bibliography in the notes, as well as this book, Chapter Eight, n. 8.

9. "The first book of Maccabees is a dynastic history of the Hasmoneans and presents an incoherent and contradictory view of the politicy of Antiochos IV" (Momigliano, *Alien Wisdom*, p. 105).

10. See Pierre Vidal-Naquet, "Du bon usage de la trahison," preface to Josephus, *La guerre des Juifs*, trans. Pierre Savinel (Paris: Minuit, 1977), esp. pp. 35–44, and id., *The Jews: History, Memory, and the Present*, trans. David Ames Curtis (New York: Columbia University Press, 1996); Gedalia Alon, *The Jews in Their Land in the Talmudic Age: 70–640 CE* (Jerusalem: Magnes Press, 1980–1984; repr. Cambridge, MA: Harvard University Press, 1989); Bickerman, *God of the Maccabees*; Fergus Millar, "The Background to the Maccabean Revolution: Reflections on Martin Hengel's 'Judaism and Hellenism,'" *Journal of Jewish Studies* 29 (1978): 1–21; Menahem Stern and Uriel Rappaport, *The History of Eretz Israel: The Hellenistic Period and the Hasmonean State*, Vol. 3 (Jerusalem: Keter, 1981; in Hebrew); Victor (Avigdor) Tcherikover, "The Third Book of Maccabees as a Historical Source of Augustus' Time," *Scripta Hierosolymitana* 7 (1961): 1–26.

11. "But in his estate shall he honour the God of forces: and a god whom his fathers knew not shall he honour" (Dan. 11:38). If we follow Bickerman's reasoning in *God of the Maccabees*, pp. 74–75, there was strictly speaking nothing Greek about the worship established at the Temple, which was a mixture of regional Syrian and Arab religion and old Canaanite traditions. That being the case, we can read the introduction to 1 Macc. 10–14 differently: "In those days went there out of Israel wicked men, who persuaded many, saying, Let us go and make a covenant with

the heathen . . . Then certain of the people were so forward herein, that they went to the king, who gave them licence to do after the ordinances of the heathen." Bickerman is criticized by scholars for his indictment of the attitude of local Jewish authorities, based on the account of Porphyry in Saint Jerome, *Ad Danielem* 11.30, especially since he explains it (p. 87) with a comparison to German and Greek Enlightenment, putting the Maccabean high priests Menelaus and Jason on the same level as the leaders of Reform Judaism Abraham Geiger, David R. Einhorn, and Gabriel Riesser, who sought to end Jewish "barbarism" by returning to the purity of religious sources. See I. Heinemann, "Wer veranlaßte den Glaubenszwang der Makkabäerzeit?" *MGWJ* 82 (1938): 145–172.

12. 1 Macc. 2:61–62.

13. Confronted in Nicolaus of Damascus with data he could not square with 1 Macc., Josephus produced duplicate versions, unchanged from the originals, according to Bickerman, *God of the Maccabees*. This theory is accepted by B. Z. Wacholder, "Josephus and Nicolaus of Damascus," in Louis H. Feldman and Gohei Hata, *Josephus, the Bible, and History* (Leiden: Brill, 1989), pp. 147–172.

14. Stern, *Greek and Latin Authors on Jews and Judaism*, 2: 343. See also Flavius Philostratus, *The Life of Apollonius of Tyana* (Cambridge, MA: Harvard University Press; London: Heinemann, 1912), 6.29.

15. 1 Macc. 13:42–43. Cf. the account of Ezra 1:1; 3:8, starting in the "first year in the reign of Cyrus," but continuing "in the second year of their arrival near the Temple," thus marking the new chronological record.

16. 1 Macc. 4:46, 14:41.

17. The place of the dead in Hebrew Scriptures, where darkness and quiet reign. See Philip Johnston, *Shades of Sheol: Death and Afterlife in the Old Testament* (Leicester, UK: Apollos; Downers Grove, IL: InterVarsity Press, 2002).—Trans.

18. 2 Macc. 12:39–45.

19. 2 Macc. 7:9, and when the mother urges her sons to die bravely at 7:23: "But doubtless the Creator . . . will also of his own mercy give you breath and life again." This recalls Jub. 23:30: "And at that time the Lord will heal His servants. . . . And the righteous shall . . . rejoice with joy for ever and ever."

20. "Can anyone in the world of the dead sing praise to the Most High? . . . the dead, who no longer exist, have no way to give him thanks" (Sir. 17: 27–28; cf. Isa. 38: 17–19 and Ps. 88:11; 115–17). The second century BCE text written in Hebrew by Ben Sira, known as *The Wisdom of Sirach* or *Sirach*, was also not included in the Jewish canon. Incidentally, its text shows by mentioning "the twelve prophets" that when it was written, the prophetic canon was already closed. See Sir. 49:10.

21. Albright, *From the Stone Age to Christianity*; Finkelstein, *Pharisees*.

22. Momigliano, *Essays on Ancient and Modern Judaism*, p. 46.

23. Ibid. Momigliano's article on Daniel focuses specifically on this, but the point is mentioned by all specialists in the era; see David Flusser, "The Four Empires in the Fourth Sibyl and in the Book of Daniel," *Israel Oriental Studies* 2 (1972): 148–175; Thomas F. Glasson, *Greek Influence in Jewish Eschatology, with Special Ref-*

erence to the Apocalypses and Pseudepigraphs (London: SPCK, 1961). For examples of other uses of this doctrine linked to consequences of the conquest, see Joseph W. Swain, "The Theory of the Four Monarchies: Opposition History under the Roman Empire," *Classical Philology* 35 (1940): 1–21. On Momigliano's views, see Joanna Weinberg, "Where Three Civilizations Meet," in *The Presence of the Historian: Essays in Memory of Arnaldo Momigliano*, ed. M. P. Steinberg (Middletown, CT: Wesleyan University Press, 1991): 13–26.

24. Dan. 11:36.

25. The era in which all or part of the text was written varies according to researchers, who identify one or several authors. The bibliography on Daniel is vast, and encyclopaedia articles are a good start for the Hellenistic and religious realms. On dates of writing, see A. LaCoque, *Daniel et son temps*; Susan Niditch, *The Symbolic Vision in Biblical Tradition* (Chico, CA: Scholars Press, 1983).

26. Uriel Rappaport, "The Book of Daniel," in *Rashi, 1040–1990: Hommage à Ephraïm E. Urbach*, ed. Gabrielle Sed-Rajna (Paris: Cerf, 1993), pp. 71–79.

27. Dan. 7:23–26.

28. Here I use the table created by Klaus Koch, "Spätisraelitisches Geschichtsdenken am Beispiel des Buches Daniel," *Historische Zeitschrift* 193 (1961): 1–32, esp. p. 28, cited by Hengel, *Judaism and Hellenism*, p. 183.

29. See Dan. 9:24–7; John J. Collins, *The Apocalyptic Vision of the Book of Daniel* (Missoula, MT: Scholars Press, 1977).

30. Jer. 25:11–12; Lev. 25:10.

31. Michael Fishbane, *Biblical Interpretation in Ancient Israel* (1985; repr., Oxford: Clarendon Press, 1988), pp. 482–489.

32. Lev. 26.

33. See "Imploration du pécheur et sa prière d'action de grâces," in *Psaumes pseudo-davidiques*, 11QPsa, 19, in *La Bible: Écrits intertestamentaires*, ed. Dupont-Sommer and Philonenko, pp. 323–325; J. A. Sanders, *The Psalm Scroll from Qumran Cave 11 (11QPs)* (Oxford: Clarendon Press, 1965), 154, 86. In "Qumran and Jewish Apotropaic Prayers," *Israel Exploration Journal* 16 (1966): 194–205, David Flusser draws a parallel with the Aramaic Testament of Levi, published by J. T. Milik, "Le Testament de Levi en araméen; fragment de la grotte 4 de Qumran" *RB* 62 (1955): 400.

34. Meg. 14a. See Urbach, *Sages*, 1:. 564–565. Ben Sira suggests, however, in "Hymn in Praise of the Fathers," 49:10, that in his era (writing around 132 BCE), the canon of the prophets was already closed. See also n. 20 above.

35. Shemaryahu Talmon, "The Emergence of Jewish Sectarianism," in *King, Cult and Calendar in Ancient Israel*, ed. S. Talmon (Jerusalem: Magnes Press, 1986), p. 192; J. T. Milik, *Ten Years of Discovery in the Wilderness of Judaea* (Naperville, IL: A. R. Allenson, 1959), p. 83; Baumgarten, *Flourishing of Jewish Sects*.

36. See also G. F. Moore, *Judaism*, 1: 193–199; Bickerman, *Jews in the Greek Age*, p. 215.

37. The solar calendar has a year of 364 days, while the lunar one contains 354. It is therefore impossible to match festivals between the two calendars.

38. Joseph M. Baumgarten, "La loi religieuse de Qoumran," *Annales HSS* 5 (1996): 1005–1025, esp. p. 1022.

39. JT Sanh. 10:6, 29c. S. Lieberman, "New Light on Cave Scrolls from Rabbinic Sources," in *Texts and Studies* (New York: Ktav, 1974), pp. 190–199; see also on the rabbinic use of the term *kat*, which is translated as "sect," Baumgarten, *Flourishing of Jewish Sects*, p. 4.

40. "Un, deux, trois, soleil" (1, 2, 3, sun) is a French-language children's counting game popular in schoolyards, in some ways comparable to the American "Red light, green light, 1, 2, 3!"—Trans.

41. See Annie Jaubert, "Le calendrier des Jubilés et de la secte de Qoumran: Ses origines bibliques," *VT* 3 (1953): 250–264, and id., *La date de la Cène: Calendrier biblique et liturgie chrétienne* (Paris: J. Gabalda, 1957). This research is sharply contested by some, followed by J. C. VanderKam, "The Origin, Character and Early History of the 364-Day Calendar: A Reassessment of Jaubert's Hypotheses," *CBQ* 41 (1979): 390–411. James C. VanderKam, *Calendars in the Dead Sea Scrolls: Measuring Time* (London: Routledge, 1998), pp. 52–70, surveys the development of these theories and all the calendrical questions raised by biblical and postbiblical texts. On the documentary hypothesis, see Chapter Two, pp. 245–247.

42. This inspired the title of Chyutin's *War of the Calendars*. Also see Lawrence H. Schiffman, "Jewish Sectarianism in Second Temple Time," in *Great Schisms in Jewish History*, ed. Raphael Jospe and Stanley M. Wagner (Denver: Center for Judaic Studies, University of Denver; New York: Ktav, 1981), pp. 20–21.

43. Dan. 7: 23–26.

44. Indications of this in the Jewish calendar appear only belatedly with the Mishnah.

45. This is the viewpoint of VanderKam, "The Origin, Character and Early History of the 364-Day Calendar." P. R. Davies, "Calendrical Change and Qumran Origins: An Assessment of VanderKam's Theory," *CBQ* 45 (1983): 80–89, suggests that this calendar would have been discarded just after the return from Babylonian exile.

46. See Chapter Four, n. 14.

47. On the differences between Exodus and Leviticus, see Chapter Six, nn. 42–43.

48. Wellhausen, *Prolegomena*, pp. 108–109; also S. Talmon, "Divergence in Calendar-Reckoning in Ephraim and Judah," *VT* 8 (1958): 48–74.

49. Josephus, *Jewish Antiquities* 1.3.80–81. He adds that the Flood happened in the year 2656 after Adam (82). This number was corrected by the editor to 1656 according to the massoretic text and the *Seder 'olam rabbah*. In bks. 1–2, Étienne Nodet, the French editor of *Les antiquités juives* (Paris: Cerf, 1992), finds a genuine later Christian interpolation (1: 26n5). The English quoted here is from *New Complete Works of Josephus*, trans. Whiston.

50. Jean Bottéro, *La plus vieille religion en Mésopotamie* (Paris: Gallimard, 1998), pp. 293–294, trans. Teresa Lavender Fagan as *Religion in Ancient Mesopota-*

mia (Chicago: University of Chicago Press, 2001). See also the list of Babylonian months, below, n. 81.

51. Grumel, *Traités d'études byzantines*, 1: 208; E. J. Bickerman, *Chronology of the Ancient World: Aspects of Greek and Roman Life* (London: Thames & Hudson, 1968), pp. 44–47.

52. Rosh Ha-shanah 25a, JT RH 58b. Joshua ben Hananiah was a *tanna*, a defender of the Academy of Hillel and disciple of Yohanan ben Zakkai, whom he conveyed in a coffin during the siege of Jerusalem to negotiate with Vespasian about keeping the academy of Yavneh open, according to Gittin 56a. Like his mentor, Joshua ben Hananiah was more inclined to negotiate with the Romans than to rebel against them, and he strove to calm the relationship. He is admired for his great erudition, especially in Greek, mathematics, and astronomy, required for members of the Sanhedrin, where intercalations and the calendar were promulgated. See Hor. 10a; *EJ*, 10: 279–281; Raphael Loewe, "Rabbi Joshua ben Hanania: LL.D or D. LITT?" in *Studies in Jewish Legal History: In Honour of David Daube*, ed. Bernard S. Jackson (London: Jewish Chronicle Publications, 1974), pp. 137–154; Lieberman, *Greek in Jewish Palestine*, pp. 16–19. See also his discussion of penitence and redemption with Eliezer ben Hyrcanus Sanh. 97b.

53. These questions continued to be addressed anew. See Stéphane Saulnier, *Calendrical Variations in Second Temple Judaism: New Perspectives on the "Date of the Last Supper" Debate* (Leiden: Brill, 2012).

54. Michael Chyutin, *The Role of the Solar and Lunar Calendars in the Redaction of the Psalms* (Lewiston, NY: Edwin Mellen Press, 2002). The subheading to this section alludes to a humorous song from 1939, "Le soleil et la lune," in which the French entertainer Charles Trenet (1913–2001) declares: "Le soleil a rendez-vous avec la lune." However, this scheduled meeting between the sun and the moon can never occur, dooming the pair to frustration.—Trans.

55. See the mention of the addition of a festival occurring in the "eighth month" in 1 Kings 12:32. And see Jacob Al-Qirqasani (first half of the tenth century), *Kitab al Riyad wa-al Hada'iq* (Book of Gardens and Parks), a biblical commentary that reproduces a history of Jewish sects in its first section, the "Book of Lights," in *Karaite Anthology: Excerpts from the Early Literature*, trans. and ed. Leon Nemoy (New Haven, CT: Yale University Press, 1952); Nemoy, "Al-Qirqasani's Account of the Jewish Sects and Christianity," *Huca* 7 (1930): 317–397; Bruno Chiesa and Wilfrid Lockwood, *Yakub al-Qirqasani on Jewish Sects and Christianity* (Frankfurt am Main: Peter Lang, 1984).

56. Judah Benzion Segal, "Intercalation in the Hebrew Calendar," *VT* 7 (1957): 250–307.

57. Chyutin, *War of the Calendars*, pp. 50, 103–107.

58. JT, RH, 1:1.

59. Wellhausen, *Prolegomena*, p. 109.

60. On the dating of the text, see James C. VanderKam, *Enoch and the Growth of an Apocalyptic Tradition* (Washington, DC: Catholic Biblical Association of

America, 1984), pp. 76–178; J. T. Milik, *The Books of Enoch: Aramaic Fragments of Qumrân Cave 4* (Oxford: Clarendon Press, 1976), pp. 4–59.

61. See 1 Enoch 74:12, in *The Book of Enoch,* trans. R. H. Charles (Oxford: Clarendon Press, 1893).

62. Ibid., 72:9.

63. Ibid., 80:2–4. And see Gillet-Didier, "Temps de Dieu, temps des hommes," p. 103n70.

64. James C. VanderKam, *The Dead Sea Scrolls Today* (Grand Rapids, MI: Eerdmans, 1994).

65. Jub. 4:17–18, in *The Apocrypha and Pseudepigrapha of the Old Testament,* ed. R. H. Charles et al. (Oxford: Clarendon Press, 1913). On the book and its composition, see this book Chapter Seven, n. 5.

66. Jub., 6:30–32.

67. Two copies of the Damascus Document Scroll (4Q271Df), dated to the tenth and twelfth centuries, were discovered in the Cairo Genizah in 1896–1897 and published by Solomon Schechter in 1910. The fragments from Qumran go back to the end of the first century BCE. The events described in the text include a Jewish group from Palestine fleeing toward Damascus "390 years after the deportation of the Jews to Babylon." Historical allusions about the characters and incidents remain obscure to researchers, and both the production environment and the date of writing remain unknown.

68. These are the first lines and probably the former title of the Book of Jubilees (see Chapter Seven, n. 5). Solomon Schechter, *Documents of Jewish Sectaries,* vol. 1: *Fragments of a Zadokite Work* (Cambridge: Cambridge University Press, 1910).

69. "Rule of the Community" 10:6.

70. Hymns (*Hodayot*), Hymn U, 7–11.

71. Passover begins on the 15th of Nisan, so clearly the calculation of the first month of spring implies what is found in the Temple Scroll 25:2: "The seventh month, the first of the month will be for you a day of rest, commemoration, and plaudits, of holy gathering." See the table of the order of appearance of the months according to the lunar and solar calendars, pp. 195–196.

72. See n. 33, above.

73. See Strugnell, "Angelic Liturgy at Qumran"; Gillet-Didier, "Temps de Dieu, temps des hommes," pp. 77–101; VanderKam, "Calendrical Texts," in *Calendars in the Dead Sea Scrolls,* pp. 71–90.

74. "The motive for it [this calendar] was probably not the mere charm of symmetry, but the desire to create a distinctively Jewish distinction of time fundamentally unlike those of other peoples, and particularly that of the Greeks" (Moore, *Judaism* 1: 194). Nevertheless, Gillet-Didier, "Temps de Dieu, temps des hommes," p. 112, argues that there was a conflict between fixed and movable dates, and the solar calendar aligned them.

75. See Morton Smith, "Helios in Palestine," *Erets Yisrael: Ha-hevrah le-haqirat Erets Yisrael ve-ʿatikotea* [Eretz-Israel: Archaeological, historical and geographical

studies] 16 (1982): 199–214; Julian Morgenstern, "The Calendar of the Book of Jubilees: Its Origin and its Character," *VT* 5 (1955): 34–76; Mark Stratton Smith, "The Near Eastern Background of Solar Language for Yahweh," *Journal of Biblical Literature* 109, no. 1 (1990): 29–39, cited by Chyutin, whose proof I summarize here.

76. Jer. 25:1–3.

77. Hag. 1:15.

78. Systems of dating and dual dating in letters about, or sent by, Jews are noted by Bezalel Porten, "The Calendar of Aramaic Texts from Achaemenid and Ptolemaic Egypt," in *Irano-Judaica*, ed. Shaul Shaked and Amnon Netzer (Jerusalem: Ben-Zvi Institute, 1990), 2: 13–32. He groups them into three categories: (1) those using only Egyptian dates; (2) those using only Babylonian dates; (3) those that synchronize Egyptian and Babylonian dates, the greatest number. See also id., "The Elephantine Jewish Community: Studies in the Life and Society of an Ancient Military Colony" (PhD diss., University of Michigan, Ann Arbor, 1965).

79. Bezalel Porten et al., *The Elephantine Papyri in English: Three Millennia of Cross-Cultural Continuity and Change* (Leiden: Brill, 1996), no. B13ff., pp. 125–126.

80. *Entsiklopedia mikra'it* (Jerusalem: Mossad Bialik, 1954), 12, 3: 441–442; S. H. Horn and L. H. Wood, "The Fifth Century Jewish Calendar of Elephantine," *Journal of Near Eastern Studies* 13, no. 1 (1954): 1–20; R. A. Parker, "Some Considerations on the Nature of the Fifth Century Jewish Calendar at Elephantine," *Journal of Near Eastern Studies* 14, no. 4 (1954): 271–274, cited by Chyutin, *War of the Calendars*, p. 69.

81. JT, RH, 1, 2, 56d; Meg. 13a; Shab. 87b; Ta'an 26b, 29a. Compare the names of the Babylonian months and their order of appearance with Jewish months: (1) Nisan = March–April; (2) Ayyar = April–May; (3) Siman = May–June; (4) Dumuzzi = June–July; (5) Ab = July–August; (6) Elul = Ulul = August–September; (7) Tesrit = September–October; (8) Warahsamma = October–November; (9) Kislim = November–December; (10) Tebet = December–January; (11) Sabat = January–February; (12) Adar = February–March. See Bottéro, *La plus vieille religion*, p. 294.

82. Zech. 1:7; 7:1.

83. Neh. 1:1; 2:1; 6:15.

84. Est. 2:16; 3:7; 8:9.

85. Michael Friedländer, "Calendar, History of," in *JE*, 3: 498–501.

86. Exod. 13:4.

87. "Ba-hodesh ziv, ha-hodesh ha-sheni la-melekh" (1 Kings 6:1); "Ba-yereah ziv) (1 Kings 6:37); "Be-yereah ha-'eitanim hu ha-hodesh ha-shevi'i (1 Kings 6:38; 8:2).

88. Benjamin Nahawandi is considered by Karaite tradition to have laid the foundations for their movement by separating it from its early "Rabbanite" leanings. He wrote codifications and biblical commentaries in Hebrew that Abraham ibn Ezra valued. Brody, *Sa'adyah Ga'on*, trans. Rosenberg, p. 88, suggests that the term "Karaite" must originally have implied what is now meant by "biblical scholar." On Nahawandi, see Nemoy, *Karaite Anthology* (New Haven: Yale University Press, 1952), pp. 21–22.

89. Hag. 1:15; 2:1. The two parashiot were divided belatedly.

90. Sa'adia Ga'on's citation of Nahawandi is from the *Kitab al-Tamyiz* or the *Sefer ha-Hakkarah* (in Hebrew). See also Chyutin, *War of the Calendars*, p. 73. These connections can only be grasped with the same start of the year in Nisan, which orders the sixth and seventh months, Elul and Tishri, and functions in the ancient Greek Metonic cycle.

91. Shab. 13b.

92. Josephus, *Jewish War* 2.17.2.409; 2.20.3.564.

93. *Seder 'olam rabbah ve-seder 'olam zutta u-megillat ta'anit, ve-sefer ha-kabbalah le-ha-RaBaD, 'zal've-divrei malkei (Yisrael be) bayyit sheni, ve-zikhron divrei romiyim* (Mantua, 1514; Amsterdam, 1710–1711). The Aramean text is in *Medieval Jewish Chronicles*, ed. Neubauer, 2: 3–25, and has also been published by Zeitlin, *Megillat Ta'anit* and, in Hebrew, by Ben Zion Lurya, *Megillat Ta'anit* (Jerusalem: Mossad Bialik, 1964). It is used by Chyutin, *War of the Calendars*, pp. 82–87. For its history and analysis, see Vered Noam, *Megillat Ta 'anit: Versions, Interpretation, History, with a Critical Edition* (Jerusalem: Yad ben-Zvi 2003; in Hebrew), and id., "Megillat Ta'anit—The Scroll of Fasting," in Shmuel Saffrai et al., *The Literature of the Sages*, pt. 2 (Assen: Van Gorcum, Minneapolis: Fortress Press, 2006), pp. 339–362.

94. RH 1:1. See Chapter Six, n. 47.

95. Megillat Ta'anit (The Scroll of Fasting) shows this, celebrating the days of the repeal of foreign laws, removing seals or emblems, and in a general sense, the will to return to Judaism.

96. Baumgarten, *Flourishing of Jewish Sects*, pp. 116–136, places written culture, as opposed to previous oral culture, among the converging elements causing the growth of sects at the end of the Second Temple era.

97. Each sect had its own version of the Bible, according to F. M. Cross, "The Text Behind the Text of the Hebrew Bible," in *Understanding the Dead Sea Scrolls*, ed. H. Shanks (New York: Random House, 1992), pp. 139–155.

98. Origen, *Against Celsus*, trans. James Bellamy (London, [1709?]), 3.12.

99. See Ginzberg, *Legends of the Jews*, p. 22; Gen. R. 6:3.

100. Sacha Stern, *Calendar and Community* (Oxford: Oxford University Press, 2001), pp. 170–180, convincingly demonstrated that the existence of this Patriarch, Hillel II, who left no traces in rabbinic sources, is quite uncertain.

101. Arakh 9b.

102. According to which a lunar month has 29 days, 12 hours, and 793 *halakim*, fractions of an hour or 1/18th of a minute. Since Jewish chronology divided the hour into 1,080 fractions, each corresponds to 3 1/3 seconds. Twelve lunar months being shorter than a solar year, to fall back on equivalent cycles, the needed intervals are added or subtracted. Tradition ascribes to this third-century Babylonian *amora* authorship of a tract on intercalations, *Baraita (tekufa) de-Rav Adda*. This text has vanished, but according to *Ha-derashot be-Yisrael*, trans. Zunz and Albeck, p. 274, it was still cited in the fourteenth century. In the sixteenth

century, when the Gregorian calendar was adopted, the astronomer David Gans noted in his chronicle: "Presently the measurement of the year is very close to calculations by Rav Adda bar Ahava" (Gans, *Sefer Tsemah David* [Prague, 1592; ed. Mordechai Breuer, Jerusalem: Magnes Press, 1983], §1583, p. 412 (see Goldberg, "Jeux du temps").

103. The *Baraita of Samuel* surfaced in nineteenth-century Salonica when Nathan ben Hayyim Amram (1805–1870) claimed to have copied it from a document in his family library. Although the manuscript was never found, researchers assume that it could not be a forgery, because the astronomical incident it describes would not have allowed renewal of the calendrical system described in the text (first ed., Salonica, 1861; Frankfurt am Main, 1863). See Leopold Zunz, *Gesammelte Schriften* (Berlin: Louis Gerschel, 1876), 3: 242–249; id., *Die gottesdienstlichen Vorträge der Juden*, p. 98; Baron, *Social and Religious History of the Jews*, 8: 192–193.

104. Thanks to Sacha Stern, who kindly sent me his article "Fictitious Calendars: Early Rabbinic Notions of Time, Astronomy and Reality," later published in *JQR* 88, nos. 1–2 (1996): 103–129.

105. The fight for lawmaking supremacy between Palestine and Babylon was one of the key factors of Jewish intellectual movements during the High Middle Ages; see Bonfil, "Le savoir et le pouvoir."

106. Eliezer ben Hyrcanus, *Pirkê de Rabbi Eliezer*, trans. and ed. Friedlander, 8.56, states:

> Hence (the Sages) have said. Even when the righteous and the wise are outside the Land, and the keeper of sheep and herds are in the Land, they do not intercalate the year except through the keeper of sheep and herds in the Land. Even when prophets are outside the Land and the ignorant are in the Land they do not intercalate the year except through the ignorant who are in the land (of Israel). . . . On account of three things is the year intercalated, on account of trees, grass, and the seasons (Tekuphoth).

107. The intervals in question follow the method of Rav Adda; see n. 102 above.

108. This presentation is only a brief summary of the facts. It is not known exactly when Sa'adia arrived from Baghdad after a stay in Aleppo, nor when he became an official authority representing Babylonian Jews. The exchange of letters preceded his nomination, and only during this polemic did he assume the title of "Ga'on." Baron believes that without the intervention and tenacity of Sa'adia, the Babylonians would have given in. See these exchanges in Bornstein, "Mahloqet," and S. W. Baron, "Saadia's Communal Activities," in *Saadia Anniversary Volume* (New York: American Academy for Jewish Research, 1943), 2: 9–74. And see also Robert Brody, *The Ge'onim of Babylonia and the Shaping of Medieval Jewish Culture* (New Haven, CT: Yale University Press, 1998), esp. the chapter "Competition with the Palestinian Center." See also Stern, *Calendar and Community*, pp. 192, 195–196; and Marina Rustow and Sacha Stern, "The Jewish Calendar Controversy of 921–22: Reconstructing the Manuscripts [the Geniza fragments] and Their

Transmission History," in *Time, Astronomy, and Calendars in the Jewish Tradition*, ed. Stern and Burnett, pp. 79–96.

109. Letter reproduced in Bornstein, "Mahloqet," no. 4, pp. 87–91, 88–89; see also Alfred Guillaume, "Further Documents on the Ben Meir Controversy," *JQR* 5, no. 4 (1915): 543–557. Quotation from Baron, *Social and Religious History of the Jews*, 8: 196.

110. François de Blois, "Some Early Islamic and Christian Sources Regarding the Jewish Calendar (9th–11th centuries)," in *Time, Astronomy, and Calendars in the Jewish Tradition*, ed. Stern and Burnett, p. 76, citing Elias of Nisibis in *Fragmente syrischer und arabischer Historiker*, ed. F. B. Baethgen (Leipzig: F. A. Brockhaus, 1884), 84 (in Syriac) and 141 (in German). See also Baron, *Social and Religious History of the Jews*, 8: 374n62, and id., "Saadia's Communal Activity," in *Saadia Anniversary Volume*, p. 46n81 [38].

111. See Ben Meir, letter written at the end of summer 1233 of the Seleucid era, published by Bornstein, "Mahloqet," pp. 104–105; also Michael Friedländer, "Life and Works of Sa'adia Ga'on," *JQR* 5 (1893): 177–199. And Brody, *Sa'adyah Ga'on*, trans. Rosenberg, pp. 154–156.

112. See statement by Sa'adia Ga'on, p. 134, and Chapter Nine, n. 19.

113. Bornstein, "Ta'arikhei Yisrael," *Ha-tekufah* 8 (1920): 326; id., "Mahloket," 54, 78ff.; and "Seder 'olam Zuttah," in *Medieval Jewish Chronicles*, ed. Neubauer, 2: 79–82.

114. Maimonides, *Hilkhot Shemitta ve-yovel*, 10.

Chapter Thirteen. A Fleeting Conclusion

1. See Graetz, *Structure of Jewish History*, p. 72.

2. Eccl. 1:9.—Trans.

3. Dietrich Rössler, *Gesetz und Geschichte*, Wissenschaftliche Untersuchungen zum Neuen Testament 3 (Neukirchen: Neukirchener Verlag, 1962), p. 42, cited by Hengel, *Judaism and Hellenism*, 1: 175.

4. Hengel, *Judaism and Hellenism*, 1: 175.

5. See Chapter Ten, n. 49.

6. Al-Bīrūnī, *Chronology of Ancient Nations*, p. 18.

7. See, e.g., Neusner, ed., *Christian and Judaic Invention of History*, esp. the preface and introductory chapter.

8. Lloyd, "Views on Time in Greek Thought," in Gardet et al., *Cultures and Time*, pp. 117, 144.

9. See Chapter Eight, n. 4.

10. See Chapter Twelve, n. 28, on the story of Daniel according to Koch, "Spätisraelitisches Geschichtsdenken."

11. Wacholder, "Calendar of Sabbatical Cycles," p. 158.

12. The great nineteenth-century traveler Jacob Saphir tells us that at the service for the 9th of Av in 1859, Yemenite Jews counted this way: "This night is the 2280th after the destruction of the First Temple, the 1790th of the destruction of

the Second Temple and we have not yet been redeemed" (Saphir, *Even Sapir*, 1: 107b). Some communities adopting the Eastern or Portuguese rite still count the years that have elapsed since the fall of the Temple on the 9th of Av.

13. See Rosenzweig, *Star of Redemption*, pp. 402, 418.

14. Goldberg, "De la Bible et des notions d'espace et de temps."

15. *Baraita* in Sanh. 11a; Yoma 9b; Sota 48b.

16. See *Seder 'olam zutta, Medieval Jewish Chronicles*, ed. Neubauer, 1: 65–67, and *Seder 'olam: Critical Edition*, ed. Milikowsky, 1.30, p. 322.

17. See Chapter Two, n. 25.

18. Juda ha-Nassi, Lamentations Rabbah 69:1, line D, in Jacob Neusner, *Jeremiah in Talmud and Midrash: A Source Book* (Lanham, MD: University Press of America, 2006), p. 262; *Pesikta de-rav kahana*, "Nahamu," p. 266, English in *Pesikta de-rab-Kahana*, trans. William G. Braude and Israel J. Kapstein (Philadelphia: Jewish Publication Society of America, 1975), *piska* 16, 3, p. 289. On Josephus as a prophetic figure, see also Rebecca Gray, *Prophetic Figures in Late Second Temple Jewish Palestine: The Evidence of Josephus* (New York: Oxford University Press, 1993); and for another point of view, see Pierre Vidal-Naquet, "Flavius Josèphe et les prophètes," in *Histoire et conscience historique dans les civilisations du Proche Orient ancien* (Louvain: Peeters, 1989), trans. David Ames Curtis as "Flavius Josephus and the Prophets," in *The Jews: History, Memory, and the Present*, 1: 37–56.

19. In *Studies in Pharisaism and the Gospels* (Cambridge: Cambridge University Press, 1924; repr. New York: Ktav, 1967), 2: 120–128, Israel Abrahams suggests four arguments to grasp the idea of the "end of prophecy": (1) the increase of "false" prophets; (2) the natural characteristics of prophecy, which necessarily make it intermittent; (3) the change from prophecies to predictions; (4) the fixing of the canon.

20. The Book of Josippon, very popular in the Middle Ages, was long taken for a work by Josephus, recounting the history of the Jews between Babylon and the fall of the Temple. Since the nineteenth century, researchers have pushed back the era of its composition to around the ninth or tenth century CE. David Flusser, who published a critical edition, *Sefer Yossipon* (Jerusalem: Mosad Bialik, 1978–1980), points out that the year 953 CE is mentioned in the text itself. Yet this dating of the work has been called into question by the discovery of older manuscripts. Now some researchers think it was written during the ninth century. See, e.g., Robert Bonfil, "Reading in the Jewish Communities of Western Europe in the Middle Ages," in *A History of Reading in the West*, ed. Guglielmo Cavallo and Roger Chartier, trans. Lydia G. Cochrane (Amherst: University of Massachusetts Press, 2003), pp. 149–178. See also Bonfil, "Jewish Attitudes Toward History and Historical Writing in Pre-Modern Time," *Jewish History* 11, no. 1 (Spring 1997): 5–40; "How Golden Was the Age of the Renaissance in Jewish Historiography?" in *Essays in Jewish Historiography: History and Theory*, ed. Ada Rapoport-Albert (Middletown, CT: Wesleyan University Press, 1988), suppl. 27, 3, pp. 78–82. Also see Saskia Dönitz, *Überlieferung und Rezeption des Sefer Yosippon* (Tübingen: Mohr Siebeck, 2013).

21. A rereading of texts such as the Midrash and the Aggadah is suggested, inter alia, by the work of Moshe Avigdor Shulvass, "Ha-yedi'a be-historia ve- ha-sifrut ha-historit bi-tehum ha-tarbut ha-ashkenazit bi-yemei ha-beinayim" (Historical knowledge and literature in medieval Ashkenazi culture), in *Sefer ha-yovel le-rabbi Hanokh Albeck* (Jerusalem: Mosad Ha-rav Kook, 1963), pp. 465–495; E. E. Urbach, "Halakhah and History," in *Jews, Greeks and Christians: Essays in Honor of W. D. Davies*, ed. R. G. Hamerton-Kelly and R. J. Scroggs (Leiden: Brill, 1976), pp. 112 –128; Isaac Heinemann, *Darkhei ha-Aggada* (1970; Jerusalem: Magnes Press, 1974), esp. pp. 1–13, to be read with Daniel Boyarin, "Toward a New Theory of Midrash" in his *Intertextuality and the Reading of Midrash* (Bloomington: Indiana University Press, 1990), pp. 1–21; and Robert Bonfil, "Can Medieval Storytelling Help Understand Midrash?" in *The Midrashic Imagination: Jewish Exegesis, Thought, and History*, ed. Michael Fishbane (Albany: State University of New York Press, 1993), pp. 228–254.

22. See the section "Awareness of Time and the Sense of History" in Chapter One.

23. See, e.g., Eli Yassif, "The Hebrew Narrative Anthology in the Middle Ages," *Prooftexts* 17 (1997): 153–175; id., *The Book of Memory That Is: The Chronicles of Jerahme'el. A Critical Edition* (Tel Aviv: Chaim Rosenberg School of Jewish Studies, Tel Aviv University, 2001; in Hebrew).

24. Among these, see Abraham Zacuto, *Sefer Yuhasim* (Book of Genealogies), (Constantinople, 1566); Salomon ibn Verga, *Shevet Yehuda* (Judah's scepter), (Adrianople, Turkey, 1544); Elijah Capsali, *Seder Eliyahu Zuta* (The small order of Elijah), and *Sippurei Venezia* (Venetian stories) (1517?; Jerusalem: Makhon Ben-Tsevi, 1975–1977); Samuel Usque, *Consolaçam ás tribulaçoens de Israel* (Consolation for the tribulations of Israel) (Ferrara, 1553); Gedaliah ibn Yahya, *Shulshelet ha-Kabbalah* (The chain of tradition) (Venice, 1587; Kraków, 1596). And see Yerushalmi, *Zakhor*, pp. 71–91.

25. Joseph ha-Kohen, preface to *Dibre ha-Yamim le-Malke Zarfat we-'Otoman* (Chronicles of the kings of France and Turkey) (Venice, 1534). Ha-Kohen also wrote a Jewish historical chronicle, trans. Harry S. May as *The Vale of Tears* (The Hague: M. Nijhoff, 1971); and see also *Sefer emeq ha-bakha (The Vale of Tears): With the Chronicle of the Anonymous Corrector*, ed. Karin Almbladh (Uppsala: Uppsala University, 1981).

26. The physician and scholar Azariah dei Rossi (1511?–1577?) was born in Mantua. His masterwork, *Me'or 'einayim (The Light of the Eyes)*, contains a translation into Hebrew of the Letter of Aristeas, an account of the 1571 Ferrara earthquake, and the *Imrei binah* (Words of understanding). See the English translation of the book and the list of the sources dei Rossi used in *Light of the Eyes*, trans. Weinberg.

27. See S. W. Baron, "La méthode historique d'Azariah de' Rossi," *REJ* 96 (1928): 151–175; 97 (1929): 43–78; revised and augmented in one of the three chapters that Baron dedicates to dei Rossi, "Azariah de' Rossi's Historical Method," in *History and Jewish Historians*, pp. 205–239, where after having made a long list of authors cited by dei Rossi, he places him in the conservative wing of Italian Judaism (p. 194).

See also Giuseppe Veltri, *Renaissance Philosophy in Jewish Garb: Foundations and Challenges in Judaism on the Eve of Modernity* (Leiden: Brill, 2009), pp. 73–128.

28. The *Shulhan 'arukh* (Set table) of Joseph ben Ephraim Karo (1488–1575) codified Jewish laws, explaining sources, opinions, and customs, and is still seen as the supreme authority in matters of orthodoxy, together with the corresponding Ashkenazi work by Moses Isserles (incidentally, David Gans's teacher).

29. The mathematician, exegete, and Kabbalist Judah Loew ben Betsalel, known as the MaHaRaL of Prague (ca. 1520–1609), was an extraordinary character, uncategorizable in the rabbinic world. His works, running from ethics to praise of the Talmud, and including an explanation of redemption and commentaries, reflect his eclecticism. Although he was chief rabbi of Moravia, Poznan, and Prague, he founded no school of followers, and his teaching remained isolated until rediscovered in the twentieth century. See André Néher, *Le puits de l'exil: La théologie dialectique du Maharal de Prague (1512– 1609)* (Paris: Albin Michel, 1965; rev. ed., Paris: Cerf, 1991), pp. 98–107, citing dismissal of the MaHaRaL as an "intellectual dabbler" and "dilettante," whose books are the "typical product of charming foraging." But see, too, Giuseppe Veltri, "Maharal Against Azariah de' Rossi: The Other Side of Skepticism," in *Rabbinic Theology and Jewish Intellectual History*, ed. Meir Seidler (London: Routledge, 2013), pp. 65–76; Sarah Marcus, "The *Be'er Hagolah* and the *Me'or Einayim*: Approaches to *Aggadata*," in *Judaic Studies Journal* 3 (Fall 2014): 105–116; and *Maharal, Overtures: Biography, Doctrine, Influence*, ed. Elchanan Reiner (Jerusalem: Zalman Shazar Center for History, 2015; in Hebrew and English).

30. Here the MaHaRaL directly addresses dei Rossi's assertions in *Me'or 'einayim*, chap. 35, titled "Yemei 'olam" (Days of the world), pp. 110a–b: "Now it is also true that there is also uncertainty about the durations of the periods of the two holy Temples." Explaining the different rabbinical methods of calculating the duration of the first Temple: "When the years are reckoned on the basis of the reigns of the kings of Israel from the fourth year of Solomon until the destruction, there is a total of 410 years, but 430 when reckoned on the basis of the reigns of the kings of Judaea," he concludes that "this implies that the number of years of the duration of the first Temple, which was disseminated by our rabbis as coming to a total of 410, must be more." He meticulously discusses the numbers of the duration of the Second Temple given in the *Seder 'olam*, showing that they were considerably reduced; see his chap. 36, p. 117b: "The number of Persian kings who reigned during Temple time, which they reckon is likewise greater than that calculated by our rabbis." Quoted from dei Rossi, *Light of the Eyes*, trans. Weinberg, pp. 431, 436, 435, 456.

31. Judah Loew ben Betsalel, *Sefer be'er ha-golah*, ed. Israel ben Shabbetai (Hopsztajn) of Kozhnitz (Jerusalem: B'nei Brak, 1972), 6th well, p. 139; Deut. 32:7, p. 127.

32. This text, *Sefer Matsref la-kesef* (The refinement of silver), was later integrated into successive editions of *Me'or 'einayim*. I use Filipowski's edition based

on Oxford MS 1576 (see n. 33 below for full citation), which includes prefaces by Leopold Zunz and David Cassel.

33. Azariah ben Moses dei Rossi, *Sefer Matsref la-kesef: Haṃityaḥes la-ḥibur Me'or 'enayim*, ed. Herschell E. Filipowski, based on Oxford MS 1576, pref. Leopold Zunz (Edinburgh, 1854; repr., Vilna [Vilnius]: Y. A. Ben-Ya'akov, 1865); ed. David Cassel (Vilna, 1864–1866), pt. 2, chaps. 11–12, Filipowski, pp. 67–80; Cassel, pp. 79–94, esp. Filipowski, p. 72; Cassel, p. 84; pt. 2, chap. 3, Filipowski, p. 38; Cassel, p. 43. See also Chapter Six, n. 45, above, and RH 2b.

34. "Many people think that the aera mundi computation is Sinaitic and originates from time immemorial. In reality, as we have said, it is merely a recent innovation" (dei Rossi, *Light of the Eyes*, trans. Weinberg, p. 377; *Me'or 'enayim, Imrei binah*, chap. 25 [Cassel, p. 279]). Dei Rossi frequently stressed the "non-Sinaitic" origins of the computation and the principle of intercalation in *Sefer Matsref la-kesef*.

35. See Mordechai Breuer, "Modernism and Traditionalism of David Gans," in *Jewish Thought in the Sixteenth Century*, ed. Bernard Dov Cooperman (Cambridge, MA: Harvard University Press, 1983), pp. 49–88; André Néher, *David Gans (1541–1613): Disciple du Maharal de Prague, assistant de Tycho Bruhé et de Jean Kepler* (Paris: Klincksieck, 1974), trans. as *Jewish Thought and the Scientific Revolution of the Sixteenth Century: David Gans (1541–1613) and His Times* (Oxford: Oxford University Press, 1986).

36. The five "greats" are Nahmanides, *Pirush al ha-Torah*; Bahya ben Asher; the Ga'on Hananel ben Hushiel; Don Isaac Abravanel, *Niḥlat Avot*; and Isaac Karo, *Toledot Yishak*.

37. On Rashi, see Chapter Two, n. 6, and on Ibn Daud, the RaBaD, see Chapter Ten, n. 2; David Kimhi (1160–1235), the RaDaK, scion of a rabbinic dynasty of Spanish origin, lived in Provence; his published biblical commentaries were translated into Latin.

38. Gans, *Sefer Tsemah David*, ed. Breuer, vol. 1, § 448, pp. 23–24 (in Hebrew).

39. Ibid., § 413, p. 57.

40. Ibid., § 442, p. 58. At the end of the same paragraph, comparing the different editions of the *Seder 'olam zutta*, Gans opts for a scribe's mistake in dating. Recall that in Hebrew, numbers are represented by letters. See the Appendix for a table of the numerical values of letters.

41. *Me'or 'enayim, Yemei 'olam*, chap. 29, pp. 103a–b. Quoted from dei Rossi, *Light of the Eyes*, trans. Weinberg, pp. 405–406.

42. On the AM 1 method according to Frank, *Talmudic and Rabbinical Chronology*, who calculated starting with the second day of creation, see Chapter Eleven, n. 64.

43. Gans, *Sefer Tsemah David*, § 448, p. 24.

44. Dei Rossi, *Light of the Eyes*, trans. Weinberg, p. 543; *Me'or 'enayim* 43, p. 138a and ff. His debate should be read in the context of the recent appearance of "Migdal David" MS by the Kabbalist Mordecai Dato, which repeats the

predictions of Azaria de Fano and was part of a speculative mystical movement that troubled Italy. See David Tamar, "Ha-tsipiya be-italia li-shnat 1575 [Messianic Expectations in Italy, 1575]," *Sefunot* 2 (1958): 61–88; id., *Mehkarim be-toledot ha-yehudim be-erets yisrael u-be-italia* [Studies in the History of the Jewish People in Eretz Israel and in Italy] (Jerusalem: Rubin Mass, 1970), pp. 11–38; Moshe Idel, *Messianic Mystics* (New Haven, CT: Yale University Press, 2000).

45. Israel J. Yuval terms this a "hobby" and arithmetical pasttime; see id., "Jewish Messianic Expectations Towards 1240 and Christian Reactions," in *Toward the Millennium*, ed. Schäfer and Cohen, pp. 105–121.

46. On these conjectures, see Silver, *History of Messianic Speculation*. See also Bernard Raphael Goldstein, "Creation and the End of Days," in *Proceedings of the 1984 Meeting of the Academy for Jewish Philosophy*, ed. David Novak and Norbert Samuelson (Lanham, MD: University Press of America, 1986), pp. 261–276; B. R. Goldstein and David Pingree, *Levi ben Gerson's Prognostication for the Conjunction of 1345* (Philadelphia: American Philosophical Society, 1990).

47. *Me'or 'einayim*, 29, p. 103b; Robert Bonfil summarizes the motivations he ascribes to this work in "Some Reflections on the Place of Azariah de Rossi's *Me'or 'Einayim* in the Cultural Milieu of Italian Renaissance Jewry," in *Jewish Thought in the Sixteenth Century*, ed. Cooperman, pp. 23–48, and also see Azariah de' Rossi, *Selected Chapters from "Sefer Me'or 'einayim" and "Matsref la-kessef,"* ed. Bonfil (Jerusalem: Mosad Bialik, 1991; in Hebrew).

48. See Néher, *David Gans*.

49. On the sources used by Gans and his influences, see Breuer, "Modernism and Traditionalism of David Gans"; id., "Rabbi David Gans: Author of the Tsemah David—An Outline," *Bar Ilan* 11 (1972–1973): 97–118 (in Hebrew).

50. "For using the era of the Creation, if you examine the first days, you will see clearly that it was not customary with us since the time that the Gemara was finished or shortly thereafter, as the *Me'or 'einayim* shows" (Gans, *Sefer Tsemah David*, 1: 61). Cf. the same passage in *Me'or 'einayim*, 25, p. 95: "I had to deal with it because if you examine the first days, you will see clearly that it was not customary with us since the time that the Gemara was finished or shortly thereafter."

51. Ernest Denis, *Huss et la guerre des hussites* (Paris: E. Leroux, 1878) is still useful here; and see also Jan Macek and Robert Mandrou, *Histoire de la Bohême des origines à 1918* (Paris: Fayard, 1984); Ruth Gladstein, "Eschatological Trends in Bohemian Jewry During the Hussite Period," in *Prophecy and Millenarianism, Essays in Honour of Marjorie Reeves*, ed. Ann Williams (Harlow, UK: Longman, 1980), pp. 241–256. On millenarianism and its multiple facets, see Norman Cohn, *The Pursuit of the Millennium: Revolutionary Millenarians and Mystical Anarchists of the Middle Ages* (New York: Oxford University Press, 1970); Jean Delumeau, *Mille ans de bonheur: Une histoire du paradis*, vol. 2 (Paris: Fayard, 1995).

52. See Nicholas of Cusa, *Complete Philosophical and Theological Treatises of Nicholas of Cusa*, ed. Jasper Hopkins (2 vols.; Minneapolis: A. J. Banning, 2001, and Philipp Melanchthon, *Commentaires sur le livre des Révélations de Daniel* (Geneva,

1555); more generally, see Emil Menke-Glückert, *Die Geschichtsschreibung der Reformation und Gegenreformation* (Leipzig: J. C. Hinrichs'sche Buchhandlung, 1912).

53. Moreover, the debate was not over; see Spinoza, *Tractatus Theologico-Politicus*, chap. 9, where he points out discrepancies in the biblical chronology (Spinoza, *Theological-Political Treatise*, ed. Jonathan Israel [Cambridge: Cambridge University Press, 2007], pp. 130–143). Earlier, Joseph Justus Scaliger had published *Opus de emendatione temporum*, offering a scientific biblical chronology, in 1583; James Ussher wrote his *Annales Veteris et Novi Testamenti* in 1654, and his *Chronologia sacra* appeared posthumously in 1660. Isaac Newton would later fall prey to the temptation to construct his own biblical chronology.

54. *Seder ʿolam*, ed. Jacob Emden (Hamburg, 1757); see Chapter Eleven, n. 11. To the edition by the Vilna Ga'on (Shklov [Škłoŭ, Belarus], 1801), editions published in Vilna [Vilnius] in 1801, in Ostrog [Slovenia] in 1820, and in Vilna in 1845 must be added. The commentaries of Elijah of Vilna and Ibn Daud's *Sefer ha-Kabbalah* are included in the 1877 Vilna edition. In 1895, Neubauer included the *Seder ʿolam* in his collection of medieval chronicles. See also Dov Baer Ratner's preface to his *Mavo la-Seder ʿolam* (Vilna: Romm, 1894), which preceded his 1897 critical edition of the *Seder ʿolam*, and recently, *Seder ʿolam: Critical Edition* . . . , ed. Milikowsky.

55. See the end of Leopold Zunz's preface to *Matsref la-kesef*, which lists the omissions and mistakes of the copist. Zunz, "Toledot le- r' Azaryah min ha-'adumim," *Kerem Hemed* 5 (1841): 131–158; 7 (1843): 119–124; and id., in *Gesammelte Schriften*, 2: 156. Nathan Stern, in "The Jewish Historico-Critical School of the Nineteenth Century" (PhD diss., Columbia University, 1901), p. 9, stresses the influence of the *Meʾor ʿeinayim* on the Wissenschaft des Judentums, for whose members it was a "model" and a " precursor."

56. Wilken, *Judaism and the Early Christian Mind* (cited Chapter Five, n. 95), holds that Philo marked the last era in which fraternization between Greeks and Jews could be considered.

57. Marcel Simon and André Benoît, *Le judaïsme et le christianisme antique: D'Antiochus Épiphane à Constantin* (Paris: Presses universitaires de France, 1968).

58. Nachman Krochmal, called ReNaK (1785–1840), wrote only one work, the work of a lifetime, *Moreh nevukhei ha-zeman* (Guide for the perplexed of our time) posthumously edited and published by Leopold Zunz in *Nachman Krochmals Werke* (Lemberg [Lviv, Ukraine], 1851; 2nd enlarged ed. by Simon Rawidowicz, London: Ararat, 1961). This singular work is a mixture of history and philosophy, with the former taken for the latter. It describes the history of the Jews from the biblical age to their expulsion from Spain. By including doctrine in historical development, it creates a structure in which the concept of an absolute God is central, as well as that of spirituality. The Jewish people are permeated by their God, who himself is drawn into Jewish history. The spiritual creativity of the Jews contributes in time and history. See Solomon Schechter, *Rabbi Nachman Krochmal and the Perplexities of the Time* (London: Jewish Chronicle Office, 1887); Jay

Michael Harris, *Nachman Krochmal: Guiding the Perplexed of the Modern Age* (New York: New York University Press, 1991).

59. "Judaism is not a religion of the present but rather of the future," Graetz says (*Structure of Jewish History*, p. 72).

60. Samson Raphael Hirsch, *Collected Writings* (New York: Philip Feldheim, 1997), 8: 241.

Afterword

1. Sacha Stern, *Calendar and Community: A History of the Jewish Calendar, 2nd Century BCE to 10th Century CE* (Oxford: Oxford University Press, 2001); *Time and Process in Ancient Judaism* (Portland, OR: Littman Library of Jewish Civilization, 2003); *Time, Astronomy, and Calendars in the Jewish Tradition*, ed. Stern and Burnett.

2. Michael Chyutin, *The Role of the Solar and Lunar Calendars in the Redaction of the Psalms* (Lewiston, NY: Edwin Mellen Press, 2002).

3. Elisheva Carlebach, *Palaces of Time: Jewish Calendar and Culture in Early Modern Europe* (Cambridge, MA: Belknap Press of Harvard University Press, 2011).

4. Goldberg, *La clepsydre II*.

Select Bibliography

Abrahams, Israel. *Studies in Pharisaism and the Gospels.* 2 vols. in 1. Cambridge: Cambridge University Press, 1924; repr., New York: Ktav, 1967.

Adelman, Rachel. *The Return of the Repressed: Pirke de-Rabbi Eliezer and the Pseudepigrapha.* Leiden: Brill, 2009.

Akavia, A. A. "Arakhan shel ketuvot Tsoar le-khronologia." *Kedem* 2 (1945): 92–98.

Al-Bīrūnī, Abu-'r-Raiḥān Muḥammad ibn-Aḥmad. *The Chronology of Ancient Nations: An English Version of the Arabic Text of the "Athâr-ul-bâkiya" of Albîrûnî, or "Vestiges of the Past," Collected and Reduced to Writing by the Author in A.H. 390–1, A.D. 1000.* Translated and edited by Carl Eduard Sachau. London: W. H. Allen, 1879; repr., Frankfurt: Minerva, 1969.

Albo, Joseph. *Sefer ha-'Ikkarim.* In *Sefer ha-'Ikkarim: Book of Principles,* ed. Isaac Husik. 4 vols. Philadelphia: Jewish Publication Society of America, 1929–1930; repr., 1946.

Albright, William Foxwell. "The Biblical Period." In Finkelstein, ed., *The Jews,* 1: 3–69.

———. *From the Stone Age to Christianity: Monotheism and the Historical Process.* 1940; 2nd ed., Baltimore: Johns Hopkins University Press, 1967.

Allony, N., ed. *Ha-Egron: Kitab Usul al-shir al-Ibrani me-et Rav Se'adyah Ga'on.* Jerusalem: Academy of Hebrew Language, 1969.

Alon, Gedaliah. *Toledot ha-yehudim be-'eretz Yisrael bi-tekufat ha-mishnah ve-ha Talmud.* Jerusalem: Magnes Press, 1980–1984. Translated and edited by Gershon Levi as *The Jews in Their Land in the Talmudic Age (70–640 C.E.)* (Cambridge, MA: Harvard University Press, 1989).

Al-Qirqasani, Jacob. *Kitab al Riyad wa-al Hada'iq.* In *Karaite Anthology: Excerpts from the Early Literature,* trans. and ed. Leon Nemoy, 42–68. New Haven, CT: Yale University Press, 1952.

Altmann, Alexander, and S. M. Stern. *Isaac Israeli: A Neoplatonic Philosopher of the Early Tenth Century: His Works Translated with Comments and an Outline of His Philosophy.* Chicago: University of Chicago Press, 1958.

The Apocrypha and Pseudepigrapha of the Old Testament. Edited by R. H. Charles et al. Oxford: Clarendon Press, 1913.

Arenhoevel, Diego. *Die Theokratie nach dem 1 um 2 Makkabäerbücher*. Mainz: Grünewald, 1967.

Ariès, Philippe. *Le temps de l'histoire*. Paris: Seuil, 1954; repr. with an introduction by Roger Chartier, 1986.

Aristeas to Philocrates (Letter of Aristeas). Edited and translated by Moses Hadas. New York: Harper, 1951; repr., New York: Ktav, 1973.

Aristotle. *Physics*. Translated by Robin Waterfield. Edited by David Bostock. Oxford: Oxford University Press, 2008.

Aronius, Julius. *Regesten zur Geschichte der Juden im fränkischen und deutschen Reiche bis zum Jahre 1273*. Berlin: Nathansen & Lamm, 1887–1902; repr., Hildesheim: Olms, 1970.

Artom, Elia Samuele. *Ha-Sefarim ha-hitsonim*. Tel Aviv: Yavneh, 1958; 3rd ed., 1967. In Hebrew.

Ascoli, Graziadio Isaia. "Iscrizioni inedite o mal note greche, latine, ebraiche di antichi sepolcri giudaici del Napolitano." In *Actes du IVe congrès des Orientalistes*, 239–383. Florence, 1878. Reprinted as *Iscrizioni inédite o mal note greche, latine, ebraiche di antichi sepolcri giudaici del Napolitano* (Turin: E. Loescher, 1880).

Ashkenazi, Jacob ben Isaac. *Tse'enah u-Re'enah* [Go forth and gaze]. Hanau, 1622.

———. *Tzeenah u-reenah: A Jewish Commentary on the Book of Exodus*. Translated by Norman C. Gore. New York: Vantage Press, 1965.

———. *The Weekly Midrash: Tz'enah Ur'enah; The Classic Anthology of Torah Lore and Midrashic Commentary*. Translated from the Yiddish by Miriam Stark Zakon. 2 vols. Art Scroll Judaica Series. Brooklyn, NY: Mesorah, 1983; repr., 2007.

———. *Zennah u-Reenah. Frauenbibel. Nach dem Jüdisch-Deutschen bearbeitet von Bertha Pappenheim. Bereschith. Erstes Buch Moses*. Frankfurt am Main: Kauffmann, 1930.

Attridge, Harold W. "Jewish Historiography." In Kraft and Nickelsburg, eds., *Early Judaism and Its Modern Interpreters*, 311–343.

Attridge, Harold W., and Gohei Hata, eds. *Eusebius, Christianity and Judaism*. Detroit: Wayne State University Press, 1992.

Augustine of Hippo. *The City of God*. Translated by Henry Bettenson. Rev. ed., London: Penguin Classics, 2003.

———. *The City of God*. Translated by Marcus Dods. Peabody, MA: Hendrickson, 2009.

———. *Confessions*. Translated with an introduction and notes by Henry Chadwick. Oxford: Oxford University Press, 2009.

The Babylonian Talmud, translated into English with notes, glossary and indices by Isadore Epstein. London: Soncino Press, 1935–1952; repr., 1961.

Baethgen, Friedrich B., ed. *Fragmente syrischer und arabischer Historiker*. Leipzig: F. A. Brockhaus, 1884.

Bagnall, Roger S., and Klaas A. Worp. *Chronological Systems of Byzantine Egypt*. Leiden: Brill, 2004.

Baillet, Maurice, Joseph Thadée Milik, and Roland de Vaux. *Les "petites grottes" de Qumran: Exploration de la falaise, les grottes 2Q, 3Q, 5Q, 6Q, 7Q à 10Q, le rouleau de cuivre.* 2 vols. Discoveries in the Judaean Desert of Jordan 3. Oxford: Clarendon Press, 1962.

Balslev, Anindita Niyogi, and J. N. Mohanty. *Religion and Time.* Leiden: Brill, 1993.

Bar Hiyya, Abraham ha-Nassi Savasorda. *Hegyon ha-nefesh ha-ʿatsuva.* 1145. Edited by Isaac (Eisak) Freimann. Leipzig: Vollrath, 1860. Translated by Geoffrey Wigoder as *The Meditation of the Sad Soul* (New York: Schocken Books, 1969).

———. *Hibbur ha-meshiha ve-ha-tishboret.* Berlin: Mekitsei Nirdamim, 1895. Translated in *Liber Embadorum*, by Plato de Tivoli (1145). In *Urkunden zur Geschichte der Mathematik im Mittelalter und der Renaissance*, ed. Maximilian Curtze, 1–183. Leipzig: Teubner, 1902.

———. *Sefer ha-ʿIbbur.* 1122. Edited by Herschell E. Filipowski. London: Longman, Brown, Green & Longmans, 1851.

———. "Yesodei ha-tevunah u-migdal ha-ʾemunah: Die Encyklopädie des Abraham bar Chijja." Edited by Moritz Steinschneider. *Hebräische Bibliographie* 7: 84–95. Berlin: A. Asher, 1864.

Bar Ilan Responsa Project. *The Global Jewish Database Responsa.* CD-ROM, Version 17. Ramat Gan, Israel: Bar Ilan University, 2009.

Baraita de-Shmuel ha-katan ha-nimtsah be ʾerets yishmaʿel. Salonica, 1861; repr., Frankfurt am Main, 1863.

Baron, Salo W. "Azariah de' Rossi's Historical Method." In Baron, *History and Jewish Historians*, 205–239.

———. *History and Jewish Historians: Essays and Addresses.* Philadelphia: Jewish Publication Society of America, 1964.

———. "La méthode historique d'Azariah de' Rossi." *Revue des études juives* 96 (1928): 151–175; 97 (1929): 43–78.

———. "Saadia's Communal Activities." In *Saadia Anniversary Volume*, ed. Boaz Cohen and Aron Freimann, 9–74. Texts and Studies 2. New York: American Academy for Jewish Research, 1943; repr., Tel Aviv: Zion, 1970.

———. *A Social and Religious History of the Jews.* 2nd ed. 18 vols. New York: Columbia University Press, 1952–1983.

Barr, James. *Bible and Interpretation: The Collected Essays of James Barr.* Edited by John Barton. 3 vols. Oxford: Oxford University Press, 2013–2014.

———. *Biblical Words for Time.* Naperville, IL: A. R. Allenson, 1962; repr., London: SCM Press, 1969.

———. *Comparative Philology and the Text of the Old Testament.* Oxford: Oxford University Press, 1968.

———. *Old and New Interpretation: A Study of the Two Testaments.* London: SCM Press, 1966.

———. *The Semantics of Biblical Language.* Oxford: Oxford University Press, 1961.

Barreau, Hervé. "La construction de la notion de temps." 3 vols. PhD diss., Université Paris X, 1982.

Barthélemy, Daniel. *Les devanciers d'Aquila.* Vetus Testamentum Supplementae 10. Leiden: Brill, 1963.

———. "Eusèbe, la LXX et les autres." In *La Bible et les Pères: Colloque de Strasbourg,* 51–65. Paris: Presses universitaires de France, 1971.

———. "Qui est Symmaque?" 1974. Repr. in *Études d'histoire du texte de l'Ancien Testament,* ed. Dominique Barthélemy, 307–321. Orbis Biblicus et Orientali 21. Fribourg: Éditions universitaires; Göttingen: Vandenhoeck & Ruprecht, 1978.

Bartlett, John R. *Jews in the Hellenistic World: Josephus, Aristeas, The Sibylline Oracles, Eupolemus.* Cambridge: Cambridge University Press, 1985.

Bartolocci, Giulio. *Bibliotheca Magna Rabbinica . . . de scriptoribus et scriptis hebraicis, ordine alphabetico hebraice et latine digestis.* 4 vols. Rome, 1675–1693.

Barton, George Aaron. *A Critical and Exegetical Commentary on the Book of Ecclesiastes.* Edinburgh: T. & T. Clark, 1908.

Baslez, Marie-Françoise. *Bible et histoire: Judaïsme, hellénisme, christianisme.* Paris: Fayard, 1998.

Baumgarten, Albert I. *The Flourishing of Jewish Sects in the Maccabean Era: An Interpretation.* Leiden: Brill, 1997.

Baumgarten, Joseph M. "La loi religieuse de Qoumran." *Annales HSS* 5 (1996): 1005–1025.

Bazin, Louis. "Les calendriers turcs anciens et médiévaux." PhD diss., Université de Lille, 1974.

Beckwith, Roger T. "Daniel 9 and the Date of the Messiah's Coming in Essene, Hellenistic, Pharisaic, Zealot and Early Christian Communities." *Revue de Qumran* 10, no. 4 (1981): 521–542.

———. "The Significance of the Calendar for Interpreting Essene Chronology and Eschatology." *RQ* 10, no. 2 (1980): 167–202.

Benoît, Pierre, J. T. Milik, and Roland de Vaux. *Les grottes de Murabba'ât.* Discoveries in the Judaean Desert of Jordan 2. Oxford: Clarendon Press, 1961.

Bensa, Alban. "De la micro histoire vers une anthropologie critique." In *Jeux d'échelles: La micro-analyse à l'expérience,* ed. Jacques Revel, 37–70. Paris: Seuil, 1996.

Berger, David. "Three Typological Themes in Early Jewish Messianism: Messiah Son of Joseph, Rabbinic Calculations, and the Figure of Armilus." *Association for Jewish Studies Review* 10, no. 2 (1985): 141–164.

Berzbach, Ulrich. "The Varieties of Literal Devices in a Medieval Midrash: Seder Eliyahu Rabba, Chapter 18." In *Jewish Studies at the Turn of the 20th Century,* ed. Judit Targarona Borrás and Angel Sáenz-Badillos, 1: 384–391. Leiden: Brill, 1999.

Biale, David. *Gershom Scholem: Kabbalah and Counter-History.* Cambridge, MA: Harvard University Press, 1979.

Biberfeld, Philip Leon. *Dina de-malkhuta dina.* Berlin: Hebräischer Verlag "Menorah," 1925. In Hebrew.

Bickerman, Elias J. *Chronology of the Ancient World: Aspects of Greek and Roman Life*. London: Thames & Hudson, 1968.

———. *From Ezra to the Last of the Maccabees: Foundation of Post-Biblical Judaism*. New York: Schocken Books, 1978.

———. *Der Gott der Makkabäer: Untersuchungen über Sinn und Ursprung der Makkabäischen Erhebung*. Berlin: Schocken, 1937. Translated as *The God of the Maccabees: Studies on the Meaning and Origin of the Maccabean Revolt* (Leiden: Brill, 1979).

———. "The Historical Foundations of Postbiblical Judaism." In Finkelstein, ed., *The Jews*, 1: 70–115.

———. *Institutions des Séleucides*. Paris: P. Geuthner, 1938.

———. "The Jewish Historian Demetrios." In Neusner, ed., *Christianity, Judaism, and Other Greco-Roman Cults*, vol. 3, 72–84.

———. *The Jews in the Greek Age*. New York: JTS, 1988.

Biram, A. "Millennium." In *The Jewish Encyclopedia*, ed. Singer et al., 8: 593.

Blau, Lajos [Ludwig]. *Die jüdischen Ehescheidung und der jüdische Scheidebrief: Eine historische Untersuchung*. Strassburg: K. J. Trübner, 1911–1912.

Blieffert, H. J. *Weltanschauung und Gottesglaube im Buch Kohelet. Darstellung und Kritik*. Rostock: R. Beckmann, 1938.

Bloch, Marc. *Apologie pour l'histoire, ou Métier d'historien*. Paris: A. Colin, 1974. Translated by Peter Putnam as *The Historian's Craft* (New York: Knopf, 1953).

Blois, François de. "Some Early Islamic and Christian Sources Regarding the Jewish Calendar (9th–11th Centuries)." In Stern and Burnett, eds., *Time, Astronomy, and Calendars in the Jewish Tradition*, 65–78.

Blumenkranz, Bernard, ed. *Les juifs et la Révolution française*. Toulouse: Privat, 1976.

Bonfil, Robert [Reuven]. "Bein Erets Yisrael le-beyn Bavel" [Between Israel and Babylonia]. *Shalem* 5 (1987): 1–30.

———. "Can Medieval Storytelling Help Understand Midrash?" In *The Midrashic Imagination: Jewish Exegesis, Thought, and History*, ed. Michael Fishbane, 228–254. Albany: State University of New York Press, 1993.

———. "How Golden Was the Age of the Renaissance in Jewish Historiography?" In Rapoport-Albert, ed., *Essays in Jewish Historiography*, 78–82.

———. "Jewish Attitudes Toward History and Historical Writing in Pre-Modern Time." *Jewish History* 11, no. 1 (Spring 1997): 5–40.

———. "Reading in the Jewish Communities of Western Europe in the Middle Ages." In *A History of Reading in the West*, ed. Cavallo and Chartier, 149–178. Oxford: Polity, 1999; repr., Amherst: University of Massachusetts Press, 2003.

———. "Le savoir et le pouvoir: Pour une histoire du rabbinat à l'époque prémoderne." In *La société juive à travers l'histoire*, ed. Shmuel Trigano, 1:115–195. Paris: Fayard, 1992.

———. "Some Reflections on the Place of Azariah de' Rossi's *Me'or 'einayim* in the Cultural Milieu of Italian Renaissance Jewry." In Cooperman, ed., *Jewish Thought in the Sixteenth Century*, 23–48.

The Book of Enoch. Translated by R. H. Charles. Oxford: Clarendon Press, 1893.

Bornstein, Hayyim Yehiel. "Heshbon shemitim ve-yovelot" [The count of sabbaticals and jubilees years]. *Ha-tekufah* 11 (1921): 230–260; 14–15 (1923): 321–372; 16 (1924): 228–292. In Hebrew.

———. "Mahloqet RaSaG u-ben Meir" [The dispute between Saadia Gaon and ben Meir]. In *Sefer ha-yovel: Huval shai li-khevod Nahum Sokolow be-yom melot hamesh ve-'esrim shanah la-'avodato ha-sifrutit* [Jubilee Volume for Nahum Sokolov], 19–189. Warsaw: Bi-Defus Shuldberg, 1904.

———. "Ta'arikhei Yisrael" [The dates in Israel]. *Ha-tekufah* 8 (1920): 281–338.

———. "Ta'arikhei Yisrael." *Ha-tekufah* 9 (1921): 202–264.

Bottéro, Jean. *Babylone et la Bible: Entretiens avec Hélène Monsacré.* Paris: Les Belles Lettres, 1994.

———. *Naissance de Dieu: La Bible et l'historien.* Paris: Gallimard, 1986.

———. *La plus vieille religion en Mésopotamie.* Paris: Gallimard, 1998. Translated by Teresa Lavender Fagan as *Religion in Ancient Mesopotamia* (Chicago: University of Chicago Press, 2001).

Bouché-Leclercq, Auguste. *L'astrologie grecque.* 1899. Brussels: Culture et Civilisation, 1963.

Boyarin, Daniel. *Intertextuality and the Reading of Midrash.* Bloomington: Indiana University Press, 1990.

Bregman, Marc. "Past and Present in Midrashic Literature." *Hebrew Annual Review* 2 (1978): 45–59.

Breuer, Mordechai, ed. "Modernism and Traditionalism of David Gans." In Cooperman, ed., *Jewish Thought in the Sixteenth Century*, 49–88.

———. "Rabbi David Gans, Author of the Tsemah David—An Outline." *Bar Ilan* 11 (1972–1973): 97–118. In Hebrew.

———. *Tsemah David le-Rabi David Ganz.* Jerusalem: Magnes Press, Hebrew University of Jerusalem, 1983.

Briend, Jacques. "La composition du Pentateuque entre hier et aujourd'hui." In *Naissance de la méthode critique: Colloque du centenaire de l'École biblique et archéologique française de Jerusalem*, 197–204. Paris: Cerf, 1992.

Brody, Robert. *The Ge'onim of Babylonia and the Shaping of Medieval Jewish Culture.* New Haven, CT: Yale University Press, 1998.

———. *Sa'adyah Ga'on.* Translated by Betsy Rosenberg. Oxford: Littman Library of Jewish Civilization, 2013.

Buttrick, George Arthur, et al., eds. *The Interpreter's Dictionary of the Bible.* 4 vols. Nashville, TN: Abingdon Press, 1962.

Capsali, Elijah (16th century CE). *Seder Eliahu Zuta: Toledot ha-'Otomanim u-Venitsi'ah ve-korot 'am Yisra'el be-mamlekhot Turkiyah, Sefarad u-Venitsi'ah* [Seder Eliyahu Zutta: History of the Ottomans and of Venice and that of the Jews in Turkey, Spain, and Venice, published for the first time based on four manuscripts with an introduction and notes by Rabbi Eliyahu ben Elkana Capsali]. Edited by Ariyeh Shmulevitz and Shlomo Simonsohn. 3 vols. Vols. 1

and 2, Jerusalem: Institute Ben-Tzvi and the Hebrew University, 1975–1977; vol. 3, Tel Aviv: Tel Aviv University, 1983.

——. *Sippurei Venezia* [Venetian stories]. 1517s? Jerusalem: Makhon Ben-Tsevi, 1975–1977.

Caquot, André, and Arnaud Sérandour. "La périodisation: De la Bible à l'Apocalyptique." In *Proche-Orient ancien: Temps vécu, temps pensé*, ed. Françoise Briquel-Chatonnet and Hélène Lozachmeur, 83–98. Antiquités sémitiques 3. Paris: J. Maisonneuve, 1998.

Carlebach, Elisheva. *Palaces of Time: Jewish Calendar and Culture in Early Modern Europe*. Cambridge, MA: Belknap Press of Harvard University Press, 2011.

Caro, Joseph. *See* Karo, Joseph ben Ephraim.

Cassius Dio. *Cassii Dionis Cocceiani Historiae romanae*. Leipzig: K. Tauchnitz, 1818.

——. *Dio's Roman History*. Translated by Earnest Cary. 9 vols. Cambridge, MA: Harvard University Press; London: W. Heinemann, 1914–1927.

Cassuto, Moshe David [Umberto]. *The Documentary Hypothesis and the Composition of the Pentateuch*. Translated by I. Abrahams. Series Publications of the Perry Foundation for Biblical Research in the Hebrew University of Jerusalem. Jerusalem: Magnes Press, 1961; repr., 1983.

——. "Ha-ketubot ha-ivriot shel ha-me'a ha-teshi'it be-Vinossa." *Kedem* 2 (1945): 99–120.

——. "Ha-ta'arikhim she-beketuvot Tsoar." *Kedem* 2 (1945): 90–91.

——. "Seforan shel shetei matsevot min ha-me'a ha-teshi'it be-derom Italia." In *Yehudim be-italia: Mehkarim = Jews in Italy: Studies Dedicated to the Memory of U. Cassuto, on the 100th Anniversary of His Birth*, ed. Haim Beinart, 1–23. Jerusalem: Magnes Press, 1988.

Cavallo, Guglielmo, and Roger Chartier, eds. *Storia della lettura nel mondo occidentale*. Rome: Laterza, 1995. Translated by Lydia G. Cochrane as *A History of Reading in the West* (Oxford: Polity, 1999; repr., Amherst: University of Massachusetts Press, 2003).

Charlesworth, James H., ed. *The Old Testament Pseudepigrapha*. 2 vols. Garden City, NY: Doubleday, 1983.

Charlesworth, James H., and Carol A. Newsom. *Angelic Liturgy: Songs of the Sabbath Sacrifice*. Tübingen: Mohr Siebeck; Louisville, KY: Westminster John Knox Press, 1999.

Chazan, Robert. *Barcelona and Beyond: The Disputation of 1263 and Its Aftermath*. Berkeley: University of California Press, 1992.

Chiesa, Bruno, and Wilfrid Lockwood. *Yakub al-Qirqasani on Jewish Sects and Christianity*. Frankfurt am Main: Peter Lang, 1984.

Chwolson, Daniel, ed. *Corpus inscriptionum hebraicarum, enthaltend Grabschriften aus der Krim und andere Grab- und Inschriften in alter hebräischer Quadratschrift . . . .* St. Petersburg: H. Schmitzdorff, 1882; repr., Hildesheim: Georg Olms, 1974.

Chyutin, Michael. *The Role of the Solar and Lunar Calendars in the Redaction of the Psalms.* Lewiston, NY: Edwin Mellen Press, 2002.

———. *The War of the Calendars in the Period of the Second Temple and the Redaction of the Psalms According to the Calendar.* Tel Aviv: Moden, 1993. In Hebrew.

Clement of Alexandria [Clemens Alexandrinus], Saint. *Miscellanies [Stromata],* Book 7. Edited and translated by Fenton John Anthony Hort and Joseph Bickersteth Mayor. London: Macmillan, 1902; repr., Cambridge: Cambridge University Press, 2010. See also under *Seventh Book of the Stromateis.*

Clinton, Henry Fynes. *Fasti Hellenici.* Vol. 3, app. 4. Oxford: Oxford University Press, 1895.

Cohen, Gerson David, ed. *Sefer ha-Kabbalah: The Book of Tradition.* Oxford: Littman Library of Jewish Civilization, 2005.

———. "The Story of the Four Captives." *Proceedings of the American Academy for Jewish Research* 29 (1960–1961): 55–131.

Cohen, Shaye J. D. "History and Historiography in the *Against Apion* of Josephus." In Rapoport-Albert, ed., *Essays in Jewish Historiography,* 1–11.

———. "The Significance of Yavneh: Pharisees, Rabbis, and the End of Jewish Sectarianism." *Hebrew Union College Annual* 55, no. 1 (1984): 27–29.

Cohn, Leopold, and Paulus Wendland, eds. *Philonis Alexandrini opera quae supersunt I–VII.* Berlin: G. Reimer, 1896–1930.

Cohn, Norman. *The Pursuit of the Millennium: Revolutionary Millenarians and Mystical Anarchists of the Middle Ages.* New York: Oxford University Press, 1970.

Collins, Adela Yarbro. *Cosmology and Eschatology in Jewish and Christian Apocalypticism.* Leiden: Brill, 1996.

Collins, John J. *The Apocalyptic Vision of the Book of Daniel.* Harvard Semitic Monographs 16. Missoula, MT: Scholars Press, 1977.

———. *The Scepter and the Star: The Messiahs of the Dead Sea Scrolls and Other Ancient Literature.* New York: Doubleday, 1995.

Colson, Francis Henry. *The Week: An Essay on the Origin and Development of the Seven-Day Cycle.* Cambridge: Cambridge University Press, 1926.

Cooperman, Bernard Dov, ed. *Jewish Thought in the Sixteenth Century.* Cambridge, MA: Harvard University Press, 1983.

Corbin, Alain. *Les cloches de la terre: Paysage sonore et culture sensible dans les campagnes au XIXe siècle.* Paris: Albin Michel, 1994. Translated by Martin Thom as *Village Bells: Sound and Meaning in the Nineteenth-Century French Countryside* (New York: Columbia University Press, 1998; repr., London: Macmillan, 1999).

Coudert, Allison P., and Jeffrey S. Shoulson, eds. *Hebraica veritas? Christian Hebraists and the Study of Judaism in Early Modern Europe.* Philadelphia: University of Pennsylvania Press, 2004.

Cowley, Arthur Ernest. "A Jewish Tombstone." *Palestine Exploration Fund Quarterly Statement* 57, no. 4 (October 1925): 207–210.

Croke, Brian, and Alanna M. Emmet, eds. *History and Historians in Late Antiquity.* Sydney: Pergamon Press, 1983.

Cross, Frank Moore. "The Text Behind the Text of the Hebrew Bible." In *Understanding the Dead Sea Scrolls: A Reader from the Biblical Archaeology,* ed. Hershel Shanks, 139–155. Harvard Semitic Studies 27. New York: Random House, 1992.

Crouch, James E. *Demetrius the Chronographer and the Beginnings of Hellenistic Jewish Historiography.* Nishinomiya, Japan: Kwansei Gakuin University, 1981.

Cullmann, Oscar. *Christ and Time: The Primitive Christian Conception of Time and History.* Translated by Floyd V. Filson. Philadelphia: Westminster Press, 1950.

Cusa, Nicholas of. *Complete Philosophical and Theological Treatises of Nicholas of Cusa.* Edited by Jasper Hopkins. 2 vols. Minneapolis: A. J. Banning, 2001.

Dahan, Gilbert, ed. *Gersonide en son temps: Science et philosophie médiévales.* Louvain: Peeters, 1991.

Dan, Joseph. "Armilus: The Jewish Antichrist and the Origins and Dating of the Sefer Zerubbavel." In Schäfer and Cohen, eds., *Toward the Millennium,* 73–104.

Dastur, Françoise. *Dire le temps: Esquisse d'une chronologie phénoménologique.* Paris: Encre Marine, 1994.

Dato, Mordechai. "Migdal David." 16th century. MS Opp. Add. 4e 153, Bodleian Library, Oxford University.

Davenport, Gene L. *The Eschatology of the Book of Jubilees.* Leiden: Brill, 1971.

Davies, Philip R. "Calendrical Change and Qumran Origins: An Assessment of VanderKam's Theory." *Catholic Biblical Quarterly* 45 (1983): 80–89.

Delumeau, Jean. *Mille ans de bonheur: Une histoire du paradis.* Vol. 2. Paris: Fayard, 1995.

Denis, Ernest. *Huss et la guerre des hussites.* Paris: E. Leroux, 1878.

Derenbourg, Joseph. "Les anciennes épitaphes des Juifs dans l'Italie méridionale." *Revue des études juives* 2 (1881): 131–134.

Des Vignoles, Alphonse. *Chronologie de l'histoire sainte et des histoires étrangères qui la concernent, depuis la sortie d'Égypte jusqu'à la captivité de Babylone.* Berlin: Chez Ambroise Haude, 1738.

Dimant, Devorah. "The Seventy Weeks Chronology (Dan 9, 24–27) in the Light of New Qumranic Texts." In *The Book of Daniel in the Light of New Findings,* ed. Adam S. van der Woude, 57–76. Leuven: Leuven University Press, 1993.

———. "Signification et importance des manuscrits de la mer Morte: L'état actuel des études qoumrâniennes." *Annales HSS* 5 (1996): 975–1004.

Dimant, Devorah, and John Strugnell. "4Q Second Ezekiel." *Revue de Qumran* 13 (1988): 45–58.

———. "The Merkabah Vision in Second Ezekiel (4Q 385 4)." *Revue de Qumran* 14 (1990): 331–348.

Diodorus Siculus. *Diodorus of Sicily in Twelve Volumes. With an English translation by C. H. Oldfather.* Loeb Classical Library. Cambridge, MA: Harvard University Press, 1935.

———. *The Historical Library of Diodorus the Sicilian in Fifteen Books to Which Are*

Added the Fragments of Diodorus and Those Published by H. Valesius, I. Rhodo-mannus, and F. Ursinus. Translated by G. Booth. London: J. Davis, 1814.

Dönitz, Saskia. *Überlieferung und Rezeption des Sefer Yosippon.* Tübingen: Mohr Siebeck, 2013.

Donnolo, Shabbetai (913–ca. 982). *Sefer hakhemoni.* In *Il commento di Sabbatai Donnolo sul libro della creazione pubblicato per la prima volta nel testo ebraico,* ed. David Castelli. Pubblicazioni del Regio Istituto di Studi Superiori. Florence: Tip. dei successori Le Monnier, 1880. In *Sefer Yetsirah* (Warsaw, 1884), 121–148, and Adolf Neubauer, "Un chapitre inédit de Sabbetai Donnolo," *Revue des études juives* 22 (1891): 213–218.

Droysen, Johann Gustav. *Geschichte des Hellenismus.* 3 vols. Hamburg: F. Perthes, 1836–1843.

Dupont-Sommer, André, and Marc Philonenko, eds. *La Bible: Écrits intertesta-mentaires.* Bibliothèque de la Pléiade. Paris: Gallimard, 1987.

Dupront, Alphonse. *Du sacré: Croisades et pèlerinages, images et langages.* Paris: Gallimard, 1987.

Dupuy, Bernard. "Temps et eschatologie dans le judaïsme." In *Temps et eschatolo-gie: Données bibliques et problématiques contemporaines,* ed. Jean-Louis Leuba, 39–53. Paris: Cerf, 1994.

Efros, Israel. *The Problem of Space in Jewish Medieval Philosophy.* New York: Co-lumbia University Press, 1917.

Ehrman, Bart D., ed. and trans. *The Apostolic Fathers: Volume II.* Cambridge, MA: Harvard University Press, 2003.

Einstein, Albert. *Relativity: The Special and the General Theory: A Popular Exposi-tion.* New York: Crown, 1961.

Elbogen, Ismar. *Jewish Liturgy: A Comprehensive History.* Translated by R. P. Scheindlin. Philadelphia: Jewish Publication Society of America, 1993.

———. *Der jüdische Gottesdienst in seiner geschichtlichen Entwicklung.* Leipzig: Fock, 1913.

Eleazar, Kallir. *Kerovot.* In *Jubelschrift zum neunzigsten Geburtstag des Dr. L. Zunz.* Berlin: Louis Gerschel, 1884.

Eliade, Mircea. *Le mythe de l'éternel retour.* Paris: Gallimard, 1962. Translated by Willard R. Trask as *The Myth of the Eternal Return: or, Cosmos and History* (Princeton, NJ: Princeton University Press, 1954); reprinted as *Cosmos and His-tory: The Myth of the Eternal Return* (New York: Harper, 1959, 2012).

Elias, Norbert. *Über die Zeit.* Frankfurt am Main: Suhrkamp, 1984. Translated as *Time: An Essay* (Oxford: Blackwell, 1992) and as *An Essay on Time,* in *The Col-lected Works of Norbert Elias,* vol. 9 (Dublin: University College Dublin Press, 2007).

Eliezer, Rabbi. *Pirké* [chapters] *de Rabbi Eliezer, according to the text of the manu-script belonging to Abraham Epstein of Vienna.* Translated and edited by Gerald Friedlander. London: Kegan Paul, Trench, Trubner; New York: Bloch, 1916; repr., New York: Hermon Press, 1965.

———. *Pirke de-Rabbi Eliezer: Nach der Edition Venedig 1544 unter Berücksichtigung der Edition Warschau 1852*. Translated and edited by Dagmar Börner-Klein. Frankfurt am Main: Peter Lang, 2004. In Hebrew.

———. *Pirkei de Rabbi Eliezer*. Edited by Chaim M. Horowitz. Jerusalem: Makor, 1972.

———. *Pirkei de-Rabbi Eliezer: Text, Redaction and a Sample Synopsis*. Edited by Eliezer Treitl. Jerusalem: Yad Yitshak Ben Tsevi, 2012. In Hebrew.

———. *Sefer pirķei Rabi Eliʿezer im Biʾur*. Edited by Rabbi David ben Yehuda Luria [RaDaL]. Warsaw: H. E. Bomberg, 1852; repr., New York: Om, 1946; Jerusalem, 1969. In Hebrew.

Encyclopaedia Judaica. Edited by Cecil Roth et al. 16 vols. Jerusalem: Keter; New York: Macmillan, 1971–1972.

Entsiklopedia mikraʾit (Encyclopedia Biblica). 9 vols. Jerusalem: Mosad Bialik, 1950–1988.

Epstein, Abraham. "Le livre des Jubilés: Philon et le Midrasch Tadsché." *Revue des études juives* 21 (1890): 1–25; 22 (1891): 80–97.

Erech Hatephilot: Rituel des prières. Tel Aviv: Durlacher, 1989.

The Ethiopic Version of the Hebrew Book of Jubilees. Edited by R. H. Charles. Oxford: Clarendon Press, 1895.

Eusebius of Caesarea. *Praeparatio Evangelica*. 4th century CE. Translated by Edwin Hamilton Gifford as *Preparations for the Gospel* (Oxford: Clarendon Press, 1903; repr., Eugene, OR: Wipf & Stock, 2002).

Even Shemuel (Kaufman), Yehudah. *Midreshei Geullah*. Tel Aviv: Mosad Bialik, 1954.

Feldman, Louis H. *Josephus: A Supplementary Bibliography*. London: Garland, 1986.

———. *Josephus and Modern Scholarship (1937–1980)*. Berlin: Walter de Gruyter, 1984.

Feldman, Louis H., and Gohei Hata, eds. *Josephus, the Bible, and History*. Leiden: Brill, 1989.

Finkelstein, Louis. *Jewish Self-Government in the Middle Ages*. New York: Feldheim, 1924.

———, ed. *The Jews: Their History, Culture, and Religion*. 2 vols. New York: Harper & Brothers, 1949.

———. *The Pharisees: The Sociological Background of Their Faith*. 2 vols. Philadelphia: Jewish Publication Society of America, 1938; repr., 1946.

———. "The Sources of the Tannaitic Midrashim." *JQR*, n.s., 21 (1941): 211–243.

Firkowitsch, Avraam. *Sefer abne zikkaron*. Vilna [Vilnius]: S. J. Fin & A. G. Rosenkranc, 1872.

Fishbane, Michael. *Biblical Interpretation in Ancient Israel*. Oxford: Clarendon Press, 1985, 1988.

———, ed. *The Midrashic Imagination: Jewish Exegesis, Thought, and History*. Albany: State University of New York Press, 1993.

Flavius Philostratus. *The Life of Apollonius of Tyana*. Cambridge, MA: Harvard University Press; London: Heinemann, 1912.

Fleischer, Ezra. "Haduta, Birebi Avraham, rishon le-payyetanei Italia." *Italia* 2 (1980): 7–29.

———. *Shirat ha-kodesh ha-ivrit be-yemei ha-benayim.* Jerusalem: Keter, 1975.

Flusser, David. "The Four Empires in the Fourth Sibyl and in the Book of Daniel." *Israel Oriental Studies* 2 (1972): 148–171.

———. *Judaism and the Origins of Christianity.* Jerusalem: Magnes Press, 1988.

———. "Qumran and Jewish Apotropaic Prayers." *Israel Exploration Journal* 16 (1966): 194–205.

———, ed. [Josephus Gorionides] *Sefer Yossipon* [The Josippon]. Edited with an introduction, commentary, and notes. 2 vols. Jerusalem: Mosad Bialik, 1978–1980. In Hebrew.

Fraenkel, Jonah [Yonah Frenkel]. *Darkei ha-aggadah ve-ha-midrash.* 2 vols. Givatayyim, Israel: Masada, 1991.

———. "Time and Its Role in the Aggadic Story." In *Binah: Studies in Jewish Thought*, vol. 2, ed. Joseph Dan, 31–56. New York: Praeger, 1989.

Frank, Edgar. *Talmudic and Rabbinical Chronology: The System of Counting Years in Jewish Literature.* New York: Philip Feldheim, 1956.

Frankel, Jonathan. *Prophecy and Politics: Socialism, Nationalism and the Russian Jews, 1862–1917.* Cambridge: Cambridge University Press, 1981.

Frazer, James George. *Folklore in the Old Testament: Studies in Comparative Religion, Legend and Law.* 3 vols. London: Macmillan, 1918.

Freudenthal, Gad, ed. *Studies on Gersonides: A Fourteenth-Century Jewish Philosopher-Scientist.* Leiden: Brill, 1992.

Freudenthal, Jacob. *Alexander Polyhistor und die von ihm erhaltenen Reste jüdäischer und samaritischer Geschichtswerke.* Vol. 1: *Hellenistische Studien.* Breslau: H. Skutsch, 1874.

Frey, Jean-Baptiste. *Corpus inscriptionum iudaicorum: Recueil des inscriptions juives qui vont du IIIe siècle avant J.-C. au VIIe siècle de notre ère.* Vol. 1. Vatican City: Pontificio Istituto di archeologia cristiana, 1936–1952. Translated as *Corpus of Jewish Inscriptions: Jewish Inscriptions from the Third Century B.C. to the Seventh Century A.D.* (New York: Ktav, 1975).

Freyman, Eli. "Le commentaire sur le Pentateuque de Gersonide, éditions et manuscrits." In Dahan, ed., *Gersonide en son temps*, 117–132.

Friedländer, Michael. "Calendar, History of." In *The Jewish Encyclopedia*, ed. Singer et al., 3: 498–501.

———. "Life and Works of Sa'adia Gaon." *Jewish Quarterly Review* 5 (1893): 177–199.

Friedman, Mordechai Akiva. "Ha-ketubot ha'arets-yisraeliot mi-tekufat ha-ge'onim" [Palestinian marriage contracts from the Gaonic period]. *Te'uda* (Tel Aviv) 1 (1980): 57–82.

———. *Jewish Marriage in Palestine: A Cairo Geniza Study.* 2 vols. Tel Aviv: Tel Aviv University, 1980.

———. "On Linguistic Chronology in Rabbinic Literature." *Sidra* 1 (1985): 59–68. In Hebrew.

Friedmann, Meir-Ish Shalom, ed. *Seder Eliyahu rabbah ve-zutta*. Vienna, 1902; repr., Jerusalem: Wahrmann Books, 1969.

Fuks, Alexander, and Victor Tcherikover. *Corpus Papyrorum judaicarum*. Cambridge, MA: Harvard University Press for the Magnes Press, Hebrew University, 1957–1964.

Funkenstein, Amos. "Collective Memory and Historical Consciousness." *History and Memory* 1 (1989): 5–26.

———. *Maimonides: His Nature, History, and Messianic Beliefs*. Tel Aviv: MOD Books, 1997.

———. *Perceptions of Jewish History*. Berkeley: University of California Press, 1993.

Gadamer, Hans-Georg. *Truth and Method*. Translation revised by Joel Weinsheimer and Donald G. Marshall. London: Continuum, 2004.

Gager, John G. "Messiahs and Their Followers." In Schäfer and Cohen, eds., *Toward the Millennium*, 37–46.

Gandz, Solomon. "The Origin of the Planetary Week, or the Planetary Week in Hebrew Literature." *Proceedings of the American Academy for Jewish Research* 18 (1948–1949): 213–254.

Gans, David. *Sefer Tsemah David*. Frankfurt am Main, 1692. Edited by Mordechai Breuer. Jerusalem: Magnes Press, 1983. In Hebrew.

Gardet, Louis, et al., eds. *Cultures and Time*. Paris: UNESCO, 1976.

Gaster, Moses. "Demetrius und *Seder 'olam*: Ein Problem der hellenistischen Literatur." In *Festskrift i anledning af professor David Simonsens 70-aarige fødselsdag*, ed. Aron Freiman, 243–252. Copenhagen: Hertz's Bogtrykkeri, 1923.

Geiger, Abraham. *Melo hofnayim: Likutim shonim mi-kitvei hakhmei kadmonei 'amenu*. Berlin: Ze'ev Vulf Viltsig, 1839.

Gelzer, Heinrich. *Sextus Julius Africanus und die byzantinische Chronographie*. Vol. 1. Leipzig: Teubner, 1880; repr., New York: B. Franklin, 1967.

Gilbert, Pierre. *Bible, mythes et récits de commencement*. Paris: Seuil, 1986.

Gillet-Didier, Véronique. "Temps de Dieu, temps des hommes: Généalogie, calendrier et tradition dans le judaïsme de l'époque hellénistique et romaine." PhD diss., École Pratique des Hautes Études, Paris, 1997.

Ginzberg, Louis. *The Legends of the Jews*. 7 vols. Philadelphia: Jewish Publication Society of America, 1909–1938; repr., 1968.

Ginzburg, Carlo. *Myths, Emblems, Clues*. Translated by John and Anne C. Tedeschi. Baltimore: Johns Hopkins University Press, 1989; repr. with a new preface, 2013.

Ginzel, Friedrich Karl. *Handbuch der mathematischen und technischen Chronologie: Das Zeitrechnungswesen der Völker*. 3 vols. Leipzig: J. C. Hinrichs, 1906–1914; repr., Leipzig: Deutsche Buch-Export und Import, 1958.

Gladstein, Ruth. "Eschatological Trends in Bohemian Jewry During the Hussite Period." In *Prophecy and Millenarianism: Essays in Honour of Marjorie Reeves*, ed. Ann Williams, 241–256. Harlow, UK: Longman, 1980.

Glasson, Thomas Francis. *Greek Influence in Jewish Eschatology, with Special Reference to the Apocalypses and Pseudepigraphs*. London: SPCK, 1961.

Glatzer, Mordechai. "'Iṭur sofrim: (Sefer ha-'Iṭur) le-Rav Yitshak ben Rav Aba Mari: Pirke mavo." PhD diss., Hebrew University of Jerusalem, 1983.

Glatzer, Nahum Norbert. *Untersuchungen zur Geschichtsleher der Tannaiten*. Berlin: Schocken, 1933. Translated by Rivka Ulmer as "The Tannaim and History," in Neusner, ed., *The Christian and Judaic Invention of History*, 125–142.

Golb, Norman. *Who Wrote the Dead Sea Scrolls? The Search for the Secret of Qumran*. New York: Scribner, 1995.

Goldberg, Sylvie Anne. "Categories of Time: Scales and Values in Ashkenazi Culture." *Jewish Studies* 39 (1999): 87–96.

———. *La clepsydre II: Temps de Jérusalem, temps de Babylone*. Paris: Albin Michel, 2004.

———. "Common Law and Jewish Law: The Diasporic Principle of *dina demalkuta dina*." *Behemoth* 2 (2008): 39–53.

———. *Crossing the Jabbok: Illness and Death in Ashkenazi Judaism in Sixteenth-Through Nineteenth-Century Prague*. Berkeley: University of California Press, 1996.

———. "De la Bible et des notions d'espace et de temps: Essai sur l'usage des catégories dans le monde achkénaze du Moyen Âge à l'époque moderne." *Annales HSS* 5 (September–October 1997): 987–1015.

———, ed. *Dictionnaire encyclopédique du Judaïsme: Esquisse de l'histoire du peuple juif*. Paris: Cerf, 1993; repr., Laffont, 1996.

———. "L'étude du judaïsme: Science historique ou religieuse?" *Préfaces* 19 (June–September 1990): 88–95.

———. "Histoire juive, histoire des Juifs: D'autres approches." Special issue. *Annales HSS* 5 (1994): 1019–1029.

———. "Les jeux du temps dans la culture ashkénaze." *Revue des études juives* 160, nos. 1–2 (2001): 155–168.

———. "Temporality as Paradox: The Jewish Time." In *Jewish Studies in a New Europe: Proceedings of the Fifth Congress of Jewish Studies in Copenhagen 1994 under the Auspices of the European Association for Jewish Studies*, ed. Ulf Haxen, Hanne Trautner-Kromann, and Karen Lisa Goldschmidt Salamon, 284–293. Copenhagen: Det Kongelige Bibliotek, 1998.

———. "La tolérance des Juifs en France: Cimetières et émancipation." In *Louis XVI: Du serment du sacre à l'édit de tolérance de 1787*, 55–67. Exhibition catalogue. Paris: Bibliothèque historique de la Ville de Paris, 1988.

———, ed. *Histoire juive, histoire des Juifs: D'autres approches*. Special issue of *Annales HSS* 5 (1994).

Goldstein, Bernard Raphael. *The Astronomy of Levi Ben Gerson, 1288–1344: A Critical Edition of Chapters 1–20*. New York: Springer, 1985.

———. "Creation and the End of Days." In *Proceedings of the 1984 Meeting of the Academy for Jewish Philosophy*, ed. David Novak and Norbert Samuelson, 261–276. Lanham, MD: University Press of America, 1986.

———. "Levi Ben Gerson's Astrology in Historical Perspective." In Dahan, ed., *Gersonide en son temps*, 287 –300.

Goldstein, Bernard R., and David Pingree. *Levi ben Gerson's Prognostication for the Conjunction of 1345*. Philadelphia: American Philosophical Society, 1990.

Goldstein, Jonathan Amos. *II Maccabees: A New Translation with Introduction and Commentary*. Garden City, NY: Doubleday, 1983; repr., New Haven, CT: Yale University Press, 2011.

Goode, Alexander D. "The Exilarchate in the Eastern Caliphate, 637–1258." *Jewish Quarterly Review*, n.s., 31, no. 2 (1940): 149–169.

Gould, Stephen Jay. *Questioning the Millennium: A Rationalist's Guide to a Precisely Arbitrary Countdown*. New York: Harmony Books, 1997.

Gourevitch, Édouard. *Rabbi Yehudah Loew: Le puits de l'exil*. Paris: Berg, 1982.

Graetz, Heinrich. "Die allerneueste Bibelkritik: Wellhausen-Renan." *Monatsschrift für Geschichte und Wissenschaft des Judentums* 35 (1886): 193–204, 233–251.

———. *Die Construction der jüdischen Geschichte*. Berlin, 1846.

———. "Fälschungen in dem Texte der Septuaginta von christlicher Hand zu dogmatischen Zwecken." *Monatsschrift für Geschichte und Wissenschaft des Judentums* 2 (1853): 432–436.

———. *Geschichte der Juden von den ältesten Zeiten bis auf die Gegenwart*. 11 vols. Leipzig: Leiner, 1900.

———. *The Structure of Jewish History, and Other Essays*. Translated, edited, and introduced by Ismar Schorsch. New York: Jewish Theological Seminary of America, 1975.

Grant, Robert M. *Eusebius as Church Historian*. Oxford: Clarendon Press, 1980.

Graves, Robert, and Raphael Patai. *The Hebrew Myths: The Book of Genesis*. Garden City, NY: Doubleday, 1964.

Gray, Rebecca. *Prophetic Figures in Late Second Temple Jewish Palestine: The Evidence of Josephus*. New York: Oxford University Press, 1993.

Greenberg, Moshe. *Studies in the Bible and Jewish Thought*. Philadelphia: Jewish Publication Society of America, 1995.

Greenspahn, Frederick. *New Insights and Scholarship in Hebrew Bible*. New York: New York University Press, 2008.

Grelot, Pierre. "Du sabbat juif au dimanche chrétien." *La Maison-Dieu* 123 (1975): 79–107; 124 (1976): 15–124.

Gressmann, Hugo. *Der Ursprung der israelitisch-jüdischen Eschatologie*. Vol. 6 of *Forschungen zur Religion und Literatur des Alten und Neuen Testaments*, ed. W. Bousset and H. Gunkel. Göttingen: Vandenhoeck & Ruprecht, 1905.

Grintz, Yehoshua M. "Jubilees, Book of." In *Encyclopaedia Judaica*, ed. Roth et al., 10: 324–325.

Gruen, Erich. *Heritage and Hellenism: The Reinvention of Jewish Tradition*. Berkeley: University of California Press, 1998.

Grumel, Venance. *Traité d'études byzantines*. Vol. 1: *La chronologie*. Paris: Presses universitaires de France, 1958.

Guggenheimer, Henrich W. *Seder 'olam: The Rabbinic View of Biblical Chronology.* Northvale, NJ: J. Aronson, 2005.

Guillaume, Alfred. "Further Documents on the Ben Meir Controversy." *Jewish Quarterly Review* 5 (1915): 543–557.

Günther, Horst. *Zeit der Geschichte: Weltfahrung und Zeitkategorien in der Geschichtsphilosophie.* Frankfurt am Main: Fischer Taschenbuch, 1993.

Gurevich, Aron. *Les catégories de la culture médiévale.* Translated from the Russian by Hélène Courtin and Nina Godneff. Paris: Gallimard, 1983.

———. *Categories of Medieval Culture.* Translated by G. L. Campbell. London: Routledge & Kegan Paul, 1985.

———. "Time as a Problem of Cultural History." In Gardet et al., eds., *Cultures and Time,* 229–245.

Guttmann, Julius. *Die Philosophie des Judentums: Geschichte der Philosophie in Einzeldarstellungen.* 3 vols. Munich: Ernst Reinhardt, 1933. Translated by David W. Silverman as *Philosophies of Judaism: The History of Jewish Philosophy from Biblical Times to Franz Rosenzweig* (New York: Holt, Rinehart & Winston, 1964).

Hadas-Lebel, Mireille. *Flavius Josèphe: Le juif de Rome.* Paris: Fayard, 1989.

Ha-derashot be-Yisrael ve-hishtalshelutan ha-historit. Translated by Leopold Zunz and Chanoch Albeck. Jerusalem: Mosad Bialik, 1954; repr., 1999.

Halbertal, Moshe. *Maimonides: Life and Thought.* Translated by Joel Linsider. Princeton, NJ: Princeton University Press, 2014.

Halevi, Yehudah [Judah]. *Judah Hallevi's Kitab al Khazari.* Ca. 1140 CE. Translated from the Arabic with an introduction by Hartwig Hirschfeld. London: Routledge, 1905.

———. *The Kuzari (Kitab al Khazari): An Argument for the Faith of Israel.* Translated by Henry Slonimsky. New York: Schocken Books, 1986.

———. *Sefer ha-Kuzari.* Fano, 1506.

Halpern, Baruch. *The First Historians: The Hebrew Bible and History.* San Francisco: Harper & Row, 1988.

Hannah, Robert. *Time in Antiquity.* London: Routledge, 2009.

Hanson, John. "Demetrius the Chronographer." In *The Old Testament Pseudepigrapha,* ed. James H. Charlesworth, 2: 843–854. Garden City, NY: Doubleday, 1983.

Harkavy, Abraham Elija. *Altjüdische Denkmäler aus der Krim.* St. Petersburg: Académie impériale des sciences, 1876.

———. *Zikhron la-rishonim, ve-gam la-aharonim. Heleq Rishon Zikhron la-rishonim: Ha-sarid weha-Palit mi-Sefer ha-Egron we-sefer ha-Galuy. Leben und Werke des Saadjah Gaon.* St. Petersburg: Mekitsei Nirdamim, 1891.

Harkavy, Abraham Elija, and H. L. Strack. *Catalog der hebräischen Bibelhandschriften der Kaiserlichen offentlichen Bibliothek.* 2 vols. St. Petersburg: C. Ricker; Leipzig: J. C. Hinrichs, 1875.

Harl, Marguerite, Gilles Dorival, and Olivier Munnich. *La Bible grecque des Septante: Du Judaïsme hellénistique au Christianisme ancien.* Paris: Cerf, 1994.

Harris, Jay Michael. *Nachman Krochmal: Guiding the Perplexed of the Modern Age*. New York: New York University Press, 1991.

Harvey, Warren Z. "Albo's Discussion on Time." *Jewish Quarterly Review* 70 (1980): 210–238.

———. *Physics and Metaphysics in Hasdai Crescas*. Amsterdam Studies in Jewish Thought 6. Amsterdam: J. C. Gieben, 1998.

———. "A Third Approach to Maimonides' Cosmogony-Prophetology Puzzle." *Harvard Theological Review* 74 (1981) 287–301.

Heidegger, Martin. *Being and Time*. Translated by John MacQuarrie and Edward Robinson. New York: Harper, 1962.

Heinemann, Isaac. *Darkhei ha-Aggada*. Jerusalem: Magnes Press, 1970; repr., 1974.

———. "Wer veranlaßte den Glaubenszwang der Makkabäerzeit?" *Monatsschrift für Geschichte und Wissenschaft des Judentums* 82 (1938): 145–172.

Heinemann, Joseph. "The Messiah of Ephraim and the Premature Exodus of the Tribe of Ephraim." *Harvard Theological Review* 68 (1975): 1–15.

Hengel, Martin. *Judentum und Hellenismus: Studien zu ihrer Begegnung unter Berücksichtigung Palästinas bis zur Mitte des 2 Jh.s v. Chr.* Tübingen: Mohr, 1973. Translated by John Bowden as *Judaism and Hellenism: Studies in Their Encounter in Palestine During the Early Hellenistic Period* (London: SCM Press, 1974; repr., 1981).

Hermann, L. "La lettre d'Aristée à Philocrate et l'empereur Titus." *Latomus* 25 (1966): 58–77.

Heschel, Abraham Joshua. *God in Search of Man: A Philosophy of Judaism*. New York: Farrar, Straus & Cudahy, 1955.

———. *The Sabbath: Its Meaning for Modern Man*. New York: Farrar, Straus & Young, 1951.

Himmelfarb, Martha. *The Apocalypse: A Brief History*. Chichester, UK: Wiley-Blackwell, 2010.

———. "Sefer Zerubbabel." In *Rabbinic Fantasies: Imaginative Narratives from Classical Hebrew Literature*. Edited by D. Stern and M. J. Mirsky. New Haven, CT: Yale University Press, 1998.

Hippolytus of Rome, Saint. *The Writings of Hippolytus, Bishop of Rome*. Edited by J. H. McMahon and S. D. F. Salmond. Edinburgh: T. & T. Clark, 1868–1869.

Hirsch, Samson Raphael. *Collected Writings*. Vol. 8: *Mensch-Yisroel: Perspectives on Judaism*. New York: Philipp Feldheim, 1997.

Hoffman, Lawrence A. *Covenant of Blood: Circumcision and Gender in Rabbinic Judaism*. Chicago: University of Chicago Press, 1996.

Holladay, Carl R. *Fragments from Hellenistic Jewish Authors*. Vol. 1: *Historians*. Vol. 2: *Poets*. Society of Biblical Literature Texts and Translations 20. Chico, CA: Scholars Press, 1983, 1989.

Holmes, Michael W. "The Epistle of Barnabas." In *The Apostolic Fathers in English*, ed. M. Holmes, 370–441. 3rd ed. Grand Rapids, MI: Baker Academic, 2006.

Horn, S. H., and Lynn H. Wood. "The Fifth Century Jewish Calendar of Elephantine." *Journal of Near Eastern Studies* 13, no. 1 (1954): 1–20.

Hughes, Jeremy. *Secrets of the Times: Myth and History in Biblical Chronology. Journal for the Study of the Old Testament*, suppl. ser., no. 66. Sheffield, UK: JSOT, 1990.

Ibn Daud, Abraham [RaBaD]. *Sefer ha-Kabbalah*. 1514. Edited by Gerson D. Cohen. Philadelphia: Jewish Publication Society of America, 1967.

Ibn Shahin, Nissim Ben Jacob. *Sefer mafte'ah manulei ha-Talmud*. Vienna, 1847. Translated by William M. Brinner as *An Elegant Composition Concerning Relief after Adversity* (New Haven, CT: Yale University Press, 1977).

Ibn Verga, Solomon. *Shebet Yehudah* [Judah's scepter]. Adrianople, Turkey, 1544.

———. *Shevet Jehuda: Ein Buch über das Leiden des jüdischen Volkes im Exil*. Translated by Meír Wiener. Edited by Sina Rauschenbach. Jüdische Geistesgeschichte 6. Berlin: Parerga, 2006.

Ibn Yahya, Gedaliah. *Shalshelet ha-Kabbalah*. Venice, 1587; Kraków, 1596.

Idel, Moshe. *Kabbalah: New Perspectives*. New Haven, CT: Yale University Press, 1988.

———. *Maïmonide et la mystique juive*. Paris: Cerf, 1991.

———. *Maimonides and the Jewish Mystic*. Cluj-Napoca, Romania: Dacia, 2001.

———. *Messianic Mystics*. New Haven, CT: Yale University Press, 1998.

———. "Mystique juive et histoire juive." *Annales HSS* 5 (1994): 1223–1240.

Ideler, Ludwig. *Handbuch der mathematischen und technischen Chronologie*. 2 vols. Berlin: A. Rücker, 1825–1826.

Idelsohn, Abraham Zebi. *Jewish Liturgy and Its Developments*. New York: Sacred Music Press, 1932; repr., New York: Schocken Books, 1967.

Ifrah, Georges. *Une histoire universelle des chiffres*. 2 vols. Paris: Seghers, 1981; repr., Paris: Laffont, 2000. Translated by David Bellos as *The Universal History of Numbers: From Prehistory to the Invention of the Computer* (New York: J. Wiley, 2000).

Isaac ben Abba Mari. *Sefer ha-Ittur*. Venice, 1608. Reprinted from Joseph Unterhandler's 1874–1885 Warsaw ed., *Sefer ha-Ittur: Code of Laws* (New York: Sepher-Hermon Press, 1979).

Isaac Israeli ben Joseph. *Sefer yesod 'olam*. Toledo, 1310. Edited by Jacob Shklover. Berlin, 1777. In *Liber Jesod Olam seu Fundamentum Mundi: opus astronomicum celeberrimum*, ed. Dov Beer Goldberg and Ariyeh Leib Rozenkranz. 2 vols. Berlin: Kornaggi, 1844–1846.

Ivry, Alfred L., Elliot R. Wolfson, and Allan Arkush, eds. *Perspectives on Jewish Thought and Mysticism*. Amsterdam: Harwood Academic, 1998.

Jacob ben Asher [Rabbi Yaakov ben Raash]. *Arba'ah Turim*. Piove di Sacco, Italy, 1475; 7 vols., Jerusalem: Me'orot, 1976.

Jacob, Meir ben [Rabbenu Tam]. *Sefer ha-yashar*. Vienna, 1811.

———. *Sefer ha-yashar le-rabbenu Tam. Heleq ha-she'elot ve- ha-teshuvot, im tikkunim ve-hagahot by Efrayim Zalman Margaliot*, ed. Shraga Fish Rosenthal. Berlin: T. H. Ittskovski, 1898; 2nd ed., Jerusalem, 1992.

Jacob, Benno. *Das Erste Buch der Tora: Genesis; übersetzt und erklärt von Benno Jacob*. Berlin: Schocken Verlag, 1934.

Jacobs, Joseph. "Chronology." In *The Jewish Encyclopedia*, ed. Singer et al., 4: 64–75.

Jacobson, Howard. *A Commentary on Pseudo-Philo's Liber Antiquitatum Biblicarum, with Latin Text and English Translation*. Leiden: Brill, 1996.

Jacoby, Felix. *Die Fragmente der griechischen Historiker*. 3 vols. Berlin: Weidmann, 1923–1955.

Japhet, Sarah. "In Search of Ancient Israel: Revisionism at All Costs." In *The Jewish Past Revisited: Reflections on Modern Jewish Historians*, ed. David N. Myers and David B. Ruderman, 212–233. New Haven, CT: Yale University Press, 1998.

Jastrow, Marcus. *A Dictionary of the Targumim, the Talmud Babli and Yerushalmi, and the Midrashic Literature*. 2 vols. Philadelphia: Pardes, 1886–1903.

Jaubert, Annie. "Le calendrier des Jubilés et de la secte de Qoumran: Ses origines bibliques." *Vetus Testamentum* 3 (1953): 250–264.

———. *La date de la Cène: Calendrier biblique et liturgie chrétienne*. Paris: J. Gabalda, 1957.

Jellinck, Adolf. *Bet ha-Midrash*. 6 vols. Leipzig: C. W. Vollrath, 1853–1878; repr., Jerusalem: Wahrmann Books, 1967. In Hebrew.

———. *Der Mensch als Gottes Ebenbild*. Leipzig: J. Rosenberg, 1854.

Jenni, Ernst. "Das Wort *'olam* im Alten Testament." *ZATW* 64 (1952): 197–248; 65 (1953): 1–35.

Jewish Bible. See *Tanakh*.

The Jewish Encyclopedia: A Descriptive Record of the History, Religion, Literature, and Customs of the Jewish People from the Earliest Times to the Present Day. Edited by Isidore Singer et al. 12 vols. New York: Funk & Wagnalls, 1901–1906.

Johnston, Philip. *Shades of Sheol: Death and Afterlife in the Old Testament*. Leicester, UK: Apollos; Downers Grove, IL: InterVarsity Press, 2002.

Joseph ha-Kohen. *Dibre ha-Yamim le-Malke Zarfat we-'Otoman* [Chronicles of the kings of France and Turkey]. Venice, 1534. Reprints, Amsterdam, 1733; Leipzig, 1858.

———. *Sefer emek ha-bakha*. 1500s. Vienna, 1852. Translated and edited by Harry S. May as *The Vale of Tears: Emek Habacha* (The Hague: M. Nijhoff, 1971).

———. *Sefer emeq ha-bakha (The Vale of Tears): With the Chronicle of the Anonymous Corrector*. Edited and translated by Karin Almbladh. Uppsala: Uppsala University, distributed by Almqvist & Wiksell, 1981.

Josephus, Flavius. *Against Apion*. With an English translation by Henry St. John Thackeray. Vol. 1. Loeb Classical Library. Cambridge, MA: Harvard University Press, 1976.

———. *Against Apion*. Translation and commentary by John M. G. Barclay. Vol. 10 of *Flavius Josephus: Translation and Commentary*, ed. Steve Mason. Leiden: Brill, 2007.

———. *Les antiquités juives*. Translated and edited by Étienne Nodet. 4 vols. Paris: Cerf, 1992–2010.

————. *Le contre Apion*. Translated by Léon Blum. Edited by Théodore Reinach. Paris: Les Belles Lettres, 1930.

————. *Flavius Josephus: Translation and Commentary*. Edited by Steve Mason. 10 vols. in 12. Leiden: Brill, 2000–2007.

————. *La guerre des Juifs*. Translated by Pierre Savinel. Paris: Minuit, 1977.

————. *Jewish Antiquities*. 9 vols. Loeb Classical Library. Cambridge, MA: Harvard University Press, 1998.

————. *The Jewish War*. Translated by Henry St. John Thackeray. Loeb Classical Library. Cambridge, MA: Harvard University Press, 1928.

————. *The Life of Flavius Josephus*. Vol. 3 of *The Whole Genuine Works of Flavius Josephus*. Translated by William Whiston. Glasgow: Blackie, 1859.

————. *Life of Josephus: Translation and Commentary*. Vol. 9 of *Flavius Josephus: Translation and Commentary*. Edited by Steve Mason. Leiden: Brill, 2001.

————. *The New Complete Works of Josephus*. Translated by William Whiston. Grand Rapids, MI: Kregel, 1999.

————. *Oeuvres complètes de Flavius Josèphe*. Edited by Théodore Reinach. 7 vols. Paris: E. Leroux, 1900–1932.

Judah ben Jehiel [Judah Messer Leon]. *Nofet tsufim: Sefer ha-halatsah le-romem Kitve ha-ḳodesh*. Mantua, 1475. Edited by Adolf Jellinek. Vienna: Bi-defus shel Bendiner u-Shlosberg, 1863. Facsimile of the 1475 edition, Jerusalem: National Library, 1981.

Judah Loew ben Betsalel [the MaHaRaL of Prague]. *Be'er ha-golah*. Prague, 1598. Edited by Israel ben Shabbetai (Hopsztajn) of Kozhnitz. Jerusalem: Bnei Brak, 1972. In *Be'er hagolah: The Classic Defense of Rabbinic Judaism Through the Profundity of the Aggadah*, adapted by Yitzchok Adlerstein (Brooklyn, NY: Mesorah, 2000).

Kaestli, Jean-Daniel, and Otto Wermelinger, eds. *Le canon de l'Ancien Testament: Sa formation, son histoire*. Geneva: Labor et Fides, 1984.

Kahana, Abraham. *Ha-Sefarim ha-hitsonim: La-Torah la-Nevi'im la-Ketuvim u-she'ar sefarim hitsonim*. 2 vols. [1931 or 1932]. Tel Aviv: Otsa'at Mekorot, 1956, 1970. In Hebrew.

Kahn, Léon. *Histoire de la communauté israélite de Paris: Le Comité de bienfaisance, l'hôpital, l'orphelinat, les cimetières*. Paris: A. Durlacher, 1886.

Kantor, Máttis. *Codex Judaica: Chronological Index of Jewish History*. New York: Zichron Press, 2005.

Karo, Joseph ben Ephraim. *Kesef Mishneh*. Venice, 1574–1575.

————. *Shulḥan arukh* [Set table]. 1563. 4 parts. Venice, 1564–1565.

Kasher, Aryeh. *Jews in Hellenistic and Roman Egypt: The Struggle for Equal Rights*. Tübingen: J. C. B. Mohr, 1985.

Kasher, Menahem, ed. *Torah Shelemah* [Complete Torah]. 45 vols in 12. Jerusalem: Torah Shelema Institute, 1927–1983. Abridged and translated by Harry Freedman as *Encyclopedia of Biblical Interpretation: A Millennial Anthology* (9 vols.; New York: American Biblical Encyclopedia Society, 1953–1979).

Kaufmann, Yehezkel. *Toledot ha-'emunah ha-yisraelit.* 8 vols. Tel Aviv: Dvir, 1936–1956. Abridged and translated by Moshe Greenberg as *The Religion of Israel: From the Beginnings to the Babylonian Exile* (Chicago: University of Chicago Press, 1960; repr., New York: Schocken Books, 1972).

Koch, K. "Spätisraelitisches Geschichtsdenken am Beispiel des Buches Daniel." *Historische Zeitschrift* (Munich) 193 (1961): 1–32.

Kochan, Lionel. *The Jew and His History.* New York: Macmillan, 1977; repr., Chico, CA: Scholars Press, 1985.

Koffmann, Elisabeth. *Die Doppelurkunden aus der Wüste Juda: Recht und Praxis der jüdischen Papyri des 1. und 2. Jahrhunderts n. Chr. samt Übertragung der Texte und deutscher Übersetzung.* Leiden: Brill, 1968.

Kohler, Kaufmann. "Jubilees, Book of." In *The Jewish Encyclopedia*, ed. Singer et al., 7: 301–304.

Kovetz al-yad [*Kobez Al yad*; annual of the Mekitsei Nirdamim (Mekize Nirdamim) Society] 9 (1947).

Kraft, Robert A. *Barnabas and the Didache.* Vol. 3 of *The Apostolic Fathers: A New Translation and Commentary.* Edited by Robert M. Grant. New York: Nelson, 1965.

Kraft, Robert, and Georges W. E. Nickelsburg, eds. *Early Judaism and Its Modern Interpreters.* Atlanta: Scholars Press, 1986.

Krochmal, Nachman [ReNaK]. *Moreh nevukhei ha-zeman* [The guide for the perplexed of our time]. Edited by Leopold Zunz in *Nachman Krochmals Werke.* Lemberg [Lviv, Ukraine], 1851; Berlin: Lamm, 1923; 2nd enlarged ed. by Simon Rawidowicz, London: Ararat, 1961.

LaCocque, André. *Daniel et son temps.* Geneva: Labor et Fides, 1983. Translated by David Pellauer as *The Book of Daniel*, with a foreword by Paul Ricoeur (Atlanta: J. Knox Press, 1979).

Landes, David. *Revolution in Time: Clocks and the Making of the Modern World.* Cambridge, MA: Harvard University Press, 1983.

Landes, Richard. "Lest the Millennium Be Fulfilled: Apocalyptic Expectations and the Pattern of Western Chronography 100–800 C.E." In *The Use and Abuse of Eschatology in the Middle Ages*, ed. W. Verberke, D. Verhelst, and A. Welkenhuysen, 137–212. Leuven: Leuven University Press, 1988.

Lapin, Hayim. *Rabbis as Romans: The Rabbinic Movement in Palestine, 100–400 CE.* Oxford: Oxford University Press, 2012.

Laqueur, Richard. *Der jüdische Historiker Flavius Josephus: Ein biographischer Versuch auf neuer quellenkritischer Grundlage.* Giessen: Münchow, 1920; repr., Rome: "L'Erma" di Bretschneider, 1970.

Le Goff, Jacques. *Histoire et mémoire.* Paris, Gallimard, 1986. Translated by Steven Rendall and Elizabeth Claman as *History and Memory* (New York: Columbia University Press, 1992; repr., 1996).

———. *Pour un autre Moyen Âge: Temps, travail et culture en Occident; 18 essais.* Paris: Gallimard, 1977.

————. *Time, Work, and Culture in the Middle Ages*. Chicago: University of Chicago Press, 1980.

————. *Un autre Moyen Âge*. Paris: Gallimard, 1999.

Le Goff, Jacques, and Pierre Nora, eds. *Faire de l'histoire*. 3 vols. Paris: Gallimard, 1974–1986.

Lehman, M. R. "Studies in the Murabba'at and Nahal Hever Documents." *Revue de Qumran* 4, no. 13 (1963): 53–81.

Leibowitz, Yeshayahu. *The Faith of Maimonides*. Tel Aviv: MOD Books, 1996.

Lemaire, André. "Israël." In *Dictionnaire encyclopédique du Judaïsme: Esquisse de l'histoire du peuple juif*, ed. Sylvie Anne Goldberg, 1241–1260. Paris: Cerf, 1993; repr., Laffont, 1996.

Leuba, Jean-Louis, ed. *Temps et Eschatologie: Données bibliques et problématiques contemporaines*. Paris: Cerf, 1994.

Leveen, Jacob. Supplementary volume (vol. 4) to George Margoliouth, *Catalogue of the Hebrew and Samaritan Manuscripts in the British Museum*. London, 1935.

Levi ben Gershom [RaLBaG]. *Commentary of Levi ben Gerson on the Book of Job*. Translated by Abraham L. Lassen. New York: Bloch, 1946.

————. *Commentary on Song of Songs*. Translated and edited by Menachem Kellner. New Haven, CT: Yale University Press, 1998.

————. *Creation of the World According to Gersonides*. Translated by Jacob Staub. Chico, CA: Scholars Press, 1982.

————. *Les guerres du Seigneur*. Books 3 and 4. Translated and edited by Charles-Touati. Paris: Mouton, 1968.

————. *The Wars of the Lord*. Translated by Seymour Feldman. 3 vols. Philadelphia: Jewish Publication Society of America, 1984–1999.

Lévinas, Emmanuel. *Le temps et l'autre*. Paris: Presses universitaires de France, 1991. Translated by Richard A. Cohen as *Time and the Other and Additional Essays* (Pittsburgh, PA: Duquesne University Press, 1987).

Lewin, Benjamin Menasheh. *Otsar ha-ge'onim* [Otzar ha-Geonim: Thesaurus of the Gaonic Responsa and Commentaries Following the Order of the Talmudic Tractates]. 13 vols. Haifa: N. Warhaftig, 1928–1962; Jerusalem: Mosad ha-Rav Kuk, 1929–1943.

Lewis, Jack P. "Jamnia Revisited." In *The Canon Debate*, ed. Lee M. McDonald and James A. Sanders, 146–162. Peabody, MA: Hendrickson, 2002.

————. "What Do We Mean by Jabneh?" *Journal of Bible and Religion* 32, no. 2 (April 1964): 125–132.

Lewy, Hildegard, and Julius Lewy. "The Origins of the Week and the Oldest Asiatic Calendar." *Hebrew Union College Annual* 17 (1942–1943): 8–18.

Licht, Jacob. "Time and Eschatology in Apocalyptic Literature and in Qumran." *Journal of Jewish Studies* 16 (1965): 177–182.

Lieberman, Saul. *Greek in Jewish Palestine: Studies in the II–IV Centuries C.E.* New York: JTS, 1942.

————. *Hellenism in Jewish Palestine: Studies in the Literary Transmission, Beliefs and Manners of Palestine in the I Century B.C.E.–IV Century C.E.* New York: JTS, 1950.

———. *Texts and Studies.* New York: Ktav, 1974.

Lloyd, Geoffrey E. R. "Views on Time in Greek Thought." In Gardet et al., eds., *Cultures and Time,* 117–148.

Lobel, Diana. *Between Mysticism and Philosophy: Sufi Language and Religious Experience in Judah Halevi's Kuzari.* Albany: State University of New York Press, 2000.

Lods, Adolphe. *Histoire de la littérature hébraïque et juive, depuis les origines jusqu'à la ruine de l'État juif, 135 après J.-C.* Edited by André Parrot. Paris: Payot, 1950.

Loeb, Isidore. "Notes sur l'histoire des Juifs: La chronologie juive." *Revue des études juives* 19 (1889): 202–205.

Loewe, Raphael. "Rabbi Joshua ben Hananiah: LL.D or D. LITT?" In *Studies in Jewish Legal History: In Honour of David Daube,* ed. Bernard S. Jackson, 137–154. London: Jewish Chronicle Publications, 1974.

Löwith, Karl. *Meaning in History: The Theological Implications of the Philosophy of History.* Chicago: University of Chicago Press, 1949.

Luneau, Auguste. *L'histoire du salut chez les pères de l'Eglise: La doctrine des âges du monde.* Paris: Beauchesne, 1964.

Lurya, Ben Zion. *Megillat Ta'anit.* Jerusalem: Mosad Bialik, 1964.

Macek, Jan, and Robert Mandrou. *Histoire de la Bohême des origines à 1918.* Paris: Fayard, 1984.

Mahler, Eduard. *Handbuch der Jüdischen Chronologie.* Leipzig: Fock, 1916; repr., Hildesheim: Georg Olms, 1967.

Maiello, Francesco. *Histoire du calendrier de la liturgie à l'agenda.* Paris: Seuil, 1993.

Maimonides [Moshe ben Maimon, RaMBaM]. *The Code of Maimonides (Mishneh Torah).* 22 vols. Yale Judaica Series. New Haven, CT: Yale University Press, 1949–.

———. *Crisis and Leadership: Epistles of Maimonides.* Translated by Abraham S. Halkin. Edited by Abraham S. Halkin and David Hartman. Philadelphia: Jewish Publication Society of America, 1985; repr., 1992.

———. *The Guide of the Perplexed.* Translated and edited by Shlomo Pines. 2 vols. Chicago: University of Chicago Press, 1963; repr., 1979.

———. *Hilchot gerushin = The Laws of Divorce: A New Translation with Commentary, Diagrams, and Notes.* Translated by Eliyahu Touger. Brooklyn, NY: Moznaim, 1995.

———. *Maimonides' Mishneh Torah (Yad ḥazaḳah).* Translated by Philip Birnbaum. New York: Hebrew Publishing, 1967.

———. *Mishneh Torah, Sefer Yad Ha-Hazakah.* 1180. 14 vols. Mantua, 1566; Leipzig, 1862.

———. *Moses Maimonides' Epistle to Yemen: The Arabic Original and the Three Hebrew Versions.* Edited by Abraham S. Halkin and translated by Boaz Cohen. New York: American Academy for Jewish Research, 1952.

———. *Responsa.* Edited by Abraham Haim Freimann. 4 vols. Jerusalem: Mekitsei Nirdamim, 1934.

———. *Responsa of R. Moses ben Maimon.* Edited by Joshua Blau. 4 vols. Tel Aviv: Papiros, 1958–1961; repr., Jerusalem: Mekitsei Nirdamim, 1984.

———. *Sefer ha-Mitsvot.* Translated by Moses ibn Tibbon. Rome, 1480. Edited by H. Heller. Jerusalem: Mosad Harav Kook, 1946.

Malter, Henri. *Saadia Ga'on: His Life and Work.* Philadelphia: Jewish Publication Society of America, 1921; repr., 2009.

Mancuso, Piergabriele. *Shabbetai Donnolo's Sefer Hakhmoni.* Leiden: Brill, 2010.

Mann, Thomas. *The Magic Mountain.* Translated by John E. Woods. New York: Everyman's Library, 2005.

Manns, Frédéric. "Les rapports Synagogue-Église au début du IIe siècle après J.-C. en Palestine." *Liber annuus* 31 (1981): 125–146.

Marcus, Ralph. "Jewish and Greek Elements in the Septuagint." In *Louis Ginzberg: Jubilee Volume on the Occasion of His Seventieth Birthday,* ed. Saul Lieberman et al., 227–245. 2 vols. New York: American Academy for Jewish Research, 1945.

Marcus, Sarah. "The *Be'er Hagolah* and the *Me'or Einayim*: Approaches to *Aggadata.*" *Judaic Studies Journal* 3 (Fall 2014): 105–116.

Margalioth, Mordecai. "Le-be'aiat kadmuto shel sefer Seder Eliahu." In *Sefer Assaf: Kovets ma 'aleph amarey mehkar muggash likhevod S. Assaf,* ed. M. D. Cassuto, J. Klausner, and Y. Colman, 370–390. Jerusalem: Mosad ha-Rav Kook, 1953.

Margoliouth, George. *Catalogue of the Hebrew and Samaritan Manuscripts in the British Museum.* 4 vols. London: British Museum, 1899–1915.

Margolis, Max Leopold. *The Hebrew Scriptures in the Making.* Philadelphia: Jewish Publication Society of America, 1922.

Mason, Steve. *Flavius Josephus on the Pharisees: A Composition-Critical Study.* Studia Post-Biblica 39. Leiden: Brill, 1991.

Mauss, Marcel. *Oeuvres.* Vol. 2. Paris: Éditions de Minuit, 1974.

———. *Techniques, Technology and Civilisation.* Translated by Nathan Schlanger. New York: Durkheim Press; Berghahn Books, 2006.

McDonald, Lee M., and James A. Sanders, eds. *The Canon Debate.* Peabody, MA: Hendrickson, 2002.

Mekhilta de-Rabbi Ishmael. Edited by Jacob Zallel Lauterbach. Philadelphia: Jewish Publication Society of America, 2004.

Melanchthon, Philipp [Philipp Schwartzerdt]. *Commentaires sur le livre des Révélations de Daniel.* Geneva, 1555.

Menke-Glückert, Emil. *Die Geschichtsschreibung der Reformation und Gegenreformation: Bodin und die Begründung der Geschichtsmethodologie durch Bartholomäus Keckermann.* Leipzig: J. C. Hinrichs'sche Buchhandlung, 1912.

Merleau-Ponty, Maurice. *Phénoménologie de la perception.* Paris: Gallimard, 1945. Translated by Colin Smith as *Phenomenology of Perception* (London: Routledge & Kegan Paul; New York: Humanities Press, 1962).

———. *The World of Perception.* Translated by Oliver Davis. London: Routledge, 2004.

Midrash Eikhah rabbah. Edited by Solomon Buber. Vilno [Vilnius], 1899.

Midrash rabbah. Constantinople, 1512.

Midrash rabbah, Shir ha-shirim. Parma, 1240. Edited by Samson Dunsky. Jerusalem: Devir, 1980. In Hebrew.

Midrash Rabbah: Translated into English with Notes, Glossary and Indices. Edited by Harry Freedman and Maurice Simon. 10 vols. London: Soncino Press, 1939; repr., 1992.

Midrash Seder olam, im be'urim ve-hagarot me-harav Yaakov Emden u-me-harav Eliyahu mi-Vilna. Jerusalem: Agudat midrash ha-pardes, 1987.

Midrash Tanhuma. Constantinople, 1522. Edited and with an introduction by Solomon Buber. Vilno [Vilnius], 1885; repr., Jerusalem, 1964.

Migne, Jacques-Paul, ed. *Patrologiæ cursus completus. Series græca: seu, Bibliotheca universalis, integra, uniformis, commoda, oeconomica omnium SS. patrum, doctorum, scriptorumque ecclesiasticorum.* 162 vols. in 168. Paris: Migne, 1857–1866.

———, ed. *Patrologiæ cursus completus. Series latina.* 217 vols. Paris: Migne, 1842–1855.

Mikhael, Joseph Haim. *Or ha-hayyim, hakhmei Yisrael ve siffrehem.* Frankfurt am Main, 1881; repr., Jerusalem: Mosad ha-rav Kook, 1965.

Milik, Józef Tadeusz. *The Books of Enoch: Aramaic Fragments of Qumrán Cave 4.* Oxford: Clarendon Press, 1976.

———. "Un contrat juif de l'an 134 après J.-C." *RB* 61 (1954): 182–190.

———. "Deux Documents inédits du désert de Juda." *Biblica* 38 (1957): 245–268.

———. *Ten Years of Discovery in the Wilderness of Judaea.* Naperville, IL: A. R. Allenson, 1959.

———. "Le Testament de Levi en araméen; fragment de la grotte 4 de Qumran." *RB* 62 (1955): 398–406.

Milikowsky, Chaim Joseph. "The Date of the Destruction of the First Temple According to the *Seder 'olam*, the Tossefta and the Babylonian Talmud: Studies in the Development of a Tradition." *Tarbiz* 62, no. 4 (July–September): 485–500.

———. "*Seder 'olam*: A Rabbinic Chronography." PhD diss., Yale University, 1981.

———. "*Seder 'olam* and Jewish Chronography in the Hellenistic and Roman Periods." *Proceedings of the American Academy for Jewish Research* 52 (1985): 115–139.

———. "*Seder 'olam* and the Tosefta." *Tarbiz* 49 (1979): 246–263.

———. "Ta'arikh ha-Hurban ha-Bayit ha-rishon al-pi 'Seder 'olam', ha- Tosefta ve- ha-Bavli, Iyyunim be-hitpathuta shel massoret." *Tarbiz* 62 (1993): 485–500.

———, ed. *Seder 'olam: Mahadurah mada'it, perush u-mavo. Critical Edition, Commentary and Introduction.* 2 vols. Jerusalem: Yad ben Zvi, 2013. In Hebrew.

Millar, Fergus. "The Background to the Maccabean Revolution: Reflections on Martin Hengel's 'Judaism and Hellenism.'" *Journal of Jewish Studies* 29 (1978): 1–21.

Miller, Carl I. "A Study of Gedaliah ibn Yahya's *Shalshelet ha-Kabbalah*." PhD diss./rabbinic thesis, Hebrew Union College–Jewish Institute of Religion, 1931.

Milo, Daniel Shabetaï. *Trahir le temps: Histoire.* Paris: Les Belles Lettres, 1991.

Mimouni, Simon C. *Le Judéo-christianisme ancien: Essais historiques.* Paris: Cerf, 1998.

Momigliano, Arnaldo. *Alien Wisdom: The Limits of Hellenization*. Cambridge: Cambridge University Press, 1975.

———. *The Classical Foundations of Modern Historiography*. Berkeley: University of California Press, 1990.

———. *Essays in Ancient and Modern Historiography*. Middletown, CT: Wesleyan University Press, 1977; repr., Chicago: Chicago University Press, 2012.

———. *Essays on Ancient and Modern Judaism*. Translated by Silvia Berti. Chicago: University of Chicago Press, 1994.

———. "The Romans and the Maccabees." In *Jewish History: Essays in Honour of Chimen Abramsky*, ed. Ada Rapoport-Albert and Steven Zipperstein, 231–244. London: Peter Halban, 1988.

———. *Studies in Historiography*. New York: Harper & Row, 1966.

———. "Time in Ancient Historiography." *History and Theory* 6, suppl. 6 (1966): 1–23.

Moore, George Foot. *Judaism in the First Centuries of the Christian Era: The Age of the Tannaim*. 2 vols. Cambridge, MA: Harvard University Press, 1950.

Mor, Menahem, and Uriel Rappaport. "The World of the Historical Bibliographer." *Jewish History* 1, no. 2 (Autumn 1986): 65–78.

Morgenstern, Julian. "The Calendar of the Book of Jubilees: Its Origin and Its Character." *Vetus Testamentum* 5 (1955): 34–76.

———. "Jubilee, Year of." In *The Interpreter's Dictionary of the Bible*, ed. George Arthur Buttrick et al., 2: 1002. New York: Abingdon Press, 1962.

Mosshammer, Alden A. *The Chronicle of Eusebius and Greek Chronographic Tradition*. Lewisburg, PA: Bucknell University Press, 1979.

Müller, Karl, ed. *Fragmenta historicum graecorum*. 5 vols. Paris: A. F. Didot, 1841–1870.

Müller, Karlheinz. "Die rabbinischen Nachrichten über die Anfänge der Septuaginta." In *Wort, Lied und Gottesspruch: Festschrift für Joseph Ziegler*, ed. Josef Schreiner, 1: 73–93. 2 vols. Würzburg: Echter Verlag, Katholisches Bibelwerk, 1972.

Munk, Élie. *Le monde des prières*. Paris: Durlacher, 1958.

———. *La voix de la Thora: Commentaire du Pentateuque*. Paris: Fondation Samuel et Odette Levy, 1969.

Nahmanides [Moses ben Naḥman Girondi, RaMBaN]. *The Disputation at Barcelona*. Translated and annotated by Charles Ber Chavel. New York: Shilo, 1983.

Nahon, Gérard. "La nation juive portugaise en France, XVIe–XVIIIe siècles: Espaces et pouvoirs." *Revue des études juives* 153 (1994): 353–382.

Nathan ben Jehiel of Rome. *Sefer he-ʿArukh*. Rome, ca. 1469–1472.

———. *Sefer he-ʿArukh. Hebero Natan Bar Yehiel ve-ʿalav sefer musaf ha-ʿarukh me-ha-hakham Binyamin Mosfiya*. Amsterdam, 1655. Tel Aviv: Beyt Refael, 1968.

Nathan, Rabbi [Nathan the Babylonian], et al. *Aboth de Rabbi Nathan*. Edited by Solomon Schechter. 1887; repr., New Haven, CT: Feldheim, 1945. In Hebrew.

———. *The Fathers According to Rabbi Nathan*. Translated and edited by Judah Goldin. New Haven, CT: Yale University Press, 1956.

————. *The Fathers According to Rabbi Nathan (Abot de Rabbi Nathan) Version B: A Translation and Commentary.* Translated and edited by Anthony J. Saldarini. Leiden: Brill, 1975.

Néher, André. *David Gans, 1541–1613: Disciple du Maharal de Prague, assistant de Tycho Brahe et de Jean Kepler.* Paris: Klincksieck, 1974. Translated as *Jewish Thought and the Scientific Revolution of the Sixteenth Century: David Gans (1541–1613) and His Times* (Oxford: Oxford University Press, 1986).

————. "La philosophie hébraïque et juive dans l'Antiquité." In *Histoire de la philosophie*, vol. 1: *Orient—Antiquité—Moyen Âge*, ed. Brice Parain, 50–81. Bibliothèque de la Pléiade. Paris: Gallimard, 1969.

————. *Le puits de l'exil: La théologie dialectique du Maharal de Prague (1512–1609).* Paris: Albin Michel, 1965; rev. ed., Paris: Cerf, 1991.

————. "The View on Time and History in Jewish Culture." In Gardet et al., eds., *Cultures and Time*, 149–168.

Nemoy, Leon. "Al-Qirqasani's Account of the Jewish Sects and Christianity." *Hebrew Union College Annual* 7 (1930): 317–397.

————, trans. and ed. *Karaite Anthology: Excerpts from the Early Literature.* New Haven, CT: Yale University Press, 1952.

Neubauer, Adolf. "Un chapitre inédit de Sabbetaï Donnolo." *Revue des études juives* 22 (1891): 213–218.

————, ed. *Medieval Jewish Chronicles and Chronological Notes.* 2 vols. Oxford: Clarendon Press, 1887–1895; 2nd ed., Jerusalem: n.p., 1967.

Neugebauer, Paul V. *Hilfstafeln zur technischen Chronologie.* Kiel: Verlag der Astronomischen Nachrichten, 1937.

Neuman, Abraham A. *The Shebet Yehudah and Sixteenth Century Historiography.* New York, 1945.

Neusner, Jacob, ed. *The Christian and Judaic Invention of History.* Atlanta: Scholars Press, 1990.

————, ed. *Christianity, Judaism, and Other Greco-Roman Cults: Studies for Morton Smith at Sixty.* Studies in Judaism in Late Antiquity 12. Leiden: Brill, 1975.

————. *Confronting Creation: How Judaism Reads Genesis; An Anthology of Genesis Rabbah.* Columbia: University of South Carolina Press, 1991.

————. *Foundations of Judaism.* Philadelphia: Fortress Press, 1989.

————. *The Foundations of Judaism: Method, Teleology, Doctrine.* 3 vols. Philadelphia: Fortress Press, 1983–1985; repr., Atlanta: Scholars Press, 1988.

————. *A History of the Jews in Babylonia.* Vol. 1: *The Parthian Period*; vol. 2: *The Early Sasanian Period.* Leiden: Brill, 1965–1966.

————. *Jeremiah in Talmud and Midrash: A Source Book.* Lanham, MD: University Press of America, 2006.

————. *A Life of Rabban Yohanan ben Zakkai, ca. 1–80 C.E.* Leiden: Brill, 1962.

————. *Messiah in Context: Israel's History and Destiny in Formative Judaism.* Philadelphia: Fortress Press, 1984.

———. "The Religious Uses of History: Judaism in First-Century A.D. Palestine and Third-Century Babylonia." *History and Theory* 5 (1966): 153–171.

Newsom, Carol Ann. *Megillot genuzot: Shirot Olat ha-Shabbat; Songs of the Sabbath Sacrifice. A Critical Edition.* Atlanta: Scholars Press, 1985.

Niditch, Susan. *The Symbolic Vision in Biblical Tradition.* Chico, CA: Scholars Press, 1983.

Noam, Vered. *Megillat Ta 'anit: Versions, Interpretation, History, with a Critical Edition.* Jerusalem: Yad ben-Zvi, 2003. In Hebrew.

———. "Megillat Ta'anit—The Scroll of Fasting." In *The Literature of the Sages,* ed. Shmuel Saffrai, Zeev Saffrai, Joshua Schwartz, and Peter J. Tomso, pt. 2: 339–362. Assen: Van Gorcum; Minneapolis: Fortress Press, 2006.

Nodet, Étienne. *Le Pentateuque de Flavius Josèphe.* Paris: Cerf, 1996.

Nora, Pierre. "Le retour de l'événement." In *Faire de l'histoire,* ed. Jacques Le Goff and Pierre Nora, 1: 210–228. Paris: Gallimard, 1974; repr., 1986.

Noris, Henrico [Enrico], cardinal. *Annus et epochae Syromacedonum in vetustis urbium Syriae nummis præsertim mediceis expositæ: Additis fastis consularibus anonymi omnium optimis: Accesserunt nuper dissertationes de Paschali Lantinorum cyclo annorum LXXXIV, ac Ravennate annorum XCV.* Florence: Typis sereniss. magni Ducis, 1689. Leipzig: Fritsch, 1696.

Noth, Martin. *Amt und Berufung im Alten Testament Rede zum Antritt des Rektorats der Rheinischen Friedrich Wilhelms-Universität zu Bonn am 9. November 1957.* Bonn: Hanstein, 1958.

Novenson, Mathew V. "Why Does R. Akiba Acclaim Bar Kokhba as Messiah?" *Journal for the Study of Judaism* 40, no. 4 (2009): 551–572.

Noy, David [Dov]. *Jewish Inscriptions of Western Europe.* 2 vols. Cambridge: Cambridge University Press, 1993–1995.

Origen. *Against Celsus.* Translated by James Bellamy. 1660. London, [1709?].

———. *The Writings of Origen.* 2 vols. Edinburgh: T. & T. Clark, 1869–1872.

Otzen, Benedikt, Hans Gottlieb, and Knud Jeppesen. *Myths in the Old Testament.* London: SCM Press, 1980.

Panofsky, Erwin. *Studies in Iconology: Humanistic Themes in the Art of the Renaissance.* 1939; repr., New York: Harper & Row, 1972.

Parker, Richard A. "Some Considerations on the Nature of the Fifth Century Jewish Calendar at Elephantine." *Journal of Near Eastern Studies* 14 (1954): 271–274.

Patai, Raphael, ed. *The Messiah Texts.* Detroit: Wayne State University Press, 1979.

Pearson, Brook W. R. "The Book of the Twelve, Aqiba's Messianic Interpretations, and the Refuge Caves of the Second Jewish War." In *The Scrolls and the Scriptures: Qumran Fifty Years After,* ed. Stanley E. Porter and Craig A. Evans, 221–239. Sheffield, UK: Sheffield Academic Press, 1997.

———. "Dry Bones in the Judean Desert: The Messiah of Ephraim, Ezekiel 37 and the Post-Revolutionary Followers of Bar Kokhba." *Journal for the Study of Judaism* 29, no. 2 (May 1998): 192–201.

Pelletier, André. *La lettre d'Aristée à Philocrate.* Paris: Cerf, 1962.

Pesikta de rab-Kahana: Rabbi Kahana's Compilation of Discourses for Sabbaths and Festal Days. Translated by William G. Braude and Israel J. Kapstein. Philadelphia: Jewish Publication Society of America, 1975.

Pesikta de-Rav Kahana: According to an Oxford Manuscript; with Variants from All Known Manuscripts and Genizoth Fragments and Parallel Passages. Edited by Bernard Mandelbaum. 2 vols. New York: Jewish Theological Seminary of America, 1962.

Pesikta rabbati. 845 CE. Prague, 1603; Shklow, Belarus, 1806.

Pesikta rabbati: Midrasch für den Fest-Cyclus und die ausgezeichneten Sabbathe, ed. Markus Friedmann. Vienna, 1880; Tel Aviv: n.p., 1963.

Pesiqta rabbati: A Synoptic Edition of Pesiqta rabbati Based upon All Extant Manuscripts and the Editio Princeps. Edited by Rivka Ulmer. 3 vols. Vols. 1 and 2, Atlanta: Scholars Press, 1997–1999; vol. 3, Lanham, MD: University Press of America, 2002.

Philo of Alexandria. *On the Creation of the Cosmos According to Moses.* Leiden: Brill, 2001.

———. *Philonis Alexandrini opera quae supersunt.* 7 vols. Edited by L. Cohn and P. Wendland. Berlin: G. Reimer, 1896–1930.

———. *The Works of Philo.* Loeb Classical Library. 12 vols. Vols. 1–10 translated and edited by Francis H. Colson and George Herbert Whitaker; vols. 10–12 translated and edited by Ralph Marcus. Cambridge, MA: Harvard University Press; London: William Heinemann, 1929–1953.

———. *The Works of Philo: Complete and Unabridged.* Translated by Charles D. Yonge. Peabody, MA: Hendrickson, 1995.

Photius, Saint, patriarch of Constantinople. *Bibliotheca.* Edited by Immanuel Becker. 2 vols. Berlin, 1824.

———. *The Bibliotheca: A Selection.* Edited by Nigel Guy Wilson. London: Duckworth, 1994.

———. *Bibliothèque.* Edited by René Henry. 9 vols. Paris: Les Belles Lettres, 1959–1991.

———. *The Library of Photius.* Edited by John Henry Freese. London: Society for Promoting Christian Knowledge; New York: Macmillan, 1920.

Pietri, Charles. "Le temps de la semaine à Rome et dans l'Italie." In *Le temps chrétien de la fin de l'Antiquité au Moyen âge, IIIe–XIIIe siècles: [Colloque,] Paris, 9–12 mars 1981,* 63–97. Paris: Éditions du CNRS, 1984.

Pines, Shlomo. *Nouvelles études sur Awhad al-Zamân Abu-l-Barakât al-Baghdâdî* Paris: Durlacher, 1955.

———. "Les sources philosophiques du Guide des perplexes." In *La liberté de philosopher de Maïmonide à Spinoza.* Translated by Rémi Brague. Paris: Desclée de Brouwer, 1997.

———. "Spinoza's 'Tractatus Theologico-Politicus,' Maimonides and Kant." In *Further Studies in Philosophy,* ed. Ora Segal, 3–54. Scripta Hierosolymitana 20. Jerusalem: Magnes Press, 1968.

————. *Studies in Abu'l-Barakāt Al-Baghdādī: Physics and Metaphysics.* Vol. 1 of *The Collected Works of Shlomo Pines.* Jerusalem: Magnes Press; Leiden: Brill, 1979.

————. *Studies in Arabic Versions of Greek Texts and in Mediaeval Science.* Vol. 2 of *The Collected Works of Shlomo Pines.* Jerusalem: Magnes Press; Leiden: Brill, 1986.

Plato. *Timaeus and Critias.* Translated by Robin Waterfield. Oxford: Oxford University Press, 2008.

Plotinus. *The Six Enneads.* Translated by Stephen Mackenna. Chicago: Encyclopaedia Britannica, 1952.

Poliakov, Léon. *Les Samaritains.* Paris: Seuil, 1991.

Pomian, Krzysztof. *L'ordre du temps.* Paris: Gallimard, 1984.

Porphyry. *Against the Christians.* Translated and with notes by Robert M. Berchman. Studies in Platonism, Neoplatonism, and the Platonic Tradition 1. Leiden: Brill, 2005.

Porten, Bezalel. "The Calendar of Aramaic Texts from Achaemenid and Ptolemaic Egypt." In *Irano-Judaica,* ed. Shaul Shaked and Amnon Netzer, 2: 13–32. Jerusalem: Ben-Zvi Institute, 1990.

————. "The Elephantine Jewish Community: Studies in the Life and Society of an Ancient Military Colony." PhD diss., University of Michigan, Ann Arbor, 1965.

Porten, Bezalel, et al. *The Elephantine Papyri in English: Three Millennia of Cross-Cultural Continuity and Change.* Leiden: Brill, 1996.

Porter, Stanley E., and Craig A. Evans, eds. *The Scrolls and the Scriptures: Qumran Fifty Years After. Journal for the Study of the Pseudepigrapha,* suppl. ser., 26. Roehampton Institute London papers 3. Sheffield, UK: Sheffield Academic Press, 1997.

Porton, Gary G. "Diversity in Postbiblical Judaism." In Kraft and Nickelsburg, eds., *Early Judaism and Its Modern Interpreters,* 57–80.

Preuss, Eduard. *Die Zeitrechnung der Septuaginta vor dem vierten Jahr Salomo's.* Berlin: L. Dehmigke, 1859.

Prigogine, Ilya, and Isabelle Stengers. *The End of Certainty: Time, Chaos, and the New Laws of Nature.* New York: Free Press, 1997. Originally published as *La fin des certitudes: Temps, chaos et les lois de la nature* (Paris: O. Jacob, 1995).

————. *Entre le temps et l'éternité.* Paris: Fayard, 1988.

Puech, Émile. "L'acte de vente d'une maison à Kafar-Bébayu en 135 de notre ère." *Revue de Qumran* 34, no. 9 (July 1977): 213–221.

Rabin, Chaim. "The Translation Process and the Character of the Septuagint." *Textus* 6 (1968): 1–26.

Rajak, Tessa. *The Jewish Dialogue with Greece and Rome: Studies in Cultural and Social Interaction.* Leiden: Brill, 2002.

————. *Josephus: The Historian and His Society.* London: Duckworth, 1983; 2nd ed., 2002.

————. "Justus of Tiberius." *Classical Quarterly* 23 (1973): 345–368.

————. *Translation and Survival: The Greek Bible of the Ancient Jewish Diaspora.* Oxford: Oxford University Press, 2009.

Rapoport, Solomon Yehudah [SHiR]. *Sefer 'Erech milin.* Vol. 1. Prague: Moseh ha-Lewi Landau, 1852; repr., Warsaw: Ha-sefirah, 1914.

————. "Toledot rabbenu Nathan ish romi ba'al he'Arukh vekorot sefero." In *Bikkurei ha-'ittim* 10 (1829); 11 (1830); repr. in 2 vols., Warsaw: Ha-sefirah, 1943.

————. "Über die Chroniken oder Erinnerungstaflen in den israelitischen Kalendern." In *Kalender und Jahrbuch für Israeliten auf das Jahr 5605*, 247–254. Vienna, 1844–1845.

Rapoport-Albert, Ada, ed. *Essays in Jewish Historiography: History and Theory.* Studies in the Philosophy of History, suppl. 27. Middletown, CT: Wesleyan University Press, 1988.

Rapoport-Albert, Ada, and Steven Zipperstein, eds. *Jewish History: Essays in Honour of Chimen Abramsky.* London: Peter Halban, 1988.

Rappaport, Uriel. "The Book of Daniel." In *Rashi 1040–1990: Hommage à Ephraim E. Urbach*, ed. G. Sed-Rajna, 71–79. Paris: Cerf, 1993.

Ratner, Dov Baer. *Mavo la-Seder 'olam.* Vilna [Vilnius]: Romm, 1894.

————. *Midrash Seder 'olam.* Vilna [Vilnius], 1897. Edited by Shemuel Mirski. Jerusalem, 1966; repr., 1988.

Reichelberg, Ruth. *L'aventure prophétique: Jonas menteur de vérité.* Paris: Albin Michel, 1995.

Reinach, Théodore, ed. *Textes d'auteurs grecs et romains relatifs au Judaïsme.* Paris: Ernest Leroux, 1895.

Reiner, Elchanan, ed. *Maharal, Overtures: Biography, Doctrine, Influence.* Jerusalem: Zalman Shazar Center for History, 2015. In Hebrew and English.

Reznikoff, L. A. "Jewish Calendar Calculations." *Scripta Mathematica* 9 (1943): 191–195, 274–277.

Richard, Edward Graham. *Mapping Time: The Calendar and Its History.* Oxford: Oxford University Press, 1998.

Ricoeur, Paul. "Événement et sens." In *L'événement en perspective*, ed. Jean-Luc Petit, 41–56. Raisons pratiques 2. Paris: Éditions de l'École des hautes études en sciences sociales, 1991.

————. *Temps et récit.* 3 vols. Paris: Seuil, 1983–1985; repr., 1991. Translated by Kathleen MacLaughlin and David Pellauer as *Time and Narrative* (Chicago: University of Chicago Press, 1984–1988).

Ricoeur, Paul, and André LaCocque. *Penser la Bible.* Paris: Seuil, 1998.

Riegler, Michael. "Colophons of Medieval Hebrew Manuscripts as Historical Sources." PhD diss., Hebrew University of Jerusalem, 1995. In Hebrew.

Ringgren, Helmer. *Israelitische Religion.* Stuttgart: W. Kohlhammer, 1963. Translated by David E. Green as *Israelite Religion.* Philadelphia: Fortress Press, 1966.

Roberts, Bleddyn Jones. *The Old Testament Text and Versions: The Hebrew Text in Transmission and the History of the Ancient Versions.* Cardiff: University of Wales Press, 1951.

Rosenblatt, Samuel. *The Interpretation of the Bible in the Mishnah.* Baltimore: Johns Hopkins University Press, 1935.

Rosenzweig, Franz. *Der Stern der Erlösung.* Frankfurt am Main: J. Kauffmann, 1921. Translated by Barbara E. Galli as *The Star of Redemption* (Madison: University of Wisconsin Press, 2005).

Rossi, Azariah ben Moses dei. *Selected Chapters from "Sefer Me'or 'einayim" and "Matsref la-Kessef."* Edited by Robert (Reuven) Bonfil. Jerusalem: Mosad Bialik, 1991. In Hebrew.

———. *Me'or 'einayim.* Mantua, 1573. Translated by Joanna Weinberg as *The Light of the Eyes* (New Haven, CT: Yale University Press, 2001).

———. *Sefer Matsref la-kesef: Hamityahes la-hibur Me'or 'enayim.* Edited by Herschell E. Filipowski, based on Oxford MS 1576, Edinburgh, 1854; repr., Vilna [Vilnius]: Y. A. Ben-Ya'akov, 1865. Edited by David Cassel, Vilna, 1864–1866.

Rossi, Paolo. *The Dark Abyss of Time: The History of the Earth and the History of Nations from Hooke to Vico.* Translated by Lydia G. Cochrane. Chicago: University of Chicago Press, 1984.

Rössler, Dietrich. *Gesetz und Geschichte: Untersuchungen zur Theologie der jüdischen Apokalyptik und der pharisaischen Orthodoxie.* Wissenschaftliche Untersuchungen zum Neuen Testament 3. Neukirchen: Neukirchener Verlag, 1962.

Rowley, Harold Henry. "The Chronological Order of Ezra and Nehemiah." In *The Servant of the Lord and Other Essays on the Old Testament.* 2nd rev. ed. Oxford: B. Blackwell, 1965.

Rubin, Nissan. "Historical Time and Liminal Time: A Chapter in Rabbinic Historiosophy." *Jewish History* 2, no. 2 (1987): 7– 22. In Hebrew.

Rubin, Nissan, and Admiel Kosman. "The Clothing of the Primordial Adam as a Symbol of Apocalyptic Time in the Midrashic Sources." *Harvard Theological Review* 90, no. 2 (1997): 155–174.

Rubio, Mercedes. "The First Hebrew Encyclopedia of Science: Abraham bar Hiyya's *Yesodei ha-Tevunah u-Migdal ha-Emunah.*" In *The Medieval Hebrew Encyclopedias of Science and Philosophy: Proceedings of the Bar-Ilan University Conference*, ed. Steven Harvey, 140–153. Amsterdam Studies in Jewish Thought 7. Dordrecht: Kluwer Academic, 2000.

Rühl, Franz. "Der Ursprung der jüdischen Weltära." *Deutsche Zeitschrift für Geschichtswissenschaft*, n.s., 2 (1898): 185–203.

Rustow, Marina, and Sacha Stern. "The Jewish Calendar Controversy of 921–22: Reconstructing the Manuscripts and Their Transmission History." In Stern and Burnett, eds., *Time, Astronomy, and Calendars in the Jewish Tradition*, 79–96.

Sa'adiah ben Yosef Ga'on. *The Book of Beliefs and Opinions.* Translated by Samuel Rosenblatt. Yale Judaica Series. New Haven, CT: Yale University Press, 1948.

———. *Sefer emunoth ve-de'oth* [The book of beliefs and opinions]. Translated from the Arabic by Judah ibn Tibbon. 1186; repr., Constantinople, 1562. In Hebrew.

———. *Sefer emunot ve-de'ot.* Jerusalem: Hotsa'at Makor, 1972.

Sacks, Steven Daniel. *Midrash and Multiplicity: Pirke de-Rabbi Eliezer and the Renewal of Rabbinic Interpretive Culture*. Berlin: Walter de Gruyter, 2009.

Saldarini, Anthony J. "Apocalyptic and Rabbinic Literature." *Catholic Biblical Quarterly* 37 (1975): 348–358.

———. "Johanan ben Zakkai's Escape from Jerusalem: Origin and Development of a Rabbinic Story." *Journal for the Study of Judaism* 6 (1975): 189–204.

———. *Pharisees, Scribes and Sadducees in Palestinian Society*. Grand Rapids, MI: Eerdmans, 2001.

———. "The Uses of Apocalyptic in the *Mishnah* and the Tosefta." *Catholic Biblical Quarterly* 39 (1977): 396–409.

Samaritan Documents: Relating to Their History, Religion, and Life. Translated and edited by John Bowman. Pittsburgh Original Texts and Translations Series 2. Pittsburgh: Pickwick Press, 1977.

Sander, Nathaniel Philippe, and Isaac Léon Trenel. *Dictionnaire hébreu-français*. Paris: Bureau des Archives israélites, 1859; repr., Geneva: Slatkine, 1982.

Sanders, James A. *The Psalm Scroll from Qumran Cave 11 (11QPs)*. Discoveries in the Judaean Desert of Jordan 4. Oxford: Clarendon Press, 1965.

Sanhedrin Translated into English with Notes, Glossary and Indices. Chapters 1–6, trans. Jacob Shachter; chapters 7–9, trans. H. Freedman. Edited by I. Epstein. London: Soncino Press, 1935.

Saphir, Jacob. *Even Sapir*. 2 vols. Lyck [Ełk, Poland]: Mekitsei Nirdamim, 1866–1874; Mainz, 1874; repr., Jerusalem: R. Kohen, 1998.

Saulnier, Christiane, and Charles Perrot. *Histoire d'Israël: De la conquête d'Alexandre à la destruction du Temple*. Paris: Cerf, 1985.

Saulnier, Stéphane. *Calendrical Variations in Second Temple Judaism: New Perspectives on the "Date of the Last Supper" Debate*. Leiden: Brill, 2012.

Scaliger, Joseph Justus. *Opus de emendatione temporum*. 1583; repr., Geneva, 1629.

Schäfer, Peter. "Diversity and Interaction: Messiahs in Early Judaism." In Schäfer and Cohen, eds., *Toward the Millennium*, 15–36.

———. *History of the Jews in Antiquity: The Jews of Palestine from Alexander the Great to the Arab Conquest*. London: Routledge, 1995.

———. *The History of the Jews in the Greco-Roman World*. London: Routledge, 2003.

Schäfer, Peter, and Mark R. Cohen, eds. *Toward the Millennium: Messianic Expectations from the Bible to Waco*. Leiden: Brill, 1998.

Schalit, Abraham. "Demetrius." In *Encyclopaedia Judaica*, ed. Roth et al., 5: 1490–1491.

Schechter, Solomon. *Rabbi Nachman Krochmal and the "Perplexities of the Time."* London: Jewish Chronicle Office, 1887.

———, trans. and ed. *Documents of Jewish Sectaries*. Vol. 1: *Fragments of a Zadokite Work*. Cambridge: Cambridge University Press, 1910; repr., 1970.

Schiffman, Lawrence H. "Jewish Sectarianism in Second Temple Time." In *Great Schisms in Jewish History*, ed. Raphael Jospe and Stanley M. Wagner, 1–46. Denver: Center for Judaic Studies, University of Denver; New York: Ktav, 1981.

Schmidt, Francis. "L'étranger, le Temple et la Loi dans le judaïsme ancien." *Annales HSS* 5 (1996): 939–953.

———. *How the Temple Thinks: Identity and Social Cohesian in Ancient Judaism*. Sheffield, UK: Sheffield Academic Press, 2001.

———. *La pensée du Temple: De Jerusalem à Qoumrân*. Paris: Seuil, 1994.

Scholem, Gershom. "Gematria." In *Encyclopaedia Judaica*, ed. Roth et al., 7: 369–374.

———. *The Messianic Idea in Judaism: And Other Essays on Jewish Spirituality*. New York: Schocken Books, 1971.

———. *Sabbatai Sevi: The Mystical Messiah, 1626–1676*. Translated by R. J. Zwi Werblowsky. Bollingen Series 18. Princeton, NJ: Princeton University Press, 1973.

Schrader, Eberhard. *Die Keilinschriften und das Alte Testament*. 3rd ed. Revised by Heinrich Zimmern and Hugo Winckler. Berlin: Reuther & Reichard, 1903.

Schreckenberg, Heinz. *Die Flavius-Josephus-Tradition in Antike und Mittelalter*. Arbeiten zur Literatur und Geschichte des hellenistischen Judentums 5. Leiden: Brill, 1972.

———. *Rezeptionsgeschichte und textkritische Untersuchungen zu Flavius Josephus*. Arbeiten zur Literatur und Geschichte des hellenistischen Judentums 10. Leiden: Brill, 1977.

Schürer, Emil. *Geschichte des jüdischen Volkes im Zeitalter Jesu Christi*. Leipzig: J. C. Hinrichs, 1886–1890; 4th ed., 1901–1909. Translated by T. A. Burkill et al. as *The History of the Jewish People in the Age of Jesus Christ (175 B.C.–A.D. 135)*, rev. and ed. Geza Vermes and Fergus Millar (3 vols.; Edinburgh: T. & T. Clark, 1973–1987).

———. "Die siebentägige Woche im Gebrauche der christlichen Kirche der ersten Jahrhunderte." *Zeitschriften für die Neutestamentliche Wissenschaft* 6 (1905): 1–66.

Schwab, Moïse. *Rapport sur les inscriptions hébraïques de la France*. Paris: Imprimerie nationale, 1904.

Schwartz, Daniel R. "On Abraham Schalit, Herod, Josephus, the Holocaust, Horst R. Moehring and the Study of Ancient Jewish History." *Jewish History* 2, no. 2 (1987): 7–28.

———. *Studies in the Jewish Background of Christianity*. Tübingen: Mohr Siebeck, 1992.

Schwartz, Seth. *The Ancient Jews from Alexander to Muhammad*. Cambridge: Cambridge University Press, 2014.

Seder ʿolam: Critical Edition, Commentary and Introduction. Edited by Chaim Milikowsky. 2 vols. Jerusalem: Yad ben Zvi, 2013. In Hebrew.

Seder ʿolam: The Rabbinic View of Biblical Chronology. Translated and with commentary by Heinrich W. Guggenheimer. Northvale, NJ: Jason Aronson, 1998.

Seder ʿolam rabbah me-ha-tanna Yose ben Ḥalafta. Vilna [Vilnius]: Bi-defus Menaḥem Man ve-R. Śimḥah Zimel, 1845.

Seder ʿolam rabbah ha-shalem: Le-ha-tana rabbi Yose ben rabbi Halafta; Divrei ha-

yamim me-yemot adam rishon ad ha-bayit ha-sheni. Edited by Yossef Menahem Weinstock. Jerusalem: Hotsa'at Metivta Torat Ḥesed, 1956; repr., Bnei Brak: Mishor, 1990.

Seder 'olam rabbah le-ha-tana rabbi Yose ben rabbi Halafta, im bi'ur maran Eliyahu mi-Vilna. Shklov [Škłoŭ, Belarus], 1801; repr., Jerusalem, 1971.

Seder 'olam rabbah ve-seder 'olam zutta u-megillat ta'anit, ve-sefer ha-kabbalah le-ha-RaBaD, zal've-divrei malkei (Yisrael be) bayyit sheni, ve-zikhron divrei romiyim [*Seder olam rabbah* and *Seder olam zutta, megillat taanit, sefer ha kabbalah* from the RaBaD, acts of the kings of Israel during the Second Temple period, and some remembering from the Romans]. Mantua, 1514; Amsterdam, 1710–1711; with additions, Jerusalem: Ha-mossad le 'idud ha-torah, 1997.

Segal, Judah Benzion. "Intercalation and the Hebrew Calendar." *Vetus Testamentum* 7 (1957): 250–307.

The Seventh Book of the Stromateis: Proceedings of the Colloquium on Clement of Alexandria (Olomouc [Czech Republic], *October 21–23, 2010.* Edited by Matyáš Havrda, Vít Hušek, and Jana Plátová. Leiden: Brill, 2012.

Sharf, Andrew. *The Universe of Shabbetai Donnolo.* Warminster, UK: Aris & Phillips, 1976.

Shavit, Yaacov, and Mordechai Eran. *The Hebrew Bible Reborn: From Holy Scripture to the Book of Books. A History of Biblical Culture and the Battles over the Bible in Modern Judaism.* Translated from the Hebrew by Chaya Naor. Studia Judaica 38. Berlin: Walter de Gruyter, 2007.

Shazar, Zalman [Rubashov]. "Sofero shel Mashiah, le-toledotiv shel Shmuel Fano, mazkiro shel Shabbetai Tsvi" [The Messiah scribe]. *Ha-shiloah* 29 (1913): 36–47; repr., Jerusalem: Mosad Bialik, 1970.

Shear, Adam. *The Kuzari and the Shaping of Jewish Identity 1167–1900.* Cambridge: Cambridge University Press, 2008.

Shilo, Shmuel. *Dina de-malkhuta dina* [The law of the state is law]. Jerusalem: Academic Press, 1974. In Hebrew.

Shmueli, Efraim. *Seven Jewish Cultures: A Reinterpretation of Jewish History and Thought.* Translated by Gila Shmueli. Cambridge: Cambridge University Press, 1990.

Shulvass, Moshe Avigdor. "Ha-yedi'a be-historia ve-ha-sifrut ha-historit bi-tehum ha-tarbut ha-ashkenazit bi-yemei ha-beinayim." In *Sefer ha-yovel lĕ-rabbi Ḥanokh Albeck, mugash 'al yĕdé talmiday yĕdiday u-moḳiray li-mĕlot lo shiv'im shanah,* 465–495. Jerusalem: Mosad Harav Kook, 1963.

Sibony, Moïse. *Le jour dans le judaïsme: Son histoire et ses moments significatifs.* Tours: Moïse Sibony and Centre national de la recherche scientifique, 1986.

Siderski, Daniel. "L'origine de l'ère juive de la création du monde." *Journal asiatique* 227 (1935): 325–329.

Siegel, Jonathan Paul. "The Employment of Palaeo-Hebrew Characters for the Divine Names at Qumran in the Light of Tannaitic Sources." *Hebrew Union College Annual* 42 (1971): 159–172.

Silver, Abba Hillel. *A History of Messianic Speculation in Israel: From the First to the Seventeenth Centuries.* New York: Macmillan, 1927.

Silverstone, Alec Eli. *Aquila and Onkelos.* Manchester, UK: Manchester University Press, 1931; repr., 1970.

Simhah ben Samuel of Vitry. *Mahzor Vitry le-rabbenu Simha: Nach der Handschrift im British Museum.* Edited by Simon Hurwitz. Nuremberg: Bulka, 1889; repr., Jerusalem, 1988. In Hebrew.

Simon, Marcel, and André Benoît. *Le judaïsme et le christianisme antique, d'Antiochus Épiphane à Constantin.* Paris: Presses universitaires de France, 1968; repr., 1994.

Simon, Uriel. "Time and Space in Biblical Thinking." PhD diss., Hebrew University of Jerusalem, 1961. In Hebrew.

Singer, Rabbi Simeon. *The Authorised Daily Prayer Book of the United Hebrew Congregations of the British Empire.* London: Eyre & Spottiswoode, 1890.

Sirat, Colette. "Les lettres hébraïques: Leur existence idéale et matérielle." In *Perspectives on Jewish Thought and Mysticism,* ed. Alfred L. Ivry, Elliot R. Wolfson, and Allan Arkush, 237–256. Amsterdam: Harwood Academic, 1998.

Skehan, Patrick William. "The Biblical Scrolls from Qumran and the Text of the Old Testament." *Biblical Archeologist* 28, no. 3 (1965): 87–100.

Smith, Mark Stratton. "The Near Eastern Background of Solar Language for Yahweh." *Journal of Biblical Literature* 109, no. 1 (1990): 29–39.

Smith, Morton. "Helios in Palestine." *Erets Yisrael: Ha-hevra le-haqirat Erets Yisrael ve-ʿatikotea* [Eretz-Israel: Archaeological, historical and geographical studies] 16 (1982): 199–214.

Sperber, Manès. *Et le buisson devint cendre: Trilogie romanesque.* Paris: Odile Jacob, 1990; repr., 2008. Translated by Constantine Fitzgibbon as *Like a Tear in the Ocean: A Trilogy* (3 vols; New York: Holmes & Meier, 1987–1988).

Spinoza. *Theological-Political Treatise.* Edited by Jonathan Israel. Cambridge: Cambridge University Press, 2007.

Stambaugh, Joan. "Existential Time in Kierkegaard and Heidegger." In Balslev and Mohanty, *Religion and Time,* 46–60.

Steensgaard, P. "Time in Judaism." In Balslev and Mohanty, *Religion and Time,* 63–108.

Steinschneider, Moritz. "Christiche Hebraisten." *Zeitschrift für die hebraische Bibliographie* 2 (1897): 50–54.

———. "Die Encyklopädie des Abraham bar Chijja." In *Hebräische Bibliographie (Ha-mazkir)* 7: 84–95. Berlin: A. Asher, 1864.

———. *Jewish Literature from the Eighth to the Eighteenth Century, with an Introduction on Talmud and Midrash.* Translated from the German by William Spottiswoode. London: Longman, Brown, Green, Longmans, & Roberts, 1857; repr., New York: Hermon Press, 1970.

Steinzalz, Adin. *Jerusalem.* New York: Institute for Talmudic Publications, 1989.

Stern, Menahem. *Greek and Latin Authors on Jews and Judaism.* 3 vols. Jerusalem: Israel Academy of Sciences and Humanities, 1974.

Stern, Menahem, and Uriel Rapaport. *The History of Eretz Israel: The Hellenistic Period and the Hasmonean State.* Vol. 3. Jerusalem: Keter, 1981. In Hebrew.

Stern, Nathan. "The Jewish Historico-Critical School of the Nineteenth Century." PhD diss., Columbia University, 1901; repr., New York: Arno Press, 1973.

Stern, Sacha. *Calendar and Community: A History of the Jewish Calendar, 2nd Century BCE to 10th Century CE.* Oxford: Oxford University Press, 2001.

———. "Fictitious Calendars: Early Rabbinic Notions of Time, Astronomy and Reality." *Jewish Quarterly Review* 88, nos. 1–2 (July–October 1996): 103–129.

———. *Time and Process in Ancient Judaism.* Portland, OR: Littman Library of Jewish Civilization, 2003.

Stern, Sacha, and Charles Burnett, eds. *Time, Astronomy, and Calendars in the Jewish Tradition.* Leiden: Brill, 2013.

Strack, Hermann Leberecht. *Einleitung in Talmud und Midrasch.* Leipzig: J. C. Hinrichs, 1900.

———. *Introduction to the Talmud and Midrash.* Philadelphia: Jewish Publication Society of America, 1931.

Strack, Hermann Leberecht, and Günther Stemberger. *Introduction to the Talmud and Midrash.* Translated by M. Bockmuehl. Edinburgh: T. & T. Clark, 1991.

Strauss, Leo. *Leo Strauss on Maimonides: The Complete Writings.* Chicago: University of Chicago Press, 2013.

Strugnell, John. "The Angelic Liturgy at Qumran: 4Q Serek Shirot 'Olat Hassabbat." In International Organization of Old Testament Scholars, *Congress Volume: Oxford, 1959,* 318–345. Vetus Testamentum Supplementae 7. Leiden: Brill, 1960.

Sukenik, Eleazar Lipa. "Matsevot yehudiot me-Tsoar." *Kedem* 2 (1945): 83–88.

Swain, Joseph Ward. "The Theory of the Four Monarchies: Opposition History under the Roman Empire." *Classical Philology* 35 (1940): 1–21.

Tacitus. *The Histories.* Translated by Clifford Herschel Moore. *The Annals.* Translated by John Jackson. 4 vols. London: W. Heinemann; New York: G. P. Putnam's Sons, 1925–1937.

Talmon, Shemaryahu. "Divergence in Calendar-Reckoning in Ephraim and Judah." *Vetus Testamentum* 8 (1958): 48–74.

———. *King, Cult and Calendar in Ancient Israel.* Jerusalem: Magnes Press, 1986.

Tamar, David. "Ha-tsipiya be-italia li-shnat, 1575" [Messianic Expectations in Italy, 1575]. *Sefunot* 2 (1958): 61–88.

———. *Mehkarim be-toledot ha-yehudim be-erets yisrael u-be-italia* [Studies in the History of the Jewish People in Eretz Israel and in Italy]. Jerusalem: Rubin Mass, 1970.

Tanakh: A New Translation of the Holy Scriptures According to the Traditional Hebrew text: Torah, Nevi'im, Kethuvim. Philadelphia: Jewish Publication Society of America, 1985.

Tanna Devei Eliyahu [The lore of the School of Elijah]. Translated by William Gershon, Zev Braude, and Israel J. Kapstein. Philadelphia: Jewish Publication Society of America, 1981.

Tcherikover, Victor [Avigdor]. *Hellenistic Civilization and the Jews.* Translated by S. Applebaum. Philadelphia: Jewish Publication Society of America, 1966.

———. "The Ideology of the Letter of Aristeas." *Harvard Theological Review* 51 (1958): 59–85.

———. "Jewish Apologetic Literature Reconsidered." *Eos* 48, no. 3 (1956): 169–193.

———. "The Third Book of the Maccabees as a Historical Source of Augustus' Time." *Scripta Hierosolymitana* 7 (1961): 1–26.

Theological Dictionary of the Old Testament. Edited by G. Johannes Botterweck and Helmer Ringgren. Translated by John T. Willis et al. Grand Rapids, MI: Eerdmans, 1974–2006.

Theological Lexicon of the Old Testament. Edited by Ernst Jenni and Claus Westermann. Translated by Mark E. Biddle. 3 vols. Peabody, MA: Hendrickson, 1997.

Thompson, Thomas L. *The Historicity of the Patriarchal Narratives: The Quest for the Historical Abraham.* Zeitschrift für die alttestmentamentliche Wissenschaft 133. Berlin: Walter de Gruyter, 1974; repr., Harrisburg, PA: Trinity Press International, 2002.

Tigay, Jeffrey H. "Notes on the Development of the Jewish Week." *Erets Yisrael* 14 (1978): 111–121.

Tobiah ben Eliezer. *Midrash Leḳaḥ Ṭov: ʿal hamisha humshei Tora = Lekach-tob.* Venice, 1746. Edited by Solomon Buber. Vilna [Vilnius]: Romm, 1884.

———. *Perush Lekah tov ʿal Megillat Shir ha-shirim.* Edited by Albert Willis Greenup. London, 1909. In Hebrew.

Torat Kohanim (Sifra): Seder Eliyahu rabbah ve-zutta. Jerusalem: Makor, 1972.

Touati, Charles. *La pensée philosophique et théologique de Gersonide.* Paris: Gallimard, 1992.

Tov, Emmanuel. "Jewish Greek Scripture." In Kraft and Nickelsburg, eds., *Early Judaism and Its Modern Interpreters,* 221–238.

———. *Textual Criticism of the Hebrew Bible.* Minneapolis: Fortress Press, 1992.

Töyrylä, Hannu. *Abraham Bar Hiyya on Time, History, Exile and Redemption: An Anaylsis of Megillat ha-Megalleh.* Leiden: Brill, 2014.

Trigano, Shmuel, ed. *La société juive à travers l'histoire.* 4 vols. Paris: Fayard, 1992.

Twersky, Isadore. *Introduction to the Code of Maimonides (Mishneh Torah).* New Haven, CT: Yale University Press, 1980.

Tykocinski, Chaim. "Bustenai rosh ha-golah" [Bustanay the exilarch]. *Dvir* 1 (1923): 145–179.

Urbach, Ephraim E. "Halakhah and History." In *Jews, Greeks and Christians: Religious Cultures in Late Antiquity; Essays in Honor of W. D. Davies,* ed. Robert G. Hamerton-Kelly and Robin Jerome Scroggs, 112–128. Leiden: Brill, 1976.

———. "Li-sheelat leshono u-mekoretiv shel Sefer ʿSeder Eliahu.ʾ" *Leshonenu* 21 (1957): 183–197.

———. *The Sages: Their Concepts and Beliefs.* Translated by Israel Abrahams. 2 vols. Jerusalem: Magnes Press, 1975; repr., 1987.

———. "When Did Prophecy Cease?" *Tarbiz* 17 (1946): 1–11.

Usque, Samuel. *Consolaçam ás tribulaçoens de Israel.* Ferrara, 1553. Translated by
    Martin A. Cohen as *Samuel Usque's Consolation for the Tribulations of Israel*
    (Philadelphia: Jewish Publication Society of America, 1965; repr., 1977).
Ussher, James. *Annales Veteris and Novi Testamenti.* London, 1654. Translated as
    *The annals of the world: deduced from the origin of time, and continued to the
    beginning of the Emperour Vespasians reign, and the totall destruction and aboli-
    tion of the temple and common-wealth of the Jews: containing the historie of the
    Old and New Testament, with that of the Macchabees, also the most memorable
    affairs of Asia and Egypt, and the rise of the empire of the Roman Caesars under
    C. Julius, and Octavianus: collected from all history, as well sacred, as prophane,
    and methodically digested* (London, 1658).
———. *Chronologia Sacra.* Oxford: W. Hall, 1660.
Valensi, Lucette. *Les fables de la mémoire: La glorieuse bataille des trois rois.* Paris:
    Seuil, 1992.
van der Horst, Pieter W. *Philo's Flaccus: The First Pogrom.* Leiden: Brill, 2003.
van der Ploeg, Johanes Petrus Maria. "Recente Pesittà-Studies (sind 1927)." *Jaar-
    bericht Ex Oriente Lux* 10, no. 3 (1944–1948): 392–399.
van der Woude, Adam S., ed. *The Book of Daniel in the Light of New Findings.*
    Leuven: Leuven University Press, 1993.
van Oort, Johannes. *Jerusalem and Babylon: A Study of Augustine's City of God
    and the Sources of His Doctrine of the Two Cities.* Leiden: Brill, 1991; repr. 2013.
VanderKam, James C. *Calendars in the Dead Sea Scrolls: Measuring Time.* Lon-
    don: Routledge, 1998.
———. *The Dead Sea Scrolls Today.* Grand Rapids, MI: Eerdmans, 1994.
———. *Enoch and the Growth of an Apocalyptic Tradition.* Catholic Biblical Quar-
    terly Monograph Series 16. Washington, DC: Catholic Biblical Association of
    America, 1984.
———. "The Origin, Character and Early History of the 364-Day Calendar: A
    Reassessment of Jaubert's Hypotheses." *Catholic Biblical Quarterly* 41 (1979):
    390–411.
———. *Textual and Historical Studies in the Book of Jubilees.* Missoula, MT: Scholars
    Press, 1977.
———, ed. and trans. *The Book of Jubilees.* 2 vols. English and Ethiopic. Corpus
    scriptorum Christianorum orientalium 510–511; Scriptores Aethiopici 87–88.
    Louvain: E. Peeters, 1989.
VanderKam, James C., and William Adler, eds. *The Jewish Apocalyptic Heritage in
    Early Christianity.* Compendia rerum iudaicarum ad Novum Testamentum 4.
    Assen: Van Gorcum; Minneapolis: Fortress Press, 1996.
Veltri, Giuseppe. "Maharal Against Azariah de' Rossi: The Other Side of Skepti-
    cism." In *Rabbinic Theology and Jewish Intellectual History,* ed. Meir Seidler,
    65–76. London: Routledge, 2013.
———. *Renaissance Philosophy in Jewish Garb: Foundations and Challenges in Ju-
    daism on the Eve of Modernity.* Leiden: Brill, 2009.

Veyne, Paul. *Comment on écrit l'histoire.* Paris: Seuil, 1979. Translated by Mina Moore-Rinvolucri as *Writing History: Essay on Epistemology* (Middletown, CT: Wesleyan University Press, 1984).

Vidal-Naquet, Pierre. "Du bon usage de la trahison." Preface to Flavius Josephus, *La guerre des Juifs,* trans. Pierre Savinel, 9–115. Paris: Éditions de Minuit, 1977.

———. *Le chasseur noir: Formes de pensées et formes de sociétés dans le monde grec.* Paris: Maspero, 1981. Translated by Andrew Szegedy-Maszak as *The Black Hunter: Forms of Thought and Forms of Society in the Greek World* (Baltimore: Johns Hopkins University Press, 1986).

———. "Flavius Josèphe et les prophètes." In *Histoire et conscience historique dans les civilisations du Proche Orient ancien: Actes du Colloque de Cartigny 1986,* ed. Albert de Pury, 11–20. Les Cahiers du CEPOA. Louvain: Peeters, 1989. Translated by David Ames Curtis as "Flavius Josephus and the Prophets," in Vidal-Naquet, *The Jews: History, Memory, and the Present,* 1: 37–56. New York: Columbia University Press, 1996.

———. *Les Juifs, la mémoire et le présent.* Paris: La Découverte, 1991. Translated by David Ames Curtis as *The Jews: History, Memory, and the Present* (3 vols.; New York: Columbia University Press, 1996).

———. "Temps des dieux, temps des hommes." *Revue de l'histoire des religions* 157 (1960): 55–80.

von Gutschmid, Alfred. *Kleine Schriften.* Edited by Franz Rühl. Vol. 2. Leipzig: Teubner, 1890.

von Orelli, Conrad. *Die hebräischen Synonyma der Zeit und Ewigkeit, genetisch und sprachvergleichend dargestellt.* Leipzig: A. Lorentz, 1871.

von Pauly, August Friedrich, et al. *Paulys Realencyclopädie der classischen Altertumswissenschaft.* Stuttgart: A. Druckenmüller, 1893–1978.

von Rad, Gerhard. *Theologie des Alten Testament.* 2 vols. Munich: Kaiser, 1957, 1960; repr., 1980. Translated by David Muir Gibson Stalker as *Old Testament Theology* (London: Oliver & Boyd, 1962–1965).

von Schelling, Friedrich Wilhelm Joseph. *The Ages of the World.* Translated by Frederick de Wolfe Bolman, Jr. New York: Columbia University Press, 1942.

von Waldow, Hans-Eberhard. "Anlaß und Hintergrund der Verkündigung des Deuterojesaja." Diss., Bonn, 1953.

Wacholder, Ben Zion. "Biblical Chronology in the Hellenistic World Chronicles." *Harvard Theological Review* 61 (1968): 451–481.

———. "The Calendar of Sabbatical Cycles During the Second Temple and the Early Rabbinic Period." *Hebrew Union College Annual* 44 (1973): 153–196.

———. *Eupolemus: A Study of Judaeo-Greek Literature.* Monographs of the Hebrew Union College, 3. Cincinnati: Hebrew Union College–Jewish Institute of Religion, 1974 [i.e., 1975].

———. "Josephus and Nicolaus of Damascus." In *Josephus, the Bible, and History,* ed. Louis H. Feldman and Gohei Hata, 147–172. Leiden: Brill, 1989.

Walzer, Michael, Menachem Lauberbaum, Noam Zohar, and Yair Loberbaum, eds. *The Jewish Political Tradition*. Vol. 1: *Authority*. New Haven, CT: Yale University Press, 2000.

Wartenberg, Ilana. "The Hebrew Calendrical Bookshelf of the Early Twelfth Century: The Case of Abraham Bar Hiyya and Jacob bar Samson." In Stern and Burnett, eds., *Time, Astronomy, and Calendars in the Jewish Tradition*, 97–112.

Weinberg, Joanna. "Where Three Civilizations Meet." In *The Presence of the Historian: Essays in Memory of Arnaldo Momigliano*, ed. Michael P. Steinberg, 13–26. History and Theory: Studies in the Philosophy of History, suppl. 30. Middletown, CT: Wesleyan University Press, 1991.

Wellhausen, Julius. *Die Composition des Hexateuchs und der historischer Bücher des Alten Testaments*. Berlin: G. Reimer, 1899.

———. *Geschichte Israels*. Berlin: G. Reimer, 1878.

———. *Prolegomena zur Geschichte Israels*. Berlin: G. Reimer, 1883. Translated by Allen Menzies and Jonathan Sutherland Black as *Prolegomena to the History of Ancient Israel: With a Reprint of the Article "Israel" from the Encyclopaedia Britannica* (New York: Meridian Library, 1957).

Wilfand, Yael. "Aramaic Tombstones from Zoar and Jewish Conceptions of the Afterlife." *Journal for the Study of Judaism* 40, nos. 4 5 (September 2009): 510–539.

Wilken, Robert Louis. *Judaism and the Early Christian Mind: A Study of Cyril of Alexandria's Exegesis and Theology*. New Haven, CT: Yale University Press, 1971.

Williams, Ann, ed. *Prophecy and Millenarianism: Essays in Honour of Marjorie Reeves*. Harlow, UK: Longman, 1980.

Wilson, William, ed. *The Writings of Clement of Alexandria*. Edinburgh: T. & T. Clark, 1867–1872.

Windisch, Hans. "Der Barnabasbrief." In *Handbuch zum Neuen Testament. Ergänzungsband: Die apostolischen Väter*, 3: 393–395. Tübingen: Mohr Siebeck, 1920.

Wogue, Lazare. *Histoire de la Bible et de l'exégèse biblique jusqu'à nos jours*. Paris: Imprimerie nationale, 1881.

Wohlman, Avital. *Thomas d'Aquin et Maïmonide: Un dialogue exemplaire*. Paris: Cerf, 1988.

Wolfson, Harry Austryn. *Crescas' Critique of Aristotle: Problems of Aristotle's Physics in Jewish and Arabic Philosophy*. Cambridge, MA: Harvard University Press, 1929.

———. *Philo: Foundations of Religious Philosophy in Judaism, Christianity, and Islam*. Cambridge, MA: Harvard University Press, 1947.

Wrathall, Mark A., ed. *The Cambridge Companion to Heidegger's "Being and Time."* Cambridge: Cambridge University Press, 2013.

Xeravits, Géza G., Tobias Niklas, and Isaac Halimi. *Scriptural Authority in Early Judaism and Ancient Christianity*. Berlin: Walter de Gruyter, 2013.

Yassif, Eli. *The Book of Memory That Is: The Chronicles of Jerahme'el. A Critical Edition*. Tel Aviv: Chaim Rosenberg School of Jewish Studies, Tel Aviv University, 2001. In Hebrew.

———. "The Hebrew Narrative Anthology in the Middle Ages." *Prooftexts* 17 (1997): 153–175.

Yerushalmi, Yosef Hayim. *Zakhor: Jewish History and Jewish Memory*. Seattle: University of Washington Press, 1982; repr., 1989.

Yuval, Israel J. "Jewish Messianic Expectations Towards 1240 and Christian Reactions." In Schäfer and Cohen, eds., *Toward the Millennium*, 105–121.

Zacuto, Abraham. *Sefer yuhasin* [*Sefer yuhasin ha-shalem*]. Constantinople, 1566; ed. Herschell Filipowski, Frankfurt am Main: M. A. Vahrmann, 1924; ed. Jacob Emden, Jerusalem: Yerid ha-sefarim, 2004.

Zeitlin, Solomon. *Megillat Ta'anit as a Source for Jewish Chronology and History in the Hellenistic and Roman Periods*. Philadelphia: Dropsie College for Hebrew and Cognate Learning, 1922.

Zeligman, Israel. *The Treasury of Numbers*. New York: Shulsinger, 1942. In Hebrew.

Zerubavel, Eviatar. *Hidden Rhythms: Schedules and Calendars in Social Life*. Chicago: University of Chicago Press, 1981.

———. *The Seven Day Circle: The History and Meaning of the Week*. New York: Macmillan, 1985.

Zevit, Ziony. "Converging Lines of Evidence Bearing on the Date of P." *Zeitschrift für die Altestamententliche Wissenschaft* 94 (1982): 481–511.

Zuckermann, Benedict. "Über Sabbatjahrcyclus und Jobelperiode: Ein Beitrag zur Archäologie und Chronologie der vor- und nachexilischen Zeit, mit einer angehängten Sabbatjahrtafel." In *Jahresbericht des jüdisch-theologischen Seminars 'Fraenckelscher' Stiftung*. Breslau: Korn, 1857. Translated by A. Löwy as *A Treatise of the Sabbatical Cycle and the Jubilee: A Contribution to the Archaeology and Chronology of the Time Anterior and Subsequent to the Captivity. Accompanied by a Table of Sabbatical Years* (New York: Hermon Press, 1974).

Zunz, Leopold. *Gesammelte Schriften*. 3 vols. Berlin: Louis Gerschel, 1875–1876.

———. *Die gottesdienstlichen Vorträge der Juden historisch entwickelt: Ein Beitrag zur Alterthumskunde und biblischen Kritik, zur Literatur- und Religionsgeschichte*. 1832. Piscataway, NJ: Gorgias Press, 2003.

———. "Toledot le- r' Azaryah min ha-'adumim." *Kerem Hemed* 5 (1841): 131–158.

———. "Toledot le- r' Azaryah min ha-'adumim." *Kerem Hemed* 7 (1843): 119–124.

Zuroff, Abraham N. "The *Responsa* of Maimonides." PhD diss. (D.H.L.), Yeshiva University, 1966.

Index

355